Library of
Davidson College

The *Designs* of Carolean Comedy

Eric Rothstein
and
Frances M. Kavenik

Southern Illinois University Press
Carbondale and Edwardsville

Copyright © 1988 by the Board of Trustees,
Southern Illinois University
All rights reserved
Printed in the United States of America

Edited by Carol A. Burns
Designed by Laura D. Niemann
Production supervised by Natalia Nadraga

91 90 89 88   4 3 2 1

Library of Congress Cataloging-in-Publication Data

Rothstein, Eric.
    The designs of Carolean comedy / by Eric Rothstein and Frances M. Kavenik.
    p.   cm.
    Bibliography: p.
    Includes index.
    ISBN 0-8093-1460-6
    1. English drama—Restoration, 1660–1700—History and criticism.
2. English drama (Comedy)—History and criticism. 3. Comedy.
I. Kavenik, Frances M., 1944–   . II. Title.
PR698.C6R68   1988
822'.0523'09—dc19   87-36552
                                                                                                                                        CIP

The paper used in this publication meets the minimum requirements of American National Standard for Information Sciences—Permanence of Paper for Printed Library Materials, ANSI Z39.48-1984. ∞

Contents

Acknowledgments	vii
1. Introduction	1
2. A Model of Carolean Comedy	6
3. Establishing the Repertory: 1659–68	41
4. *The Tempest, or, The Enchanted Island*	85
5. The French Connection: 1668–72	108
6. *Marriage A-la-Mode*	138
7. The *Moraliste* Comedy of the 1670s	165
8. Durfeyan Comedy and *The Spanish Fryar*	202
9. The Last Years of Carolean Comedy	228
10. Retrospect	254
Appendix 1: Formation of the Repertory and Use of Repertory Data	261
Appendix 2: The Carolean Comic Repertory	268
Bibliography	280
Index	290

Acknowledgments

In addition to the warm support of family and friends, we would like to acknowledge, with thanks, the generosity of the Newberry Library and the American Society for Eighteenth-Century Studies for a Newberry Library Summer Fellowship which allowed Frances Kavenik to work on this project in 1983, and of the National Endowment for the Humanities and the Graduate School of the University of Wisconsin-Madison, which enabled Eric Rothstein to spend the summer of 1980 working in the British Library. We are also grateful to Professor Robert D. Hume for his advice on this manuscript as well as for his invaluable scholarship on Carolean drama.

Introduction

Since Good King Charles' gilt-edged days, the major comedies written for his loyal servants the actors have stirred more attacks and defenses than any other literature in English. Some critics have insisted that they are good, airy (if not clean) fun. Some have found them orthodox underneath a bold front: lively sheep—even lambs of God—dressed in wolf's clothing. And some have agreed with the persona of *God's Revenge against Punning* (1716), who found them an "Abomination" that might incite "Even Infants [to] disfigure the Walls of holy Temples with exhorbitant Representations of the Members of Generation" (269–70). More sophisticated readers, who have seen that many of the plays do not gel into something "unified," have elaborated dualistic but unitary schemes, based on satire, by which to salvage the comedies from being mere, "all in fun" entertainment. These schemes may focus on ideology, for example, describing morality and fashionable pragmatism at loggerheads in plays that mediate "libertine ideology and traditional social values" (Brown, *English* 47); or the schemes may be representational, like that of "a double-faced mirror that reflects simultaneously upward and downward," ideality and experiential facts (Zimbardo 76–77). We find all these views useful, though to different degrees. We also find them all misleading.

These critics have in common an assumption that we wish to challenge. It is that good, "serious" plays would ideally cohere in the (re)presentation of belief or attitude (an attenuated form of belief). Here belief relies upon some kind of advocacy, at times quite complex, whether skeptical or Christian or ethical (one can take one's pick). And to help instill belief, the plays manipulate the audience's desires for wish fulfillment, for vicarious participation into the action, for a splash of romance to brighten their drab lives. (We are evoking "belief" and "desire" as common philosophical categories that comprise world-directed mental acts and states: the field of cognition, the field of volition.) Most assignments of literary value exalt belief over desire, of course. Academic brows furrow over "poetic truth" and "exploration of ideas and motifs" and "ethical profundity," whereas wish fulfillment is somehow disreputable, a criterion that would demote Art to the level of entertainment. "The artistic character of a work," insists Hans Robert Jauss, "is to be measured by the aesthetic distance with which it opposes the expectations of its first audience"; those works that cater to audiences come close to " 'culinary' or entertainment art [*Unterhaltungskunst*]" (25). If one applies these criteria to the best Carolean plays—surely "serious" literature, since they have intrigued cultivated, sophisticated audiences over three centuries—each of them ipso facto, so their defenders have often claimed, at least challenges its audience's received ideas through a better-considered, coherent vision of the world. But why then do critics have such a hard time agreeing on what that "vision," that syndrome of belief in Carolean comedy, is, even broadly? The reason may be that although the corpus of Carolean comedies is arguably the finest in the English language, these are popular comedies, and popular comedy must be among the most likely genres to make "truths" auxiliary to wishes, not vice versa. Comedy above all, we urge, demands to be known in terms of "human will and desire and . . . the particular social formation within which will and desire are produced, directed, controlled, satisfied, frustrated" (Pechter 292).[1]

Therefore we would like to shift perspective a bit. Our method will be first, in chapter 2 and part of chapter 3, to propose a new, desire-based model for discussing the comedies, rooted in the playwrights' common assumptions not about the world but about what audiences wanted and how to provide them with what they wanted. Then, in the rest of the book, we describe the history of Carolean comedy (1660–85) through reference to that model. We concentrate on this method of description because we assume readers are familiar with the more general historical grouping and chronicling superbly done in Robert D. Hume's *Development of English Drama in the Late Seventeenth Century*. "Comedy," for our purposes, includes tragicomedies and plays of Spanish honor. Our mode of approach, we believe, allows us to be generous in what we claim as our scope. Our broad definition responds, too, to some indifference in the Restoration about "comedy" and "tragicomedy": *The Surprisal* is called "comedy" on its title page and "tragicomedy" in the Stationers' Register, and plays like *Secret Love* and *All Mistaken*, classic examples of "tragicomedy," are listed (in the Stationers' Register and on the title page respectively) as "comedy." The looseness of terminology implies something that we too

---

[1] As we mean to announce by this reference, which is to "new historical method," our willingness on the one hand to treat the plays seriously although we take them as popular literature, and on the other to criticize them in terms of desire, effect on an audience, discontinuity and indeterminacy, and ideology owes a great deal to critical theory in the 1980s. But, then, modern critical theory owes a great deal to a disposition to take modes of popular literature "seriously," and indeed to sap distinctions between "serious" and its antonyms.

wish to stress, the heterogeneity of Carolean comedy.[2]

Our model derives from the comedies of the 1670s, those that fit the lay public's image of Restoration comedy. We recognize that to launch off with the 1670s, in medias res, risks endorsing a stubbornly selective canon and even of making "organic" a "period" in literary history. In this vein, the comedies of the 1660s would caper in a sprightly and innocuous youth, and those of the early and mid-1670s strut in a tough, willful prime down paths of glory toward the 1680s' senility of empty giggles (*The London Cuckolds*) and cynical brooding (*The Souldiers Fortune*). We disclaim such mythical biographies. The Carolean repertory theatre ensured that after the mid-1660s no one kind of play dominated the stage, and if change in new plays is pronounced during these twenty-five years—because repertory competition put a premium on the market value of being up-to-date—what the daily audience got was continuity, old comedies and new, so that even more plainly than usual, any notion of a "period" with "organic" development is bankrupt here. We also disclaim any notion that new Carolean comedy reached some sort of apogee or felicitous stability with the early to mid-1670s, for as we shall show, the new repertoire kept on restlessly changing, experimenting, responding to both internal and external demands.

In fact, we begin where we do for three reasons. First, the familiar comedies of Dryden, Etherege, and Wycherley have long intrigued and puzzled critics. These plays have resisted efforts to place them at the center of an orthodoxy, and they therefore provide a rigorous test for any theory about Carolean comedy. Second, because these comedies have been canonical, any theory about Carolean comedy must deal well with them if it is to make scholarly headway. And third, comedies of the early to mid-1670s fall in the middle of the Carolean years, so the issues they raise, the devices they use, and the rationale behind their construction are likely to be usefully similar to those of comedies in the dozen years before and after them. In proposing a model rather than offering a list of normal surface features, we will focus on these issues, these devices, and this rationale as components of a structural logic, parts of a sort of elaborate verbal diagram. Each comedy embodies the logic of the model to a greater or lesser extent. The usefulness of the model depends on its explanatory range, the features to which it calls attention and the features

---

[2]Our practice, since we are dealing with active repertory, is to give the year of first performance in parentheses after a play title and to cite the first edition of the play unless we have indicated otherwise.

it relates to one another, rather than on its fully fitting all—or, indeed, any—of the actual comedies. In chapter 7, we test it upon three actual comedies of the mid-1670s by Shadwell, Behn, and Wycherley: *The Virtuoso*, *The Rover*, and *The Plain-Dealer*. Here, as throughout, we aim not to assimilate plays but to reveal, through reference to the model, the nature and scale of their differences from each other.

For further pragmatic reasons we expand the theory backward to 1660 and forward to 1685 by devoting our most detailed analyses to Dryden, the only writer of comedy to come close to spanning the reign of Charles. Here we have benefited by the superb editorial work done on Dryden, as well as from his having been the greatest, most articulate, and one of the most ductile writers of his time. He helped create some fashions and responded to most of the rest. In that sense he was a typical Carolean comic playwright, though obviously his genius makes him atypical of any group of authors in any genre at any time. His plays, like those to which our model principally refers, keep to the fore how much the better Carolean comedies reward close, traditional analysis. In our accounts of these comedies we have tried to use such analysis, usually saved for "literary" rather than popular culture, to help bypass this dubious distinction.

By dwelling on one playwright and therefore on one mind and its preferred body of themes, we of course cannot illustrate the full range of Carolean comedy. We hope, though, to display its generative forces in practice. Plays by other women and men will not submit to any formula or algorithm we provide; again, we hope that Dryden's practice will instead point to the kinds of questions that one might most profitably ask when coming to these other plays. Though others' comedies embody their own forms, their own themes, they yet share with Dryden's an audience and a dramatic grammar that this audience and those who wrote for them alike understood. Because we are not trying to typify Carolean comedy—we do not believe that good Carolean comedies can be reduced to types—but to instantiate the workings of generative principles, we have chosen to focus on three comparable plays of Dryden, in chapters 4, 6, and 8. They are artistic and popular successes, with double-plot structures that exhibit heterogeneity in very clear form: *The Tempest* (1667), *Marriage A-la-Mode* (1671), and *The Spanish Fryar* (1680). The first responds to the pre-War repertory as so many comedies naturally did in the 1660s; the second is à la mode des années 1670; the third appeared during the Exclusion Crisis and sets a tone adopted by other plays in the last years of Charles' reign.

One final point: in a historical explanation where the function of belief is largely to propel and legitimize desire, certain descriptive terms raise even more problems than usual. One might argue that any normative idea—like "nature," "truth," "reality," "the moral," "seriousness," and "normality," with their derivatives—ought always to be handled with oven mitts by a historian who does not want to get burned. Every one of these compulsorily pretends to be free of the ideology or ideologies within which it has been created. Each is also part of both the historian's explanatory system and that of his or her subjects. We cannot avoid such troublesome ideas, however: they take center stage in our account of Carolean comedies, for these plays depend on distinguishing nature from art, reality from artifice, and so forth. As we will illustrate, the plays often make such distinctions with enormous self-awareness, toying with, blurring, or inverting the sense of their demarcations. They dwell on and thereby revalidate the hierarchies about which they are simultaneously ironic. No one could accuse Dryden's comedies of too little sophistication. Like Dryden, we want to be cagey with these ideas, but since our text puts belief first and its audience's desires second, we want neither to toy with nor to validate the natural, the real, and the moral. The following request or exhortation to our reader, then, governs the whole of this book: every time we employ these normative terms, their variants, or their antitheses, please read them as though they were picketed with quotation marks. They allude to systems of belief to which we usually have no interest in subscribing. (The same holds for terms that we inherit from old literary critical systems, like "period," "moral vision," and any abstraction ending with "-ism.") At the same time we want to stress that we have no interest in subscribing to a twentieth-century ideology of suspicion, so as to reveal the playwrights' complicity in seventeenth-century ideological terms as bad faith or false consciousness. Quite the contrary: we relish the Carolean playwrights' warm, fascinating flirtation with these beliefs as one of the many great delights of their comedies.

A Model of Carolean Comedy

The Latitude of Carolean Comedy

After discussing the need for infants and children to sort out their environments, David Knight remarks, "Great scientists are Peter Pans, still anxious to classify and explain at an age when most people are concerned with money, power, and sex" (17). We suggest that seventeenth-century audiences, as opposed to the ingenuous and volatile critics of Carolean comedy, were likely to be concerned with money, power, and sex, and as matters less to be intellectually explored than to be emotionally exploited. The audience valued consistency, or more exactly the sense of consistency, intellectual or formal, only as one desideratum for entertainment, in competition with such local effects as flights of rhetoric, displays of passion, and "poetic justice" for the sake of moral or retributive or aesthetic pleasure. We doubt that Carolean audiences would have been as ready as those born in the mid-twentieth century to exalt as virtues the interpretive needs of academic criticism or even the explanatory, dignifying needs of seventeenth-century formalism. We doubt that Carolean playwrights, whose livelihood could be, and sometimes was, strangled by those audiences' purse strings, inflicted on them what they were indifferent to seeing.

If all this is so, to understand a Carolean play calls for understanding its strategy for entertainment. Therefore we should like to start with what we infer to have been the desires of Carolean audiences and thence to propose a generative principle that includes goals for Carolean Comedy and available procedures for achieving them. (We will use the capital letters when we would like to keep in view that we are presenting a model, not a direct statement about a genre or about all plays from 1660 to 1685.) We see our model, Carolean Comedy, then, as heuristic for the playwrights, a guide and stimulus for their comic invention, and more obliquely, for the audience. We might add that for the critic, there is a tactical as well as a heuristic advantage in approaching the plays through such a mechanism of generation, rather than beginning with a body of themes and attitudes in terms of which a "vision of the world" is to be developed. S/he runs less risk of either reducing the plays, individually or collectively, to specious unity or, at the other extreme, of seeing a repertory as a heterogeneous blooming and buzzing that can never be discussed as a system of choices.

Our hypothesis is as follows. Carolean Comedy primarily entertains not through wit, farce, or bawdry for their own sake but by allowing the audience to entertain (in another sense of that verb) desired, provisional images of themselves. The audience came to the theatre for distraction and society; the plays gave them what they came for by letting them don social roles different from and better than those in which they lived their daily lives, often bored, harassed, and frustrated. We take this kind of substitutive design to characterize popular literature of many periods, to be in the nature of popular literature as a social mode. How it works depends on three quite obliquely interdependent factors: the possibilities in a given idiom or genre, the nature of the desires that a given society legitimates, and the social restraints placed upon public expression and encouragement of those desires. In the early 1660s and again in the years of the Exclusion Crisis, the theatrical versions of the provisional images that people wished for themselves, by and large, clustered around a single social orthodoxy, not because society then was homogeneous but because as a public institution the theatre was politically sensitive. When the crown was or had recently been endangered, public orthodoxy looked good. In the later 1660s and most of the 1670s, however, these images in the theatre more often diverged from conventional orthodoxy and—because not everyone was comfortable imagining him- or herself a Dorimant or Horner—they also diverged from each other within a given play. Comedies of the 1670s therefore offer different provisional images to different members of the same audience. To stress this splitting of an audience and individuating of its members in desire, as opposed to the communal functions of belief, "audience" appears throughout this book as a plural noun.

Carolean comedies of the 1670s typically make the moral of the rakish plot, if there is one, ambivalent and also set the rakish plot vis-à-vis a more conventional plot. The formulaic mode of a multi-plot rakish comedy with a pair of moral endings, we suggest, can be explained by the hypothesis of accommodating a diverse audience; one need not resort to the usual reductive either/or expedient, which ferrets out the theatre's "real" underlying orthodoxy or a cynicism glimmering through a sham morality. For some members of the audience, no doubt, such a play did signal a standard ethic; for some a morality professed (rudely?, slyly?, drolly?, deliciously?) tongue in cheek. The viewer has a number of options, deliberately left open, for resolving the comedy. Its idiom neither resists nor imposes a given closure. We do not mean that the play as seen is indeterminate but rather that its determinacy rests, and is meant to rest, in the responses of the audience, in what they desire to see rather than in what they might prefer to resist seeing but are presented with for their belief. If one reads the play analytically, it may be (mis)interpreted as an example of the literature of "entrapment," defined by Vieth as disorienting, puzzling, lacking explicit shared values, and aiming for maximum response, even multiple or self-contradictory response. The comedies may appear "hopelessly disunified and inexplicably contradictory, . . . encompassing poetic justice and the interpositions of Providence, along with cynical doctrines of hedonistic appetite" (Thompson 49). Yet the viewer tossed happily in the high exuberance of a Carolean comedy is likely to get the lift s/he has paid for, enjoying the ideological flight(s) that suit him or her, and needing for the rest only that his or her understanding of it suffices for the duration, or, in the happy neologism that Herbert Simon has popularized, "satisfices."

The first supposition of our hypothesis, then, is the kind of heterogeneity of possible responses which we have just indicated. The second supposition follows from the patterning of that heterogeneity so that those responses are not limited to simple identification with the rakish or the moral plot. Rather, the comedies allow what we will call a "compromise formation," a term we have borrowed from Freud. Freud uses this term for a behavioral structure—a neurotic symptom, perhaps, or a dream—which represents both the gratifying of an illicit wish and also its repression or punishment. And while this process can be hidden, as when one gratifies a wish in a repressed (toned-down or symbolic) form, we are interested in a visible process corresponding to dramatic narrative, actions of sequentially doing and undoing or, in Freud's German, *ungeschehenmachen*, "making unhappened" (see, e.g., Freud 45–46). For example, in narrative, not psychotherapeutic terms, a sinner repents and is cleansed of guilt, a criminal "pays his debt to society" and is restored to it, a whoremonger turns over a new leaf and can start afresh. These are acts that in some sense officially annul a past in which a wish for "sin," crime, or whoring has been gratified. A social, therefore non-"neurotic" version of the procedure appears in the magic of purification rituals which have "the status of a rite of annulment" (Douglas, *Purity* 136).

As a compromise formation, the rakish comedy permits spectators to fancy themselves rakes painlessly. It does so by a sharp reduction of the cognitive dissonance implicit in at once admiring and disapproving of the rake; for example, admiration is fulfilled by the rake's reward of money, sex, and power (a beautiful heiress, in attaining whom he discomfits his rivals), while morality is fulfilled by his social alignment through marriage. The happy ending gratifies the audience who identify with the rake, while its moral propriety purges them, if need be, of uneasiness about that identification. The problem of possible unease is especially acute in Carolean comedy because, moral or no moral, the rake hero usually ends up with the choice lady, the most obvious reward the play provides. One cannot guess how many members of a given, mixed audience would feel ambivalent, but the point of the moral ending is to discommode the sensibilities of no one important, no likely paying customer. A similar principle informs twentieth-century politicians' speeches or television ads: reinforce the audience's preferred images of themselves and minimize as much as possible the risk of any umbrage. In shunning risk, modern marketers assume, as we do, that the bolder public will be less outraged by a bow to convention, like the moral ending, than the righteous or timid public would be by convention's being flouted for five full acts. Such a moral ending satisfies those who would be disturbed by its absence, but because it is only a conventional ending, it invites active moral decision (pro or con) less than would more openly ideological alternatives. Thus, by offering up a small, ready-baked moral ending, a Carolean comedy of this sort may appease—but also avoid prompting—the faculties of personal moral judgment in the audience. The ending relies on consensual morality, tailored for the idiom of stage comedy, in that the members of the audience might well have quite various notions of what was moral but be willing to accept a substitute from among the consensual possibilities. The essential is that the audience enjoy vicariously both freedom and social approval: freedom must take forms that they can enjoy and social approval take forms that have a satisfying plausibility.

A good example of the comedies' operating as we have suggested is their treatment of marriage. Within the body of the plays, in keeping with a prevalent ideology during the Restoration, marriages work badly; we cannot think of a single good marriage, in fact, exhibited in any Carolean comedy. We take this misogamy, moreover, to be part of an image of the world widely preferred among the audience for an empowering of worldly cynicism and sexual freedom, among other things. Yet, in keeping with a reigning convention, playwright after playwright "rights" rakery with the promise rather than the threat of nuptial rites and writings. By dramatic alchemy, the experience of real marriages, some better and some worse, is thus distilled, with the bitter sludge silting up during the play and the pure aetherial spirits bottled for the end. In fact, such a stage marriage is staged to marry the audience to the comic action with which they have been having a fling.

Thus the vagrant attitudes (realistic, cynical, eager) toward marriage might be exploited to produce four different potential readings of *The*

Man of Mode, say, with individual members of the audience accepting a mix of the four in accord with their predilections. (1) The Righteous: "As scandalous as the general attack on marriage may be in these sorry times, the institution of marriage can still thrive despite the cynics. Look at Emilia and Bellair. Even look at Harriet and Dorimant, brought into line and bound for the country." (2) The Aesthetic: "The general attack on marriage is the cant of the town, amusing enough, but just as easily countered by another kind of conventional cant, romantic love. The first four acts serve up the one, and the last provides the other for dessert." (3) The Practical: "Sow your wild oats while you can, God love you! But, you know, life is not a bowl of cherries; that sort of thing just doesn't last and you want a bit of comfort when you settle down." (4) The Hedonistic: "Boy, is that guy lucky. He gets to sleep with all the girls and then ends up with the best one plus the money and the land." The four readings reflect four dominant, mutually exclusive positions taken by modern critics of Carolean comedy, as admirably spelled out, for instance, by John T. Harwood (and on this play, see Brown, *English* 45–47; Corman). We would argue that the conventionality of the ending, the marriages that may happen by default without their implying any specific social or moral point, makes any of the four a reasonable closure for a given play—the choice rests with the eye of the beholder. Onstage these plays are unambiguous; but for a reader who treats these dramatic narratives as fables, the ambiguity or polysemy of the play increases in proportion to his or her sensitivity.

The hypotheses of the compromise formation and of heterogeneous response, then, identify a comic idiom that fosters ideological discrepancy within a play. They assume an audience who did not share one notion of what was moral or one notion of whether plays should be moral, and they treat stage morality as a source for an audience member's cognitive dissonance or harmony, not as an independent, "objective" issue. If accepted, these hypotheses moot or redirect much previous controversy about ethics and structure in the multi-plot comedy of the 1670s. Our emphasis in presenting them, however, raises an obvious question: should one presume, as we do, that plot is really important in itself? Or is it merely a vehicle for satire, wit, amusing incident, displays of energy, suspense, and other such momentary charms and exhilarations of Carolean comedies? Our model of Carolean Comedy stresses that members of the audience may well treat the play as wish fulfillment, treat the rake or other heroic characters as their proxy, treat the particulars of escapades as making visible a trajectory for the success of their own desires. A critic like our Aesthete, (2) above, would not need a compromise formation for *The Man of Mode* any more than s/he would need one for *The Importance of Being Earnest*. No doubt Carolean authors wrote comedies in which the plot does act largely as a vehicle for satire and energy. The best example is *The London Cuckolds* (1681), a play about as entertaining as *The Importance of Being Earnest*. We do not believe that many such plays, except for spoofs like *The Rehearsal*, predate the 1680s, though.

In the next chapter, we shall develop an intrageneric reason for presenting our model as we do. Carolean Comedy, we shall argue, adapts the early seventeenth-century mode of Fletcher and his associates so as to take over an idiom based on affectivity and then to develop characters as consistent agents in an unfletcherian manner. In this chapter, we would like to advance an extrageneric reason beyond the obvious, hard-to-interpret fact that Restoration social critics wailed about people's imitating stage rakes as no one, we guess, imitates Gwendolyn Fairfax and Algernon Moncrief. We propose that the Aesthete's aloof response depends on his or her having a secure perch upon a set of settled values relative to what s/he is watching. In the Carolean audience some—libertines, the pious, the romantic—might well have had such a perch, but by all accounts many members of Carolean audiences might have been likely, even eager, to entertain any number of provisional images of themselves.

Certainly since the work of Paul Hazard fifty years ago we have become accustomed to reading about the great changes the seventeenth century saw in the ways people understood their world. Learned books and articles have presented us with an almost Spenserian pageant of abstractions—skepticism, secularism, materialism, science, Hobbesian realpolitik—in whose chariots ride many if not most of the artists and thinkers who have interested later ages. The seventeenth century, we have been told, saw for better or for worse the decline of hell, of witchcraft, of unquestioned hierarchies in the state and the home, of pseudodoxia gullibly gobbled down, and of old doctrines of macro- and microcosmic correspondences. Kings became answerable to the law as well as to God, and in Keith Thomas' words, "In place of a natural world redolent with human analogy and symbolic meaning, [scientists] constructed a detached natural scene to be viewed and studied by the observer from the outside, as if by peering through a window, in the secure knowledge that the objects of contemplation inhabited a separate realm, offering no omens or signs, without human meaning or significance" (89). At the same time, according to social historians, what Lawrence Stone has labeled "affective individualism" gradually replaced patriarchal domination. "Self-awareness," "autonomy," "feeling," and the "pursuit of pleasure" became values increasingly praised. Still more generally, Susan Staves has argued from the evidence of law courts and pamphleteers that "secular democratic myths of authority"—authority governing relations between individuals, members of families, ruler and ruled, and persons subject to moral and ethical imperatives—"replaced religious and feudal myths" (xiv).

One inference from all this exceptionally valuable, interrelated scholarship is the strong form of an argument: in the course of the seventeenth century there was a conceptual revolution. It is the revolution suggested by Marshall Sahlins' dry comment in regard to Hobbes' idea of man in a state of nature: "So far as I know, we [Americans and Europeans] are the only people who think themselves risen from savages; everyone else believes they descend from gods" (53). Adam and Eve, shaped by the Lord in his image, began to look less like our ancestors than did Montaigne's cannibals, say, or maybe even Rochester's monkey. Indeed, people may well have rapidly altered the way in which they saw themselves and their fellows. The forty-seven changes in the government of England that Henry Jessey tabulated between 1640 and the time of his writing, 1661, no doubt emerged from and caused great conceptual upheavals (Capp 171). Nonetheless, we do not want to endorse this strong form of the argument. The term "revolution" signals a view of cultural history as melodrama; it ignores that individuals' social attitudes are commonly both confused and inconsistent and that those of a populace are far more so, especially at "revolutionary" times. Accounts of cultural phenomena on the "revolutionary" model at best suffer from intrinsic reductiveness; still more likely is they employ largely invented reifications. J. C. D. Clark, for instance, protests that "none of the grand revolutions beloved of recent historiography are to be observed in the quantifiable data of seventeenth-century society" (36).

Since reductive and factitious scenarios are just what we hope to avoid, we endorse a weak form of the argument about the changing climate of beliefs in the seventeenth century: there was a sharp, pervasive change in the way public discourse defined things. This point has less to do with private thoughts than with appearances, with words and representations. From the bare fact that so many scholars have been struck with changes in the material they examine, one may infer that the realm of the publicly acceptable must have changed. There was now both the latitude and the language to say what previously had not been said. And to say something—as a number of "muted cultures" are proving in the late twentieth century—is to permit its being entertained as legitimate, to give it objective expression within the bounds of the socially recognizable.

During the middle of the seventeenth century, as our cursory list indicates, an open questioning of values pervaded public statements of attitudes about the most central issues of value and conduct. It also affected a wide range of Englishmen and -women. For example, challenges to old hierarchies emerged into speech from the populist agitation of the Civil Wars, but on Staves' evidence they also appeared in the practice of post-Restoration law courts, institutions that by definition are voices of the Establishment. Staves shows that Restoration judges "discovered a class of married women [whom they were] willing to treat as though [these wives] had the autonomy of single women," including those who had separated from their husbands and enjoyed maintenance agreements which seem, moreover, to have been enforceable (150–51, 155). The portrayal of women in comedy, generally as well as in matters of divorce, plainly emerges from attitudes that were not only changing but also were perceived as in flux. So-called "libertine" arguments, in and out of the drama, are similarly broad-based. A Dorimant or Horner, whether openly or not, proclaims his freedom from dependence on the wills of others and from all relations except those into which he voluntarily enters with a view to his own interest; he sees himself as sole proprietor of his own person and capacities. But these "libertine" principles are the very ones that C. B. Macpherson has pointed out as underlying the political theories of the Levellers, of Hobbes, and later of Locke (263–67). Still another broadly significant set of questions about values is associated with "status inconsistency." Without subscribing to contentions that mid-to-later seventeenth-century society was tormented by questions about the value of status from inherited position vis-à-vis personal accomplishment (see Clark 30–32), we agree with Michael McKeon that such questions were very much in public awareness, as indicated by the pervasiveness of these issues in a wide variety of prose narratives throughout these years (*Origins* 150–75); McKeon also locates them in *Marriage A-la-Mode* ("Marxist" 156–62). They recur too in comedy after comedy, as issues of rank, individual appetite, savoir faire, social and moral virtue, and socially valued qualities (beauty, money, intelligence) become dramatic counters in a game of reconciliation.

Perhaps, given that during the Civil Wars many people made many shifts in ideological allegiance, one might expect such promiscuous bedfellows in London and in its playhouses. Christopher Hill, in *The World Turned Upside Down*, remarks that "Restoration comedy does not merely pick up the old Inns of Court naughtiness: it has also learnt something from the Ranters" (358), that rowdy lower-class sect who revelled in whoring, drinking, smoking, swearing, and a conviction of sinlessness. Hill obviously assumes an upward migration of ideas, just as upper-class ideas had earlier migrated down to the Ranters. This "Puritan" group had "links . . . with the royalist aristocracy, whose oaths and whose compliments the Ranters aped. Much of Ranterism was less a new ethic than an expression of traditional attitudes, some of which derived from the leisured ruling class" (340; see Brown, *English* 41–42). The Ranters and related groups, like the Seekers and the early Quakers, had wide appeal and much turnover (Hill 197–99, 236–40). "Men and women, faced with an unprecedented freedom of choice, passed rapidly from sect to sect, trying all things, finding all of them wanting. Again and again in spiritual autobiographies of the time we read of men who passed through Presbyterianism, Independency and Anabaptistry before ending as Seekers . . . as Ranters . . . or as Quakers," with the young especially susceptible (189–91). In 1655, the clergyman John Pordage, an associate of the Ranters and father of the poet and playwright Samuel Pordage (b. 1633), wrote that "notions of Ranterism . . . were everywhere frequently discoursed of" (qtd. in Hill 224). Since Hill thinks that "Restoration comedy . . . learnt something from the Ranters" (358), we suspect that an appreciable number of the audience had either sampled a form of Ranterism during the Interregnum or envied those who had, like middle-aged adults in the 1980s who lived through the flower-strewn "sexual revolution" of the 1960s. The Ranters appealed to apprentices, who might well have been among theatre audiences twenty years later (189). If so, young Carolean rakehells on stage were creatures of nostalgia as well as of fantasy, disowned in real life but reinhabited for an afternoon. In any case, some "royalist" values overlapped some "Puritan" values, both of them subversive of established order, and these would surely have been widely familiar to a Carolean audience.

Although present-day historians are tempted, with good reason, to set cits and libertines (including ex-Ranters) apart, one as supporting and the other as challenging accepted order and, as Marxists call it, "labor discipline," one may challenge the thoroughness of that dichotomy. Mary Douglas suggests an anthropological link between the unconstrained leader, like the rake, and the "total dropout," like the Ranter: both, she suggests, "see the cosmos as a rational order not dominated by people but by manipulable objects. These objects are the impersonal rules which govern their transactions. . . . There is no sin: only stupidity" (*Symbols* 136–37). But this ideology has been extended to precisely those who insist on order and "labor discipline," all of whom are practitioners of the "instrumental reason" polemically described by Horkheimer and Adorno as a post-Baconian phenomenon associated with nascent capitalism. Reason, that is, becomes a tool for dominating nature, including one's fellow people, for one's own benefit. Without subscribing to the social values or historical account expressed in this description, we agree that such "instrumental reason" is in accord with an individualistic, competitive ethos, whether that of a rake who thrives on immediate power and pleasure or that of a cit who thrives on power and pleasure mediated through cash. McKeon argues, as in general would we, that "what early modern thought achieved was, in a sense, the 'neutralization' of human nature" from moral to descriptive terms, leading to a "rehabilitation of desire." And "what is human behavior if not appetitive?" (*Origins* 202–3). We submit, then, that the entrepreneurial rake, rewarded for his enterprise and yet brought into social order at the end of the play, might appeal to a seventeenth-century cit on an afternoon's holiday, at least in the tolerant 1670s. If so, no wonder compromise formation was so widely and obligatorily practiced.

Just as heterodoxy affected so considerable a variety of people as perhaps not to be heterodox at all, the theatres attracted an audience varied enough to reflect most shades of opinion. Recent scholarship has scrapped the old canard that a coterie of blasé, sexy men-about-town made up the theatre audiences, a knot of wits, fops, and their hangers-on who would have received into their minds only a narrow range of socially and sexually convenient new opinions. (The countervailing myth, that the theatres largely drew sturdy Christians, has never won converts despite the evangelism of some American academics. This version adds to the false assumption of a uniform audience the false assumption that Restoration Christians would have been in accord as to what constituted moral behavior.)[3] As Scouten and Hume write, "the whole theory of a coterie audience, long dominant, seems to have no better foundation than the limited knowledge and moral prejudices of later commentators" (48). Instead, the theatres catered to a mixed group of literate Londoners. This group should ipso facto have been among the most alert to the new, broadly sanctioned diversity of opinions and attitudes in society as on stage, for they themselves would have represented a considerable range of such attitudes.

Added plausibility for our view of Carolean comedies comes from another prolific, broadly familiar, popular body of Restoration literature, the ballads. Such ephemera could be read, and apparently were, by anyone able to read, and the market for them was lucrative enough

---

[3] The providential reading of these plays has had more attention, mostly in rebuttal, than it deserves. Its assumptions have largely been demolished by Hawkins ("Example Theory," *Likenesses*) and the scholarship behind those assumptions by Scouten.

to enrich the London publishers' consortium, the Ballad Partners, whose presses churned them out (Spufford 83–91). Simple in verse form and usually adorned with crude, comfortable old woodcuts, ballad broadsheets decorated walls, like those pasted up by Swift's Baucis and Philemon in his poem of that name (written 1706?). Nonetheless, ballads were not a cheap lower-class pursuit of marginal interest to sophisticates. Among those who collected them were that acerbic Oxonian snob, the historian Anthony à Wood, and that middle-level bureaucrat (and insatiable playgoer) Samuel Pepys. The ballads, then, had a varied and wide audience, like the theatres, though because the ballads are traditional culture, perhaps a more conservative audience than the theatres'. In some sense, then, the ballads make a useful test case for an a fortiori argument about the heterodoxy of the theatre. They are particularly useful because the simplicity of the ballads and their crude handling of irony leave them easy to interpret, unlike the better comedies. They also lack the verbal sparkle and detachment from all parties which underlie the Aesthete's response to Carolean Comedy; in fact, they traditionally had didactic freight of some sort. The "moral" of a ballad therefore probably represents a position that people were willing to take seriously, at least for the moment.

The kinship of ballads and comedies, moreover, appears in obvious parallels in subject matter and even, for narrative ballads, in motifs and plots. We can provide some examples from the Roxburghe collection of ballads, many of them once Wood's. (Our datings come from Wing's *Short-Title Catalogue*.) The stock figure of the country clown whose years at college help him make a fool of himself in London appears in the ballad "The Great Boobee" (1656) and in Durfey's *The Fool Turn'd Critick*. "The Woman's Victory: or, the Conceited Cuckold Cudgel'd into Good Qualities" (1684–95) and Shadwell's *The Woman-Captain* both portray wives who beat jealous, miserly husbands into submission. In "The Westminster Frolick, or, A Cuckold is a Good Man's Fellow" (1670–82) and in Ravenscroft's *The London Cuckolds*—as earlier in Dryden and Caryll (*Sir Martin Mar-all* and *Sir Salomon*, both following Molière)—one finds a gallant whose loose talk leads to his cuckold's discovering his betrayal. The woman in man's apparel follows her sailor lover in "The Valiant Virgin: Or Philip and Mary" (1670–75) as well as in *The Plain-Dealer* and Durfey's *The Royalist*. Another Durfey play, *Madam Fickle*, shares with "The Deceiver's Deceiv'd: Or, the Virgin's Revenge" (1680–85) a lady who is cruel to revenge a lover's treachery and cruelty. J. D.'s *The Mall* shows a man contriving his own cuckolding by making an assignation with a servant and sending a friend to keep it, not knowing that his wife had substituted herself for the servant upon learning of the assignation; the same plot occurs in "The Wanton Vintner, and the Subtile Damosel" (1684–88). Of course those ballads that have plots like Durfey's plays may have been written by Durfey himself, but that supposition only reinforces the closeness of ballads and plays.

If the ballads indicate popular taste in the morality of popular entertainment, one ought to read the comedies, contemporary with them and complementary to them, as morally very tolerant. For if some ballads continued to preach goodness and decry sin, like "A New Wonder" (1681; Rollins 210–14): "O *England* then in time Repent, / For fear you may too late Lament," at least as often the diverse mores of the ballads make one despair of reading the comedies as faithful to Christian or socially benificent tenets. At this popular level, no social consensus seems to have existed for what had previously been thought orthodox on some of the touchiest issues of conduct. Three examples will show what we mean: drunkenness, the extremities of love, and marriage. All three seem especially pertinent to the uneasy relations between social order and personal appetite in Carolean comedies, in which all three so often appear.

Drunkenness would seem to be the epitome of disorder, making men so brutish, as Richard Allestree warns, that "thou mayest as well say there is no Heaven, as that drunkenness shall not keep thee thence" (Sunday VIII, 75). But if Christian moralists were likely to treat drunkenness on the axis of order/disorder, balladeers were likely to treat it on the axis of natural/unnatural. While tracts contrast its disorder with the proper order of monarchist loyalty, ballads pair drinking with such loyalty, as equally "natural." This latter scheme appears in such ballads as "England's Triumph: or, The Subjects' Joy" (1660–75), "The Courtiers Health; or, The Merry Boyes of the Times" (by the loyalist poet Matthew Taubman, 1681–82), "Content's a Treasure; or, The Jovial Loyalist" (1684?), "Merry Boys of Christmas" (1660?), and "The King of Good Fellows" (1684?). In "The Merry Boys of Europe" (1682?) the loyalist toasts the King and recommends drowning the senses until "our selves do not know what we say or think," and the pledge in "The Oxford Health or, The Jovial Loyalist" (1681) is "We'l drink our brisk Wine till each his Soul drenches." One must assume, we believe, that these ballads support what they seem to support, even if only for the duration of the ballad reading. We know of no direct evidence that they either use irony against loyalty to a monarch or that they merely portray a contemporary type, the sodden cavalier—arguments that parallel two anti-Collierite defenses at the century's end, that the comedies satirize or simply imitate the libertine rowdiness they seem to relish.

As to suicide, many ballads accept it for the sake of love. We are not speaking here of Cato or Lucretia, saving honor while losing their lives, but of amorous youth for whom the canons of excessive passion outweigh those against self-slaughter. Although suicides do not come up in comedies, tolerance for them suggests a fortiori that if girls or boys can kill themselves for love without being blamed for it, then less extreme actions for the sake of love should also be excused. Christian moralists would groan to find no censure of the maiden who stabs herself in "Love's Downfal" because her parents refuse a mésalliance between her and the stable-groom whom she loves. Bloody handed, she commends her soul to Christ, and the balladeer frowns only at the parents. Love-suicide remains uncensured in "The Maiden's Tragedy" (1685–92), "The Unfortunate Lady; or, The Young Lover's Fatal Tragedy" (1684), and "The Unfortunate Forrester" (1670–77). Indeed, still other ballads, "Phillis and Philander"(?) and the paired "The True Lovers Tragedy" (by Nathaniel Lee?, 1680–82) and "A Strange Apparition" (1680?), represent the suicidal lovers happily mated in the postmortem joys of Elysium. As in "Love's Downfal" (1684), sympathy for deprived lovers leaves little for the traditional rights of offended parents. So, for example, in the (nonsuicidal) "The Seaman's Renown in Winning His Fair Lady" (1670?) the balladeer praises a secretly married sailor for gaining his curmudgeonly father-in-law's blessings by direct means: the "Noble stout Seaman" "cut[s] him & lashes him" into submission. "The Master-piece of Love Songs" (1670–80) has a very similar plot. We remarked earlier that libertines and Levellers alike thought of individuals as sole proprietors of their persons and capacities. Plainly the same notion legitimizes disposing of one's own person when the freedom to exercise one's proper capacities for love—the paramount affective value—is lost. In accord with this scheme of values, meddlesome parents get punished for balking "nature."

We have been dealing with extensions of "libertine" ideas beyond the specific platform, so to speak, of Restoration libertines. Rochester and Sedley would have cheered for drunkenness, in which they themselves delighted, but sneered at love-suicides. Attacks on marriage, our third example from the ballads, are associated with libertine notions but were too widespread to be limited to a coterie's defiant code. As Staves says, "Especially after about 1670, many writers expressed fear that marriage itself was under attack" (136). To her examples (136–38) can be added many others, claims that "our great men . . . undervalue and disgrace [marriage]," that *"Marriage* [is] almost forgotten in the World, and made among the *Wits* of our Age, the Character of Fools, or badge of Necessity," that there is a "present great *Contempt* of *Matrimony*," and that "nothing is more cried down in the World, than Marriage" (Hunt? 7; *Marriage Promoted* 3; *Guardian's Instruction* 27; *Bachelor's Directory* 2; see also Novak, "Margery" 5-12). As one would expect, many roistering ballads have men declaring for the free life: "The Politick Countreyman" (1670-82), "Advice to Young Gentlemen; or, An Answer to the Ladies of London" (1685-88), "The Bachelors Delight"(?), "The Bachelor's Triumph: Or, The Single-Man's Happiness" (1672-95), "A Young Man Put to His Shifts, or, The Ranting Young Man's Resolution" (1670), and so forth. What one might not expect, since popular libertinism has generally been posted as a male preserve, is that numerous ballads depict women who reject marriage. That "Marriage brings Sorrow and Care" underlies the counsel of "The Maidens Counsellor" (1685-88), the craft of "The Crafty Maid: or, The Young Man Put to His Trumps" (1672-95), the victory in "The Young Mans Labour Lost" (1680?), the advice in Tobias Bowne's "The West-Country Maids Advice" (1672-95). Nor does the single state mean the solitary state, not when one finds "The Maids Complaint for the Want of a Dil-doul" (in this ballad, 1680-90, a natural rather than an artificial anatomical part).

Fornication had always been a part of ballads about rustic Jocky and Nancy or nymph and swain, but without so much as a twitch of horror, ballads like "The Secret Loves, or, The Jealous Father Beguil'd"(?) bring illicit sex from fantasy and low life into the middle class. Some ballads do the same with adultery, like "The Doting Old Dad" (1685-88) and Walter Pope's "The Forc'd Marriage, or, Unfortunate Celia" (1676-85), both of which approve a resolution to cuckold an old fumbling husband. Even female rakery has its day unscathed in "Unconstant William: or, The Damosels Resolution to Love Indifferently All Men Alike, from Her Experience of His Disloyalty" (1690). The damosel "never will value the name of a Bride, / To one Huffing Gallant I'll never be ty'd." She claims a bachelor's privilege from city to court, "And there with young Gallants in Pleasure I sport. . . . With Twenty or more, I will reap my Delight." Because the balladeer has "justified" her rakery with William's disloyalty, he almost surely does not mean to exhibit the lady as a tramp.

We do not want to ignore the very many moral ballads with traditional lessons. Quite the contrary: we want to insist on them. Ballads of various moralities and amoralities thrived in the same people's hands, just as in October 1676 Nell Gwyn, whose bastard son by

Charles II was two months later to be created Baron Heddington and Earl of Burford, could comfortably go to Dorset Gardens to see Shadwell's libertine Don John pulled down to Hell by devils (*The Libertine*), Etherege's Dorimant drawn off only to the wealth and wit of Harriet, and Tuke's lovers in *The Adventures of Five Hours* remain punctiliously chaste (*LS* 250–51). A collection of ballads or a succession of comedies in a repertory was likely to be heterogeneous; our argument extends that heterogeneity to individual plays. If new plays could have been sampled as quickly as ballads or had been rated like modern movies (G, PG, PG-13, R, and X, as of the mid-to-late 1980s), so that the rakish, the prudish, and the timid could all have been good, selective customers at the theatres, perhaps individual comedies could have been ethically simpler, as, indeed, were many of the older plays in the repertory. But those frazzled moguls, Killigrew, Betterton, and the rest, did not have the economic leeway to take an easy course till 1682, when the United Company reigned alone in London and the managers could fall back on a trusty repertory. Before that, with a varied audience to entice and to please for their economic survival, the theatres tried to speak at once to as many tastes as they could. By the 1670s, the idiom of their comedies and the broad-mindedness of their public let them speak to a good many.

Both in its double plots and within its rakish plots, we submit, Carolean Comedy embodied the new public latitude that we have indicated in large cultural terms and in the specific, popular world of the ballads. "Latitudinarian" comedies might expect from their audiences a good measure of at least preliminary tolerance for diverse attitudes, along the lines of Dryden's modest and diffident "skepticism," with its allegiance to "freedom of inquiry," such as Phillip Harth has described (9–15). The public recognition that heterodoxy was socially tolerable, in fact socially tolerated, echoed through comedies in which a viewer could equally accept the life of a Dorimant (an existence developed in plot one) or of a Young Bellair (an existence developed in plot two), holding in equal embrace a newfangled code and a morality distinctly old-fashioned, even if deviously achieved. Moreover, the members of the audience might feel freer themselves to try on for size what one now calls "nonconformist"—in varying degrees antisocial—attitudes. Through the principle of compromise formation, with its free trial offer of vicarious sampling, Carolean Comedy offers exceptionally complex stimuli for projection (or "identification" with characters) and judgment, different degrees of appetite and aversion, different extensions of one's own power and proprietorship. And to this end, the categories of belief subserve the categories of desire.

The Logic of Carolean Comedy

Desire and Contempt

If we are right in seeing Carolean Comedy as providing its audience with society and distraction by offering them a social role they desire, purged of the troubles, embarrassments, and ennui of everyday life, then across the heterogeneity of values among the audience lies a consistent view of these men and women as desiring beings. From this psychological insight are developed the complex means by which to market social roles and desires. To explore them, we should start by defining the term "desire," for it covers very general senses (as in, "The people of the United States have a sincere desire to see true democracy for their Latin American friends") and technical ones (as in the work of Jacques Lacan, from which it flowed into critical theory of the 1970s and 1980s). Our rather simple, commonsense use of the term belongs to a currently credible drive/structure psychological model that seems apt for explaining the thrust of these plays and that in gross terms would have been quite comprehensible to someone living in the Restoration. (We are not committed to its general applicability.) From a dilute Lacanianism we adopt the notion that desire focuses on social tokens, like money, power, and sexual conquest, to which a culture assigns value. The pursuit and acquisition of these tokens slake drives that may originate elsewhere. By "drive" we mean an internally produced impulse to perform a certain type of action; this action must be oriented towards an objective, an object of desire, which may be a concrete thing (money, a lover) or a quality (honor, power, freedom). The specific actions and objects are not fixed by the drive but are contingent, hence open to cultural direction. Carolean Comedy ratifies its culture's choice of objects of desire in two ways, by disguising them as pure products of "human nature" and natural drives and by dangling them before the eyes of the audience in immediate, available form through stage representations (the bag of guineas, the rake and his baffled cuckold, the melting heroine). These objects are established—more accurately, reinforced—as things one naturally wants to have, for which one has a natural disposition to act.

The text performed on stage then prompts a viewer to an inner performance of wish fulfillment, moral, immoral, amoral, or some mixture of these. It does so through showing the stage actors themselves behaving in a way both determined and free: free in that characters have autonomy (at least the heroes and heroines do) and determined in that they act from drives. In Carolean Comedy, the primary drives are for sex, power, and freedom, all or any mixture of the three requiring social expression. Other motives, like hunger, virtue, decorum, simple greed, or curiosity, tend to subserve or act as foils for these primary drives. Stage personages and therefore the audience are supposed to have these natural energies, drives; the play on stage offers an action and objects that cannot satisfy but do slake the drives, the comic version of Aristotelian catharsis. Carolean Comedy thereby also declares the drives valid, though some of their expressions, as in a Pinchwife, may be undesirable. The drives, which have wide moral potential, must themselves be outside moral categories, prior to them, if the play is to have the moral indeterminacy for which we have been arguing; different viewers must make their different moral judgments on the expressions of the drives, not the natural impulses themselves. Carolean Comedy, in harmony with this requirement, treats the drives as universal human energies, and their expressions as socially conditioned. Partially as a result of this arrangement, the relation between "nature" and "culture" runs thematically throughout these plays. What the audience want for cultural reasons is declared natural and thus properly secured for them through what happens on stage.

In its emphasis on action, our use of "desire" jibes with that of Hobbes, who describes "desire" as an endeavor in the imagination to attain something (*Leviathan* 1: 6). He groups desire, the senses, and the imagination as basic modalities of interaction with the world, and to "desire" he traces secondary modes of interaction, pleasure and pain, will, and the passions. Later he claims it as the source of Felicity, "a continuall progresse of the desire, from one object to another; the attaining of the former being still but the way to the later" (1: 11). In his use as in ours, "desire" therefore involves continuing acts of adjustment of the relation between self and world, the self as it appropriates the world, the world as it becomes available for the self. Carolean Comedy, in our reading, directly eases and specifies this adjustment by giving people something that will pass for what they want. The process of doing this, of representing a trajectory of desire, so to speak, in which self and world are happily, safely adjusted, is relatively simple in socially orthodox plots: there the idiom limits the range of self-image that a member of the audience can fancy for her- or himself, the range of ways in which the world can become available, and the degree of threat in the world. But in the rakish plots of Carolean Comedy, to which we shall now devote most of our attention, the idiom poses wider limits and the management of the play gets a good deal more difficult.

So far, in discussing the heterogeneity and audience investment in

Carolean Comedy, we have concentrated on self rather than world, to the extent that those can be separated. For example, we have stressed the role of compromise formation for people's images of themselves. When a comedy punishes (by exclusion) or supersedes (by marriage) the socially questionable conduct it has hitherto been rewarding, however, it protects not only people's images of themselves but also their sense of security in the society around them. The satire of society, as Traugott insists (597), "is an anatomy of a *necessary condition of existence*"—through these witty, aggressive, ethically savvy comedies, the audience control the necessary conditions of social life. Furthermore, by encouraging closure, the sequence of events used in compromise formation also provides social comfort for residents in the now uncertain, nonconsensual society of later Stuart England. For the entire audience, those who take the play as a compromise formation and those who do not, Carolean Comedy reenacts the latitude familiar to all of them outside the theatre, and yet allows them enough internal latitude of judgment to let different viewers resolve or order that version of outside heterogeneity differently. In its potential to (re)affirm shared values which, at least on stage, hold good for a group of glamorous, powerful figures, such a play pleases not only by satisfying the imagination of its audience but also by making the uneasy among them feel easier within the troublingly chaotic surroundings of everyday life. The double plot and conventional denouements of many comedies work toward this end of reassuring each viewer that the world is stable in the manner that s/he prefers.

Because the plays challenge and reassure their audiences in terms of attaining wishes and maintaining a flattering sense of status, only two basic types of scenes appear in our model of Carolean Comedy once exposition is out of the way. Typically, Carolean playwrights gear every scene for enacting the movements of desire and/or eliciting admiration or contempt. Thus each scene deals with movement to or from a specific object of desire, movement that is at times free, at times thwarted or retrograde; and/or it deals with the display of a character or characters who are cynosures, sympathetic or satiric. Scenes that do not shift characters closer together or farther apart fall into the latter category, display. An example is the presentation of Dufoy in his tub (*The Comical Revenge*). Festive scenes, like some in *As You Like It* and *Twelfth Night*, appear only to wrap up the denouement; scenes of mere humor, like the clown scenes in *Two Gentlemen of Verona* and *The Merchant of Venice*, rarely appear. Nor do tender scenes, except in "high" plots of mixed-mode comedies, nor do passages that call the tone of the play itself into question, such as Feste's song in *Twelfth Night* about the rain that raineth every day. The dramaturgical moves in Carolean Comedy, then, are highly restricted and purposeful, like the options at any moment in the most sophisticated games, like chess, or sports. One can mark the plays up or down for these restrictions, as one can spurn family picnics for chess or vice versa. Our point is that these constitutive restrictions are part of a sound, supple logic, not the results of chance, "neoclassicism," lack of imagination, or a coterie's chronic depravity.

Since desire implies aversion, admiration implies contempt, satire must have a central part in Carolean Comedy, as we have just been indicating. It may seem, though, to contravene our hypothesis, in that the latitude in Carolean Comedy is pinched by intolerant satire of the witless, the witlings, sometimes even the wits. Etherege cheerfully lets characters be demolished by smart laughter (Old Bellair, for example) or social Darwinism (Loveit, Bellinda) and, strikingly, embarrasses Dorimant himself. Our model accommodates comic satire by distinguishing four kinds not always distinct in practice: mockery of fools and social failures; of the audience, in prologues and epilogues; of the rake at given points during the play; and of the rake for the folly or failure of his (rarely "her") mode of life. In Carolean Comedy this last category simply confirms our model, since the rakery seems foolish only to those viewers who resolve the comic heterogeneity that way. Such overall ethical reactions can—with reasonably similar interpretive validity—vary markedly from one person to another, as witness the Collier controversialists, the argument of Steele and Dennis over *The Man of Mode*, and the to-and-fro of all their clever and dull epigones to the present time. Those who believed that Horner ended up badly with Mrs. Fidget and family may have seen him the butt of satire, while others probably envied his access to "that Fountaine of Love so juicy so Plump / That delicate Compound of Spiritt & Rump" who was Mary Knepp, the first Mrs. Fidget (Highfill, Burnim, and Langhans 9: 58; Milhous and Hume 85). Given our model, the last category does not need further explanation. But we should elaborate on the first three categories, mockery of fools, jibes at the audience, and undeniable embarrassment of the rakes.

Carolean Comedy does not exercise ideological latitude as an item of belief. It does so to gratify the pursuit of objects of desire common to characters and audiences. Characters who fail to attain these objects—money, power, and sexual goals (in various hierarchies or mixtures established by various plays)—are set apart by ridicule from characters who do attain them, who perform and thereby specify, if not actually create, the audience's desires. By lowering esteem for the have-nots, the playwright obviously raises the value assigned to what the haves have. As well as their lacking in money, power, and sexual prowess, have-nots are usually also made offensive to a broad spectrum of other values: they are posturing, fatuous, grasping, bungling, boorish (before a London audience), and/or unsuccessfully immoral. Within an idiom that at least toys with accepted values and often calls them derisively into question, the ridicule of such characters provides reassuring stability, what everyone can comfortably agree on. The audience as members of a society happily reinforce boundaries based on social image, certainly not primarily ethical behavior and not even simply success.

We would underline, moreover, that social failure (lack of money, power, and sexual prowess) does not cause the fools' posturing, fatuity, etc., as in a psychological play, but often results from these faults. A character's taint, as if under anthropological laws of pollution, is a nonexplanatory given, not extenuated by circumstances (poor Pinchwife as a case for Adlerian psychotherapy rather than laughter). Ridiculed characters in Carolean Comedy in fact are not so much persons as they are givens, punctuating the hero's progress, speeding or blocking his or her movement in the plot, calling attention to elements of his or her behavior. It is to these buffoonish fops, cits, prudes, and the like that one may refer the persistent claims of the playwrights to be generally instructive in their satire, for here the laughter of the crowd, unified in scorn, has the consensual power of social judgment. In making other ethical decisions, as we have argued, even the most upright members of the audience, some rigorous, some utilitarian, some more casuistical, would have veered in different ways. But at this level, they could agree, so that the hero(in)es, who initiate much of the ridicule, thereby reinforce their roles as the whole audience's agents.

To sharpen the willingness to make judgments—that is, to reinforce the consensual values of which we have just spoken and to reinforce the individual decisions that reduce the perception of ambiguity and promote closure—prologues and epilogues of Carolean comedies often make fun of the audience, thereby raising the audience's level of aggressivity. Such direct addresses also help ratify the plays' realism, in that they typically identify in the playhouse those groups targeted within the plays themselves, such as fops, witlings, pedants, Whigs (in the early 1680s), whoremongers who lacked wit and style, and vizard masks peddling their flesh. These specific purposes make unnecessary Thompson's speculation that these direct attacks testify to "a peculiarly hostile relationship between playwright and [an] audience" that he, like us, sees as "without center, and without unifying interests, political, financial, or aesthetic" (49, 54).[4]

We think Thompson's speculation is also off track. Hungry Carolean writers probably had better sense than to flaunt whatever hostility they felt, especially in that they had so fractioned a constituency. In fact, the outspoken prologues and epilogues usually exhibit the same sort of bravado, joviality, wisecracking, bluffness, independence, and aggressive chaffing that marks the exchanges between male friends or between "gay couples" in the comedies themselves. A gentler approach is less "masculine," more closely associated with sexual wooing and inequality. We suggest, therefore, that the "satire" of the audience serves a social purpose of bonding, in a mode then as now continually in play among men (less among women) of all classes in Western society. The license to insult, up to a mutually and tacitly understood point, ratifies the cooperation between the parties. The audience is situated in near-equality with the playwright (and s/he with them), suitable for the reciprocal relationship of judgment they have, a feature often mentioned in prologues and epilogues. All know, of course, that the audience, as paying customers, have the last word. Audience and hero(ine) do not have a reciprocal relationship, to be worked out in social terms outside the dramatic narrative, and here the audience needs a mode of self-assertion. They may be given a pleasing irritant to be more aggressive through the tone set in prologues and epilogues, a tone that intensifies their reaction to the characters on stage and alters the scope of permissible behavior. But they also get a chance to laugh at, as well as with, the hero(ine).

The satiric modes set out in our first two categories fix points of reference for dealing with the relation between a competitive, aggressive audience and competitive, aggressive rakes who—through successes and failures—enact their desires. Mockery of onstage fools wields a power of contamination, so to speak, by means of which the comedies undermine the rakish or witty protagonist who begins to

---

[4]The social functions of Carolean Comedy resemble those often assigned to ideology. Geertz helpfully summarizes these as the draining off of individuals' emotional tension through displacement onto symbolic enemies, denying strain or "legitimizing it in terms of higher values," "knit[ting] a social group or class together," and calling attention to social conflicts (205). Satire and wish fulfillment in Carolean Comedy serve the first three functions, and compromise formation serves the last by thematizing and resolving conflict as the viewer likes. Geertz argues that ideologies arise to reorient a society under social, cultural, and psychological strain (219), exactly the kind of argument we are putting forth for Carolean Comedy as a "system of interacting symbols" (207) with ideological force.

challenge the audience, making them feel that they are being outdone by the superior wit, panache, and aplomb of a Rhodophil or a Dorimant. Thus in act III of *The Man of Mode* Loveit is allowed to embarrass Dorimant by "contaminating" him, equating him as a beau with Sir Fopling Flutter. More often the threat of contamination occurs through more covert potential analogies between wit and fool, like Horner and Pinchwife. Making the hero vulnerable to ridicule or to being debased by mirroring keeps the rake at his main dramatic task of feeding the audience's fantasies, but with a difference. His discomfiture reassures them of their own superiority to enviable figures and perhaps of their own ethical soundness. Reassured, they can—if they are so minded—sympathize more freely with him and cheer on his eventual victory. (We observe that the only chief figures in these plays who do not meet with satire are those who succeed in their own limited spheres without endangering the self-esteem of the audience, like the moral Bellair in *The Man of Mode* or the amoral, though loyal Freeman in *The Plain-Dealer*.) Analogous states of affairs have been examined by René Girard, who points to the rivalry for a desired object once "by the example of his own desire . . . the model conveys to the subject the supreme desirability of the object" (146). The Girardian "model" in Carolean Comedy is the dashing figure who "conveys to the subject," a member of the audience, "the supreme desirability" of his present and future attainments (wit, women, willfulness), and so becomes the viewer's proxy and rival. Though on stage s/he serves the audience, s/he also threatens to compete with them as an image of someone whom they might meet in real life—one thinks of the mixture of envy and awe, of identification and hostility that attaches to modern celebrities who act to define and fulfill the fantasies of television viewers. The temporary embarrassment of the protagonist of Carolean Comedy sets to rights the rivalry between her or him and the audience.

One can frame a similar argument about the craftsmanship of a Carolean comedy, a craftsmanship that tacitly gives value to some sort of unity and asserts the force of a single controlling mind. On one level, the well-wrought play marks control, purposiveness, and savoir faire as sources of pleasure so as to insure one's prizing the well-wrought phrases that come from the witty characters, just as the play's satiric gusto insures one's prizing the ridicule they initiate. On another level, the playwright's craftsmanship lends the audience the illusion of control, for a sense not only of safety and of freedom akin to that which heroines and heroes enjoy, but also of superiority to those heroines and heroes. The playwright allows the audience a perspective above that of even the most individual characters, who appear as parts of a pattern. Moreover, when witty protagonists display their skill at arranging the action verbally or in other ways, they in a sense emulate what the author has done for the public, but of course they never succeed quite so well. The scheme is one which in Fujimura's terms sets the Truewits above the Witwouds, but sets the audience—with the playwright their compliant host—above anyone. Thus Carolean Comedy keeps the audience secure, and it allots value to its protagonists in ways that allow them to fulfill their functions.

We should note that the endorsement and hedging of the comic protagonists facilitate their approval but does not entail their being approved by all the audience, does not, that is, reduce the heterogeneity of Carolean Comedy. Whatever the eventual response to the hero and heroine, everyone would have agreed that they must have admirable traits and skills. As that moralist John Dennis protested in defending *The Man of Mode*, Dorimant "has pass'd for [a fine Gentleman] with all the World, for Fifty Years together. And what indeed can any one mean, when he speaks of a fine Gentleman, but one who is qualify'd in Conversation, to please the best Company of either Sex?" (2: 245). Unless the audience depreciate themselves mightily, therefore, they will be pleased by the conversation of fine ladies and gentlemen. But, like Dennis, they may also disapprove of the fine people's conduct. Mastery of wit helps the heroine or hero act out the desires of those who do not disapprove and those whose disapproval can be assuaged by the protagonists' embarrassment and the moral balm of the ending. For those, like Dennis, who do disapprove, mastery of wit increases the charm and elegance of the play and, in the manner of tragic denouements, reinforces the moral: if even a Dorimant gets his comeuppance, surely anyone less talented will; and it suggests, too, the speciousness of these elegant but treacherous virtues. "*Loveit*," Dennis advises, "has Youth, Beauty, Quality, Wit, and Spirit. And it was depending upon these, that she repos'd so dangerous a Trust in *Dorimont*, which is a just Caution to the Fair Sex, never to be so conceited of the Power of their Charms, or their other extraordinary Qualities" (2: 249). The more one admires the faculty of wit, the more one may regret what the witty person says and deplore what s/he does.

In our model, then, for the play to work well its most glittering protagonist must have a visibly dangerous charisma, able to draw the audience into a wary identification. Engagement by such a Carolean hero differs from engagement with Shakespearean lovers, who demand far more univocal responses and demand them from the whole audience. In Carolean Comedy, the more aggressive and individualistic the hero is, the more he fascinates and also challenges the men in the audience, ethically if they disapprove of his behavior or of their own attraction to it, socially if they see him as a sort of rival who at once directs and vicariously fulfills their appetites through his actions. With Carolean women, we propose, a still more complex relationship seems likely. Some women who went to plays in which a man was the most absorbing character, with the most stage time and action, might respond exactly like male playgoers. Other women, or the same women at other plays, might respond in terms of their own roles in a society that at once kept strongly patriarchal institutions and yet rewarded entrepreneurial acts; that is, they might identify with images of other women who use themselves as "erotically alive and desirable objects" (Symons 182) to get and keep the man (as key to sexual freedom and security) that they seek. To put this another way, sexual politics in Carolean Comedy usually involves strong males' refusal and violations of contracts (vows, marriages) with women, and strong women's trying to enforce such contracts through manipulating male fear and desire. We hypothesize, then, that men among the audience who defined themselves in terms of their public lives would respond strongly to the prospect of private freedom, refusals and violations such as rakes enjoy but that the more vulnerable women who were defined by their husbands' status would be attracted by the pointed maneuvers of both sexes (as has been argued for films; see de Lauretis 141–45).

Maus argues provocatively for two changes in the Restoration which we believe support this argument: first, that on stage, gender polarities replaced the hierarchical "rhetoric of an earlier generation," at the same time that women in some ways withdrew more from public life; second, that contrary to pre-War practice, the audience became intrigued with "the personalities of both male and female players" and that the actresses' sexuality appeared "part and parcel of their histrionic vocation" ("Playhouse" 610, 612–13, 598, 603). Female characters, we would argue, therefore had a peculiar license to act in a way that was no doubt deeply appealing in itself when women's status was so especially uncertain, that shone with a naughty glamor reflected from the actresses' supposed lives of sin, and yet that was sufficiently segregated from everyday life to be taken with varying degrees of seriousness as an ideal. These are plain conditions for the heterogeneity of response and the compromise formations of the Carolean Comedy model.

The ardent pursuit of the beautiful lady by the dashing hero, and usually vice versa, she distinguished by her virginity and her portion, he by his status among other men, satisfies what is both a typical and a historically enforced fantasy of both sexes. Playwrights continuously marketed characters to different interest groups in the audience. Given that, this plot pattern of pursuit and domination imposes a certain delicacy of timing. To please both sexes, the rake's embarrassment should come in a context specific to courtship, preferably with the courted woman present. This principle holds good whether or not the rake is embarrassed through what we called "contamination" by some ridiculed character. To the women in the audience (and, for other motives, to the men), the courted woman is made more erotically alive and therefore more valued through her being desired enough for the rake to risk humiliation for her. (This, of course, is an old pattern from "courtly love," as with Chrétien's Lancelot in his dung cart.) Often, as in *The Gentleman Dancing-Master*, the hero, suddenly at a loss, survives only because the ingenious heroine prompts him, thus further increasing her power and lessening his.

In more conclusive combat between hero and heroine, where he is irremediably victorious over her, as when Dorimant gives Loveit a coup de grace, her defeat renders her useless; hence Loveit is replaced on the spot with Harriet, Dorimant's equal. (Since the heroine must fix her man's affections without his being lowered as the prize of her victory, she is never irremediably victorious.) On rare occasions, because Carolean Comedy assumes the need for equality between combatants of different sexes, the victorious hero may relinquish his advantage, thus to create equality. In John Lacy's *Sauny the Scot* one can see how peremptory in Carolean Comedy such an equalizing treatment of male and female leads is, for this play adapts the most famous, or glaring, example of masculine triumph disguised as "nature" in Elizabethan comedy, Shakespeare's *The Taming of the Shrew*. Lacy not only turns into madcap farce his predecessor's lesson about the order of nature, he also makes his "shrew" spunkier than Katherine, blots out the "tamed" woman's last-act schoolmarmery about wives' kneeling for peace (*Shr.* V.ii.136–79), and has his Petruchio respond to her submission by immediately making her "mistress both of myself and all I have," ready "to change kindnesses, and be each other's servant" (V; 394). But, as we say, such a denouement remains very much atypical.

Spectacle and Roles

We may now round out our argument by ceasing to neglect what no audience can neglect, that they are in a theatre watching actors act. An emphasis on the audience's investment in the characters and even rivalry with them implies the audience's willingness to treat the characters like real people with whom they share a world, much as modern soap opera audiences view the television creatures at whose agonies they gaze daily. We conjecture that actual Carolean comedies to some extent induced and made psychologically acceptable a similarly "naive" response, but that in the setting of Restoration theatres, such naivete thrived together with enforced detachment. Siegfried Kracauer compares the moviegoer, and perhaps the watcher of television, to a hypnotized person, "spellbound by the luminous rectangle before his eyes" and open to suggestion, reverie, and "trance-like immersion" in the spectacle (160–67). But Dorset Gardens or Drury Lane presented a play to a throng in a lighted auditorium, without close-ups or tracking shots. Even with actors nearby on an apron stage, the kind of intimacy was very different, allowing Carolean playgoers to be more like fans at a sports event, a spectatorial fact that enters into the logic of our model.

Of course in crucial ways a Carolean comedy is not like a sports event, constituted by competing participants supposed to be equally matched, nor is the comedy's outcome uncertain. Still, comparison between sports events and these plays offers analogies that strikingly clarify the model of Carolean Comedy, as with other forms of popular art. John G. Cawelti, for example, in his study of "formula stories," notes that in both the stories and in sports "the highly varied ways in which [a set of rules] can be embodied in particular characters and actions produce a patterned experience of excitement, suspense, and release that . . . can be perennially engrossing no matter how often the game is repeated. In the formula world, as in play, the ego is enhanced because conflicts are resolved and inescapable tensions and frustrations temporarily transcended." He quotes Piaget as saying that "conflicts are foreign to play, or, if they do occur it is so that the ego may be freed from them by compensation or liquidation. . . . it is because the ego dominates the whole universe in play that it is freed from conflict" (19–20). These observations plainly tally with our model of Carolean Comedy as an idiom into which members of the audience translate their wishes, so that stage triumphs of an accepted sort for men and women can act as vehicles for more general kinds of desire. At one level, Carolean Comedy involves play with its connotations of freedom, as in the wordplay and play of ideas which one may find in dramatic wit with its *moraliste* character (see chapter 5; Lewis). At another, it involves play as violent assertion of wills, as in physical competition. Both kinds of play are watched for finesse as well as vicariously played by a team's fans.

The mixture of conflict and nonconflict, pleasure in finesse and fandom, concentration on the game as itself but also as an idiom into which other sorts of conflicts may be translated—these obvious characteristics of the sports event bear directly on Carolean Comedy. For example, our Carolean Comedy nicely accommodates traits that some previous critics have considered opposites, such as "realism" and "stylization," "cynical brutality" and "fairy tale telling," "amorality" and a moral frame for the "right way" and the "wrong way." This inclusiveness is latent in any play between representative agents. Think of a World Series or a World Cup soccer game between rival teams representing hostile constituencies. Such a game of representatives can be in various senses "serious" and bear an enormous weight of wish fulfillment, so that a sportswriter, contemplating the fourteen-inch gold statuette that goes to the World Cup winner, can fly off into a rhyming triplet from emotion, like a Carolean tragedien(ne): "Its value is priceless. All the world vies for it. Men die for it. Nations cry for it" (*Dallas Morning News*, 29 June 1986). Yet the game is still, inescapably, a game. However brutal for its players and however played to be won at almost any cost, it will yet be stylized, sequestered by its occasion and rules from the brutality of "real life." Among the crowd, one can be fiercely partisan ("right way"/"wrong way") but need not be.

Again for example, we have argued that each play not only provides a range of closures (satisfactory ways of reducing cognitive dissonance) but recognizes that each viewer has multiple roles. Such roles go beyond those on which we have touched: the viewer may at a given moment identify with the action, judge it, judge the quality of the acting or the play, compare him- or herself to characters per se or in situations, and/or laugh at what s/he sees. A continuously trackable, public version of such mixed reactions appears in the running commentary on a broadcast sports event. There one can hear professional spectators who sometimes judge the action, enclosing it within their own sense of the rules and the space for improvisation, and who sometimes grow more absorbed in that action, though on the air a sportscaster rarely becomes (like the fans) a violent and profane critic or a giddy Walter Mitty. Obviously in the sports event—and, we suggest, also in Carolean Comedy—the fan's Mittyism has to do partly with a given player's prowess, partly with the player's representative heroism, partly with the spectator's own blocked urge to play the game.

"Identification" at the game and in the theatre, then, results from a series of differences. The player is reduced to his or her function, executing rule-governed sequences of action, which the spectator converts into a supplement for his or her daily life where s/he is thwarted from fulfilling appropriate analogues to that function. But in addition to this function, a good player brings a personal style to the game, as does an actor, with which one can identify differently; and a celebrated player or actor is likely to have a public personal life to which a spectator may also react. When one speaks of an audience, one is speaking of a group of members each of whom reacts in terms of changing variables such as these. Carolean Comedy acknowledges and makes use of that fact more powerfully than any English comedy before our own time.

The analogy between these popular spectacles, the sports event and Carolean Comedy, can help develop as well as clarify our model still further. One of the plays' most perceptive readers, Robert D. Hume, observes that "Carolean . . . comedy is formulaic in the extreme" and that "what is most widely characteristic of late seventeenth-century comedies is . . . above all a boisterous *energy* which is greatly invigorating" (*Development* 128, 148). As in our earlier citation from Cawelti, formula and energy, of course, have specifiable roles in spectator sports. In terms of three principles, these roles recur in the comedies. (1) A sport valorizes its own procedures. To play well is to play in terms of the rules, the current practice, the needs of a given contest between given teams in a rule-governed environment. No doubt some form of this proposition holds true of every human activity, but sports events make it visible. Players exist as players because they can take preexisting roles in the sport. What one delights in is not their raw individuality but their intensity and skill in accomplishing something standard, something comparable to what others do. Besides the obvious parallel here to different actors playing specific parts or character types or role types—rake, ingenue, old fumbler—in formulaic plots, we also see a parallel to the conduct of the game or play as a whole. Both take meaning from an idiom to which they contribute meaning. Both, through their formulas, constitute themselves as gripping, aesthetically pleasing, communicative, and relevant to the strivings and pains of "real life." (2) A sport has a double unity. It has an organized, asymmetrical relation (that of winners and losers) and it has a generic pattern, in which all the divergent happenings typify rule-governed possibilities (a strikeout, a pop-up, a force play). The people actually playing the sport of course always see the winner/loser relation but in reflective or strategic moments (the huddle, the time-out) must also weigh generic possibilities, thus in some sense impersonating the spectators. Again, the application to formulaic comedy with scheming, self-conscious, sometimes ratiocinative protagonists is clear. So is the way in which formula can be suffused with an energy of thought, an energy of the potential, precisely because it is "formula." (3) As in the boisterously energetic comedy that Hume discerns, a sport gives pleasure from the display of energy it occasions, such that the spectator reacts in muscular sympathy, applies a kind of body English when the ball is struck, the sprint started, the uppercut landed flush on an unhappy jaw.

To place our earlier remarks on Carolean Comedy in a fuller context, we may expand on these principles, starting with (1) "A sport valorizes its own procedures." Restoration comedy has been blamed as a "comedy of habit"; yet these plays share their use of formulas with not only tennis and basketball but also "high" cultural stage spectacles like the opera or the Kathakali dance theatre of India. These latter seem different from comedy in being high-flown, ceremonious, and mythopoetic theatre, to take up the descriptive terms of Herbert Lindenberger's *Opera: The Extravagant Art*. But all these cultural modes distance and "universalize" their actions. Thus Carolean Comedy's high degree of patterning and plot formulas, perceived as such, fence off the action from that of "real life" so as to permit the audience to engage with it without feeling impugned as a result. Heroines and heroes take preexisting roles and so reinforce a mythopoeia of desire in which they are representative figures. One does not find many elaborately or subtly characterized roles in Carolean comedies because that kind of art would individualize too much and also perhaps channel moral judgment too much. Instead, again as in the opera or in a sport, the playwright tries for and often achieves intensity through a combination of prowess, glamor, and focused energy: Isolde sung by the famous diva with her powerful and gorgeous high notes; the quarterback with his enormously lucrative contract and strong, accurate arm; Dorimant or Horner, wittier, sexier, and more determined-than-thou. The rules of the game are the sole constraints, though fierce constraints, on the will that expresses itself, necessarily, through them.

A sport, as we have remarked, is an autonomously chosen, socially acknowledged activity, and its main rewards come in some form of socially acknowleged specie (a ring, a trophy, an entry in record books) defined by the rules and contexts of the game. The "specie," that is, has value as it represents freedom and power in one's own mind and others'. To apply our analogy, whereas in Shakespeare or Franz Lehár lovers fall in love, in Carolean Comedy lovers more often attain an appropriate object of desire, a symbol of victory. Protagonists are at once agents and rewards, the audience's representatives and their chosen "specie." Thus the playwright follows social and generic principles of endogamy a good deal narrower than those in the ballads we earlier surveyed. By these rules, no King Cophetua and his beggar maid, no Squire B. and Pamela can appear in Carolean Comedy, because the spouse-to-be of a hero must be marked as a reward through inherited status (birth, money). By the 1670s, to be a hero's worthy prize, "gay" heroines also need earned status, the ability to be as strong as the men they bring to the altar; in a society of status inconsistency, personal and social status must coincide for the stability of marriage to be earned. No reverse mésalliance—a comic version of Jaffeir and Belvidera or Mellors and Lady Chatterley—can appear either. The spouse-to-be of a heroine needs earned status, power over or preeminent respect among his nominal peers. He must make men, and no doubt also women, want to identify with him, to see him as an agent who can exercise freedom of sexual choice. She in turn must make women, and no doubt also men (as they deal with their own envy or disapproval of the rake), want to identify with her, to see her as a surrogate means of fixing male sexual appetite, hence marital desire. As we have noted, the Carolean stage simplified this task by developing star actresses. In fulfilling these typical courtship roles, and in having few traits of character that do not help fill these roles, heroine and hero satisfy the wishes of both men and women in the audience. Let us stress once again that by necessity, unlike the stock, docile, placeholder lovers in many earlier and later romantic comedies, characters designed for the terms of Carolean Comedy remain vivid, full of life, and fascinating, as the better heroes and heroines of Dryden, Wycherley, Etherege, Shadwell, and Behn plainly are. The heroines in particular may, and typically do, have more charisma than any in pre-Restoration drama, before actresses.

In valorizing its own procedures, Carolean Comedy liberates itself from, or conceals, competing modes of valuation. Here the motif of freedom is crucial. Since the chosen mate is awarded to acknowledge a competitive victory, no need of the heroine or hero should steal center stage from that competition. S/he must be perceived as needing nothing but the freedom to compete. Even a stated need for money (on his part) or more general liberty (on hers) is largely a pretext for action. In Carolean Comedy, protagonists remain unconstrained by serious ties or duties. No one has an old mother to support, no single parent has a minor child—the Widow Blackacre is a proof of this rule rather than an exception to it—although such familial ties were frequent in a society with seventeenth-century London's mortality rate. Wish fulfillment (by definition?) requires relative independence and views compulsion as an enemy. As we will suggest in more detail, the only acceptable compulsion is from within, that of psychological drives that focus appetite on classes of objects (sexual, political, financial) and thus create the possibility of wish fulfillment by creating the possibility of wishes.

Although we do not claim that Carolean Comedy developed the independent, intensely realized, representative hero so as to prompt audience identification, that end, we believe, was well served by such a hero. In identification the audience have reciprocal relationships with what they see on stage. The character creates or extends, directs, and enacts their desires; the character's success, however, hangs on their social judgment, as is implied by our historical argument about a range of self-images that might be wished for in the Restoration. Even where a character strategically forfeits the good opinion of his own represented society, as Horner in part does, those in the know must see him as acting for ends within society and social expectations. Horner just goes on horning as he did before his fatal trip to France; he could not really become a eunuch, a hermit, or a man of business like Sir Jaspar Fidget. As Sedgwick says:

> If [Horner] gives up the friendship and admiration of other men, it is only in order to come into a more intimate and secret relation to them—a relation over which his cognitive mastery is so complete that they will not even know that such a bond exists. . . . Because he is willing not to undergo but to represent "castration" himself and because he himself assumes the role of passive and circulable commodity—because in one register he withdraws from the role of rival to that of object—he is able in another register to achieve an unrivaled power as an active subject. (232–33)

The audience, preeminently in the know, arbitrates all values in the play from its own varying standards, adapted of course for the genre of dramatic comedy. Carolean Comedy thus not only engages the desires of its audience, it also authenticates the range and tenor of values by which they weigh those desires. (In contrast, some comedies of the 1660s, like *The Adventures of Five Hours*, did not feed desires in the same way; some comedies of the 1680s, like Otway's, did not authenticate the system of values.)

(2) "A sport has a double unity." Most of the bonding between audience and protagonist comes from his or her display of wit, grace, power, and glamor. But additional bonding between audience and characters occurs when a character, in the phrase we used earlier, impersonates the spectator by stepping back from the competition to comment on the action. Carolean Comedy lends a double self-consciousness to its protagonists, who not only act for socially under-

standable ends but also display themselves doing so, thereby turning "private" behavior into a performance. S/he survives the risk of fixity in a role, like Sir Fopling Flutter or Pinchwife, through, so to speak, gazing at her- or himself playing that role. In evincing this liberating awareness of the role s/he takes within a larger, grasped situation, the heroine or hero stands with the audience. As a knowledgeable, therefore privileged interpreter of the action, s/he becomes the vehicle for the audience's thoughts as well as their fantasies. Sometimes this function involves making generalizations about human nature, sometimes simply about a local situation or a figure in the play, but whatever the scope of the commentary, the audience is meant to accept the generalizations when they are uttered. In the world of *The Country-Wife* a quack is as fit for a pimp as a midwife for a bawd, since they are still but in their way both helpers of nature. We do not mean to imply that the maxims of the spectatorial rake become the play's gospel, an argument that would run directly counter to the principle of heterogeneity on which we have insisted. But they do valorize the rules of the game, defining the world within which the rakish action takes place. The ending of the play may (at least for some members of the audience) cancel out this world, but it nevertheless is inhabited for five acts.

Typically the hero-commentator's stepping out of his or her involvement has a counterpart in mimicry and disguise, where the plot itself compels someone to be aware of playing a role. Mimicry and disguise capture a character type, a set of motives, or formulas of response not in words, like a commentator's generalizations, but in actions. To be a convincing gentleman dancing master demands an understanding of the genre in which one finds oneself. And just as generalizations give the effect of freedom and power by their verbal mastery of the subject, so does mimicry by its practical mastery: high characters in Carolean Comedy almost always buy freedom and power through mimicry of figures of less freedom and power, as in Horner's pretense of being a eunuch or in Dorimant's of being a conventional civil gentleman who can charm Harriet's mother. (In Carolean Comedy, to mimic one's equals or betters is affectation, which usually leads to disaster. The one exception to this rule is women's disguising themselves as men, which sometimes leads to no overall increase in freedom—Doralice and Melantha in *Marriage A-la-Mode*, Margery and "Fidelia" in Wycherley's two last plays—and sometimes purchases added freedom by added risk—Mrs. Gripe in Shadwell's *The Woman-Captain*.) The price of freedom for those who seek it through disguise is to have their mastery tested before they can triumph.

Of course, any kind of mastery produces bonding with many of the audience. Verbal mastery in addition gives the spectators a voice through a principal character. Paradoxically, the mastery in mimicry produces still firmer bonding by being achieved through a principal's accepting, so to speak, a mode of surrogate loss by pretending to be a dutiful son, a clergyman, a suitor to the egregious Blackacre, or something degrading of the sort. The fuller mastery of the audience remains, as they like it, unchallenged. Still more important, it gains strength through watching the hero or heroine make such splendid capital of a slumming expedition into those very roles that represent the audience's real fears and real lives, the impotent, the workaday, the obligated. The audience thus find their desires authenticated by the plot and their self-image as knowing and powerful also reinforced through the characters' function as commentators in words and acts.

(3) "A sport gives pleasure from the display of energy it occasions." We earlier set up as a point of comparison between Carolean Comedy and a sporting event the vicarious expression of energy given to someone watching a game. The same sort of pleasure comes from ceremonious forms of art, like dance or opera, in which the text (like the "text" of a sports event) is a stimulus for a consummating practice. Entrechats and coloratura, stick smartly smacking puck into the net, are parts of a virtuoso effort that is both text-determined and spontaneous. So is the performance of a great farceur, for whom enacting a text involves treating it as a set of parameters that govern his or her display. Although the intricate plotting and designed repartee scripted into Carolean Comedy does not transmit the energy of practice in quite this way, the farce in the plays does, as do the rapid peripeteias of the action. Moreover, the acting style probably fitted these kinds of liveliness. Charles Gildon claimed that the greatest actor of the period, Betterton, took as a first principle that "the Eye is caught by any thing in Motion, but passes over the sluggish and motionless things as not the pleasing Objects of its View. . . . [T]he Attention of the Audience is fixt by any irregular or even fantastic Action on the Stage of the most indifferent Player; and supine and drowsy, when the best Actor speaks without the Addition of *Action*" (26). We see the energy of action on stage as a means of intensifying the vividness we mentioned earlier and thus of setting forth a persuasive, immediate action that stages and fulfills the audience's appetites.

A second kind of energy in Carolean Comedy arises from the bustling, plotting world, so prone to boredom, in which the action occurs. A London that might be disturbing if it were real, the lustful and predatory town of Dryden's, Etherege's, and Wycherley's comedies, needs to exist on stage so as to display everyone in pursuit of desires and thereby set up an ethical framework in which the desires of the audience are valid. In Carolean Comedy, this world undergoes a crucial isolation so that ordinary standards of behavior do not apply with ordinary force nor do they have the utility that they have in ordinary life: here, as usual, comedy displays a freedom from the everyday run of consequences. The plot itself isolates the world through its own energy and intricacy, as well as its formal balance, so as to define an arena in which the protagonists meet and usually defeat specific threats to their progress or aura. This arrangement helps the protagonists, coping with a dangerous world on the move, to define the point of view within the play. To avoid the isolation's rendering the action a mere game, however, Carolean Comedy insists on the correspondence of that dangerous world with the "real world" of the audience's experience; hence the portraits of current behavior and other signs of "realism." In so doing, these plays offer a paradigm of conquest over what is genuinely disturbing to the audience, the everyday world that stunts their desires, by showing it, as Polly Peachum would say, troubled, bubbled, bamboozled, and bit. The energy of Carolean Comedy is an assurance of vitality and, in part, of triumphant reprisal.

Carolean Comedy, then, defines the appetites of the audience, performs actions and presents objects that those appetites crave, and helps the members of the audience to define themselves in ways that they find most comfortable. In formulating the process this way, we are refusing to distinguish—as moral defenders and attackers insist on doing—between the plays' mimetic and rhetorical functions with regard to desire: do the plays vicariously satisfy desires that are already there, or do they, like modern advertizing, create and stoke desires? We do not believe these two functions can be separated in practice, since the plays exist within and as an instrumentality of a society that forms its members' desires through all its symbol-making activities. We would, however, argue that these comedies try to make the audience feel good about themselves, not (as, for instance, in Shakespeare) by displaying to them a world where all's well that ends well, but by making them victorious over a world like that envisioned by pragmatic seventeenth-century scientists, a potential garden of profit and delight, of energies that can be mastered and put to use. This is the secular, extraverted, entrepreneurial version of the older, lingering creed in which human energies ("passion") were properly to canter under the reins of divinely ordered purpose ("reason"). Members of the audience may take the protagonists' road to this entrepreneurial end or may treat all the characters, including the protagonists, as events or stops in their own progress, or, of course, do both. Carolean Comedy poses no obstacles to the audience's imagined achievement of glamor, success, power, or even their notion that justice, poetic justice, reigns. This comedy, often brilliantly, stages the world as you or you or you like it.

3

Establishing the Repertory 1659–68

We have outlined an approach to Carolean comedy that accounts both for the critical controversy over the plays and for the peculiar mingling of distance and intimacy such comedy provokes in its audiences. In the process, we have touched upon some social and political reasons why this kind of comedy might differ from its predecessors. But we have only mentioned, not explained, a generic reason that is equally distinctive and essential. We refer, of course, to the development of the repertory, that hotbed warmed by the rivalry of two "houses," two companies, which vied for public favor. There the flourishing repertory of the moment was constantly being crowded by the possible repertory—new plays or new revivals—that might replace it. As a money-making enterprise, the Carolean theatre was an unsubsidized business, depending on gate receipts that in turn depended on pleasing the public. Each new play produced, therefore, had to win its place against old London favorites; as Joseph Donahue says, because "the traditional English repertory theatre maintains a large number of plays, sometimes altered, sometimes withdrawn, sometimes revived, all to suit the changing tastes of demanding audiences. . . . the author of a new play must compete not only with those of his contemporaries but with [older] works of proven merit" (7). Such a system led to moderate conservatism, for "managers needed [a] stock of proven box-office appeal as their base of annual operation" (G. Stone 181). But as long as rival theatres existed, the enticements of novelty meant that conservatism could not be more than moderate. "In the height of theatrical warfare," Milhous writes about the 1670s and late 1690s, "each company often staged ten or a dozen new plays each year, and a production could be gotten up from scratch in three to six weeks" ("Company" 27).

These comments about caution and novelty apply peculiarly to the Carolean theatre in the early 1660s, for as never before or since in Britain there was a clear beginning, a time after the Great Lord Protector's Void when there was Light, at first glimmering, then abundant. In appendix 1, we have summarized current information about the problems of initial production during the first few years of the period. But during most of the 1660s, practical conditions forced theatrical managers to rely more on old than on new repertory, even

41

beyond the reasons suggested previously. Possibly the impetus to put on new plays was also greater than usual at this time especially because theatregoers had a sharp sense of their own historical position and of the pastness of the pre-War past. Except for reasons of nostalgia, these audiences presumably wanted plays that mirrored their own time, yet such plays could only appear slowly to edge out the trusty repertory of Jonson, Middleton, Shirley, Fletcher, and the rest. These pre-War classics had to provide shelter when good new plays were not at hand or when new plays at hand turned out not to be good, while cramped finances made managers experiment unusually widely and unusually carefully with new plays to gauge as well as to meet the public fancy.

In the Carolean theatre, as in any active, competitive repertory environment, these new plays sometimes capitalized on a popular formula, sometimes tried to create a new fashion, but more often, combined both and were innovative in terms of what the playwright and management had reason to think would sell. Because of this peculiar kind of innovative conservatism, repertory development can be traced by observing the alterations of inherited conventions of plot, character, and ethos in successive seasons. For this purpose, one must categorize plays, and we have tried to do so in terms that the playwrights themselves might have found useful. One such term is that of popularity, and although performance records are wretchedly skimpy, we have made such distinctions at least in the years when Pepys was recording his play going, up to the 1668–69 season (see appendix l). We have, that is, not considered comedies of which fewer than two performances have been recorded.

The other terms we have used are modal, like "fletcherian" and "jonsonian," because we can refer them to admired repertory pieces, define them, and with them bypass such vague, inclusive rubrics as "comedy of manners" and "Jacobean comedy." Carolean playwrights did not use these modal terms, but they did cite Fletcher and Jonson as models, and they did write within idioms set by the formats of older comic drama. Such modal characteristics, of course, are not absolutes but tendencies of plot, character, and other variables. In each case, their defining force derived from specific comedies popular in the repertory rather than from the entire printed canon of a given author; with Fletcher, the popular comedies typified the canon as a whole, but this was not true with Jonson or Shakespeare.

The Beginnings to 1665

Fletcherian and Jonsonian Modes: Old Plays

Thirty-seven comedies are recorded as having three or more performances from the opening of the theatres to the time of the Plague, when the theatres were temporarily shut down (see appendix 2). Only nine are new, and some of these are new versions of plays written before 1660, like Davenant's *The Law Against Lovers* and *The Rivals* or Cowley's *Cutter of Coleman Street*. Of the twenty-eight "old" plays, fourteen are wholly or in part by one man, Fletcher, and three more by his collaborators and followers. In fact, plays by Fletcher and other "fletcherian" plays account for almost half the total performances for the most popular comedies—96 of 194—and about two-thirds of the total performances for pre-War comedies—96 of 149. As Arthur C. Kirsch has said, "Beaumont and Fletcher . . . clearly dominated the repertory of the English stage for the better part of the seventeenth century. . . . No English dramatists before or since have had so extraordinary an influence" (*Jacobean* 3–4). By this, of course, he means more than the prevalence of Fletcher's plays on stage: the greatest importance of Fletcher for dramatic history has to do with the mode for which his plays were such popular ambassadors. To what extent this mode came from the influence of Fletcher himself and to what extent it grew from the social or other theatrical demands of its time is unanswerable. To what degree the idiom of Carolean Comedy followed this mode, however, is answerable, along with the extent to which this mode meshed with the peculiar audience/stage relationship described in chapter 2. In Fletcher can be found the pattern of a highly energetic, formulaic comedy with representative heroines as well as representative heroes, all designed to serve desire and affectivity.

The fletcherian mode—we use the lowercase "f" to detach the word from the practice of John Fletcher alone—originated not in comedy but in tragicomedy. The mixture of emotions in this new genre lent itself to rapid reversals from laughter to tears to fear to joy: tragicomedy has a logical, if not an obligatory claim to emotional comprehensiveness. As a result, fletcherian plays bring forth, dish by dish, a banquet for the emotions. In Arthur Mizener's words:

> Beaumont and Fletcher's aim was to generate in the audience a patterned sequence of responses, a complex series of feelings and atti-

tudes so stimulated and related as to give to each its maximum effectiveness and yet to keep all in harmonious balance. The ultimate ordering form in all their plays is this emotional form, and the narrative, though necessarily the ostensible object, is actually with them only a means to the end of establishing this rich and careful arrangement of responses.   (135)

Of course, any dramaturgy, even that of Brecht when most fascinated by *Verfremdung*, produces an effective series of emotional responses, at least if the audience is to be kept seated and awake. Here and elsewhere, the fletcherian mode differs from others in degree, not kind. Nonetheless, a combination of an affective emphasis (rather than one on narrative development or cognitive values) and an impulse toward variety leads to consequences that one can isolate and identify.

Fletcherian plays contain an exceptional sum of energy. They are likely to have several near-simultaneous, independent actions which may or may not achieve the status of separate plots. Each of these actions moves forward with changes in velocity, so to speak, through surprising revelations, twists of fortune, and character reversals, with discoveries and peripeteias marking its slalom. In counterpointing the multiple actions in his play, a fletcherian playwright's main interest is not cognitive, is not increased understanding, but formal (through analogies that lend the play structural coherence), contrastive (through differences in tone or emotional force that add to the variety of the fare), and rhythmic (through changes from dynamic characters, like a pair of witty lovers, to static ones, like humours characters; from rage and passion to languor or melancholy; from one set of asserted or assumed values to another). Form, contrast, and rhythm are neither exhaustive nor mutually exclusive ends, but all three direct and contain the high energy of fletcherian drama.

Although a fletcherian play may move toward a final climax, an eleventh-hour unveiling or reversal right before the denouement, such a climax is merely the last, though often the biggest, in a series. Typically, an action looks as though it might conclude more or less satisfactorily early in a play, but then a reversal unravels everything. A ruse is discovered, parents intervene, someone changes his or her mind for a reason that might or might not have been necessary. Thus, although fletcherian comedies tend to use a few basic plot patterns, nearly all having to do with courtships obstructed by rivals, parents (and brothers), and/or the wilfulness or folly of the lovers themselves, the plays sustain their audiences' attention by focusing on the "how," the intricate and unforeseen means to the obvious end.

Such a structure is wonderfully elastic. It allows the playwright the widest range of actions, characters, and effects, even if its pliability and speed tend to deny him or her much chance of developing profound cognitive meaning. At the same time, the movement of the play, however ingeniously wrought, has an underlying clarity from the division of a plot line into a series of episodes or actions nearly as discrete as the three tasks in *Rumpelstiltskin* or the stops in Odysseus' perilous tourism on his way home from Troy. Furthermore—as in *Rumpelstiltskin* or the *Odyssey*—in the fletcherian play a conclusion often does not follow more than generally from the episodes that precede it. Fletcher's own plays often have predictable, broadly moral conclusions; but the moral ending, as for example in *A King and No King*, may run counter to the apparent thrust of the plot and the "truth" of the characters.[5] In a given fletcherian play (like *A King and No King*), one might interpret such an ending as ironic, but the moral ending is more rightly seen as convenient, a contrivance to please the audience and satisfy their sense of rightness. Because of the artificiality of fletcherian comedy, such a device is less necessary or calculated than the "compromise formation" of Carolean Comedy; but it is certainly in the same vein of authorial control. As Kirsch remarks, sudden moral resolutions which in earlier tragicomedy or romance had been marks of Providence are no longer used to organize the action in fletcherian drama (*Jacobean* 38). Instead, they are God's gift to the prestidigitator playwright.

Because affective concerns rule these plays, characters are constructed in the service of emotional effects. Eugene Waith calls such characters "Protean," "monsters and saints, living abstractions and combinations of irreconcilable extremes" who "elude our grasp by changing shape from moment to moment" (38). Kirsch expands upon this:

> Psychologically considered, the characters in [serious fletcherian drama] simply do not have enough substance to explore. They are all primarily elements in a spatial design and they follow completely from the design, not the design from them. They are accordingly portrayed with radical discontinuities, capable of Protean change . . . or with

---

[5] "An atmosphere of encompassing evil is created in *A King and No King* and increases in density until the end of the last act, when it is dispelled by the discovery that Arbaces is the son of an old counselor and was adopted by the Queen. . . . His incestuous passion becomes legitimate romantic love, and (illogically) his other objectionable traits disappear, as if they were functions of the false position in which he was placed. . . . The evil of the play seems in retrospect to have been no more than a bad dream." (Waith 35–36)

> consistent but stereotyped humours . . . which are equally in the service of a peripatetic action. (*Jacobean* 47)

On the face of it, such evaluations would suggest that three or four generations of seventeenth-century audiences were profligate with their tears, when "sympathy" made "A glowing Tide of Wo gush from each Eye" that watched *The Maid's Tragedy*, the play Kirsch uses as an example (*Jacobean* 38). But, in fact, unless one is an analytic critic, such characters appear quite substantial on stage, where the actor's physical presence helps guarantee a continuous identity for the character and invests with life what looks like a stock part on paper.

But not even a Betterton can provide what does not exist. Fletcherian characters do not allow one to infer an underlying psychological life with subtleties of motive, growth of experience, and nuances of feeling. What one sees and hears is pretty much what one has: the limits of inference about character compensate for the "radical discontinuities" of portrayal just as the limits of inference about "meaning" in the play as a whole compensate for the variety and energy of events. Disorder is thus held within a restricted field; to remove the restrictions on character or meaning would create a broad interpretative problem, how to make sense of events and characters despite their radical unpredictability. Fletcher and his immediate school maintained these restrictions on the number and range of questions it is appropriate to ask of their drama (and which apply, of course, only to the way the audience sees the play, not the way the poor, puzzled characters in the plays see their surroundings). Carolean playwrights chose to modify those restrictions.

A better term than "Protean" for these characters, since Proteus metamorphosed himself ad libitum, is A. O. Lovejoy's "adjectival" (79–81). Adjectival values, in Lovejoy's use, refer to roles (self-image, projection of an image to others) rather than goals of action. The roles may be images one wants to avoid—coward, fool, cuckold—as well as desired ones—lover, arch-manipulator—but their grounding in either case is in opinion, the judgment of oneself and others, rather than in ends of either a more solid or a more ideal sort. Thus, fletcherian characters modify themselves for themselves and others, and the task is made easier by the simplification of "self" with which the plays operate, since if there is no "underlying psychological life," as we have called it, characters can move themselves freely and alter radically. The fletcherian playwright also creates "adjectival" characters as he attunes their "selves" to the effect they will produce on the audience rather than to some independent measure (as in morality plays) or conception of thematic coherence (as in Shakespearean or Shavian plays) which controls both character and action.

Some other characteristics of the fletcherian mode identified by Waith and others—like the vague, pervasive atmosphere of evil, the improbable hypothesis, and the rhetorical elaborations of its debates and set speeches—are either limited to tragedy and tragicomedy and do not really concern us here, or when they appear in comedy, serve different purposes. Improbability, for instance, is often a virtue in comedy. So, perhaps, is a form of elaborate rhetoric which, when turned into wit, establishes the rhythms of a particular kind of comedy. Kirsch notes that these also can add to the psychological verisimilitude of the characters. He points to a scene in *The Scornful Lady* where the Lady appears to be moved by a diatribe from her lover, the Elder Loveless, whom she has already sent into exile, then duped and rejected. Loveless' fervent denunciation brings her to kiss his hand and swoon, at which he predictably begs her forgiveness and reavows his faith, causing the Lady and two companions to burst into laughter at him and reject him again. As he rushes out in a rage, the Lady genuinely repents of her behavior. Kirsch remarks about this scene (IV.i):

> Like [two scenes in *The Maid's Tragedy*, this one] consists of extreme turns and counterturns, of characters whose emotions oscillate violently, of declamations which are at once passionate and contrived. . . . The difference is that whereas in *The Maid's Tragedy* the extreme discontinuities of character and the turns of passionate debate which are their consequence can be accepted only as theatrical conventions, in *The Scornful Lady* they represent credible human behavior. Elder Loveless's contortions are the reflections of a young man in love, while the artifices of the Lady are the expression of a woman who finds herself incapable of accepting not only the love of a man but the reality of her own feelings. Interacting with one another, the two form a pattern representing the dynamics of a recognizable human relationship.   (*Jacobean* 49–50)

Without necessarily accepting Kirsch's judgments of *The Maid's Tragedy* or *The Scornful Lady*, one can agree that the more the situation seems to prompt characters to pretense, to be like Proteus in willing their changes adaptively, the more illusion the audience has of such characters' inner psychological life, perhaps even a complex integrity. And fletcherian comedy, needless to say, is largely made up of such disguise-inducing situations.

What the fletcherian mode meant in comic practice can be seen by looking at an example: *The Scornful Lady* (Bowers ed.) will do as well as any, in being both typical of Fletcher and quite popular throughout the Restoration (six performances recorded before 1665, eight thereafter). The central action involves three attempts by the Elder Loveless to win the Lady in marriage, though she has ordered him to spend a penitential year abroad for the crime of having stolen a kiss from her in public. His first maneuver is to come back in disguise to report his own death, but he is secretly recognized by the Lady, who thereupon mournfully announces to the "messenger" that she will take another husband, her suitor Welford, even though the Elder Loveless would have been her first choice. When he then unmasks, she laughs and reenjoins his penitential exile.

His second attempt at her is in the scene we earlier summarized. Here the courtship dance begins with a reversal of previous positions, as he adopts her scornful role, she his of entreaty, until her pretended melting before his diatribe causes first him, then her, to reverse positions. Finally, Loveless' third and eventually successful attempt repeats and reverses the first (disguise, threat of marriage to another). He appears with the Lady's former suitor Welford disguised as a woman and announces that he will marry "her." Afraid of losing the Elder Loveless forever, and conscious of having acted dishonorably to him (as she has earlier accused him of acting dishonorably to her), the Lady allows herself to be whisked off to an immediate marriage. Welford, meanwhile, has been taken in pretended tears to the bedroom of the Lady's sister, Martha, for comforting, and by the end of the play, he and Martha have comforted each other so generously that their marriage too is impending.

Alongside this tripartite, peripatetic central action are episodes analogous to it. Some deal with the Lady's old, lecherous maid, Younglove, who doubles her mistress through a parallel pattern of mockery/entreaty/marriage with the Lady's chaplain, Roger. More important are episodes that involve the Younger Loveless, a profligate brother who offsets Martha, the Lady's profligate sister, in the scheme of the play. A spendthrift with a troupe of four parasites (captain, poet, tobacco-man, and traveller), the Younger Loveless corrupts his brother's steward, swindles (through no ingenuity of his own) his chief creditor, the usurer Morecraft, and marries a rich widow who will keep him and his parasites in drink ad infinitum. His squandering of money stands in contrast to the Elder Loveless' prudence, his company of parasites to the Elder Loveless' lonely exile, his fraternal indifference to his brother's fraternal care, and his effortless successes to his brother's laborious courtship. He supplants his brother as master of the estate (while the Elder Loveless is supposedly on his way abroad) at the same time that Welford supplants the Elder Loveless as suitor. The Younger Loveless' destitution when the play opens is like his brother's—one man bereft of money, one of love—and just as his brother brings the Lady to give herself to him, so the Younger Loveless, without really trying, brings the Widow to be his wife and the usurer Morecraft to imitate his mindless liberality. In short, each of his acts parodies or inverts an element in the main plot, usually an element directly juxtaposed to it in the sequence of scenes in the play, and his career from bankrupt to seeming heir to successful swindler of Morecraft (precisely through losing his position as heir) and at last to betrothed man is as peripatetic and unpredictable as is his brother's in the main plot.

This high degree of patterning in *The Scornful Lady* can be taken as typical of the manufacture of fletcherian comedy. So can the fact that none of it carries any cognitive burden at all: one learns nothing about either brother (or sister) from the other. Both plots end well, and the siblings remain in amity throughout (despite the Younger Loveless' joy at the news of his brother's "death" and his windfall inheritance). The sharply different value systems to which they adhere never seem to be in open conflict.

On the other hand, we do not mean to suggest that the counterpointing of the Loveless brothers (and, to a lesser extent, the two sisters) simply pads out the play. Both the clear patterning and the marbling of irresponsible levity added by the Younger Loveless episodes prevent one from taking the play too soberly. In such a mixed atmosphere, it is only right that the Elder Loveless's ingenuity rather than his passion wins the Lady, though the passion too has its place, in reassuring her that marriage will mean neither absolute submission nor lonely nights. Moreover, Fletcher must let us know that the Elder Loveless has enough good sense and reason to contrive a strategy, although for reasons of plot those qualities would be inappropriate in his early addresses to the Lady. Thus, the subplot lets us know about them by presenting the Elder's prudent, sympathetic counsel to his profligate brother. Meanwhile, the Widow's doting on the appearance of honor—she insists on marrying a knight—parodies the Lady's imposition on the Elder Loveless of a task from chivalric romance ("almost invincible labours performed for your mistres" [I.i.116–17]); the Widow's capitulation to one brother foretells the Lady's to the other, and in fact the Elder Loveless' triumph is enhanced by his having set up not one but three rich marriages: for Welford, his own brother, and himself. Even if this counterpointing does have some cognitive function, in preparing for the Lady's capitulation through the Widow's prior one, that function is shrunk by its being largely unnecessary: the comic tone of the play has already told everyone what to expect, if not when or how.

Counterpointed actions teach the audience, then, what it does not have to learn. What about the characters? None learns anything from any other, except for the usurer who turns spendthrift when he sees the Younger Loveless wealthy and wedded as a result of wholehearted imprudence. Aside from that mock-learning, only the Lady develops, and that is because of self-realization. Fletcher might have chosen to show the Elder Loveless, twice duped and rebuffed, learning from experience that he must force the Lady to commit herself in action as well as in words. That is, in fact, the course Loveless takes successfully at the end. But experience has not taught him his tactics, for his earlier failure has simply come from the Lady's penetrating his disguise when he reports his "death." She would not have committed herself in action no matter how clever he had been. One might argue that Loveless' final successful trick comes from his having seen the effects of jealousy upon himself and then trying to produce those effects in the Lady. But however much this parallelism may show the lovers as like-minded, and therefore suited to one another, it hardly gives the sense of one individuated human being with special insights into the mind of another whom he loves.

Throughout the whole play, characters who presumably know each other well surprise each other: to judge by the Elder Loveless' puzzled dismay, the Lady never before has shown her dominant humour of capricious scorn, though they are so intimate that "all the howers of day and night have seene us kisse" (I.i.128–29), nor does the older brother know the extent of the younger's callousness. This underscores an important characteristic of fletcherian drama. In plays by Shakespeare or Jonson, characters are rapidly made known to the audience, old acquaintances surprise each other only on extraordinary occasions (except for practiced hypocrites or practiced-upon fools), and individual nature is taken seriously. In contrast, the fletcherian mode whets more than it satisfies our curiosity about individual characters or motives. Character is an alterable element of situation, "adjectival" for the playwright who wants to develop an effect.

A highly patterned plot filled with reversals, divided into three complete episodes and counterpointed with two lesser actions; "adjectival" characters; thinning of cognitive meaning to a minimum; and inconsistency of ethical codes—*The Scornful Lady* exemplifies fletcherian practice in all these regards. Its ending is also typical. Fletcher wants a big scene for his last reversal, so it is longer, more elaborate in its interactions, and more ornamented with analogies (Martha's affair, the rehabilitation of the Lovelesses' steward Saville, Morecraft's conversion) than the earlier confrontations between the Lady and

Elder Loveless. Yet as a resolution of the play's problems (principles of disorder), this "big" ending lacks force, partly because Fletcher simply extends the already established pattern of development from which the disorder itself proceeded.

The Younger Loveless, still (one supposes) wagging his sycophants behind him, seems ready to fritter away his new wife's fortune on ale, if not whores. More important, the newly married Lady chafes at her lost ascendancy, telling the Elder Loveless: "By this light, had I but sented out your traine [trick], ye had slept with a bare pillow in your armes, and kist that, or else the bed-post, for any wife yee had got this twelve-month yet. I would have vext you more than a tyr'd post-horse: and bin longer bearing, then ever after-game at *Irish* was. Lord, that I were unmaried againe!" (V.iv.78–83). Most of her remaining speeches in the play are to wish Welford had not had Martha, to declare herself shamed by having Young Loveless as a brother-in-law, and to be snide and threaten her new husband with cuckolding. These actions can be interpreted as final in that they parody rather than continue the earlier conflicts, but at the same time they also establish the oscillation of fletcherian characters and actions. Certainly the Lady's new husband continues the conflict, since she, who exiled him at the beginning of the play for stealing a kiss and telling the company that he had had many like it, now must put up with his sexual boasts: "How like you this dish, *Welford*, I made a supper on't, and fed so heartily, I could not sleepe" (V.iv.76–77). One may compare with this the ending of Shakespeare's *Taming of the Shrew* where Katherine's new consciousness of her role in home and society comes from an enhanced awareness of her previous self which Petruchio therapeutically had mirrored for her inspection. In the course of the play, she discovers her real self and he uncovers—the theatrical sense of "discovers"—his. Fletcher's plot, unlike Shakespeare's, would be open-ended if one could imagine the characters with any life offstage. This sense of the action going on adds spice and tartness to the play. It does not, however, endanger the closure because the whole comedy is so plainly ruled by the conventions of the theatre. In fletcherian drama, the best guarantee for the harmony of the denouement is the pliability and noncontinuousness of the characters, even when, like the Lady, they seem to be feisty and restive.

The fletcherian mode contrasts with those typical of Shakespeare and Jonson, Fletcher's older contemporaries in the Carolean repertory. Shakespeare, even in his most fletcherian plays (*Cymbeline*, *The Winter's Tale*, *The Tempest*, and, if it is by Shakespeare, *Pericles*), is much less given to what one might call "strophic" structure, a consecutive series of analogous episodes. Instead, he presents characters with their full range of capabilities suggested, so that the play moves forward in ways that one can anticipate. In Fletcher, nothing is assured in a world of surprising changes, and the audience's formulations are in a perpetual state of ironic tension. For a similar effect, Shakespeare provides a deepening emotional response through a deepening cognitive awareness: there is a logic (at times in the tragedies even a ruthless logic) to his procedures. Thus in *Much Ado About Nothing* he prepares the audience through knowledge of Claudio's character for the loss of faith in Hero, and what seems like a sudden reversal—what would be a sudden reversal in Fletcher—is more likely to stun those on stage than the observant spectator in the theatre. If the audience is fooled, as happens occasionally, it is only so that Shakespeare can create a greater effect thereby, like the magical joy when Hermione's statue comes to life, or a realization, as when Iachimo climbs out of the chest, of how vulnerable certain characters are. In Shakespeare, such surprises create and sustain empathy between characters and audience, whereas in Fletcher, surprises are common coin, empathy a thing of the moment. Similarly, double plots in Shakespeare far more often have cognitive force than in Fletcher, and Shakespeare's endings have a finality and harmony which makes noninclusion—Shylock, Malvolio—a shocking exception. None of this, let us be quick to say, makes Shakespeare's mode in and of itself better or worse than Fletcher's. Each, however, can accomplish something different.

In fact, the "something different" of Shakespearean comedy was not very successful after the Restoration.[6] Jonson's comedies, though limited by the Lord Chamberlain's edict to the King's Company alone (see appendix 1), were more popular (about 14 percent of the total recorded performances of popular comedies, 18 percent of the old comedies during the 1659–65 period). Jonson's four popular comedies—*Epicoene, The Alchemist, Bartholomew Fair,* and *Volpone* (with, respectively, nine, seven, seven, and three recorded performances)—were also held up by Carolean critics as models of playwrighting. Although these plays differ from each other in many ways, one can draw from them some general principles of a jonsonian mode which

---

[6]Only *The Merry Wives of Windsor* appears among the most popular comedies in the 1659–65 period, during which time there is a single recorded performance of *A Midsummer Night's Dream* and two of *Twelfth Night*. Adaptations, such as Davenant's *Law Against Lovers* (*Measure for Measure* and *Much Ado About Nothing*) and *The Rivals* (*Two Noble Kinsmen*) did somewhat better.

was important for Carolean drama. The primary function of the plot is to ridicule various moral, ethical, and social failings. The mechanism for this is a cozening action or actions established early in the play, with characters essentially divisible into wits or cozeners and their dupes who (except for those in *Epicoene*) come together, as Robert Ornstein puts it, "where bourgeois greed meets underworld guile" (44). The main conflict is enhanced and varied by the wide range of fools who appear in the play, a range made coherent by analogies of action and function. And the plot moves toward punitive unveilings at the end for both "bourgeois greed" and "underworld guile."

From this it follows that Jonson's characters do not change, that character is condemned to play itself out through the drama's circumstances and confrontations until the final humiliating moment. Jonson stabilizes these satirized figures in three associated ways. He fits them into a typology which has both moral (humours) and social (druggist, gentleman-scholar, pickpocket) coordinates. Except in *Epicoene*, he individualizes them most often in terms of their dreams of self-aggrandizement, the millenial delusions of personal, secular grace. Characters invariably try to escape their type by fantasies that are so situated within that type as to reconfirm their rootedness in it. Thus Morose envisions a perfect wife who leavens his solitude without disturbing it, and Adam Overdo sees perfect justice coming only from his personal intervention and judgment. Finally, Jonson localizes his characters visually so as to reinforce both the typology and the delusions: "The shrine of gold stands ominously behind all the action of Volpone's bedroom, bogus laboratory equipment surrounds Face and Subtle, and stocks appear on the grounds of Bartholomew Fair so that Justice Overdo can sit in them" (Teague 177–78). As object is metaphor for Jonson's characters, so it is for Jonson's audience, though the metaphoric object does not mean the same thing to both groups. Moreover, Jonson not only stabilizes his satirized figures, he devotes most of his play to displaying them with introductory sketches, dialogue and soliloquy, and situations designed to reveal greed and gracelessness under pressure.

The first and second means of stabilizing his satirized figures— typology and individualization through dreams of self-aggrandizement—also serve Jonson as moral devices. The typology gives the satire breadth of inference, so that the figures seem to be a legitimate sampling of the world in a manner that Jonson borrowed, scholars have suggested, from the "estates" moralities of the 1590s (where, say, courtier, soldier, priest, and scholar represent the "estates" or social classes so as to generalize an indictment). Thus *Volpone* offers, as principals, "an Aduocate," "an old Gentleman," "a Merchant," "a Knight," and "a Gent. trauailer," and *The Alchemist*, a clerk, a tobacco-man, a knight, Puritans, and so forth. Individualization balances the moral effect of typology by localizing sin or folly in the person rather than in society.

It follows that the cozeners, along with their typed, self-deluded victims, may be subject to moral judgment through a similar pattern; they too are likely to be humours characters with some specific social footing (Volpone is "a Magnifico," Face a servant, Dol Common a whore) and to cozen with their own self-aggrandizement in mind. They are more efficient than their dupes but just as driven, and it is only those who stand outside the delusive mechanisms of desire who control the denouement. One of the peculiarities of this arrangement is that these outsiders, like Lovewit in *The Alchemist*, need not be moral figures. Jonson's comedy remains free of the "moral" conclusions so often—if casually and unevenly—provided by fletcherian comedy's last-minute reversals, unveilings, and reconciliations. It is a comedy of only local purgation and of values rarely more than implicit in the midst of pervasive social disorder.

Wherever one places Jonson's comedy in terms of moral intention between the poles of moral seriousness and punitive malice, the principle of full poetic justice is not his, any more than it is Fletcher's, as Dryden remarked in the Preface to *An Evening's Love, or, the Mock Astrologer*:

> *Ben. Johnson* himself, after whom I may be proud to erre, has given me more than once the example of [rewarding the vicious]. That in the *Alchemist* is notorious, where *Face*, after having contriv'd and carried on the great cozenage of the Play, and continued in it without repentance to the last, is not only forgiven by his Master, but inrich'd by his consent, with the spoiles of those whom he has cheated. And which is more, his Master himself . . . is introduc'd taking his Man's counsel, debauching the Widow first, in hope to marry her afterward. In the *Silent Woman*, *Dauphine* . . . professes himself in love with all the Collegiate Ladies: and they likewise are all of the same Character with each other . . . yet this naughty *Dauphine* is crown'd in the end with the possession of his Uncles Estate, and with the hopes of enjoying all his Mistresses. And his friend Mr. *Truwit* (the best Character of a Gentleman which *Ben. Johnson* ever made) is not asham'd to pimp for him. As for *Beaumont* and *Fletcher*, I need not alledge examples out of them; for that were to quote almost all their Comedies.   (CD 10: 208)

To be sure, there may be moral questions of another sort in jonsonian comedy; in *Epicoene*, for example, the wits seem to torment

Daw, La Foole, Otter, and to some extent Morose simply for sport, not because it does them or Jonson's audience any good. To "expose" self-exposing folly appeals first, as Dryden also says, to "the ill nature of the Audience [who] are mov'd to laugh by the representation of deformity" and next, in principle, are moved to avoid those vices themselves (*CD* 10: 209). The audience, then, is driven to complicity, even if temporary, with all jonsonian cozeners, and for anything that the play itself brings about, to a more lasting complicity with cozeners who escape satire themselves, like Dauphine, Clerimont, and, largely, Truewit. Jonson comes very close, in this regard, to the Fletcher who lets the Younger Loveless cheat Morecraft with impunity or, in *Rule a Wife and Have a Wife*, cheerfully lets Estefania manipulate Michael Perez and Leon cozen his way to an heiress.

Whatever the deep values of Jonson's morality may have been and however masterful the logic of his plots, in fact his comedies share many traits with Fletcher's, like casualness about "poetic justice." Both men dwell on fixed, eccentric characters ruled by some standard or inexplicable passion: Morose's aversion to noise, everyone's greed in *Volpone*, the Puritans' zeal in *The Alchemist* are donneés as unchallengeable as the Scornful Lady's scorn or the toxins from within and without that give the Humorous Lieutenant his humours and humor. What is moral or cognitive in Jonson may be used for a shock, a laugh, or a flourish in Fletcher, but the same kinds of characters get put on the stage, the same stress on wit and outwitting shapes their lines, and the same quest for variety informs their depicted worlds.

Our argument then is, first, that a fletcherian mode can be sketched out, different from the modes of Shakespeare and Jonson, but also, second and at least as important, that this fletcherian mode was in some respects similar enough to Jonson's, and elastic enough, for Carolean playwrights to use it without abandoning the devices and kinds of scenes popular in Jonson. This elasticity of structure enabled the Caroleans to take comedic advantage of contemporary social and political issues, fashionable ideologies such as libertinism, and changing theatrical conditions.

Fletcherian and Jonsonian Modes: New Plays, New Directions

The new plays written during the early Carolean period adapted fletcherian and jonsonian models in response to theatrical and social conditions that stimulated and reinforced dramatic change. These same circumstances help explain not only the way the new comedies altered their inherited patterns but also the continued popularity of fletcherian and jonsonian comedies in the repertory. To get some idea of the directions charted by the new plays, we refer to four of the new or newly revised comedies from the nine popular comedies in the repertory between 1659 and 1665: the two from the King's Company—Sir Robert Howard's *The Surprisal* (1662) and *The Committee* (1662)—and the two most popular from the Duke's Company—Sir Samuel Tuke's *The Adventures of Five Hours* (1662) and Abraham Cowley's *Cutter of Coleman Street* (1661). To these we will add Dryden's first two comedies—*The Wild Gallant* (1663) and *The Rival Ladies* (1664), both at the King's Company, which demonstrate Dryden's earliest efforts to match the prevailing comic modes.

The plots of all six plays display the energy, multiplicity and variety, the affectivity and rapid reversals characteristic of fletcherian comedy. Formal balance of action and character appears in two different formats in these new plays. In *The Surprisal, The Wild Gallant,* and *Cutter of Coleman Street,* as in Fletcher's *The Humorous Lieutenant* or *The Maid in the Mill,* one finds two interlocking actions of relatively equal weight, with central characters who "cross over" and function differently in the two plots. In *Cutter of Coleman Street,* for example, Colonel Jolly, in one plot the hero trying to extricate himself from poverty by cozening and marrying a rich Puritan widow, is in the other plot the wicked guardian who separates the young lovers, Truman Jr. and Lucia, and who tries to marry Lucia off to the disreputable Cutter or Worm for a share of her dowry. In *Cutter of Coleman Street,* Jolly's two roles balance one another even as the romantic and satiric plot lines of the play do; in *The Surprisal* and *The Wild Gallant,* that balance is offset, respectively, toward the serious or humorous plot lines, with generally less commingling of actions. In contrast, the other three plays—*The Adventures of Five Hours, The Committee,* and *The Rival Ladies*—achieve similar effects with two or more pairs of near-identical, intertwined lovers; a single, diversified plot; and more liberal use of disguises and misinformation to add and then dispel complications. In the "Spanish plot" of *The Adventures of Five Hours,* for example, the play's frenetic activity is almost entirely a result of characters not knowing at least one of the multiple roles (friend/future in-law/love-rival) of other characters.

All six plays produce emotional ups and downs, like Fletcher, by careful patterning, elaborate rhetoric, and neat juxtaposition of characters and actions. In *The Surprisal* and *Cutter of Coleman Street,* where the distance between plot lines and tones is the greatest, distressed lovers speak in blank verse and take time off for melancholy set speeches, while "gay" or crafty manipulators remain ruthlessly prosaic. And although the moods of *The Adventures of Five Hours, The*

Rival Ladies, The Wild Gallant, and *The Committee* are contained within a narrower spectrum (the first two more uniformly serious, the other two more humorous), they achieve similar kinds of tonal shifts by delegating changes of pace and tone to low characters decorously separated from the main antagonists and action.[7]

As in fletcherian comedy, the final climaxes in these plays seem as fortuitous and surprising as those which have occurred throughout the previous four acts, but whereas Fletcher often depends on lost heirs and identities, Carolean playwrights use less romantic devices. In the Spanish-plot mode of *The Adventures of Five Hours* and *The Rival Ladies*, the elaborately constructed edifice of conflicts and errors, misinformation and suspicion culminates in sword fights and complex resolutions among the love-rivals, who switch loyalties and mates with dazzling agility as they follow the alternate calls of love, honor, friendship, and revenge. In *The Committee*, an unanticipated eleventh-hour rescue is provided by a document the heroine discovers accidentally and then uses for blackmail. In *The Surprisal*, a fool bumbles in to prevent the heroines' rape, giving the heroes enough time to effect a proper rescue, and Howard again uses blackmail as a device to restore one hero's lost estates. Additionally, all six plays rework a common fletcherian reversal: threatening or obstructive guardians undergo last-minute about-faces whether under pressure, as in *The Committee* and *The Adventures of Five Hours*, or not, as in *The Surprisal*. Even the implacable Lord Nonesuch in *The Wild Gallant* succumbs after his niece Isabelle enjoins him—"Come, Nuncle, 'tis in vain to hold out now 'tis past remedy: 'tis like the last Act of a Play when People must marry; and if fathers will not consent then, they should throw Oranges at u'm from the Galleries: why should you stand off to keep us from a dance?" (V.v.84–88)—virtually invoking fletcherian convention as precedent for the comic denouement.

Isabelle's words proclaim that fletcherian comedy subjugates characters to plot considerations whenever the two conflict, and these "modern" comedies would seem to subscribe to the same rule. Last-minute character conversions, softenings, and reversals are one version of this; another is the cowardly Brancadoro's momentary courage when faced with a duel at the climax of *The Surprisal*; a third is the central anomaly which provides most of the conflict in *The Adventures of Five Hours*, that Antonio would betroth himself to one woman while

---

[7]In *The Rival Ladies*, Dryden avoids extra characters but achieves humorous effects from his two "breeches parts" females by putting them into confrontations where they must prove their masculinity. A similar but more elaborately ironic use of "innocents" will show up later in *The Tempest*.

intensely loving another. Yet, by and large, the plots of these new comedies, unlike their fletcherian predecessors, are constructed so as to avoid such inconsistencies whenever possible, and in consequence, their characters tend to be more plausible, less protean, than those in fletcherian comedy.

This procedure is in keeping with a general concern shared by these early plays, a concern that led to some of the most distinctive, powerful effects of Carolean comedy: resolving fletcherian problems with a nonfletcherian attention to dramatic "rules," in particular those of decorum, liaison of scenes, and probability. That these neophyte playwrights were aware of the difficulties inherent in creating modern comedy seems evident from Dryden's preface to *The Rival Ladies*:

> [The playwright] may be allow'd sometimes to Err, who undertakes to move so many Characters and Humours as are requisite in a Play, in those narrow Channels which are proper to each of them: To conduct his imaginary Persons, through so many various Intrigues and Chances, as the Labouring Audience shall think them lost under every Billow; and then at length to work them so naturally out of their Distresses, that when the whole Plot is laid open, the Spectators may rest satisfied, that every cause was powerfull enough to produce the effect it had; and that the whole Chain of them was with such due order Linck'd together, that the first Accident would naturally beget the second, till they all render'd the Conclusion necessary.   (CD 8: 95)

This dedication to Orrery displays a fletcherian concern for audience effects but also an unfletcherian concern for causality, the plausible linkage of action to action, motive to behavior. Following the principles of decorum, the two plot patterns noted earlier—the seriocomic double plot and the multilevel single plot—serve to separate the various plot elements and to parcel out the play's emotional range amongst different, parallel characters—for example, melancholy Cialto versus insouciant Miranzo, contriving Aurelia versus weeping Lucia—with the more broadly humorous or farcical actions generally confined to low characters like Teague and Diego or satiric butts like Brancadoro and Abel Day. Thus, using fewer characters and somewhat more schematic arrangements than fletcherian comedies, these new plays remain versatile and affective while channeling their own and their characters' adjectival tendencies into a set of clear motivations and goals shared by most, if not all, characters and, not incidentally, their Carolean audiences. These clear goals are the first stage toward developing a kind of comedy in which the action embodies movement towards an objective (image and possessions) which is identified as the realization of desire.

One category of such goals appears in the comedies which thrust their heroes and heroines into a hostile environment, where family, society, and the state are controlled by persons inimical to their interests. Under such conditions, adjectival characteristics—shape shifting and role playing—are necessary tactics for survival, and the disguises Cialto or Octavio wears to hide from the law are comically rendered in the self-protective bantering of Careless and Ruth, or the mannered fronts Cialto and Samira assume to hide the feelings they elsewhere reveal in private confidence or soliloquy. These plays' authors get additional credibility for their characters because, in a play where disguise figures so prominently, the audience is likely to assume an underlying layer of motive and meaning. Thus, by manipulating their characters' exterior and interior states of being—masks versus feelings—Carolean playwrights gain the coherence and affectivity of goal-directed characters who yet retain a fletcherian elasticity of movement and emotion and adaptability to rapidly changing plot conditions. Unlike fletcherian characters who simply display or enact their own changeability, characters in these early Carolean comedies seem to be real agents, acting consistently from some core of self.

At the same time that these new comedies adopted the basic structure and audience orientation of fletcherian comedy, they were also making use of new possibilities inherent in altered theatrical and sociopolitical conditions. The most radical of these innovations were correlates to theatrical changes with the reestablishment of stable theatrical companies—the introduction of actresses and the use of moveable scenery—both of which, because of their audience appeal, had very early and noticeable effects on the form of Carolean comedies (see Wilson, *Ladies*; Gilder, chapters 7–8; *CD* 8: 307–16, 319–21). The drawing power of specific dramatic presentations can be seen in Pepys' remarks on those frequent occasions when he left the theatre impressed only with Lacy's or Moll Davis' performance in a "meane" play or praised the scenes or music while deploring the writing. Recognizing the "bankability" of key actors and scenic wonders, thoughtful managers and playwrights began to choose and write plays which would show off the company's sets and costumes or which featured virtuoso performers, single or paired.

Each innovation takes advantage of one of these crowd pleasers, again, to help develop the new, probable, desire-oriented comedy, peopled by agents with some core of self. Actresses, for example, aided verisimilitude, so that the play could more closely resemble and refine upon situations into which members of the audience could project themselves. For men, actresses also served to focus desire in a way, we suspect, that the "squeaking" boys—the adjective is that of Shakespeare's Cleopatra (V.ii.220)—of the pre-War stage could not. For women, just as important, actresses offered self-representations on stage, equal in glamor, intelligence, and power to the males with whom they acted and interacted. Scenery obviously also contributed to the new realism, shifting it, if the company wished, to accommodate some degree of fantasy. The settings, for example, might be made especially opulent; or the audience might find themselves ogling a lady's boudoir. Some degree of voyeurism seems necessarily involved in the vicarious (re)presentation of desire, and scenery added to the voyeuristic illusion. In addition, the rapidly moveable scenery allowed the action to change fast but each scene to be particularized so that a quick-moving, complex play could also stay clear, with visually memorable confrontations and tête-à-têtes.

The very early introduction of actresses into Carolean acting companies probably reinforced the initial selection of fletcherian over, say, jonsonian comedies, although we would note that Carolean attitudes toward women, as touched upon in chapter 2, would have made the fletcherian model preferable even in the absence of actresses. While Jonson tends to relegate females to secondary status—as ornaments of success (Pliant) or as satiric butts (Mrs. Otter) and only occasionally offers them equal roles in the cozening game (Dol Common)—fletcherian comedies tend to provide a balance between strong male and female roles. For every clever, witty, resourceful, or romantically benighted hero in fletcherian comedy, there is invariably a counterpart or counterpoint heroine: Elder Loveless and the Scornful Lady in *The Scornful Lady*, Estefania and Leon in *Rule a Wife and Have a Wife*, Celia and Demetrius in *The Humorous Lieutenant*, Valentine and Lady Hartwell in *Wit Without Money*, Petruchio and Maria in *The Tamer Tamed*. Early Carolean theatre managers determined to play their best cards would hardly have ignored the wealth of opportunities such good female parts provided for actresses to display their talents (not to mention their legs, in breeches parts). Besides the novelty value of real women on stage, the theatre also gained, as we have said, visible objects of desire (for the male audience) and of identification (for the female audience).

Meanwhile, other kinds of strong acting roles grew out of fletcherian and jonsonian humours characters—Fletcher's foppish or foolish rivals and myopic parents, Jonson's grasping manipulators and lackwit dupes. Many of the new comedies put these humours and foibles into modern dress: avaricious or foolish Puritans (the Days, the Barebottles), bumbling, inept young men (Abel Day, Sir Timorous), cowardly or witless fops (Brancadoro, Puny). Equally contemporary are the jonsonian predators and fletcherian parasites who practice their coney catching in modern London (Cutter, Worm, Burr, Failer). Once established as an actor's or actress's prerogative, versions of these roles appear again and again in Carolean comedies played by him or her: Lacy's fools; Cartwright's and Underhill's bumbling, crusty old guardians; Corey's bawds; Long's saucy maidservants. Such character types fit neatly into the newly refurbished fletcherian plot lines as love-rivals, servants, villains, parents. The use of stellar actors in these roles served to provide more compelling characters for audience identification, while the standardization of roles reinforced decorum, especially in complex or multi-plot plays.

The new Carolean comedies' altered use of setting was similarly pragmatic—responding to the advent of moveable scenery and the use of multiple stage spaces—and it was not long before new Carolean comedies began using these techniques to amalgamate fletcherian diversity with jonsonian precision and depth. Introduced first by the Duke's Company, scenery was initially used mainly to concretize the peripatetic movement of fletcherian comedy in scenes which switch from indoors to outdoors or from city to country with graceful abandon and delight in juxtaposition and movement for their own sakes. Most of Fletcher's best scenic effects—Celia trying to bluff her way into the crowded castle reception room or Philaster and Arethusa wandering about miserably in their pastoral exile—are affective devices of the moment rather than the fully integrated usage of jonsonian comedy, where setting is a primary and substantial dramatic fact, from the greasy abundance of *Bartholomew Fair* to the exquisite detail of Captain Otter's cups. To varying degrees, most of the new playwrights make some effort to use setting to add to the drama's formal coherence and its contemporary relevance, as well as dazzle the audience with the speed and realism of the scenic movement.

The most thorough integration of setting and style appears in the three new plays which use a political framework to increase tension and immediacy and to direct their satire. Whereas politics was mainly an excuse for certain kinds of actions and climaxes in Fletcher, in these Carolean comedies it responds to the times and offers a consensual focus for the post-War audience. Both *Cutter of Coleman Street* and *The Committee* are set during the Interregnum, with villainous, avaricious Puritans and distressed Cavaliers battling over sequestered or lost estates and beleaguered heroines. *The Surprisal*, although set in Siena, tells the same tale analogically with its dispossessed young soldier-hero and corrupt politics. In all three plays, the introduction of a political framework provides, at base, a convenient shorthand for villainy and virtue. It can also enhance characterization and conflict. In *Cutter of Coleman Street*, political loyalty is used metaphorically when

Truman Jr. reacts to his father's forcing him to reject Lucia and marry someone else:

> Though I to save this Dung-hill an Estate
> Have done a Crime like theirs,
> Who have abjur'd their King for the same cause,
> I will not yet, like them, persue the guilt,
> And in thy place, *Lucia* my lawful Soverain,
> Set up a low and scandalous Usurper!   (I.ii; 271)

In *The Committee*, Howard uses his Commonwealth London setting to give political affiliations both moral and social connotations. The Puritan Days use the political turmoil of the Interregnum to feed their lust for power and gain, and each additional revelation—that Mrs. Day is a parvenue escaping her kitchen maid origins or that Day is licentious as well as avaricious—simply reinforces the audience's first impressions. Howard establishes a unified sensibility—one admires witty characters like Ruth, neutral characters like Blunt, and fools like Teague, and condemns their counterparts, the Days, the Committeemen, and Abel—and creates, in effect, exemplary comedy with its heroes—Ruth and Careless—admirable for their wit and virtue both.

A different kind of moral coherence and characterization is linked with the setting of the Spanish plays which redefines fletcherian plot and character in modern terms. Fletcher himself had been fond of Spanish settings and plots as suitably exotic opportunities for love intrigues punctuated with affective rhetoric.[8] But the Carolean versions do more than their predecessors to exploit the prejudices of the Carolean audience, for whom Spain was an overrefined country where women died for love, men protected the faintest slight to their honor with a sword, and amorous intrigues were conducted under the threat of overprotective guardians and despite restrictive rules of social conduct. Thus, in *The Adventures of Five Hours*, Spanish honor is the basic criterion for evaluating character and behavior, and the heroes' and heroines' adherence to this strict moral code ensures their ultimate success. If one learns less about these characters in the course of the play than about Howard's, one is, instead, invited to admire them in a series of tableaux in which they are caught in extravagant poses and rhetorical, as well as physical, flights. While such behavior is comparable to the conquests of heroic heroes or the efficient wit of satiric heroes, admiration for Antonio or Porcia is essentially static; activity

---

[8]John Loftis notes that about seventeen of Beaumont and Fletcher's fifty plays have Spanish sources, among them *The Chances, The Island Princess, Rule a Wife and Have a Wife*, and *The Spanish Curate*, all popular on the Carolean stage (25–27).

in Spanish-plot plays is too often frustrated and unprofitable to be a standard for judgment.

In addition to their use of setting to add coherence and identify character, Carolean comedies also dealt differently with the stage itself, although, as Colin Visser points out, many of their innovations were extensions of earlier practices:

> The physical disposition of the stage . . . fostered theatrical conventions. The proscenium walls with their doors and balconies dictated a range of dramatic possibilities; wings and shutters generated their own conventions; certain kinds of discovery became habitual, precedents were established for the use of traps and machines. Often these conventions were passed down from pre-Restoration theatres, which the Restoration playhouses in many ways resembled. The most accomplished playwrights were those who best exploited these conventions.
> (66–67)

Exploiting stage conventions meant, primarily, an almost jonsonian sense of place as a locus for certain kinds of actions. Interiors, for example, are associated with the older generation, with confinement, restriction, force, and deception in *The Committee* where the Committee of Sequestration meets and Arbella is importuned inside the Days' house. Indoors, the play's heroes and heroines are forced to dissemble and hide behind false identities, whereas outdoors or in public places like the tavern, they enjoy more freedom of speech and movement. Likewise, in *The Adventures of Five Hours* and *Cutter of Coleman Street*, flight, disguise, and dissimulation are the defenses the powerless use to advantage, eluding capture and confinement until they can obtain a more permanent kind of freedom.

Together, these pragmatic alterations in theatrical production—the allotment and popularity of acting roles and the use of stage setting devices—make new Carolean comedies even more likely than their fletcherian predecessors to exploit certain affective possibilities, particularly with prominent female roles displayed advantageously in witty or emotional scenes between hero and heroine and with farcical character parts for comedians playing fops, guardians, servants, and other stock figures. But more pertinently, these theatrical changes were used to heighten two important sources of dramatic conflict—sexual and generational—inherited from fletcherian comedy but given new life on the Carolean stage. Over time, the twin pulls of sex and money exert increasing force on characters until, by the 1670s, power itself supersedes all other motives for most comic characters and is given ideological weight in the text with references to Hobbesian psychology. In these early new comedies, they have not yet attained such eminence but must vie for attention along with other motives driving central characters—elevated status for a social climber (Mrs. Day), romantic yearnings for a young maiden (Lucia), lust for honor in a young man (Octavio). Even so, the goals of sex and money are already solidly present as sources of internal conflict and external competition for some characters and, as a kind of "gay" hedonism, together identify one of the competing value systems of the plays.

Of the two, sexual conflict is perhaps the best documented for Carolean comedy (e.g., Smith), and shows up amongst the early new plays in two forms—semiseriously in *The Adventures of Five Hours* and *The Rival Ladies*, humorously in *The Committee* and *The Wild Gallant*. While such conflicts clearly derive from battles for ascendancy in fletcherian plays like *The Scornful Lady*, *Rule a Wife and Have a Wife*, and *The Tamer Tamed*, their Carolean incarnation is partly a result of playwrights' attempts to trade off the absolute unpredictability of fletcherian characters for more plausibly motivated ones while retaining the affectivity of fast-moving, unstable love relationships. The explanation for characters' unpredictability—in both the serious and humorous forms of Carolean sex conflicts—begins to be linked with the primacy of uncontrolled and uncontrollable passion.

In the serious plays, passion works through characters for good and ill and requires delicate handling to accord with the moral framework. In *The Adventures of Five Hours*, the four star-crossed lovers are unwaveringly faithful to each other; but mistaken identities and Henrique's contrary passion for Camilla preclude any simple solution to their dilemma. Dryden brews an even more complex but less coherent mixture in *The Rival Ladies*, where Honoria and Angellina are both in love with Gonsalvo, while he loves Julia, the woman betrothed to his brother Roderigo. To support his characters' swift change of loyalties and unpredictable behavior, Dryden rather cavalierly introduces two conflicting ideologies. The first, passion's omnipotence, is invoked consistently by characters throughout the play; yet the resolution of the plot depends on a quite different set of values, when Gonsalvo, after fighting desperately to win Julia, finally gives her up to Roderigo and decides to marry Honoria whose love for him and "merit" will eventually (he hopes) overcome his love for her sister. This resolution of the play's physical and ideological complications reminds one of the last-minute resolutions of fletcherian comedy but is even less convincing because of the apparently serious arguing of the love/reason/honor conflicts permeating the play. In contrast to Dryden's, Tuke's play seems more coherent because its love/honor conflicts can be resolved within the play's value system; only Henrique's conversion is needed, and it is within the conventional fletcherian pattern.⁹

Passion as a motive produces a different kind of sex conflict in the two humorous plays, Howard's *The Committee* and Dryden's *The Wild Gallant*, where male and female characters meet and argue over issues of libertinism, more precisely, to what degree the hero's prior and potential license affects his ability to establish a lasting relationship with the heroine. Libertinism in its broadest sense is often present in fletcherian comedy with its socially and sexually active characters who spend themselves and their monies liberally until they are married or betrothed at the denouement. Like so many other conflicts in fletcherian comedy, however, this one is ephemeral: such heroes may or may not explicitly reform at the end of the play; neither case particularly affects the substance of the character or the conclusion. In Howard's or Dryden's version, the issue is made more significant, both as a source of conflict and as a possibly conflicting value system within the play as a whole.

In *The Committee*, for example, the issue seems alive, if only briefly, when in act III (iv; 85–86), after she has rescued him from her mother, the Cavalier Careless and the (apparent) Puritan Ruth face off over the double imperative of his debauching her versus her forcing him to take the Covenant.¹⁰ It is an almost perfect example of a Carolean transformation of a fletcherian confrontation. Howard manages a consummately lively scene between the two lovers, taking full advantage of the multiple referents and ambiguities of language; words like "covenant," "jointure," "principles," and "virtue" operate on sexual, social, and political levels simultaneously to good comic effect. Dramatic irony reduces the fletcherian suspense—the audience knows that Ruth's politics, birth, and virtue are in the right camp—but highlights the elegance of the lovers' patterned verbal encounter, like a duel or dance. Nor is marriage an issue. Careless' "I have no defense against thee and matrimony but thy own father and mother, which

---

⁹This may be partly attributable to the fact that Tuke used only one source, Coello's *Les Empeños des seis horas*, while Dryden, according to Loftis, used several, a Cervantes novel and its derivatives—Fletcher's *Love's Pilgrimage* and two French plays (CD 8: 103).

¹⁰By act of Parliament in 1643, Royalists' estates could be seized or sequestered by the government. If sequestered, the estate could be redeemed if its owner paid from one-sixth to one-half its value, such payment to be accompanied by taking the Covenant, an oath of allegiance to the Puritan government masquerading as a statement supporting the reformed church. In act II, Careless and Blunt have refused when called before the Committee of Sequestration to redeem their estates by taking the Covenant.

For further details about the political background to *The Committee* see Howard 39–46; textual references are to this edition.

are a perfect Committee to my nature" and Ruth's "When the quarrel of this nation is reconciled, you and I shall agree" (III.iv; 85–86) set up the play's conclusion, wherein Ruth's false identity and Careless' libertinism are shucked off to reveal their sincere, virtuous selves.[11]

Similarly, in Dryden's *The Wild Gallant*, particularly the revised version with its added scene among Loveby, Constance, a bawd (Lady Du Lake), and her whores (IV.i.70–191), the hero's libertinism also seems a barrier to the lovers' union. But Constance's distaste for her lover's "relatives" (Lady Du Lake calls him "son," he calls her "mother") finds little sympathy with her cousin Isabelle: "The worst you can say of him, is, he loves Women: and such make the kindest Husbands I am told. If you had a Summ of Money to put out; you would not look so much whether the Man were an honest Man, (for the Law would make him that) as if he were a good sufficient Pay-master" (IV.ii.25–29). As Ned Bliss Allen points out (30), this passage is almost identical to one in Fletcher's *The Wild Goose Chase* and, as in fletcherian comedy, Loveby's license and Isabelle's defense of it prove no barrier to either couple's match.[12] Loveby and Isabelle either will or will not cuckold their respective mates (she probably will, he may not); both questions are beyond the scope of the play's ending.

The rake redeemed and the rake rampant, passion satisfied, deflected, or controlled by reason or honor—all these conflict resolutions are equally likely to appear in Carolean comedy for the next twenty years. But while these earlier playwrights choose one such resolution and force a conclusion into its confines, their successors are as likely to offer multiple responses or to preserve a delicately ambiguous solution subject to audience interpretation. At this early stage of comic development, the subject of passion and libertinism follows the pattern of fletcherian comedy, in that it is a plot device, a basis for conflict

---

[11]It is for this reason that John Harrington Smith, in his search for the origins of the "gay couple" in Restoration comedy rejects *The Committee*. Its lovers are too sincere, he says, and show "no awareness that it was passé to take love seriously" (45). The burying of such admissions, however, can be seen to develop gradually in the repertory, as it became less fashionable to profess feelings openly. The logical progression is from *The Committee* to Etherege's *She Would if She Could* (1668), where the men overhear the women admit their love, to *The Man of Mode* (1676), where Dorimant admits his feelings for Harriet in an aside.

[12]Smith and MacMillan go a step further in their introduction to the play in the California Dryden, seeing Loveby's libertinism as an integral part of the "gay couple" contest: "His rakishness is a masculine trait tending to keep him independent of her, and this too is a prerogative which, as things are managed, he is not compelled to renounce as a condition of having her . . . " (8: 238).

and witty displays, and a temporary barrier to matrimony. At the same time, however, it is laying the cornerstone for the compromise formation by offering characters who play out the audience's desires onstage, even if those desires are, as yet, only vaguely or incompletely formulated. And while Octavio, Careless, and Loveby are tamer than Almanzor, Dorimant, or Horner, they are also easier to identify with comfortably and don't require counterpoised moral figures. Their brand of license does not threaten either the social system the audience inhabits or the individual members' self-images, although it carries the potential to do both.

Equally threatening in its implications is the new comic drama's treatment of confrontations between youth and age (see Mignon). Unlike sexual conflicts, which depend on relatively equal antagonists, generational conflicts identify misused authority in terms of age and gender differences; the play's business is to upset those traditionally assigned superior and inferior positions. Generational conflicts appear in all the new plays, most centrally in the Spanish-plot comedies, *The Adventures of Five Hours* and *The Rival Ladies*, and in *The Surprisal*, as well as in the older repertory: Morose versus his nephew and company in *Epicoene*, Demetrius versus his father in *The Humorous Lieutenant*, even the older and younger Loveless brothers in *The Scornful Lady*. In Fletcher, such conflicts are used to highlight youthful distress or gaiety; in Jonson, they are subsidiary to larger considerations of character or humour. Their omnipresence in the new plays seems to indicate a signficant shift of emphasis. Susan Staves, for example, suggests (especially chapter 3) that plays which show figures of authority regularly flouted and bamboozled by their children, sisters, wards, and servants begin, by their very weight and number, to subvert the claims of custom, convention and inherited morality. In this view, the treatment of authority in these early plays can be seen as outlining issues which are more daringly exploited in later comedies: if young women demand the right to choose their own husbands, they can also make untraditional or immoral choices about sexual behavior; if young men can overset parental authority, they can also rob, cheat, or cuckold those same parents or their analogues. But even in this more serious reading, the early comedies are groundwork only, avoiding the deeper questions of authority by unseating only political outcasts (Puritans) or by easily converting blocking figures. Their youthful protagonists can take their winnings, as it were, without disrupting the social fabric.

In all of these early new comedies, the older generation is represented as having access to power—the power of law, of money, of custom, of habit—which it proceeds to abuse in various ways. The Days rob the Cavalier heroes and heroines of their estates and attempt to force Arbella to marry their son; they have Careless jailed for debt and ruthlessly hunt down his compatriots. Lord Nonesuch in *The Wild Gallant* tries to have Loveby arrested for debt and would marry his daughter to a fool. In *The Surprisal*, Cialto's estates are stolen by Brancadoro's father and his lover's uncle betrothes her to Brancadoro; that same uncle courts his own nephew's girlfriend with her father's encouragement. In *The Adventures of Five Hours* Henrique forces his younger sister into marriage while hounding her lover Octavio, and in the other Spanish play, *The Rival Ladies*, Manuel pressures his sisters into matches of his choosing, not theirs. Truman Sr. in *Cutter of Coleman Street* makes his son swear an oath to give up Lucia or lose his inheritance, while her guardian, Jolly, plans to sell her to the highest bidder. The pattern is clear. Consistently, in these plays, abuse of power, malice, faulty judgment, and dishonorable behavior are all linked with the older generation and its adherents; contrasting characteristics or virtues reside, almost by default, in the younger. The heroes and heroines must rely on their wits, their good hearts, and Providence to win them their mates and their estates. Indeed, much of the dramatic tension in these plays comes from the apparent inequality of the contests, and much of the audience's satisfaction with their endings derives from their relief when the underdogs prevail despite their feeble weapons.

We see from the examples above that, even more than the young heroes, the women in these plays evidence the younger generation's dilemma, as they are forced into or prevented from marriage by guardians exerting the authority society grants their age and sex. In Dryden's *The Rival Ladies*, for example, Julia's brother arrogantly demands she dissolve her prior betrothal to Roderigo (which he engineered) and marry Gonsalvo, because he has changed his mind:

Manuel [*to Gonsalvo*] . . . the only way
to make her happy is to force it on her.
Julia, prepare your self strait to be Married.
Julia. To whom?
Man.   You see your Bridegroom: and you know
My Fathers will, who with his Dying breath
Commanded, you should pay as strict Obedience
To me, as formerly to him: if not,
Your Dowry is at my dispose.
Jul.   O would
The loss of that dispense with Duty in me,
How gladly would I suffer it! and yet

> If I durst question it, me-thinks 'tis hard!
> What right have Parents over Children, more
> Than Birds have o'r their Young? yet they impose
> No such Plum'd Mistriss on their Feather'd Sons;
> But leave their Love, more open yet and free
> Than all the Fields of Air, their spacious Birth-right.   (II.ii.94–109)

In purely dramatic terms, such scenes in serious comedy offer useful opportunities for pathetic outpourings and love/honor conflicts; they also provoke night escapes, disguises, and clever contrivances by which heroes and heroines seek to avoid these inappropriate assertions of authority.

But there is a deeper level of contrivance operating in this structure. Conflating several realms of authority—political, familial, social, sexual—as most of these comedies do, intensifies the audience's sympathy for the comic victims without the need for the author to raise the emotive level of the play's language or acting style. Even though Tuke, Cowley, and Howard (in *The Surprisal*) resort to fletcherian rant or weeping to heighten specific scenes or characters, the format itself provides them sufficient entree to the audience's sympathy for the plays to work without it. How could it be otherwise? Victims of malice, greed, lust inspire pity automatically; compounding the victimization, as long as it is done stylishly, expands the affective level. These comedies, to be sure, do not inspire anything much more complex in their audience—Jonson's sense of implication, for example—but it is likely that the audiences of the 1660s were simply more homogeneous in their sentiments than the audiences of the 1670s, more likely to respond univocally to such stimuli. What they were prepared for, and got, were complicated, rather than complex, moral plays—admirable heroes and heroines versus nasty villains. Howard and Tuke were especially good at them; Dryden and Cowley, who saw matters less simply, were more popular in later years than they were in the early 1660s.

Both the structural and social readings of these plays, then, take us to the same place, a solid but simple view of the world, and a temporary stage in Carolean comic development. The concern for causality which ultimately produced comedies which were more coherent and contained more plausibly motivated characters than fletcherian comedies probably also resulted from some niggling dissatisfaction with the fletcherian mode. After all, Carolean dramatists sought to "improve" Shakespeare, why not Fletcher? Whatever the playwrights' motives, Carolean comedies, even as early as the 1659–65 seasons, demonstrate a shift in emphasis from plot to character as the basis of formal pattern, whether that character is displayed as in the Spanish plays or revealed layer by layer as in the more satiric comedies. It was, however, only an interim solution. Rather quickly, the "moral" structures of *The Committee* and *The Adventures of Five Hours* became passé (although these two plays themselves continued to be popular). By the 1666-68 seasons, the Spanish mode had become "anglicized," and there were not only an unusual number and variety of new comedies but also experiments with form, content, and setting that rectified the fletcherian mode's excesses while retaining its diversity. In the next section, we will examine the most popular comedies of those seasons to see what began to emerge from more assured playwrights responding to and creating a more sophisticated public.

From the Plague to The Tempest

With the plague raging in London, the Lord Chamberlain closed the theatres on 5 June, 1665 and kept them largely closed till December 1666. When the theatres reopened, for the first time new plays outnumbered old in the repertory (see appendix 2). Of the thirty-two comedies with two or more recorded performances from 1666 through 1668 (about equally divided between the King's and Duke's companies), nineteen postdate 1659 and account for 107 of the 143 recorded performances of such comedies, about 75 percent. Yet the repertory remained heavily fletcherian, and the new plays became, if anything, more fletcherian than before. While continuing the tradition of reversals, formal balance, and emotional emphasis established by the older comedies, they tended to demote the consensual morality that had marked *The Adventures of Five Hours* and *The Committee* in favor of more affectivity, more latitude, of the sort we discussed in chapter 2. Once the traumas of the Civil Wars no longer demanded healing, the comedic idioms employed by Howard and Tuke no longer achieved a measure of unity through moral structures. Plays might retain moral plots, characters, or both but would set them next to amoral counterparts, at least until it was time for the convenient moral endings of fletcherian comedy.

Stripped of their roots in consensually accepted values, then, the moral duelling of Tuke's world and the political conniving of Howard's both boiled down to a match between authority on the one hand and social efficiency on the other, and the concentrate achieved by the boiling down was reconstituted in a variety of skillful ways. Because the two strains of comedy developed somewhat differently, we shall consider them separately as "Spanish comedy" and "English comedy." A third category, "multi-plot comedy," counterpoints two or more distinct plots with different tones or interests, at least one of which is romantic or heroic. Such unity as all these plays needed came from their developing two innovations of the early 1660s: they created denser characters whose plausible motivations made actions cohere, and they increased the coherence of causal relationships among diverse plot actions. Both of these innovations depart from the inherited fletcherian model, and the comedies' growing insistence that all motivations arise from universal drives makes them depart from Jonson's model too.

Spanish Comedy

During the 1666–67 and 1667–68 seasons, for whatever reason, no record remains of a production of *The Adventures of Five Hours* in a London theatre (though it was presented once at court), but three other Spanish plays enjoyed some popularity. Sydserf's *Tarugo's Wiles* was largely translated from the Spanish (Moreto's *No puede ser*), Davenant's *The Man's the Master* from a French adaptation of a Spanish comedy (Scarron's *Jodelet, ou le maître valet*); the third play, Dryden's *An Evening's Love; or, The Mock Astrologer*, borrowed from a number of French sources that in turn had Spanish sources.[13] All three altered the rigid conventions that Tuke had brought to the Carolean stage, in each case positing an anglicized Spain, morally looser and tonally less serious than those in proper Spanish comedy. Because Tarugo, for example, is changed from a clever servant (a "gracioso") into a gentleman, a younger son bred in England and recently returned to Spain, he can stand outside the value system that governs the serious characters and therefore take on the role of objective witness. Sydserf can thereby expand the humorous effects of his play without loss of decorum or character consistency. Furthermore, Tarugo's central manipulative role in the love plot, which does not involve him directly, also influences the drawing of other characters: the heroines are more assertive than in Tuke, the restrictive guardians thoroughly mocked.

And what the novice Sydserf did cautiously, the confident Dryden did audaciously. *An Evening's Love* plucks what it likes from various works to create a play, as Maximillian Novak says, "very much in the vein of Beaumont and Fletcher, who . . . borrowed many of their plots from Spanish novels" (*CD* 10: 444). Dryden provides four intertwined

---

[13]For fuller discussion of these plays' relationship to their sources, see Loftis 87–95; *CD* 10: 433–44.

plot strands encompassing a range of character and tone from the wit of the English gentlemen Wildblood and Bellamy, with the "gay" Spanish girl Jacinta, to the seriousness of the Spanish couple, Don Lopez and Theodosia. Each action is primarily restricted to its main participants and takes its tone from them. Overall, however, the humorous characters and scenes tend to overshadow the serious ones, "lowering" the tone of the play and reflecting, as Loftis puts it, "Dryden's studied refusal to take the Spanish preoccupation with honor seriously" (111). In the two courtships where Spanish and English mores and attitudes confront one another, the Spanish side meets with ignominy at the hands of English exuberance. In effect, Tuke's neat, morally coherent structure and codified system gives way to a varied, more fletcherian pattern. The marriages with which the play ends are instructively diverse: wit to wit in Wildblood and Jacinta, and in their servants Maskall and Beatrice; wit to sober lady in Bellamy and Theodosia; sober Spaniard to précieuse in Don Lopez and Aurelia. Thus Dryden adds the newer "gay couple" pattern to a set of unequal marriages reminiscent of fletcherian comedies like *Wit Without Money* and his own *Wild Gallant*.

The popular Spanish plays of the 1666–68 seasons, then, anglicize the mode by juxtaposing conventional Spanish characters with unconventional, un-Spanish ones: gracioso-turned-gentleman or farceur, witty Spanish ladies, expatriate Englishmen. If the essence of Spanish comedy in Loftis' terms is the intermingling of tragic and comic actions and moods, a strict sense of decorum and complex love intrigue plot emphasizing action over character, the Spanish plays of 1666–68 substantially alter these tenets, tampering particularly with decorum and morality, and trading character interplay for display. Structurally, we can see this as a restoration of fletcherian affectivity through efficient rather than absolute characters, linguistic range, and emotional manipulation. Further, if true Spanish comedy is profoundly rather than conveniently moral (see, for example, Fiore), the new plays, like fletcherian comedy, are more concerned with exhibiting conflicting value systems than with explicating a single one.

The fate of the Spanish plot in the 1666–68 seasons thus bespeaks the movement of the repertory away from its temporary flirtation with a simple moral universe and back into the fletcherian arena where multiplicity is king. Wit and disguise have been raised to an art and, in characters like Bellamy, Wildblood, and Jacinta, are a confirmation of intellect and merit. Yet *An Evening's Love* is not just a return to fletcherian comedy. The lessons of *The Adventures of Five Hours*, that a moral framework provides coherence and character motivation and that plausibly different values can be subscribed to by characters separated by class or temperament, have been absorbed and utilized, even if to different ends. More important, the distance achieved by irony in fletcherian comedy and awe in Spanish comedy has been shortened by the kind of humor which invites the audience to share the fun, to identify with witty characters like Bellamy who use their intellect to puncture their opponents' self-images. For Dryden, unlike Tuke, the Spanish setting was merely a starting place, offering him a set of conventions and expectations to deviate from, tinker with, and reform along the lines of the other new comedies coexisting on the Carolean stage.

Multi-Plot Comedy

For the kind of hierarchical structure that the ideals of Spanish comedy promote, one could look at the multi-plot comedies (or tragicomedies) that were among the most popular Carolean forms. In at least one plot line of these complex plays, the voices of Fletcher and Tuke are newly tuned to the notes of heroic drama. Of course Fletcher's own double-plot comedies, like *The Humorous Lieutenant* and *The Maid in the Mill*, fathered early Carolean tragicomedies, like Robert Howard's *The Surprisal* and Etherege's *The Comical Revenge*. Etherege, in turn, set the style for his successors.

The Comical Revenge; or, Love in a Tub (1664) offers four essentially independent and simultaneous plots, or actions, connected by their London setting, family and social relationships among the characters, and parallels in language and imagery. The hero, Sir Frederick Frollick, also participates in all four, so as to bridge the range of behavior and values from the highfalutin courtship of two pairs of lovers, the witty courtship of Sir Frederick himself and the Widow Rich, and two different gulling and ridiculing actions. Otherwise, Etherege maintains decorum by distinguishing the characters in each action variously, by morality, social class, occupation, intelligence, and personality. One has a kind of roster of Carolean type characters, structurally separated in the four actions, ranging from the couplets, duelling, and debating in the highest plot down to the humiliation of the poxed valet, Dufoy, in the lowest.

Sir Frederick adumbrates the flexible, many-sided, rake hero of later Carolean plays, though his boisterous gallantry would not pass muster with Palamede or Dorimant. And his style of wooing, too, looks backward in that it reworks a number of comic turns from fletcherian repertory favorites: the midnight serenade (*Father's Own Son*, i.e., *Monsieur Thomas*), the feigned death (*The Tamer Tamed*, *The Scornful Lady*), a woman rescuing her lover from the bailiffs (*Wit Without Money*,

Middleton's *The Widow*, Dryden's *The Wild Gallant*). Nonetheless, Etherege controls the actions in this play, where values—from the highest rules of honor and quest for beauty to the diseases of Puritanism, greed, and lust—spring from self-interest, and therefore where a gentleman who can stoop to conquer and who wields acute perceptions of himself and others, can master the various strata of society.

Two further points about *The Comical Revenge* seem worth stressing. One has to do with the interconnections among the various actions. These allow Etherege to move gracefully from one level of action to another without jarring the audience's expectations, and also allow the world on stage to look like a clarified version of the real world, complex but comprehensible, so as to engage the audience's interest. But although the low characters, the socially maladroit, the fools, the fops, the pimps, keep aping the highest characters, here Bruce, Beaufort, and Sir Frederick, *The Comical Revenge* does not integrate these actions vertically. As in *The Scornful Lady*, one gains nothing cognitive from understanding the analogies. The other point is that the low actions, in which Nokes, Underhill, Sandford, and Joseph Price starred, exemplify the growing inroads of satirical farce into Carolean comedy. As noted before, serious moral framing was by the late 1660s being replaced by a different kind of "morality," in which the audience as a group was led to relish the abuse of inadequate characters, like Cully and Dufoy here, the fat Pinguister who suffers repeated purges in James Howard's *All Mistaken*, and numbers of characters in Lacy's *The Old Troop*. Because farce acting depends on some characters having mechanical responses and slow wits, farce reinforces by contrast the value of social efficiency, the protagonists' deftness, ingenuity, and skill at assessing the world. The presence of the farcical underlayer in *The Comical Revenge* thus reinforces Sir Frederick's status as wit hero, despite "the sophomoric quality about his escapades" (Fujimura 88).

Other playwrights of the 1666–68 seasons adopted the structure of *The Comical Revenge*. Easily the most successful were Dryden's *Secret Love* and *The Tempest*, both appearing in 1667. James Howard's *All Mistaken* (1665) and Sedley's *The Mulberry Garden* (1668) are far below the quality of Dryden's or Etherege's plays. In one plot Howard has a pair of lovers who pretend in blank verse to hate one another; he has jailed lovers, with a villain and a martial man of virtue ready for blood; he has the hero's "mad" kinsman pursued by three nurses carrying the kinsman's unchristened bastards; and he alternates these scenes of romance, farce, pathos, and love/honor debate, connecting them in Etherege's manner with parallels that give the play formal coherence but lack any cognitive function. Sedley hit on Puritan restraint as an analogue to Spanish restraint, thus combining the biases of *The Committee* and *The Adventures of Five Hours*, and anglicizing Spanish conventions by setting *The Mulberry Garden* in the waning days of the Commonwealth. Five characters sound off in couplets; love games in the "gay" plot include satiric commentary on contemporary social practices; a witwould weds a widow's maid rather than the intended widow; and a commonwealth's-man is discomfited and cudgeled. Even more than Etherege, Sedley shares characters among the plots and so holds the actions together with family and love relationships, and his two heroes, Wildish and Sir John Everyoung, also mediate among them somewhat in the manner of Sir Frederick Frollick.

English Comedy

We have called the third group of plays popular during the 1666–68 seasons English comedy because these plays are in their own way as dependent on setting as is the Spanish mode. While moral values still form the nucleus and exert at least partial control over other parts of the new repertory—Spanish comedies and the upper layer of multi-plot comedies—English comedies laud efficiency and wit in what appears to be a relatively unstructured, transitional world featuring the confrontation between old and new values. Derived from the earlier new comedies with political settings—*The Committee, The Surprisal, Cutter of Coleman Street*—they eliminate the politics to reveal more fully the essential amorality of socially efficient characters. They are all admixtures of satire and farce, although specific plays among them emphasize one effect over the other: Lacy's plays are more farcical, Etherege's more satiric. This mixture may seem curious to those who want satire to unveil serious social ills and abuses and assume farce aims only to "stimulate the risibilities of the audience" (Hughes 19) by whatever grotesqueries the playwright can fabricate. For in these new comedies, the dividing line between farce and satire is very thin indeed, and the Carolean dramatists use all the weapons in their arsenal—physical and verbal—against various foes: aged guardians, fops, rivals, countrified fools, overreachers, and underachievers.

This kind of farcical/satiric comedy is not unique to the Carolean period—witness Plautus and Aristophanes—but was different from the more restrictive romantic or satiric formats favored by Shakespeare, Fletcher, and Jonson. Its appearance in early Carolean comedy is more than a linkage between Jonson and Fletcher; it marks the establishment of a framework within which desire—the characters' and the audiences'—coalesces. Inadequate characters identify one boundary in rather simple terms, and Carolean comedies intensified and made more graphic these characters' punishment. In Newcastle's *The Humorous Lovers*, the neurotic hypochondriac Furrs becomes the star attraction at a dance of bellows-wielders for the crime of daring to court the hero's marital choice. The commonest coin for all love-rivals is marriage to a servant, a whore or cast mistress, or an older woman who will keep him under her thumb. This kind of updated bed trick was condign punishment for those who transgressed a broad range of social and moral values from incorrect dress, behavior, and language to sins such as coercion and avarice.

Quite often in Carolean comedies, satire dissolves into farce; some plays are dominated by it, sacrificing variety of tone for other components of the fletcherian mode—namely surprises, turns, and "heightening." Lacy's *The Old Troop* and *Sauny the Scot* are both, in Leo Hughes' terms, "fitful, full of shifts and surprises, in terms of structure, episodic," with "repetition, disguise, . . . physical violence . . . [and] a motif particularly attractive to English audiences: the exaggerated or overdrawn character" (21, 32). These are quintessentially actors' plays, dependent on stage business, timing, and improvisation, on physical over verbal humor, broad over subtle effects; they remind us that "what is dead and repetitious on the printed page may well have been very much alive in the capable hands of a trained farceur. Especially in farce where everything depends upon an instantaneous and vigorous response from the audience, the skill of the actor is paramount" (Hughes 153). At its best, the kind of comedy Lacy was writing is universal in its appeal, funny to all audiences in all times if it is well done. Authors who rely on farce need no great sensitivity to or awareness of their particular world beyond a general drawing of contemporary types. Yet farce can also serve a greater goal: unifying its audience by means of shared laughter and contempt, providing consensus and opening the door to a more complex identification.

Such identification is a part of Etherege's second comedy, *She Would if She Could*, which reproduces the objectives and foibles of present-day London characters in a structure which looks backward to Jonson and Fletcher and forward to the sex comedies of the 1670s. A fletcherian courtship motif provides the play's forward movement, while deficient characters are indirect victims of that movement insofar as they impede the hero's progress. Etherege intensifies the focus and minimizes the extravagances of the fletcherian mode by relating episodes to each other in a cumulative pattern, reducing the number of characters and incidents, deepening characters by amalgamating their romantic and satiric functions. As these characters test and to some extent create the limits of the social landscape, they reveal its boundaries and ambivalencies. In his creation of a complex wit hero, Etherege identifies the constraints contemporary society does and does not place on individual behavior and what that behavior seems to reflect about human desire and its fulfillment.

She Would is both a regular and a restricted play: the action, which covers about thirty-six hours, is contained within the perimeters of fashionable London, amongst a small group of people. At the center of *She Would*, Courtall operates on different levels of its action, his character altering to suit the occasion, but this primarily structural device also contributes to the building of a heroic character. Etherege shows Courtall intentionally adopting disguises and strategies to achieve his ends much as Jonson's Alchemist and Volpone do; at the same time Courtall performs the double role of cozener and lover much more fully than previous wit heroes, providing linkage between these two functions under the heading of "natural" capabilities and motives. As lover, he and his friend Freeman court Ariana and Gatty, and he avoids the sexual pursuit of Lady Cockwood; as cozener, he outwits and exposes Cockwood, Jolley, and Lady Cockwood to ridicule. To do this, he must possess the agility of the liveliest fletcherian lovers and the versatility of the cleverest jonsonian cozeners. Multiple levels of action provide plenty of variety, and the audience's special knowledge contributes to the irony and suspense. Climactic confrontations occur in each separate action, with more elaborate climaxes when these actions intersect. One such scene occurs when Courtall helps Lady Cockwood dupe her husband (III.ii); later Courtall is confronted, first by the girls, then by Lady Cockwood, and finally by her husband in the space of some two hundred lines and forced to defend himself as best he can (IV.ii).

Etherege uses scenic devices to enhance such confrontations. Indoor and outdoor scenes alternate with each other through most of the play, every second scene taking place in Cockwood's town house. Dale Underwood suggests that these settings are counters for the play's ideological confrontations: "the home of the Cockwoods alternates with settings which represent the libertine or 'honest-man' values espoused by the heroes and aspired to by the dupes. The Cockwoods' home, on the other hand, represents in numerous ways a violation of these values. It becomes indeed the antithesis and finally the nemesis of them" (66). In specific scenes, Etherege uses setting to display Courtall's dexterity, as when he plays three different roles in rapid succession (I.i). With Freeman, he is the witty, licentious comrade, overcome with fatigue but perking up at the news of two country heiresses. With Sentry, he is the courtly lover, charmed into butter by her mistress, Lady Cockwood. With Cockwood, he is one of the boys, an "honest" and respectful hedonist. Freeman, Sentry, Cockwood, each sees in Courtall a reflection of his/her own aspirations, needs, or self-image, inviting the audience to do so as well.

Meanwhile, the use of physical setting emphasizes Courtall's versatility: Freeman is hidden in the closet when Sentry appears, and she in turn placed in the wood-hole when Sir Oliver arrives. Thus, though each previous confidant is able to hear what happens afterwards, Courtall successfully reestablishes faith with them before they leave. Later, these three roles are joined by a fourth with Courtall playing "honest" lover to convince Gatty of the seriousness of his affection and the invalidity of his other selves. Eventually this role supersedes and contains all the others and is the one in which he ends the play. Whether or not it is yet another role is another question.

From their vantage point, the audience sees an attractively multifaceted hero who can fashion himself at will to the exigencies of situation. Without a stable moral or political superstructure provided in the play to direct their reactions, the audience are invited to respond to characters and situations in accord with their own needs and expectations. There is, of course, no real latitude here; one can only identify with Courtall, whose skills and savoir faire combine with good fortune to overcome his obstructors and win Gatty. At the same time, the play's shift away from some absolute system of virtue and vice, allied with the need to provide some kind of character motivation, impels Etherege to provide a positive wealth of possible motivations for Courtall and his fellow Londoners. Courtall seems to respond to many impulses, interior self-seeking ones and exterior, socially sanctioned ones; often he seems to be playing out a game with rules made up on the spot, to be creating some kind of self-image out of his own wants and others' expectations but also in reaction against roles which are thrust upon him—like that of Lady Cockwood's young lover. This method of characterization has much to do with the play's analogical construction.

Each of the three plot actions has its own climax, further enhanced when, as in the first act, two or more actions abut. The most jonsonian of the three actions involves Sir Joslin Jolley and Sir Oliver Cockwood, Carolean versions of jonsonian dupes more nearly descended from Thwack and Elder Pallatine of Davenant's *The Wits*, Dryden's Sir Martin Mar-all, and Sir Nicholas Cully of Etherege's *The Comical Re-*

venge.[14] Their bumbling foolishness as they try to be town gentlemen by involving themselves with predators such as Rake-Hell and Madame Rampant provides most of the farcical humor in the play, to amuse the lovers and the audience both. What are called their "humours" in the play are merely absurdities of personality—in his cups, Jolley always brings his latest drinking companions home to meet Ariana and Gatty; in his, Cockwood publicly insults his wife and is mortified and penitent the next day—while their actual humours—stupidity and overreaching—are displayed in their futile attempts to imitate gallants like Courtall and Freeman.[15] The more sympathetic Jolley gets off lightly compared to Cockwood, who pays dearly for his pretensions and self-delusion by being forced to remain married to his ill-tempered, cuckolding wife.

Cockwood also figures prominently in the Courtall/Lady Cockwood action where he plays the cuckold. Duped by both his wife and her would-rather-not-be lover, he is consistently misled and used as a pawn in their own war, thereby acting as a focus for the play's sexual and generational conflicts. The importance of this merger in *She Would* becomes clearer when one looks at the confrontation between Courtall and Lady Cockwood, the dynamic center of the play. Lady Cockwood's pursuit of Courtall develops in two distinct stages. From the beginning of the play to the end of act III, she believes that Courtall loves and is deluded by her. As the pursuer, she is a "ravenous kite" (III.1.61) whose lusts are tempered and thwarted by her own hypocrisy and self-delusion; and while in this state of overconfidence, she is easily convinced by Courtall that the postponements of their "happiness" are unfortunate mishaps rather than carefully planned obstructions. But in act IV she becomes suspicious of his attentions to Gatty and tests him; learning the truth, she determines on a course of revenge which nearly succeeds in ruining them all.

Although Lady Cockwood has analogues in other popular comedies of the 1666–68 seasons—other ladies who "would" from Newcastle's Lady Huntlove (*The Country Captain*) and Jonson's Collegiates (*Epicoene*) to Shadwell's Lady Vaine (*The Sullen Lovers*)—her function in the play is not just satiric; she is also Courtall's analogue and principal antagonist. A malicious, clever woman, she, like him, is ruled

---

[14]Note that Nokes, who played Cockwood, also played Sir Martin and Cully.

[15]This flaw is presented visually in act III, when Cockwood submits to having his "penitential suit" made even more ridiculous by Rake-Hell's fashionable accouterments: wig, hat, and sword.

by her passions but able to control and satisfy them by means of her wit; like him, she dupes and manipulates all the other characters in the play at one time or another. Both, in short, are predatory, willful, cunning, and skilled actors. Their confrontation, perforce, is a clash of Titans reminiscent of those in heroic dramas between Montezuma and Zempoalla of *The Indian-Queen* or between Almanzor and Lyndaraxa of *The Conquest of Granada*. Yet, despite her formidable wit and weapons, she loses the contest because the game is rigged: she can't compete with her youthful rival, and she's handicapped by society's double standards for male and female behavior. Thus the Courtall/Lady Cockwood action throws new light on the conflicts between old authority and young lovers and between men and women: what would previously have been her advantages—age, status—turn against her when she tries to play the love game by the new, freer rules. More than Cockwood or Jolley, who are obviously underequipped for wit and sex games, Lady Cockwood demonstrates the shift in power from the older generation to the younger in early Carolean comedy.

Courtall's second major conflict, with Gatty, is more equal in another sense, and winning Gatty is the greatest test of Courtall's skill. Although willing to flirt and able to hold her own in their witty dialogues, Gatty is chaste and intends to remain so.[16] This constitutes an impenetrable barrier to Courtall's lust, as his rejection of marriage confounds her plans for him. Differently from the conflict between Courtall and Lady Cockwood, then, the Courtall/Gatty action also raises questions about dominance, self-interest, and sexual gratification. The progress of their love affair is fitful—the close relationship between characters who know Courtall in different guises almost insuring his failure to seduce Gatty. She is also a worthy opponent, able to disconcert and humiliate him more thoroughly than anyone else because his "constant lover" pose is so thin. Try as he may, Courtall cannot get Gatty to take him seriously, the only way she will take him at all. Her knowledge of the town and common sense are more than a match for his schemes and charms, and even his ultimate capitulation, his marriage proposal, is only accepted tentatively.

As mentioned earlier, Etherege uses his three plot strands in a way which perpetuates the fletcherian tradition of climactic structure while adding the coherence of meaningful analogies which distinguish among apparently equivalent actions or characters: the sexual pursuits of Courtall, Freeman, and Cockwood; the coyness of Mrs. Cock-

---

[16]See the discussion between the girls before they take to the streets (I.ii.119–71) where they resolve to be "mighty honest."

wood and the girls; the disguises and affectations of characters who pursue recognizably similar goals.[17] Etherege does some of the sorting out for the audience, differentiating characters beyond type in terms of both motive and capability. For example, Sentry, the lovers, and Lady Cockwood qualify as wits who successfully and deliberately affect roles to manipulate others for their own purposes, but their motives are different. Sentry needs to use pretense and act humble to be a successful maidservant, while Lady Cockwood seeks to conceal her lustful and predatory nature under a guise of pious gentility. The lovers assume roles for their amusement, protection, or advancement; unlike Lady Cockwood, however, they never mistake their own motives or confuse role with reality. As Gatty says to Ariana: "I hate to dissemble when I need not; 'twould look as affected in us to be reserv'd now w'are alone, as for a Player to maintain the Character she acts in the Tyring-room" (V.i.325–28). Moreover, playing country innocents for Lady Cockwood and town ladies for Courtall and Freeman gives the girls freedom of expression and movement, while Courtall's multiple roles provide him with the sport and variety his nature craves.

In *She Would*, Etherege separates plot lines simply by principles of decorum rather than, as in *The Comical Revenge*, by genre. By so doing, he facilitates Courtall's movement among the actions, and permits his hero's multiple roles to shade into one another prismatically and thereby to offer the illusion of a consistent self with which the audience can identify. And as he resembles each of the major characters in some way, so Courtall acts as the agent of distinction, so to speak, who through analogy and contrast emphasizes these principles of decorum. One can see this clearly in Cockwood and Jolley, the two dupes who are put in their dramatic place by their inept imitation of town gallants like Courtall. Motive differentiates Rake-Hell, an impoverished younger son who cozens for gain, from Courtall (and Freeman), who are affluent and bored; Rake-Hell commits the vulgarity, in the world of Carolean Comedy heroes, of being needy, thus of having his freedom impaired. The girls have a double relationship, to the men on the one hand, to Lady Cockwood on the other—and she, as we have said, is also, like the men, principally defined by her contrast

---

[17]This leads some critics to make extremely nice and sometimes surprising distinctions between or assimilations of wit and witwould, heroine and villainess, gallant and fop. Jocelyn Powell argues that Lady Cockwood cannot be criticized because she is in a "state of innocence" and "does not possess the knowledge of good and evil" ("Etherege" 54), and Norman Holland links all the women in the play together: "The title *She Wou'd if She Cou'd* applies to any one of them" (30).

with her foe Courtall. As with some other older women in the comedies, Lady Cockwood's power comes from her having the freedom, the ruthlessness, and the directedness that characterize rakes; for being "male" is the only way, beyond physical attraction and the capacity to say "no" to suitors, that women exercise power in Carolean comedy. The rage to be "absolute Tyrants" over their gallants (I.ii.168) marks Ariana and Gatty ("Sly-girl" and "Mad-cap") as progressively Lady Cockwood's equals and the equals of the rakes whom they resemble. Although less sophisticated—or is it streetwise?—than Lady Cockwood, the girls are also freer, both less self-deluded and less encumbered with other commitments, so that they enjoy a stronger position in the courtship game.

Ultimately, a substantial part of the audience's interpretation of *She Would* depends on whether Courtall is a libertine devoted to satisfying his "natural" desires or a social man playing a variety of roles. One looks, naturally enough, to the ending for clues, to the conclusion of the courtship action. In the first case, the ending is ironic; in the second, it is open-ended, whether in service to some new realism or to Fletcher. Either interpretation is textually and dramatically supportable, thus offering various members of the audience their own preferred ending. But such delicate ambiguity is scarcely necessary, for this rake-hero, unlike Horner or Dorimant, keeps well within acceptable moral bounds; his libertinism is only hinted at, never acted upon, and his humiliations are more the humorous fumblings of a slightly inept hero than the necessary "contamination" of the dangerous rake.

Indeed, Courtall's progress is basically that of the fletcherian courtship hero—gradually enmeshed in more and greater entanglements until he extricates himself by his wit and bold devices and ends up with the prize—an advantageous marriage. Such satiric characteristics as Courtall inherits from Truewit, Dauphine, and other jonsonian ancestors are used to enhance his character as a contemporary portrait, add motivation, and make the play coherent, but they do not alter its essential pattern. Thus, Etherege's much praised and criticized "realism"[18] was as much a matter of dramaturgy as of philosophy, while the greater repertory shows Courtall's role in the greater drama of Carolean comic development. Courtall's analogues in the 1666–68 seasons include not only Celadon in Dryden's *Secret Love* and Wildblood in *An Evening's Love*, but also Dryden's heroic heroes, Cor-

---

[18]Comparing *She Would* with *The Comical Revenge*, Norman Holland praises it for just this quality: "The new play is saturated with realism, real taverns, real parks, real stores, contrasted implicitly to the outlandish atmosphere of heroic drama" (35).

tez and Guyomar of *The Indian Emperour*. It is the latter comparison which is most intriguing, and Arthur C. Kirsch points out the similarities between Etherege's comic and Dryden's heroic modes and heroes:

> Dryden's rhymed plays were written and performed during the years in which the libertine hero flourished in Restoration comedy; the production of Dryden's first and last rhymed plays coincide almost exactly with the performances of the first and last plays of Sir George Etherege. The same audience saw and presumably applauded the works of both men, and there seems no reason to believe, as many theater historians have, that this audience was uniquely capable (or guilty) of possessing one set of ethical attitudes for tragedy and another set for comedy. The evidence of contemporary reactions to the drama of the period shows precisely the opposite: to the people who saw or read them at the time the theatrical appeal of comedy and tragedy was usually very similar and their moral assumptions seemed compatible. The opposition between an allegedly romantic heroic drama and a realistic comedy of manners, the heroes of the former ideal and idealized, the heroes of the latter natural and naturalistic, is a modern and tendentious distinction. (*Dryden's* 35)

The common fletcherian origins of the two Carolean forms—English comedy and heroic tragedy—is yet another argument for their similarities, suggesting that what one knows about Dryden's tragic heroes can in some measure be applied to Etherege's comic ones. Ultimately, this means that in the 1660s Etherege's English comedy, like heroic drama, focuses on the interaction between the hero and his environment, and that "eventually [the hero's] own good is not in conflict with the good of society" (Kirsch, *Dryden's* 64).

Courtall acts as a cohesive agent and mediator for the comic environment he inhabits. Pursuing his own very personal ends, enacting his desires, he continually adjusts his relationship to the world but also affects that world. He restores harmony around him, whether by indirectly helping his friend to an heiress or directly reinstating the status quo between Cockwood and his Lady, and his actions reestablish in society the formal patterns, the order, and the congruity necessary for its life and propagation. Thus, he performs the ancient comic function in a new way. While demonstrating his own capability and self-awareness, he allows others to retain their illusions for the most part. *She Would* presents a society in which individual capabilities determine function and place but where all parts eventually work together to create some kind of social order—it offers bifurcation without dislocation, rendering fletcherian structure as levels of compromise and capability which interlock to form a coherent universe.

In a sense, then, Courtall is a more powerful agent than Careless and Blunt or Antonio and Octavio were. They merely restore what has been lost or recover what has been stolen; he creates a new set of needs and expectations, particularly appealing to some members of an audience living through a time of social transition, when old values were being tested and found wanting and when new values had not yet arisen to replace them.

Conclusion

Almost by definition, multi-plot comedies must offer divergent ways to satisfy similar underlying drives. These divergences seem obvious when class or aptitude separates characters widely; the heroic lovers in *The Comical Revenge* can hardly share tastes with Sir Frederick's valet, Dufoy, even if they (spiritually) and he (so named and so poxed) all keep faith and suffer the wounds of love. In *Secret Love*, as we shall demonstrate later, the divergences seem motivated more by genre than by person, so that members of the audience—who in their real lives can define something of their own, no doubt mixed, genre, can identify with different characters and thereby try out for themselves different allegiances, postures, points of view towards the contemporary world. Desire thus prompts and develops its own cognitive underpinning. In late 1660s comedies, the psychologically denser characters, acting within a "realistic" plot, forwarded this process. Comedies in the two post-Plague seasons continue to present "moral" answers to the questions they raise about individual and collective behavior, but in the absence of the consensual moral norms that had informed earlier Carolean comedy, these answers achieve a more than formal closure only for those spectators who choose to believe in them. Other spectators are invited to identify with witty and attractive protagonists whose use of social rules as personal tools does not make them suffer exclusion. Moral solutions are therefore presented so that they may be understood as optional, and the plays allow the audience to resolve actions that may be seen as employing morality to decorate, varnish, and explain self-interested behavior. Sex, power, and money reappear as (ab)usable ideals: love, authority, freedom, "nature," honor. This practice marks *She Would if She Could*; variants of it also mark two other extremely popular comedies of the 1667–68 season, *The Tempest* and *Secret Love*. We will turn to *The Tempest* in the next chapter and to *Secret Love* in chapter 6.

4

The Tempest, or, The Enchanted Island

The Dryden-Davenant *Tempest* (1667, published 1670) delighted Restoration playgoers with its charm, comedy, and—later on when operatic effects were added—its theatrical spectacle. It also delighted bardolatrous critics by giving them something to fulminate about. Horace Furness and Hazelton Spencer danced as wildly about the mute evidence of the desecrated Shakespeare as Dryden and Davenant's Caliban and his boozy company dance around their emptied bottle of sack (IV.ii). "One aim and one alone," cried Spencer, "animated its authors: to pander" (*Shakespeare* 201). Since we have chosen to discuss this play, perhaps we should make clear our own opinion that the revised *Tempest*—or, for ease of reference, to call it by its subtitle, *The Enchanted Island*—is an enchanting comedy. It is less good than its original since neither Dryden nor Davenant could write so well as Shakespeare: "*Shakespear's* pow'r is sacred as a King's," the reigning poet laureate and his distinguished successor agreed (Prologue, 24). By and large, though, their play is wittier, more entertaining, and if less noble and spacious than Shakespeare's, more exuberant and, in all the senses of the term, more realistic. As Maus points out, the collaborators "observe the unities of time and action . . . much more loosely than Shakespeare does in his very tightly constructed play" ("Arcadia" 190). By the terms of Davenant's grant from the Lord Chamberlain in 1660, he could present only an altered *Tempest*: we would say that both the Carolean audience, who had a play very much to their taste in *The Enchanted Island*, and the modern reader, who can enjoy both versions, benefit from the results.

More interesting to us than Spencer's and our aesthetic judgments, though, is his charge of "pandering," the kind of accusation that our discussion so far has tried to redefine. No doubt most of the particulars that bothered Spencer in the conversion of "noble serenity" to "licentious farce" (*Shakespeare* 203) will not bother anyone who has emerged from celluloid collars or laced stays. Nonetheless, the revised *Tempest* does appeal to its audience in ways less salient in or wholly absent from Shakespeare's. That change of appeal is implicit in the logic of the fletcherian mode that we have described. Unless one is referring only to sex, however, we hardly think one play "panders" more than the other. After all, the romance not accused of pandering sets forth the world largely as shaped by wish. Readings of *The Tempest* vary, but except to its most somber or cynical interpreters, by the

85

play's end good rules evil by magic, wickedness is self-confounded, and the order of nature moves toward harmony. Shakespeare stirs up and largely appeases a longing for a redemptive world, using that world's very flaws to make it seem more genuine: who can indict a play as glib when it leaves the magus laden with weary wisdom and unable to redeem major characters, Antonio and Sebastian? Through concession, the formulas of romance exercise some rights in the real world. But in Dryden and Davenant's "pandering" play, such flattery of deep human wishes ends up in shreds. Redemption, such as it is, must be built on the sexual and self-aggrandizing instincts that underlie all behavior in the play and presumably outside the play too. What may or may not be "base" is certainly basic to what all humans are, and moreover need not and should not be hated. One can find this either honest or reductive and escapist, as one can find Shakespeare's "insubstantial pageant" profound or pretentiously nostalgic and escapist.

We would like to bypass such preferences for this or that view of the world to focus on a formal difference: Shakespeare articulates his play with a moral and cognitive coherence that is of no interest within the fletcherian, heterogeneous mode of Dryden and Davenant. This difference is the more striking in that Shakespeare's last plays, written perhaps for the Blackfriars Theatre, appear to adopt some of the manner of the bright, new Fletcher of about 1610. Early collaborations between Beaumont and Fletcher, G. E. Bentley says, seem "to have been prepared for boy companies at the private theatres," so that their style reflected the tastes of an audience to whom Shakespeare's company, the King's Men, was presumably eager to appeal "when the company began acting at the Blackfriars late in 1609 or early in 1610" (3: 308). The eagerness would explain the King's Company's having secured the services of Beaumont and Fletcher, and indeed, after Shakespeare's and Beaumont's retirements (by 1614 at the latest), Fletcher became the company's leading dramatist. Shakespeare is generally assumed to have collaborated with his junior, Fletcher, on three plays, *Henry VIII*, *The Two Noble Kinsmen*, and the lost *Cardenio*. *The Tempest* (1610–11?), Shakespeare's final noncollaborative late romance, comes from a period when one may suppose him willing to write in a fletcherian style, moved (by the needs of his troupe) to do so and practiced in its techniques.

Whatever Shakespeare's situation, Dryden and Davenant certainly found congenial elements to elaborate when they came to retailor *The Tempest* along fletcherian lines for the Carolean public. Ready to hand were magic, symmetry of plots and characters, an improbable hypothesis, reversals of fortune, and an uneasy mixture of fragile comedy and of losses averted only after being grieved for. Without stylistic unease, Dryden and Davenant could employ other staples of fletcherian dramaturgy, such as character reversals, a peripatetic plot divided into episodes, sudden resolutions, role playing, a stress on a central courtship plot with a blocking character and obstacles of the lovers' own creation, and inconsistencies of moral vision. Like Fletcher's plays, originated for troupes where boys were equally (un)realistic playing adult men and women, *The Enchanted Island* gives women a much fuller role than does *The Tempest*. In the Carolean manner, they have more to do and say, and differ less from men in their saying and doing it. While the resulting play departs from its Shakespearean source nearly as much as Shakespeare's plays had departed from theirs in sixteenth-century narratives, it is nonetheless a comedy that functions smoothly and has its place in a familial line common to Shakespeare and Fletcher.

That line, as we have argued, passed through *The Comical Revenge* and other plays that handled a multi-plot structure quite differently from Shakespeare's. Unsurprisingly, Dryden and Davenant in *The Enchanted Island* change the relative stress on the three plots they adopted from Shakespeare: the "high" political plot in which Prospero punishes and tries to reclaim his enemies, the "low" plot involving Caliban and the lower-class castaways, and the love plot that unites Prospero's line and Alonso's through the marriage of Miranda and Ferdinand. Framed by Prospero's revenge and forgiveness, Shakespeare's "high" plot dominates *The Tempest*. After the courtiers endure bodily pains (hunger, thirst), inner pains (grief, pangs of conscience), and madness, Prospero manifests himself to them in all his magical power and exhibits his ultimate bit of stagecraft as the supposedly dead Ferdinand and the lost Miranda appear "playing at chess" (V.i.171), a game of mock-conflict free of chance and secrecy. The whole love plot in *The Tempest* principally acts to create and ratify this scenic metaphor of Prospero's victory over evil schemes, blindness, and mere fortune. Although this specific love affair grows through time, the love itself is atemporal, a complement and rebuke to past disorders. Its presentation in Shakespeare's play treats time as a pattern of convention, even of ritual, with love at first sight, tests of constancy and compassion, and a final ceremonious union of the newly reigning couple, Miranda and Ferdinand, by the unchanging goddesses of love and fertility. The lovers, who themselves have only the sketchiest of pasts (Miranda, one recalls, does not know hers till after the shipwreck in act I), set the seal on the "high" plot's resolution of historical conflicts and temporal developments. In *The Tempest*, then, the "high" and the love plots turn out to be one. Both converge at the end of a process of intrigue and suffering, with first the conspirators and then Prospero in control, and an overlapping, slightly later process of learning, whose beneficiaries are first Prospero and then the conspirators.

Such a relationship, in which two distinct streams of action merge into a single, typically Shakespearean, encompassing order, runs counter to fletcherian practice. In its place, Dryden and Davenant substitute a fletcherian three-episode construction, carried out through three Carolean independent plot lines. *The Enchanted Island* starts (episode one) with Prospero's exercising control over the courtiers (largely in II.i). It continues (episode two) with his attempts to control the lovers. This action moves in three stages marked by breaks: the first stage introduces Hippolito, a youthful prince who has never seen a woman; after a break (III.ii–iii) comes a second stage, Ferdinand's love plot and his rivalry with Hippolito, followed by a break (IV.ii); and the third stage ends with a seeming denouement—fletcherian reversal number one—in which Hippolito apparently dies, Ferdinand is condemned to death for killing him, and Prospero returns to the vengeful state in which he began the play. Finally, independently of Prospero, Ariel brings a salve that resuscitates Hippolito (episode three), and in act V—fletcherian reversal number two—Prospero effectively surrenders all pretensions to control. To achieve this non-Shakespearean structure, Dryden and Davenant postpone Ferdinand's meeting with Miranda (to III.v) and dispose early of the courtiers' purgative sufferings. But in another dramatic reversal Alonzo (spelled with a "z" in this play) suffers again when his newfound son Ferdinand is sentenced to death (IV.iii). Since by now Alonzo needs no more moral reformation, for him the repeated threat of losing his son serves no purpose. Dryden and Davenant's fletcherian plots, brought together formally, discard Shakespeare's cognitive and moral interaction.

Neither Fletcher nor Dryden and Davenant had any bent, like Shakespeare, to rob a courtship plot of its temporal and psychological progress so as to make it ancillary to another. *The Enchanted Island* puts the lovers, very much involved in time and process, at its center and quintuples the number of lines allotted to them. Thus the "high" plot, inasmuch as it treats of the courtiers' change of heart rather than Prospero's own self-discovery, remains largely for its elegiac and moral solemnity. Stripped as it is of old Gonzalo's ramblings and the nasty, surreptitious wit of Antonio and Sebastian, in fact without any Sebastian whatsoever, this stratum of *The Enchanted Island* becomes unified in tone, and so loses its Shakespearean role as vehicle for a range of experience. In Carolean comedies such a range derives mainly from actions that focus on the fulfillment of desire, and here Dryden and Davenant characteristically transfer that range to the love plots.

Alonzo and Antonio, close to penitence even before Prospero begins to work on them, suffer an early, short, and—by comparison with *The Tempest*—impersonal kind of punishment. They have, after all, just come from "a famous heroic combat against the Moors in defense of Christianity" (Zimbardo 70). In addition, Dryden and Davenant drop Shakespeare's analogies between "high" and "low" power struggles (Antonio and Sebastian's conspiracy against Alonso, the "low" characters' against Prospero) and "high" and "low" irrationality (the madness and drunkenness, and wild greed in the two plots of *The Tempest*). Without such moral broadening of its statement, the plot of the aged foes and their past is isolated and impoverished. Fletcherian comedy and Carolean comedy following it is no country for old men. Especially in the 1660s, the old are largely significant as blocking figures, a role that Dryden and Davenant's Prospero shares with that of victim. These roles, blocking figure and victim, repeat the Queen's in the same theatre season's *Secret Love*, though Prospero, unlike the Queen, steadily becomes less a victim, more a repressive authority.

In *The Tempest*, the "low," farcical plot parallels the serious action and includes most of Shakespeare's commentary on people's animal nature. His lovers are pure, and though his courtiers are appetitive, they act out their ferocity in ways taught by civilization. But the bestial Caliban and the castaways with dim heads more dimmed by drink are something else. Caliban's lust for a state of nature and for Miranda's body takes on new direction when Trinculo and Stephano appear, and their plots rise up in proportion as the draughts of sack, that great egalitarian leveller, go down. Slave, butler, and jester seek to usurp the natural authority of their masters, as within each of them an animal nature usurps the natural authority of reason.

In *The Enchanted Island* this plot is greatly expanded, not in length but in fascination. To the original triumvirate of Caliban, Stephano, and Trinculo (Dryden and Davenant's Trincalo), the collaborators added Mustacho and Ventoso, a ship's mate and a mariner respectively, and gave Caliban a grotesque, lustful sister named Sycorax. This doubling of roles, a fletcherian technique already found in Shakespeare's *Tempest* with his two parallel pairs, Antonio/Sebastian and Stephano/Trinculo, increases the bustle of the comic scenes. The four marooned Italians and two island monsters also pair off or form alliances that act as unstable entities, producing their own energy. With more characters, more happens in the same length of time, and ingenious stage direction undoubtedly caused still more to happen. As we remarked above, satiric farce often took up moral "slack" in Carolean comedy.

Not only do the low characters show the limits as well as the brief delights of carnival, as do Shakespeare's, they also exert political authority within a state of nature. Stephano and Trincalo are no longer mere imitative underlings, Shakespeare's butler and jester; they disembark on the Enchanted Island as previous bosses, a ship's master and a boatswain. These emissaries of Latin civilization to the island heathen, then, parody the way governments operate, the strategies, alliances, and blunders of men equally well- (or ill-) qualified to exercise control. Dryden and Davenant glance not only at such squabbles during the commonwealth period, as Novak points out (CD 10: 363), but also at the stage representations of political battles in heroic plays, the dramatic type evoked by the spectacular, operatic effects of *The Enchanted Island*. "Heroic" jostlings and shiftings of alliance for power and sex are also clearly parodied by the intrigues of Stephano, Trincalo, and the other buffoons who try to stake out their realms on the brave new island. And the bold Trincalo's appearance in II.iii, to destroy the newly settled government of the viceroys Mustacho and Ventoso under the ducal Stephano, parodies the heroic cliché of the "stranger" who strides in and makes his own laws.

But despite this playful satire, the "low" plot has an effect sharply different from its Shakespearean source. In *The Tempest* the farcical plot presents the misadventures of the free so as to underscore the need for people to suppress their baser nature. A person is to be ruled by appetite, in itself unworthy, no more than a court is to be ruled by a servant, like a butler or a jester. Thus none of the discredited claims made by Stephano, Trinculo, or Caliban come from impulses that Shakespeare elsewhere in the play shows as potentially good. Exactly the opposite holds for Dryden and Davenant. Through their treatment of the mariners' government as parody in *The Enchanted Island*, they suggest what the rest of their comedy helps confirm, that from baser nature(s) spring all government, personal as well as social. Immediate appetite may be controlled by, so to speak, enlightened appetite, but everyone, as we remarked in chapter 2, behaves in accord with drives, universal impulses that produce contingent actions. No longer the murderous, bestial little mob of *The Tempest*, these castaways show the audience a recognizable caricature of themselves, no matter how upright any playgoer might fancy her- or himself to be.

It follows that drives also govern women and men alike in the love plot, drastically altered from that of *The Tempest* by multiplication of characters and change in the conception of dramatic action. *The Tempest*, in the manner of all Shakespeare's late romances, focuses on one pair of young lovers, who serve as an archetype of concord. The singleness of their union is a badge of its significance. Dryden and

Davenant, we suggest, had not concord but a dynamic of desire in mind, and they surrendered Shakespeare's single pair for the doubled lovers of their Restoration predecessors as well as, for that matter, early Shakespeare and, occasionally, late Fletcher (*The Wild Goose Chase, Rule a Wife*). Miranda, then, receives a younger sister, Dorinda, and a foster brother in the boyish Hippolito, "One that never saw Woman" (Dramatis Personae). (In *The Tempest* Ferdinand mysteriously refers to "the Duke of Milan / And his brave son" [I.ii.437–38].) He may have his name from the mythical Hippolytus, whose associations with chastity, incest, the sea, paternal rage, and resuscitation from death (by Aesculapius) are wittily germane to the youth in this play. As Dryden and Davenant worked out their plot, Hippolito was heir not to Milan but to Mantua. He has been brought to the island by Prospero, a fellow sufferer, for Alonzo stole Hippolito's dukedom when Antonio stole Prospero's. Around him develops a love plot far livelier than Shakespeare's, through a curse placed on him at birth, a frequently altering courtship-and-rivalry plot with the other trio of young lovers, and his climactic resurrection with the help of a magic vulnerary salve after Ferdinand, unwittingly repeating his own father Alonzo's misdeed, nearly kills him in a duel.

As Shakespeare's ends, then, led him to create his chief analogies between the "high" and "low" plots, Davenant and Dryden's led them to match the love and the "low" plots. Caliban's lust, taken over from Shakespeare, has an echo in Hippolito's repeated insistence that he will have all women for himself; specifically, as it happens, those after whom Caliban has also lusted. Such are the universal workings of bawdy Dame Nature. His incestuous hope to sleep with both sisters, Miranda and Dorinda, is acted out with a difference by Caliban, who cavorts sexually with his sister Sycorax: "I found her an hour ago," reports the cuckold-"Duke" Trincalo, "under an Elder-tree, upon a sweet Bed of Nettles, singing Tory, Rory, and Ranthum, Scantum, with her own natural Brother" (IV.ii.107–9). Both "low" and love plots expose the limits of ducal power adventitiously gained, by Prospero's magical charms and Trincalo's butt of sack, another sort of fetish with power to render one irrational. In both plots the products of civilization, Trincalo and Ferdinand, train the island innocents, Caliban and Sycorax, Hippolito and the sisters. Trincalo's courtship of Sycorax for her imagined political position, Queen of the isle, parodies the political motives in part behind Prospero's choice of husbands for his two daughters. Wooers in both plots encounter fomented jealousies, and a battle royal among the drunken shipmen and island monsters (IV.ii) directly precedes the duel between Ferdinand and Hippolito (IV.iii); each fight includes a broken contract, first Stephano's agreement to submit to Trincalo, then Hippolito's to stop fighting once blood is drawn. And if the "low" plot parodies the heroic play, one might expect to find—and does find—the love plot too evoking heroic conventions, like shifting alliances, battling, and passion at first sight. Because the fools' drives and feelings counterpoint those of the lovers, both "low" and love plots display the workings of human nature when relatively loose from control; the prominence of those plots in *The Enchanted Island* over the relatively controlled revenge plot indicates the altered focus of its kind of comedy, from a Shakespearean explication of moral nature to an exhibition of political behavior. (We are using "political" in a broad sense, of course, the way Fielding uses "matrimonial politics" or Kate Millett, "sexual politics." Both these extensions of the term are quite appropriate for Carolean England.)

In Shakespeare's moral explication, his plots comment asymmetrically, the "low" upon the "high" but not vice versa. In Dryden and Davenant's exhibition of political behavior, as in fletcherian comedy and the Carolean mode we discussed in chapter 2, the plots do not really comment on each other at all. Greed and planned mayhem among Caliban and the mariners in *The Tempest*, for example, help reveal the debased savagery of Antonio and Sebastian, despite their gold lace and golden tongues. To have the low group ape the machinations of the high is Shakespeare's gesture of contempt toward their shared cravings and their impotence on his and Prospero's charmed ground. By contrast, Dryden and Davenant's analogies rarely teach or impugn. One does not need their clowns' antics to learn that the lovers' antics are foolish or that real love has its deepest roots in possessiveness and physical desire. The analogies, between explicit and self-contained actions, do as much to differentiate as to assimilate these two classes of action, about which the audience maintains its knowing tolerance. On the Enchanted Island, as we have said, the lovers, the monsters, and the seamen escape from guidance long enough to have to create their own political rules from patterns that they have learned or feel inclined to favor for the satisfaction of their desires. The play tests these rules by putting them into action and by putting them into a comedy. One watches the love plot wobble in the right direction and the "low" plot trot off in the wrong, with the analogies to remind us how much the points of departure have in common. If Shakespeare's analogies are moral convergences for disparate actions, Dryden and Davenant's, which only allude ad hoc to any moral scheme of reference, clarify how disparate actions diverge.

To turn to other functions of analogy in the two *Tempests* is to discover further differences in the formal and conceptual handling of the material. Both comedies, for instance, employ analogy as a tonal device: the "low" plot keeps the audience from taking too solemnly the "higher" plot to which the "low" has analogical ties, even if the "high" plot scenes are themselves solemn or pathetic; meanwhile the same ties keep the audience from dismissing the "low" plot as simple entertainment, mere comic relief. To choose an example from *The Enchanted Island*, if the buffoons lament the impending death of the butt of sack—"I fear the Butt begins to rattle in the throat and is departing" (IV.ii.116–17)—shortly before Hippolito "dies" at the hands of Ferdinand, one is not likely to take with full gravity Prospero's dark sentence, "He must be laid in Earth, and there consume" (IV.iii.201), however poetically eloquent the line is. But because Prospero's and the lovers' sufferings are to be intense, recalling Alonzo's when he thinks his son Ferdinand drowned, the low characters do not reappear and dispel the mood till the end of the comedy. In this sequence, Dryden and Davenant use the analogy for a quasi-cognitive, eventually affective purpose: one "knows" that Hippolito will be saved because of the tonal analogy between one kind of death and emptiness, the draining of the butt, and another, Hippolito's bleeding. One does not "know" it, however, from any external complex of knowledge that relates the boy and the butt, such as a general moral principle or a principle of faith in a redemptive, radically untragic order of nature, as in *The Tempest*.

Because in Shakespeare's and the collaborators' works tonal analogy differs in the kinds of knowledge to which it refers, it differs in its relation to moral analogies. The realm of tonal analogy is the play as play, a structure arranged for an audience and following certain mutually accepted rules of dramatic syntax. Since in what is for them "real life," the characters themselves can have no idea of tonal analogies between plots, Trincalo's using a metaphor of death can mean nothing to them about Hippolito's being wounded at the same time. By contrast, the moral analogies in both plays, like those between usurpations in the "high" and "low" plots of *The Tempest* or between naive figures' innocent incestuousness in the love and "low" plots of *The Enchanted Island*, are potentially available in hindsight to the characters. From such analogies, characters can learn.

Shakespeare is much more likely than the collaborators to make tonal analogies also serve purposes of commentary available to the characters. One can imagine, for example, a morally rectified Antonio and Sebastian who recognize with shame the raw burlesque of their own complotting in the mariners and Caliban; true penitence in some sense entails being capable of such moral recognition. In fletcherian plays, the order of the play as play, which concerns only the audience, is more likely to be separate from the sorts of judgments that concern audience and characters both. Dryden and Davenant have little interest in offering their characters opportunities to learn by example or surrogate experience of some sort. The characters do not even learn from their own inner experience: the variety of emotions they display teaches them little about themselves and nothing about others. Emotions have no cognitive force in their fletcherian role of unreflective reaction, usually unreflected upon afterward. Again, as with analogy, the characters' emotional capacity does have a cognitive function to the audience, of a predictive sort. It is a mark of prowess, grotesque or shallow for the low characters and, for the high ones, an admirable sign of the *magna anima*, akin to conventions of costume like the white hat of heroes in Western movies or the fair wig of heroes in Restoration plays. But for the characters, learning, if it occurs, is more visceral; Hippolito's is quite medical, for he "learns" temperance by having his sanguine humor tempered at the point of Ferdinand's tempered steel. As we have noted, the collaborators slight the learning in the "high" plot to which Shakespeare had devoted himself.

Analogy offers a different perspective on the handling of audience and character in these two comedies because both Prosperos take on the double role of playwright and character. By giving the action a kind of thematic symmetry, analogies in these two *Tempest*s suggest the playwright's or playwrights' control and thereby set up a relationship between the author(s) and Prospero. On his island, each Prospero exercises his control through a drama of analogy, in which his persecutors are to repeat a stylized, only seemingly real version of his own sufferings, at the mercy first of the sea and then of unseen forces that threaten to rob them, as he had been, of necessaries, loved ones, and power. His old enemies need to know what he has known before they can rise to learn what he knows now.

Shakespeare brings this pattern to completion. His Prospero succeeds with analogical teaching, even if Antonio and Sebastian lour outside the close circle of reconciliation. Dryden and Davenant, by taking Shakespeare's analogical construction further, arrive at a non-Shakespearean point. Their Prospero, having made Alonzo and Antonio suffer a version of his past, plans to make them suffer the real, not stylized killing of the newfound son Ferdinand because of his own new grief over the killing of his foster son Hippolito. The continuing analogy betokens his triple loss of power and privilege: he has failed to keep Hippolito safe; he lapses from his chosen role as magician-playwright, in which his foes' sufferings are to be seemingly real, redemptive illusions; and he does not know that the wounded youth, whose soul stands "all bare / And naked, shivering like Boys upon a Rivers / Bank" (V.ii.69–71), can still be brought back to life.

His knowledge, unlike his Shakespearean prototype's, is less than that of the audience, who have understood what the comic parodies of threat in the "low" plot of *The Enchanted Island* say, by means of analogy, about this one. Here is the assertion of the audience's superiority to any character, as in our model of Carolean Comedy: about halfway through the play, the formal structure of events stops mirroring the forms of Prospero's order and begins mirroring only the playwrights', and therefore, in this comic idiom, the audience's.

One can, that is, read *The Enchanted Island* as a damning test of Prospero's power, a very partial reading but still consistent enough to suggest the distance and the nature of the distance separating Dryden and Davenant's play from Shakespeare's. Strong rivals to the audience's own potency in Carolean comedies are liable to meet humbling discomfiture, and Prospero II is no exception. After all, his character, as with the other central figures in Carolean Comedy, elaborates the internal principle of the desiring self, which treats the world as instrumental to personal goals, and he at least temporarily denies the personal goals of the other main characters on his own social level. Unlike these other central figures, a Dorimant or a Rhodophil, however, Prospero is allowed to triumph only through (rather than despite) his confutation. The Queen of Sicily, in Dryden's immediately preceding "tragicomedy," comes closest to him when, failing to block her subjects, the lovers, she can only subject her own love to blockage. As *The Tempest* unfolds, this pattern is split and partially reversed: successful with the other old rulers, Prospero cannot deal with the young figures of his own creation, lovers not so much younger than he was, one supposes, at the time of his deposition with two tiny daughters. By making Prospero's success partial, Dryden avoids one dramatic problem that later would be solved through the audience's compromise formation. Prospero's success is made to seem still more partial by its being dealt with so rapidly—these easy conquests do not bear witness to the magnitude of Prospero's teaching.

More fundamentally, the logic of the play does not call for a compromise formation, because the figure of power does not bear with him and create the desire of the audience. Dorimant and Rhodophil have both the skills to "operate" society and an energy of desire shared, even if variably, by the audience; here Prospero has the skills but the young lovers have the sympathetic energy of desire. As a rule of thumb in Carolean Comedy, moreover, a character properly exercises power only over those who assume or allege themselves to be at least her or his equal. Ideals of natural merit, of freedom, and of fair duelling stand behind the rule. Betty the chambermaid, not Sir Frederick Frollick, can clamp the drugged Dufoy in his sweating tub

(*The Comical Revenge*). By this rule, the Duke of Milan, monarch of his isle, can neither produce nor block his subjects' love, cannot embody the empowering, legitimating force of nature.

Perhaps of more immediate effect than this general rule is a set of political beliefs of the late 1660s. Shakespeare's magus, Maximillian Novak remarks, "is certainly given power that Dryden and Davenant would never have allowed an earthly monarch" (341). One cannot read backward from the divine David of *Absalom and Achitophel* (1681), with its peculiar raison d'état, to suppose a Dryden who worshipped monarchy at the time of *The Enchanted Island*. His heroic plays, *The Indian-Queen* (1664), *The Indian Emperour* (1665), and *Tyrannick Love* (1669) center on flawed rulers—the Ynca, Montezuma, and Maximin—who bring about their own downfalls. The Queen in *Secret Love* (1667) finds her power painfully abridged. Moreover, plays by courtiers which were current on stage between 1665 and the first production of *The Enchanted Island*, like Boyle's *Mustapha*, Caryll's *The English Princess*, and Robert Howard's *The Great Favourite*, also dwell on flawed rulers, as do other currently popular plays of Fletcher's: *Rule a Wife and Have a Wife* and *The Humorous Lieutenant* among the comedies and *The Maid's Tragedy* and *The Bloody Brother* among the tragedies. However much Thomas Rymer might protest that "undoubtedly all crown'd heads by *Poetical right* are *Heroes*," he was forced to note with disgust that "the choicest and most applauded *English Tragedies* of this last age," that is, the stock influential repertory in his own age, worked on far different principles (61, 1). Although theatrical convention would probably have allowed Dryden and Davenant to keep a Prospero like Shakespeare's, they chose one much more in tune with the times, by assimilating their Prospero to the model of the "statesman," a characteristic object of distrust in the Carolean theatre. As Maus so incisively puts it, "The original Prospero dreams of a world in which repression is unnecessary, the Restoration Prospero . . . dreams instead of a world in which repression is merely unproblematic" ("Arcadia" 200).

The combination of a highly fallible older blocking figure and this vein of political allusion serve to underline that *The Enchanted Island*, like most Carolean plays after the early 1660s, demythifies power by making its sources arbitrary, dependent on force, or both. Shakespeare's Prospero regains through his humane wisdom the dukedom he has forfeited by his human folly. His acts on his island validate his natural right to rule, as the minister of an ordered nature. However, when the Dryden-Davenant Prospero had his Restoration, a Milanese might be excused for not expecting much of such an island governor. And a citizen of Mantua, about to be handed over to Hippolito, the rustic, adolescent ignoramus who happened to be the rightful heir, might suddenly and desperately become devout.

One can see, then, why *The Enchanted Island* displaces a Shakespearean cluster of analogies between the "low" plot and the "high" plot most directly under control of a sage Prospero, and instead uses such analogies to the amphibious mariners and monsters for the sake of enriching the love plot, where Prospero's rule fails before the course of passionate Nature. All direct challenges to Shakespeare's Prospero, such as the murderous schemes of Caliban and Stephano (III.ii) and retribution by Prospero's "goblins" (IV.i), exist in the "low" plot; but for Dryden and Davenant's Prospero, in the love plot. Most of their low characters do not even know of Prospero's existence. Likewise, their Prospero's ability to control these characters, though not in doubt, does not enter into the play. Except for Ariel's ironic reversal of the miracle at Cana, changing wine to water to (dis)honor Trincalo's betrothal to Sycorax (III.iii), Prospero and his agents never intervene in or spy upon the doings of Trincalo, Caliban, and their confederates. The core of analogies and the central actions of the play operate beyond the edges of Prospero's field of vision.

The motives within the love and "low" plots from which noble and ignoble behavior alike arise, sexuality and possessiveness, are basic, premoral impulses that repulse outside control. For Shakespeare's Prospero, the fixed relation between motive and behavior enables him to cauterize evil motives once he has the evidence of behavior and to predict behavior from altered motives. The Prospero of the 1660s cannot infer behavior from the passions or drives that serve as motives in *The Enchanted Island*: love is based on lust and fidelity on sexual possessiveness, but those drives also have other possible, even likely expressions. Therefore his techniques of control over the "low" and love plots have a slippage logically inherent in them. The playwrights', of course, do not, and their artifact draws further and further from Prospero's reality. Enacting the audience's present desires through the lovers, not Prospero, they stand apart from a figure who represents age and the past, the superego enfeebled by the whole tradition of fletcherian comedy. As Novak writes:

> That this demythifying of Prospero was entirely deliberate there can be no doubt. . . . The wonder of Shakespeare's Prospero is his complete control over the operations of fate. The Prospero of Dryden and Davenant has about as much control over the lives and loves of his daughters and his ward as have most of the exasperated fathers of Restoration comedy. . . . [His] ability to command a spirit falls far short of a power to control human destiny. In his soliloquy near the end of the third act, Prospero maintains that "mans life is all a mist,

and in the dark, our fortunes meet us." All we really know, he concludes, is that whatever happiness man meets in life proceeds from Heaven. (340–42)

Authority of all sorts being what it is in *The Enchanted Island*, even pious devotion might lead only to disenchantment. At the end of the play three of the characters invoke Heaven (V.ii.134,143–45,150,174–75), but Providence, though not of course openly flouted like Prospero, is a sort of machina sine deo. "God in this drama," as Gewirtz flatly states, "has no moral principle whatever" (11). Hippolito has a literal "ill Genius" (IV.iii.59) and a "good Angel" (V.i.58), who respectively threaten and aid Ariel. More important, as human power is arbitrary, so in a somewhat different way is the human sense of divine power, of which Prospero, tutor and guardian, most often speaks. When Hippolito "dies," Prospero shows his unchristian motives in declaring "No pleasure now is left me but Revenge," a sentiment he transparently and self-servingly masks slightly thereafter by the claim that his spirits "are now the Ministers of Heaven, / Whilst I revenge [Hippolito's] murder," and later, still self-servingly but also inconsistently, "Our Acts of grace / To Criminals are Treason to Heavens prerogative" (IV.iii.38,161–62; V.i.12–13). Indeed, if the incestuous Sycorax is a "Jew" to "make love in her own Tribe" (IV.ii.110), Prospero seems like one in the next scene when he cites among "Heav'ns Laws" the talionic "Blood calls for blood" (IV.iii.147,150). His standards always seem improvised out of bafflement to fit his own will, and one is not surprised to find him ending a soliloquy with only the clauses of his couplets showing any equilibrium:

> If Fate be not, then what can we foresee,
> Or how can we avoid it, if it be?
> If by free-will in our own paths we move,
> How are we bounded by Decrees above?
> Whether we drive, or whether we are driven,
> If ill 'tis ours, if good the act of Heaven. (III.vi.157–62)

No doubt Dryden and Davenant meant Prospero to be seen as invoking Heaven for his own ends, but they never give any sense that he has learned that he has done so.

Another distinction may be of use here, that between law and morality. As Herbert Morris elaborates: "Law aims at a minimum; morality at a maximum. Law is prohibitive; morality is injunctive. The aim of law is not to punish sin but to prevent certain external results" (26). In these useful, not absolute terms, Dryden and Davenant make their Prospero the agent of law, punishing deeds rather than sin and prohibiting acts "to prevent certain external results," most notably

Hippolito's foretold death. Behind Prospero's power lies mere force, overt in his threats. Some of these shows of force come from Shakespeare, such as the threat of "peg[ging]" Ariel in the "knotty Entrails" of a rent oak (I.ii.217–18), the imprisonment of Ferdinand, and the physical pains inflicted on Caliban. But though Prospero I begins largely as a figure of might and revenge, he gradually frees himself from personal rancor while in *The Tempest* as a whole, evil deeds progressively appear as acts of sin, capable of absolution. Thus he can aim, in Morris' words, "at a maximum," enjoining a moral order in various ways, such as experience (the wrecked men's purgatory), his own example, and the emblem of concord he produces in Ferdinand and Miranda. Dryden and Davenant's Prospero could hardly entertain such Olympian ambitions. He finds the natural power of Hippolito's "ill Genius" as strong as his own in menacing Ariel, and the natural power of young sexuality stronger than his to control his daughters and Hippolito. He never moves from law to morality, and to each of the Shakespearean shows of force he adds another, threatening to chain Ariel "within the burning Bowels of Mount *Hecla*" (IV.iii.65), to kill Ferdinand, and to leave his daughters in anguish.

The power he does have, of course, he misuses. Without the vulnerary salve brought him on Ariel's initiative, he would have plunged into misery or destruction the already penitent Alonzo and Antonio, his daughters, the admirable Ferdinand, and perhaps even an Ariel driven to repine: "Why shou'd a mortal by Enchantments hold / In chains a spirit of aetherial mould?" (IV.iii.274–75). In *The Tempest* the answer to Ariel would be obvious, for Shakespeare's Prospero transcends his mere mortal state. But it is a good question in *The Enchanted Island*, where law and morality, as a scheme of natural rights, stray farther apart. Prospero I has freed his island from the evil Sycorax, prefiguring the purgation and renewal he attempts in the play. Prospero II has taken his enchanted island by *force majeure* and made it a neutral testing ground for the interplay of freedom and compulsion, with his law only one element of both. Here again one strikes on a thematic of great weight in Carolean comedies, as in any literature based on desire; desire arises involuntarily and exercises compulsion but also defines freedom by creating values and thereby the possibility of choice. (For Shakespeare, values do not need to be created by individual desire; they do, however, in affective drama, especially drama written in the atmosphere of shaken authority we have evoked in chapter 2.) Platonists and Christians might insist that obeying the irrational enslaves one, but as Aristotle says in the *Eudemian Ethics* (1223a: 29–36), to be held from following one's appetites is also compulsion.

Though orthodox thought connected freedom to the nature of the chosen act (as in Milton), freedom might still be politically gauged in terms of constraints, and ethically in terms of responsibility, voluntary or involuntary action. (Constraints and responsibility are not necessarily opposed, for one can choose to do something that one is also constrained to do.) Dryden and Davenant set aside the nature of the act, which is an effect of drives, to concentrate on constraints and responsibilities. With the Queen of *Secret Love*, Dryden had treated a freedom that was constrained and voluntary; with *Sir Martin Mar-all*, in his third big hit of 1666–68, he and Newcastle had treated a freedom that was unconstrained and involuntary; here in *The Enchanted Island* he offers two implicit points of view, that of a viewer detached from the lovers and that of someone emotionally invested in them. From the former perspective, in which one has no investment in the characters, they look unfree, compelled by desire. The lovers' love, for example, has to do with bodily humours, not choice, as Hippolito's therapeutic bleeding reminds one. From the latter perspective, however, the lovers themselves and the audience emotionally invested in them feel free when they can act in accord with "nature." The physical, compulsory passion, therefore, seems to affect or afflict only Hippolito, very young, "savage," and brought up virtually alone. The other three give one more sense of a love somehow both fated and voluntary. A real audience presumably maintains some sort of double vision, different with different viewers.

In achieving such a complex effect, Dryden and Davenant set forth a "high" plot world in which choice and compulsion join. Antonio's plea sums up this paradox of intentionality, versions of which fill *The Enchanted Island*:

> Though penitence forc'd by necessity can scarce
> Seem real, yet dearest Brother I have hope
> My blood may plead for pardon with you, I resign
> Dominion, which 'tis true I could not keep,
> But Heaven knows too I would not.   (V.ii.146–50)

Love at first sight, whether from merit (Ferdinand and Miranda) or from naivete and hot pubescence (Dorinda and Hippolito), has exercised its compulsion on the lovers, and their various love wrangles then give this compulsion the force of personal choice. Ariel's goodness is in his choosing to follow the spirit of Prospero's enforced commands. Here as elsewhere material taken over directly or by extension from Shakespeare becomes thematized in quite un-Shakespearean ways. As to the Carolean Prospero, trying with free use of magic to cope with his revenge, the curse on Hippolito, his unruly young charges, refractory island denizens, and his foster son's "death," he continually reacts to events rather than effects them, submissive at last to what passes for the decrees of Heaven. Choice and responsibility are themselves compromised, deprived of any real norm, like Shakespeare's moral and natural absolutes, to guide them. At the same time, so much results from the supernatural, like both the curse on Hippolito and his rescue, so much results from natural but hardly controllable impulse, and so much results from sheer chance (Prospero's arrival with magic books, Trincalo's with a butt of sack), that even in the plot *The Enchanted Island* can only now and then—as when Ferdinand's good sense finally sorts out the still-quarreling lovers—give choice and responsibility any independent weight.

The high characters, then, find themselves all on the same compromised ground, again unlike those in Shakespeare. How that is interpreted is, as we have insisted, up to members of the audience, and it is to interpretability that we would now like to turn. We may begin with Pepys' comment, that *The Enchanted Island* was "the most innocent play that ever [he] saw" (*Diary* 7 November 1667, 8: 522). Innocence, whether one opposes it to guilt or to experience, depends on a notion of responsibility. What, then, is an "innocent play"? In *The Tempest*, purgation of sin almost, but not quite, earns a character the right of innocence so that in seeing the Italian courtiers when she does, Shakespeare's Miranda has almost as much right to cry, "O brave new world / That has such people in't," as her father has to finish her pentameter darkly, "'Tis new to thee" (V.i.183–84). She and Ferdinand alone are the truly innocent, without taint. *The Enchanted Island* damps the norms and the choice that lie behind innocence/guilt and lessens the foresight that gives meaning to innocence/experience. None of the characters in any profound way is or can be guilty or experienced, and none of the most nearly innocent is free of basic urges of appetite that underlie human nature, appetites that in Shakespeare threaten one with guilt or experience. Dryden and Davenant's play is innocent, then, by enlarging innocence to include whatever is not conscious evil, and by refusing as much as possible to enter upon moral judgments within the borders of this innocence or to endorse those made by characters themselves.

As well as replacing the Shakespearian insistence on moral principle with a morally neutral setting and situational values, *The Enchanted Island* revamps the moral thematic taken over from Shakespeare. It keeps the themes as topics for dramatic exploitation but enfeebles their traditional meanings, letting members of the audience define them and so see in the play different sorts of moral value. We have already offered one example of this technique, in the invocations of

Providence by Prospero and others. For the viewer who accepts these at face value, the denouement of this play involves the pious notion that where Prospero's human strength fails, divine righteousness preserves the innocent. For other viewers, the denouement will come as an arbitrary treat, because part of a spectacle in which Christian assumptions have no consistent weight. Either reading is possible from the same production, without any directorial choice having intervened.

Another example is provided by the most "guilty" action of the play, Ferdinand's "killing" of Hippolito. The play does not rebuke the furious Prospero for sentencing the young man to retributive death for this "crime." Indeed, after the sentence is revoked, Ferdinand's father Alonzo pronounces it "severe [but] just": "In losing Ferdinand / I should have mourn'd, but could not have complain'd" (V.ii.132–33). As we have noted, Prospero puts his condemnation on a religious plane and of course a moral one: "cruel Son of an / Inhumane Father!"; "black Crimes"; "all foul with guilt"; "that blood-thirsty / Man, that Ferdinand" (IV.iii.35–36, 81, 121, 142–43). Yet Dryden and Davenant show Ferdinand as close to morally blameless as they can. He has agreed with Hippolito that the first to draw blood in their duel will get both Miranda and Dorinda, presumably planning to cede Dorinda after he wins her in combat. The bargain is struck with Ferdinand's saying "I desire not to take / Your life" (IV.i.327–28), and once Hippolito is wounded, Ferdinand begs him to "Remember our Conditions," saying "I'm loth to kill you" and "Pray, Sir, retire," while he himself merely "*retires and wards*" (IV.iii.12, 14, 18, 13 s.d.). At most Ferdinand is guilty of negligence in his initial thrust, by which he meant only to draw blood enough to settle the contest, or perhaps—if the scene is staged that way—in letting the staggering Hippolito, faint for lack of blood, impale himself while making a last desperate thrust.

The scene exemplifies what the philosopher Thomas Nagel calls "moral luck," and it does so to finesse a moral issue. "Moral luck" depends on the common, if illogical practice of the law and of moral opinion in condemning a given negligent act more if it happens to have harmful consequences: the person who clumsily knocks a flowerpot out the window is differently guilty if the falling pot kills the postman or if it misses him by a foot, though the act performed is identical and the coincidence of pot and postman simply a piece of luck. Dryden and Davenant inform guilt with this sort of contingency—very unlike Shakespearean guilt, which is always a function of one's intentions—and they thus allow one to see in the play either an amoral arrangement of affects or a serious moral structure, like

Enchanted Island 103

Alonzo, who thinks guilt requires punishment. Or, of course, something in between, moral but not intently so.

The vagueness of "guilt" is supplemented by the psychological specificity of Prospero's deep pain, and the rapid change from condemnations to free pardon is made plausible, even consistent, by Prospero's habit throughout the play of making emotional judgments, in this scene first from his rage and stifled self-reproach at his young charge's death, then from his joy at the wonders wrought by herbal medicine. The psychological consistency masks a useful lack of moral focus upon a matter absolutely central in *The Tempest* and much talked about in *The Enchanted Island*. We would argue that at the deepest level, Dryden and Davenant follow the fletcherian mode, that the most fundamental and continuous principle of their play is to be an arrangement of affective devices. But we want to insist that audiences rarely respond to plays at the deepest level, and that playwrights may, and perhaps typically do, count on the happy selectivity of what people of different tastes will hear and think in a noisy, or even a hushed theatre.

Dryden and Davenant's handling of moral issues can be more specifically illustrated in their treatment of reclamation from guilt. Early in *The Enchanted Island*, the courtiers are being terrified into penitence. As suits a Carolean comedy, they get reasons of self-interest, their fear, to combat their earlier reasons of self-interest which led them to usurp Italian dukedoms. Here their guilt centers on an allegorical masque and expresses itself in a set of metaphors. The masque (II.i) is that of devils, Pride, Fraud, Rapine, and Murther. Alonzo, "left . . . all unmann'd," feels his sinews slacken and cries out that the fruit and "the shadows of the Trees are poisonous too: / A secret venom slides from every branch" (92–93,106–8). Dryden and Davenant then mark the courtiers' reclamation by emptying these vicious acts (fraud, rapine, murder) and baleful images (masquing, poisoned food, unmanning) of any dire significance. First, the collaborators render benign the metaphor of food the next time the courtiers appear (III.ii). Music and diabolic dancing occur as in II.i, but now with "all varieties of Meats and fruits" for the hungry, humbled penitents. Alonzo still worries about poisons (43–45). Then Dryden and Davenant begin to temper the vices by displacing them into the love plot and making them innocent. Prospero sees with some pleasure that Miranda has taken up fraud:

> I find she loves him much because she hides it.
> Love teaches cunning even to innocence,

> And where he gets possession, his first work is to
> Dig deep within a heart, and there lie hid,
> And like a Miser in the dark to feast alone.   (IV.i.133–37)

Shortly thereafter (IV.i.222–43), Hippolito and Dorinda also try to defraud each other, to maintain possession of each other's hearts. The next stage is force, the mutual threats of Ferdinand and Hippolito and their prideful allotting the women, willing or not, to the victor in the duel; and the final stage, two scenes later (IV.iii), is Hippolito's "murder." After the devils of the masque have been thus domesticated in the love plot, only the motif of poison remains to be made innocent, and Ariel's gathering of herbs for the vulnerary salve does that (V.i).

After the previous discussion we do not need to belabor the way this sequential doubling of motifs fits the pattern set by character doubling, the way a pattern initiated by Prospero's scenario for the dancing devils is repeated out of Prospero's control, or even the way he himself is implicated in the vices. He does, after all, deal with his naive charges through fraud, when he tells them that members of the opposite sex are monstrous and dangerous, through force when he threatens or imprisons them, and through a sort of murder in the planned execution of the arguably innocent Ferdinand. What is to our point here is that the abstractions Fraud, Rapine, and Murder are themselves as emptied of guilt as the metaphors of food, unmanning, and poison. No one disapproves of the fraud practiced in the love plot. The force is to some degree merely ritual, as with Prospero's first imprisonment of Ferdinand or Ferdinand's plans for the duel, or it is protective, like Prospero's sequestering the cursed Hippolito. As to the "murders," the guilt is ambiguous in itself and also in that no one dies. *The Enchanted Island* proclaims moral issues, making everyone who enters into the pattern of fraud and force suffer for doing so, the lovers and Prospero as well as the courtiers and the buffoons. Yet unlike the courtiers, Prospero and the lovers benefit in the long run by acting as they have.

The same may be said for the metaphor of unmanning, the third, along with food and poison, in II.i. Alonzo's guilt and fear "unman" him in act II, and in act IV Hippolito is also unmanned after the practice of fraud, force, and "murder." But he is reclaimed (V.ii) through some phallic play with his sword that Miranda bares and anoints as the other two lovers rankle with jealousy. "Sweet Heaven," he cries, "how I am eas'd!" (74), perhaps offering an early example of the eighteenth-century slang "ease oneself" (ejaculate seminally). He is cured by being partially unmanned, since his loss of blood lets his sexual desires slacken to the point where he is content to have only one woman (V.ii.45–50), and very likely in the original production his sexual manhood itself was toyed with by having the part of Hippolito played, innocently, by a woman (Jane Long?). The very consistency with which Dryden and Davenant keep to what had been a serious pattern of moral psychology only shows how loose and flexible they have made the moral issues and their instances. As Jocelyn Powell notes, "The curing of Hippolito by Miranda through her physical ministrations to Hippolito's sword contradicts the scene's explicit moral" (*Restoration* 74). Again, one may read the movement of *The Enchanted Island* as an aesthetic game being played with moral counters or as a gradual and benevolent passage into innocence, a renewal with ethical energy behind it. The text supports either kind of reading or an amalgam of the two, and our argument is that Dryden and Davenant would have regarded that optionality as a dramatic virtue.

As with theme, so with plot: part of the logic of *The Tempest* is that scenes should have a cumulative effect, in testing a dialectic towards harmony, and part of the logic of a fletcherian rewriting of *The Tempest* is that any dialectic has to proceed through a series of plot reversals, thus very much weakening the sense of progress. "Reality" on the island of Dryden and Davenant is too unpredictable, events too reversible, values too ambiguous for a clear movement of ideas. The contrast between the two plays is quite sharp because Shakespeare's has so deliberately visible a scheme behind it. After they end their exposition in II.ii, Dryden and Davenant work a reversal into nearly every scene or sequence of scenes involving the same group of characters; and earlier, they end II.i, the introduction of the castaway courtiers, with Alonzo's lament for his lost son so that the next scene can open with that son's appearance on stage, an effect not in Shakespeare. (They even stress this partial reversal by pepping up the earlier scene with a diabolic masque about loss.) The mariners' meeting with Caliban in *The Tempest* moves simply from acquaintance to alliance (II.ii), while the parallel in *The Enchanted Island* brings Caliban in to develop an earlier reversal in this same scene, where Trincalo rebels against his fellow seamen's rule (II.iii). Again, Shakespeare's next scene shows the simple progress of the love of Ferdinand and Miranda, but Dryden and Davenant's displays a reversal (II.iv), as Prospero tries to keep his daughters from Hippolito, only to have them disobey his ban.

And so *The Enchanted Island* goes on, with the lovers and the mariners forming and breaking alliances, Hippolito "killed" and saved, the courtiers mystified and then brought to face first Ferdinand's being alive, then his impending death, and then the repeal of that sentence. After act I of *The Tempest* only one such action occurs, in III.iii, where a mysterious banquet appears for the guilty courtiers and then is snatched from them, leaving them to dine on a moral harangue. Here Dryden and Davenant limit themselves to a sudden "Masque of fatten'd Devils" (III.ii.37) who leave a presumably nondisappearing meal behind them for the famished Alonzo and company; but they improve the occasion by shifting the reversal—the deprivation of food—to the next scene, in which Ariel changes Trincalo's wine to water. They do not, in other words, lose the chance for reversals in plot, but they drop the one in Shakespeare which reinforces a moral lesson by spectacle. Again, some might see the randomness of their enchanted island as moral, a display of human weakness in a world with its own mysterious powers of healing, and some might not.

In discussing *The Enchanted Island*, we have found ourselves apportioning conceptual territory among various senses of "nature," between two senses of "innocence," among different ways of assessing "freedom," between "law" and "morality," and between responsibility and "moral luck." That is not because the collaborators—Dryden and Davenant or Kavenik and Rothstein—are scholastic, Talmudic, neoclassically taxonomic. Quite the contrary, for Dryden and Davenant thrive on a calculated vagueness, inconsistency, and shallowness of ostensible positions; this is the genius of their flexible, emotionally astute idiom. Their play, as a revision of Shakespeare's, requires that the normative concepts of belief on which it is built, such as "nature," "freedom," "innocence," and "morality," correspond to wide, blurry expectations among a large Carolean audience. By implicitly touching on different definitions as reference points within these concepts, Dryden and Davenant moor *The Enchanted Island* to a variety of beliefs within those wide expectations. In selectively following, warping, flouting, and coopting such strong but ambiguous norms for action, the characters thereby prompt approval and disapproval among the full variety of believers in their audience.

From this sort of individual engagement comes the sympathy that, as we have suggested, is key to the dramatic fulfillment of the audience's desires. Any exploration of ideas is thus an epiphenomenon of the affective complexity so brilliantly developed. And, as we have said, that is in keeping with the modified fletcherianism of this new *Tempest*: the consistent, driven characters, the sure craftsmanship, the zigzagging through a peripatetic action, the treatment of women as equal in nature to men, the cognitive independence of the plots, the combat between authority and social efficacy, and a subtle mixture of distance and intimacy. Dryden and Davenant make a fletcherian change in amplifying the lovers well beyond Shakespeare; the attention given to the older, more rigid Prospero may be old-fashioned, but perhaps not, for as our discussion of Molière in the next chapter will show, a number of comedies in the late 1660s and early 1670s followed his frequent practice of making an older humours character—Arnolphe, Orgon, Harpagon, M. Jourdain—a central figure.

The French Connection: 1668–72

The Repertory

The Carolean repertory was highly productive during the 1668–72 seasons (see appendix 2). Although the production evidence thins with the loss of Pepys' diary after May 1669, the available information suggests strongly that audiences were hungrier and more demanding than ever, forcing companies too often to put on new plays after only a few nights' rehearsal, sometimes, as their authors attest, with disastrous results. Even allowing for the disproportionate representation of new plays in historical sources and hence in *The London Stage*, the evidence about this increased activity seems convincing: of the seventy-six comedies known to have been produced during the four seasons, twenty-nine (38 percent) are brand-new, while fifteen (20 percent) are new revivals. This many new plays meant new playwrights as well, and in addition to those who had already proven themselves (Dryden, Lacy, Shadwell, Edward Howard), one finds Orrery trying comedy for a change, Betterton putting his actor's knowledge to different uses, and a host of new faces, including Aphra Behn, Edward Ravenscroft, William Wycherley, and John Crowne.

The overall movement of comic drama during the four seasons again shows imitation of the modes which had proved popular in previous seasons. The category of foreign comedy (Spanish comedies and plays with other continental settings exclusive of those based on Molière) contains ten new plays; English comedy has three; and multi-plot comedy two. In all, about three-fifths of the brand-new plays fall into these three older categories, which show varying amounts of alteration from the plays of previous seasons. The most noticeable changes show up in the area of foreign comedy which also has the largest proportion of new offerings, most of them at the Duke's Company. This suggests that the initial impetus for these plays was competitive, a need to counter the still solidly entrenched fletcherian repertory at the King's Company,[19] and that these plays are still the closest to their fletcherian

---

[19]Looking briefly at the pre-1660 plays alone, one sees that competition showing up in other ways. While the King's Company operates from a solid base of nineteen plays by Jonson and Fletcher or his imitators (seven of which are new revivals), half of the Duke's Company's fourteen offerings are scrounged from Shirley, Ford, Cartwright,

origins and thus represent a marked contrast to the English comedies and to the Molière-based imports coexistent in the 1668–72 repertory.

Foreign comedy, like its forerunner Spanish comedy, continues to be based on hierarchy—of classes and their distinctive behaviors, speech patterns, and dress, whether these conventions are taken seriously, as in Tuke's *The Adventures of Five Hours,* Behn's *The Amorous Prince,* and Crowne's *Juliana,* or mocked, as in Edward Howard's *The Six Days' Adventure* and Arrowsmith's *The Reformation.* The linkage between all these plays set in foreign places—Spain, Italy, France, Poland, Scythia, Utopia—is their adherence to a moral code which provides the superstructure of the play, while its characters' activities often proceed along quite different paths: toward libertinism, satiric exposure of the bastions of morality, the witty undercutting of characters or ideas associated with conservatism of all sorts. Although the tonal range within individual comedies is often wide, each play tends to keep within its own boundaries by means of the devices established in the Spanish comedies of previous seasons, the most common of which identifies different characters and levels of action with levels of seriousness. In an almost entirely romanticized political play like *Juliana,* comic relief comes from the vulgar and self-serving landlord who owns the inn which all the disguised and mismatched lovers, exiles, and rebels pass through on their way to important battles, duels, and confrontations. A more uniformly humorous play like Wycherley's *The Gentleman Dancing-Master* maintains its young lovers within conventional moral bounds, allowing license only in their wit in the manner of Dryden's *An Evening's Love.* Wycherley goes one step beyond Dryden by moving his setting closer to home, ridiculing the affectations of Hippolita's father who keeps a "Spanish" household in the heart of London and his nephew who has equally thoroughly adopted the manners and behavior of a Frenchman.

In keeping with changes in other parts of the repertory, many of these plays contain stronger libertine elements than their predecessors in the Spanish-comedy mode. Yet those elements continue to be structurally controlled and counterbalanced: the more immoral the character or plot movement, the more deliberate its counterweight. In Arrowsmith's *The Reformation* and Edward Howard's *The Six Days' Adventure* and *The Women's Conquest,* control comes in the form of distance: both authors establish an improbable hypothesis at the outset

---

Habington, with a couple of newly revived plays by Fletcher himself. This still leaves them with only about two-thirds the number of old plays as their competitors have (see appendix 1).

of the play which removes its situation from reality to fantasy—a "reformation" freeing women from their guardians, a political and social takeover of Utopia by females, a country ruled solely by men where wives can be cast aside at whim. Working out these respective hypotheses affords each author free rein to parody modern social attitudes and sexual expectations, with the comfortable assurance that the unreality of the setting will prevent the audience from being offended or implicated.

Another variation appears in Behn's *The Amorous Prince* which presents the familiar rake-reformed pattern with new gusto in charting the course of the Amorous Prince, Frederick, who feels compelled to debauch all the fair women in his kingdom either by force of charm or *droit de seigneur*, whichever works best. Perhaps worried that Frederick was overstepping generic boundaries, Behn frequently interrupts the action to let characters make excuses for his behavior, explaining that he is merely spoilt and self-indulgent, and in his closing speech Frederick vows to forget the "sallies" of his youth and become a good husband and ruler. Behn's concern about extending sexual license in her play without offending her audience was not shared by other authors, and therefore one assumes it was unnecessary.

In fact, the genre's continued popularity probably results from its interweaving and balancing a variety of tones while eliminating some of the restrictions imposed by the moral parameters of earlier Spanish comedies. In his preface to *The Women's Conquest*, Edward Howard acknowledges the appeal of this kind of comedy, partly because of its wide range of affectivity, partly because specific members of the audience are more attracted by either the humorous or serious elements. Its satire is largely based on fixity external to the individual, the quirks of a strange society with odd mores, and the distance inherent in the form allows the audience a freer range of imagination and identification without the need to be shielded from its consequences: foreigners are, after all, not like Us.

Molière-based Comedy

In one respect, the foreign comedies do resemble the newest comedies in the late 1660s and early 1670s. As discussed in chapter 3, much of the inspiration for Spanish comedy came from abroad, specifically from Spanish romance, whether percolated through Fletcher, through French novelists like Madame de Scudéry or French playwrights like Thomas Corneille. To focus on the latter, in the pre-Molière era just before the Restoration (1635–60), the French stage was largely populated by translations from the Spanish comedia (ten out of fourteen of the plays by established dramatists between 1652 and 1658, according to Lancaster [3.1: 45]); the playwright Boisrobert commented in 1653 that "if we Frenchmen took the trouble of invention now and then, the Spanish would not be the sole masters of splendid inventions" (Lancaster 2.1: 728, 745). As Loftis points out, this was the very period when the English court was in exile abroad. "The fact that the Spanish vogue in France reached its height in the 1640s and 1650s meant that many Englishmen who were to be influential after the Restoration, and presumably the king himself, saw French adaptations of the comedia in Paris" (34).

At one level, then, the influx of Molière-based comedies during the 1668–72 period is part of an honored tradition of English playwrights aping French fashion, occurring later partly because Molière's plays were only acted in or near Paris beginning in the late 1650s. Because the Molière vogue didn't begin in England until the late 1660s, there is quite a gap between the earliest French production and its English adaptation in the case of *L'Étourdi* (1658) and *Sir Martin Mar-all* (1667), or *Les Fâcheux* (1661) and *The Sullen Lovers* (1668), while some later plays are predictably closer in time to their sources: *George Dandin* (1668) into *The Amorous Widow* (1670, but possibly as early as the 1668–69 season), *Tartuffe* (1669) into Medbourne's *Tartuffe* in 1669–70. But as Molière's popularity increased in France, so it did in England (see accompanying list adapted from Wilcox 180–81). Thus, by the late 1660s and early 1670s, some ten Molière-based plays were being offered on the Carolean stage, many of which would have a pervasive influence on the comedy of the mid-1670s, refining the English-comedy mode into London comedy.

These comedies were either direct translations or revised versions of Molière's major works, from *L'Étourdi* of 1655 to *Le Bourgeois gentilhomme* of 1670,[20] and they represent about a quarter of the post-1660 plays appearing during the 1668–72 seasons, the eight brand-new plays among them over one-third of the new comedies in that group. These figures alone argue for substantial impact. Looking forward and backward one also sees Molière in Carolean comedies from Dryden and Newcastle's *Sir Martin Mar-all* (1667) and Shadwell's *Sullen Lovers* (1668) all the way to Otway's *Cheats of Scapin* (1676) and Wycherley's *The Plain-Dealer* (1676), but the high density of his comic appeal in the 1668–72 seasons leads us to two pertinent questions.

---

[20]While other English comedies like *An Evening's Love* and *The Mulberry Garden* also have borrowed scenes or situations from Molière, we are concerned here only with those plays which are substantially derived from French sources.

Translations of and Derivations from Molière

Season	Play	Source
1666–67	Sir Martin Mar-all (Dryden)	L'Étourdi (1558)
1667–68	The Sullen Lovers (Shadwell)	Les Fâcheux (1661)
1668–69	Damoiselles a la Mode (Flecknoe)	L'École des maris (1661) Les Précieuses ridicules (1665) L'École des femmes (1662)
	The Hypocrite (Shadwell)	Tartuffe (1669)
	The Amorous Widow (Betterton)	George Dandin (1668)
1669–70	Tartuffe (Medbourne)	Tartuffe (1669)
	The Dumb Lady (Lacy)	Le Médecin malgré lui (1666)
	Sir Salomon (Caryll)	L'École des femmes (1662)
1671–72	The Miser (Shadwell)	L'Avare (1668)
	The Citizen Turn'd Gentleman (Ravenscroft)	Le Bourgeois gentilhomme (1670) L'Avare (1668) M. de Pourceaugnac (1669)
1674–75	The Country-Wife (Wycherley)	L'École des femmes (1662) L'École des maris (1661)
1676–77	The Cheats of Scapin (Otway)	Les Fourberies de Scapin (1671)
	Scaramouche (Ravenscroft)	Les Fourberies de Scapin (1671) Le Bourgeois gentilhomme (1670) Le Mariage forcé (1664)
	The Plain-Dealer (Wycherley)	Le Misanthrope (1666)
1677–78	Sir Patient Fancy (Behn)	Le Malade imaginaire (1673)

What is the basis of that appeal for Carolean playwrights and audiences? What use did those English playwrights make of the originals in their own work?

Molière's comedy shares plenty of ground with the fletcherian mode. Like Fletcher's, Molière's plots are episodic and also repetitive, an accretion of scenes which reproduce the same pattern of confrontation again and again. Eraste in *Les Fâcheux* walks around the park being accosted by a succession of "bores," each slightly different from but analogous to the ones before and after. Mascarille in *L'Étourdi* sets up trick after trick whereby his master Lélie can outwit his father and marry Célie; Lélie each time drops the ball or blabs to the wrong person, a device Molière repeats with Arnolphe and Horace in *L'École des femmes*. Even the more complexly structured plays—*Tartuffe* or *Le Misanthrope*—have at base a series of discrete episodes of confrontation which end when the playwright puts an end to them, not because of some causal necessity in the play itself.

A second important linkage between Molière and the Carolean stage is the use of farce, a connection recalled in many Carolean prefaces where authors inveigh against it as a vile French import. As discussed in chapter 3, several factors seem to have been responsible for the high level of farce in Carolean comedy: the mixed tone and low characters inherited from the fletcherian mode, the audience's delight in broadly drawn caricatures, and the presence of talented actors like Lacy and Nokes to play those roles. The farce in Molière's comedy is similarly rooted in its sources—here the Italian commedia dell'arte—and in its being, above all, an actor's medium. Furthermore, the episodic structures of Fletcher and Molière lend themselves to farcical "business" for two important reasons: because farce varies the tone of the plot without breaking the chain of events by its anarchy, and because the generic congeniality of a moment-by-moment technique like farce meshes with a dramatic idiom that is episodic scene by scene.

There were, of course, also differences between the two types of comedy, an analysis of which can help explain the short- and long-range effects of this particular French invasion of the English stage. These differences also help explain why the most faithful translations of Molière—like Shadwell's *The Miser* and (lost) *Hypocrite* and Matthew Medbourne's *Tartuffe*—did less well on the English stage than the more altered versions—like Dryden and Newcastle's *Sir Martin Marall* or Caryll's *Sir Salomon*. While there are numerous distinctions between the comedy of Molière and the Carolean comic format based on Fletcher, some—like Molière's greater emphasis on servant characters—are less important than others. One of the important differences is Molière's tendency to write single, linear, repetitive plot lines, most evident in early plays like *Les Fâcheux* and *L'Étourdi*. Carolean adaptations of these plays, respectively, Shadwell's *The Sullen Lovers* and the main plot of Dryden's *Sir Martin Mar-all*, have a rhythm quite different from their fletcherian competitors in the repertory, almost ponderous in their forward movement of nearly identical episodes, each of which constitutes what amounts to a complete and independent sketch.

A more important difference between the two modes of comic plotting is their emphasis. In fletcherian and early Carolean comedy, the focus is on the romantic courtships of one or more pairs of young lovers; in Molière's comedy, the courtship action is often relegated to second place or even to the background.

> Little needs to be said about the young lovers who suffer many pangs but who win approval for their marriage at the end of the play. . . . They have a basic structural function, since comedy nearly always shows the victory of youth over age, but as personalities they obviously did not interest Molière so much as the great figures to whom he gave central roles. He preferred to lavish his skill on the hypocrite, the misanthrope, the coquette, the miser, and several other unforgettable characters.[21] (Wadsworth 107).

Molière's comedy thus offers more range of subject and character interaction than the relatively simple obstructed courtship pattern of the fletcherian mode, centered on its exemplary sympathetic heroes and heroines. Molière was free to focus on clever servants and blundering masters (*L'Étourdi*), religious and social hypocrisy (*Tartuffe, Les Fâcheux*), foppery (*Les Précieuses ridicules, Le Bourgeois gentilhomme*)—in short, whatever current subject piqued his interest and provoked his amusement.

Ultimately, this gives Molière's comedy a satiric emphasis which shows up most clearly in his heroes or protagonists of the mid-l660s: Tartuffe, Don Juan, Alceste, Jupiter. All these flawed, somewhat brutal protagonists are the center of a "courtship" action very different from that found in Fletcher—one which encompasses hypocrisy, lust, avarice, and cuckolding. If one looks at the Carolean borrowings from Molière, the most popular of the adaptations seem to be of two different kinds—those which are more farcical and center on one or more objects of ridicule (*The Sullen Lovers, Sir Martin Mar-all, The Amorous*

---

[21]Wadsworth also points out, lest one forget, that the author usually wrote and "gave himself the outstanding comic part, whether as Sganarelle, Scapin, Argon, Harpagon, or Monsieur Jourdain" (106–7).

Widow, *The Citizen Turn'd Gentleman*), and those which are more satiric and center on a "hero" engaged in a debased courtship action (*Sir Salomon*, *The Country-Wife*, *The Plain-Dealer*). And although the earlier Molière borrowings lean toward farce and the later toward satire, all these plays have in common the effective displacement of the romantic tone and action from center stage. In its stead one finds satiric figures which provoke more complex reactions: an abused fool like George Dandin/Barnaby Brittle, a clever blocking figure like Arnolphe/Sir Salomon, a narrow-minded bastion of honor like Alceste/Manly. This process was begun in the Molière-derived plays of the 1668–72 seasons.

Looking at the ten plays (nine still extant), one finds some variety in the ways the different Carolean authors use their source materials. Shadwell, for example, in *The Sullen Lovers*, *The Miser*, and presumably the lost *Hypocrite*, is relatively faithful to his French sources; Dryden in *Sir Martin Mar-all* and Betterton in *The Amorous Widow* add a second, fletcherian plot line; Caryll in *Sir Salomon* enhances the courtship action of Molière's plot. The purpose of the two latter techniques is quite clear: to make Molière's comic action more acceptable to an audience accustomed to fletcherian comedy, first, by elevating the courtship action and its hero and heroine and, second, by adding more complexity and convolutions to Molière's relatively simple linear plots. In confirmation of these latter authors' choices, we note again that the more faithful translations, like Flecknoe's *Damoiselles a la Mode* and Medbourne's *Tartuffe*, were generally less successful on the Carolean stage than the looser adaptations, like Betterton's *The Amorous Widow* and Dryden and Newcastle's *Sir Martin Mar-all*; the only exception, the success of Shadwell's *The Sullen Lovers*, should perhaps be attributed to that play's personal satire against the Howards.[22] Otherwise, the more altered Carolean versions of Molière's comedy offer the best glimpse of its effect on the repertory.

The first of the plays to appear, and one of the most enduringly popular, was Dryden and Newcastle's *Sir Martin Mar-all; or, the Feign'd Innocence* (1667). *L'Étourdi*, from which *Sir Martin Mar-all* largely derives, was Molière's first full-length play, itself derived from an Italian

---

[22]Pepys' reactions are instructive here. After having seen the play twice and judging it "tedious" and "contemptible," he changed his tune: "I saw 'The Impertinents' once more, now three times, and the three only days it hath been acted. And to see the folly how the house do this day cry up the play more than yesterday! and I for that reason like it, I find, the better too; by Sir Positive At-all, I understand, is meant Sir Robert Howard" (5 May 1668; *LS* 135). By 24 June, he had decided it was "a pretty good play" (*LS* 138).

original.²³ Despite this, it follows what was to become Molière's basic comic pattern, with a strong focus on one or two characters, weak secondary roles, a format of increasingly complicated variations on a theme, and a deus ex machina ending. Here one of the two main characters is the foolish young Lélie, who loves Célie, a slave, though his father wants him to marry the well-born and well-to-do Hippolyte; the other is Lélie's servant Mascarille. The theme and variations involve Lélie's blunders, which overturn at the eleventh hour each of the plots that Mascarille has carefully wrought on his behalf. In fact the courtship is a mere vehicle to display the delightful master/servant relationship between these two. Eventually, a romantic unveiling of lost heirs and heiresses brings the comedy to an end.

In many ways, this plot is perfectly congenial with the established mode of Carolean comedy. The accelerating variations and increasing complications within the plot, the mixture of farce/satire and romance, the eleventh-hour reversal—all are familiar components of the fletcherian mode. The central cozening motif of *L'Étourdi* is reminiscent of Jonson, with Mascarille a French version of Face or Subtle: arrogant, clever, dedicated to preserving his "honor" (reputation for ingenuity) in the face of almost overwhelming odds. He is also clearly derived from the clever slave of Roman drama and thus kin to his modern incarnation, the Spanish gracioso. The distinctions between *L'Étourdi* and Carolean comedy are equally clear-cut. Imitating its Italian source, *L'Étourdi*'s stagecraft is minimal, consisting of a few neatly done entrances and exits. A fair amount of action occurs offstage or is related from the past, and there is considerable reliance on soliloquy instead of dialogue or action to provide motivation and to characterize. Moreover, in its single plot line there is little of the variety of effects and linking of disparate sensibilities typical of Carolean comedy, the strong secondary plots and roles which counterpoint the main action's forward movement. The addition of this kind of complication is, in fact, the first and most notable difference between *L'Étourdi* and Dryden and Newcastle's *Sir Martin Mar-all*.

Sir Martin Mar-all retains the basic tension between the characters of blunderer (Sir Martin Mar-all) and servant (Warner) in the main action of what has essentially become a double-plot play. Sir Martin is an arrogant fop, as confident of his own wit as the long-suffering Warner is of his master's stupidity. The focus of this action, like that of *L'Étourdi*, is the abortive attempts by Warner to help his master court Millisent—the authors eliminate the obstructive father and in-

---

²³For a detailed comparison of *L'Étourdi* and *L'Inavvertito* see chapter 2 of Wadsworth.

stead elaborate the action by elevating a number of secondary humours characters to important roles: Lady Dupe, Mar-all's cousin; Moody, Millisent's father who longs for Elizabethan times; Sir John Swallow, Millisent's betrothed; and Millisent herself. They also add a secondary plot wherein Lady Dupe and Christian cozen Lord Dartmouth, Christian's seducer, with an elaborate ploy: Mrs. Christian at first evades him with her "feign'd innocence," then capitulates, becomes pregnant, and cozens him into supporting her. The two plots are linked in acts IV and V when Warner intervenes to marry Christian off to Sir John and are linked metaphorically in that Mar-all's "innocence" (ignorance) is not feigned, but all too real.

Some of the differences between *Sir Martin Mar-all* and *L'Étourdi* are pragmatic: adding the second plot leaves less time for complicated contrivances in the main action which has, therefore, fewer miniplots than *L'Étourdi*. Other differences may be attributable to English versus French types of cozeners, fools, and lovers. Warner is a less elaborate planner but faster on his feet and more quick-witted than Mascarille; Sir Martin is more foppish and less likeable than Lélie. Molière's romantic lost heirs have been supplanted by fletcherian disguises and substitutions to provide a denouement, a twist of "poetic justice" wherein Warner is revealed as an indigent gentleman and gets the girl. Women have a far greater role in *Sir Martin Mar-all* than in *L'Étourdi* and are generally more clever than the men, except for Warner. (Even Millisent suspects the truth about Sir Martin and requires proof of his wit before she throws her life away.)

There are plenty of purely gratuitous farcical scenes in *Sir Martin Mar-all*, such as Sir Martin's lute playing (V.i.165–229), Warner's hiding from Sir John (II.ii.80–121), the hoisting on stools of Sir John and Moody at the climax (V.ii.41–126), and Sir Martin's East Indian disguise and subsequent beating (V.i.281–475). The last two are both from *L'Étourdi*, and some of the other stage business may also have been part of the French production. Despite the abundance of farce in both versions, there is a major distinction between the French and English plays. In the former, the cozener, Mascarille, is the more central figure, having more stage time and attracting the audience's sympathy with asides and direct appeal; in the English play, Mar-all's foolishness is central, and Warner is sometimes tainted by association, as his plots are confounded by his master one by one. Indeed, contemporary accounts of *Sir Martin Mar-all* all indicate that the character of Mar-all, with Nokes in the role, was responsible for the play's success, while Underhill, in the role of Old Moody, was also praised (*CD* 9: 353). This shift of emphasis—from witty characters as controllers of the action to satiric objects controlled by forces outside and inside themselves, a shift which we have noted in *The Tempest*—seemingly goes against the grain of the development of witty heroes like Courtall in *She Would if She Could*, but in fact is part of the same process.

What one finds in the late 1660s and early 1670s are comedies which rely on satiric distinctions between characters and actions that are increasingly similar. Whereas comedies of the earlier 1660s sharply contrasted the motives and methods of antagonists like Careless and the Days, the newer comedies show almost all characters seeking the same kinds of gratification. Sir Martin and Warner, outwardly distinguished by their master/servant role, both seek the same object—Millisent—and are only marginally different from Lord Dartmouth or Sir John Swallow. Once moral distinctions have thinned to this point, the satiric distinctions provided by Molière's comedy take over. The courtship activity becomes both more and less important—it is the crowning of the hero's achievement in other areas: deception, manipulation, agility, perception. In short, what Carolean comedies borrowed from Molière's comedies were primarily satiric central figures and other more complex characters inhabiting more realistic, less romantic settings.

Yet, as *Sir Martin Mar-all* indicates, other elements of Molière had either to be eliminated or altered to suit a public accustomed to fletcherian structure and style. A courtship plot had to be elaborated, variety introduced, and the roles taken by the stellar farceurs of the two companies—Nokes, Underhill, Lacy—had to be beefed up. Two approaches to this amalgamation were commonly used by Carolean playwrights writing successful adaptations of Molière's comedy: the enhancement of the courtship action within a single plot and the addition of another plot. One finds these methods used respectively in Caryll's *Sir Salomon* (1670) and Betterton's *The Amorous Widow* (ca. 1669), both of which successfully borrow from Molière plays which are later than *L'Étourdi* and have richer, more ambiguous characters.

Caryll's *Sir Salomon* owes a strong debt to Molière (*L'École des femmes*) openly acknowledged in the Epilogue, yet it remains distinctively fletcherian (see also Taylor). Caryll integrates the English and French strains into a single, but complex plot with two foci: Sir Salomon and his son, Mr. Single. The play begins with Sir Salomon disinheriting his son, thus preventing his son's marriage to Julia, so that he himself can marry the country-bred innocent (Betty) whom he, calling himself "Mr. Evans," is keeping in town. Meanwhile, Young Single and Julia have the traditional obstructed lovers' laments and doubts (she decries his jealousy), and an additional obstruction in the rivalry of Sir Arthur Addell, who employs Single as his intermediary with Julia. Single's friend Peregrine Woodland adds the final linkage to the entanglement when he courts Betty (taking the role of Horace, Arnolphe's rival in *L'École des femmes*).

From this point on, the Sir Salomon action is a close derivation of Molière's play, but the added action—his son's problematical courtship of Julia—is given almost equal time and status. The two plots frequently intersect—as when Sir Arthur blunders into a trap set for Peregrine or young Single helps his friend, and Caryll goes Molière one better by adding a second deus ex machina ending to resolve the play's complications. Thus, Caryll retains the core of the Molière play mostly intact but makes it share center stage with a pair of fletcherian obstructed lovers and adds an inferior rival (played by Nokes [Downes 64]) to provide much of the farcical humor in the play.

Because the plot of *Sir Salomon* is more active and complicated than that of *L'École des femmes*, there is no time for Molière's long soliloquies, instructions to the young, innocent girl, or extensive comments on society. Instead, there is constant movement, as fletcherian surprises, disguises, and unexpected encounters provide and alter the pace. Yet Sir Salomon (Arnolphe)—the role originated by Molière and taken by Betterton—remains the most interesting character in the play, retaining enough of Arnolphe's introspections to make him more psychologically intriguing than his role as fletcherian obstructor would generally warrant. In Molière's play where he is the center, he represents "the rights of authority, the rights of property [and] is defeated ultimately both by nature itself working through the love of Horace and Agnes, and also by the unseen webs of relationship which make up society" (Grene 41). In *Sir Salomon*, the position of the audience with regard to the Sir Salomon/Arnolphe figure is more complex. As a symptom of contemporary society, the cynic determined to avoid cuckoldom by molding an innocent to his needs is a satiric object; but his success in outmaneuvering his son and Peregrine attracts the admiration due to a wit hero.[24] Indeed, as competitor for the latter role, Single Jr. lacks his father's finesse or his ingenuity, and their respective success and failure are clearly more the playwright's moral contrivance than a reflection of the characters' relative merit.

Throughout, *Sir Salomon* uses its fletcherian elements to counterbalance Molière's single-mindedness. It conveys a powerful double message that lust is innate but that romance exists, that loyalty is passé but that friendship is possible, and that the likely end of modern

---

[24]In *The Country-Wife*, a later play also based on *L'École des femmes*, Wycherley solves the problem of Sir Salomon as attractive/repulsive character by splitting the role: Horner becomes the sympathetic object, Pinchwife the satiric.

marriage is adultery but that marriage is a desirable end. The play never suggests that Sir Salomon's cynicism is unwarranted, while the "innocent" deceptions of his bride-to-be, as in *The Tempest*, reinforce assumptions about the naturalness of sexual license. Because, as in Molière's play, there is no attempt to draw Sir Salomon into the festive comic conclusion, his forceful personality lingers on to cast a pall over the happiness of the young couples and the rest of the doting parents. What one perceives, then, is that Molière-influenced Carolean comedy moves a step away from pat fletcherian endings toward a courtship resolution more appealing to a sophisticated audience. As the potentially disruptive, unattached male, Sir Salomon stands aside and casts doubt upon simple answers for those in the audience who would eschew romance; yet his rejection by the society of the play is comfortable for those who desire a hopeful comic conclusion.

Another kind of French/English amalgamation occurs in Betterton's *The Amorous Widow*, a double-action comedy, half original, half derived from Molière's *George Dandin*, with some borrowings from *Les Précieuses ridicules*. The play begins with the added fletcherian courtship action: Philadelphia, the witty heroine, is being pursued by Cunningham, a young man of the town; obstructions come from her jealous and lustful aunt, Lady Laycock, and Philadelphia's own doubts about Cunningham's stability and character. Cunningham sets his friend Lovemore the task of keeping Lady Laycock busy, but Lovemore, like Courtall in *She Would if She Could*, shrinks at the crucial moment. When Cunningham finds himself the unwilling object of Lady Laycock's affections, he disguises his falconer, Merryman, as Viscount Sans-Terre and aims him at her, while he works to convince Philadelphia of his sincerity. This plot is also reminiscent of *She Would if She Could* in its abundance of fletcherian disguises and the fancy footwork the lovers employ to elude their obstructors and assuage their own doubts about constancy and marriage.

The Molière plot appears midway through act II when Lovemore confides to Cunningham his own plans to cuckold Barnaby Brittle, a rich cit married to a young, unhappy gentlewoman. From Brittle's entrance shortly thereafter, this action is a fairly close translation of *George Dandin*; Lovemore provides the main bridge between the two plots, and there is some social interaction between the two sets of characters. Like those of *L'Étourdi* and *Sir Martin Mar-all*, the Brittle plot consists of three near-identical episodes: the wife meets her would-be lover, is discovered by her husband who sends for her parents and has his revenge thwarted when she escapes discovery at the last minute. Within this plot are some very frank discussions, taken from Molière, about the perils of unequal marriages, and Betterton also follows Molière in preventing the actual cuckolding.

The need to conjoin the two plots at the conclusion creates some problems of sense and sensibility for both author and audience; despite Betterton's valiant attempt to link the two endings, there are some obvious questions still pending. Her plans thwarted, Mrs. Brittle apparently converts, saying: "Well, Husband, seeing so many join'd in Happiness, if you'll promise never to be jealous, I'll promise from this moment never to give you Cause, and endeavour to make you as happy as I can" (V; 86). But this reconciliation is a good deal more open than had been true in earlier comedy. If the viewer's predilection creates a happy ending, it can serve the purpose. But if the viewer takes the Brittle plot as a psychologically realistic depiction of a doomed marriage, the reconciliation rings false. Members of the audience who take the characters as having an ongoing psychic life must assume that Brittle will eventually be cuckolded, even if not now by Lovemore. For them, Betterton's forcing a happy ending convention on to such material produces irony and shows the conventional ending inadequate in an atmosphere in which the issue of unequal marriage seems more serious than in previous comedies.

The openness arises from the impact of Molière upon the ambiguity typical of fletcherian comedy. The two plots offer a before-and-after view of marriage rarely seen in fletcherian or Carolean comedy before the 1670s, in which near-cuckoldings had been used only satirically to enhance a hero's status or to ridicule one or both marital partners. While *The Amorous Widow* superficially follows this pattern, it dwells in Molière's fashion so heavily on the motives and emotions of Barnaby Brittle and his scornful lady that these characters begin to have an inner life and almost invite our sympathy. Betterton makes his audience feel the frustration of a young gentlewoman sold into an inferior marriage by her money-hungry parents and the anger of a social-climbing citizen humiliated by the wife for whom he paid good money. The connotations of the glass that Barnaby Brittle has grown so rich selling—its fragility, its expensiveness in the mid-seventeenth century, its connection with windows as viewing places and as places for surreptitious entrances and exits—all come into force in this comedy, so as to relate the cuckolding action to the occupation that brought Barnaby his refractory bride. Because he and she, especially he, seem more than conventional humours characters acting out their ineluctable roles, one can treat the resolution ironically, either as Betterton's sop to the "moral," or as a real but temporary resolution that confirms the cynical truths it purports to deny; one can also take it straight, for if Mrs. Brittle has a mind, she also can learn how fleeting and unsatisfactory for her a prospective affair is likely to be, and indeed, the more sympathetic Barnaby becomes, the more tolerable he may appear as a person, hence as a husband.

This is exactly the sort of openness that exploits an audience's heterogeneity of reponse, as we believe *The Amorous Widow* does, and that makes compromise formation a device of the late 1660s and 1670s, here because one can enjoy the "immoral" antics of Mrs. Brittle and Lovemore without having to take the consequences of that enjoyment at the end. In this play, more than in its predecessors or successors, the way in which one understands the Brittle plot affects one's attitude towards the other plot. Unlike analogous earlier plays like *The Scornful Lady*, *The Country Captain*, or *She Would if She Could*, *The Amorous Widow* juxtaposes, not just degrees of seriousness and moral tones, but planes of verisimilitude.

As a result, *The Amorous Widow* treats sexuality differently from previous Carolean or fletcherian comedies. Hume and others have identified *The Amorous Widow* as "the first real comedy of sex and cuckoldry" (*Development* 90), even though cuckolding is only a threat in *The Amorous Widow* as it is in *She Would if She Could*, *The Country Captain*, or Fletcher's *The Coxcomb*. Yet these commentators correctly sense that the equivocal ending and mixed tone of this comedy set it apart from its predecessors. The perhaps shaky conversion of Mrs. Brittle conjoined with the hesitancy of the young lovers' hopes and the availability of Lovemore, a sometimes sympathetic and sometimes menacing single rake-about-town, suggest that matrimony may not be a stable or a final condition allied with love. The high degree of ambiguity in *The Amorous Widow* has to do in part with Betterton's having hitched a wholly fletcherian plot (despite its borrowings from early Molière) with a plot taken from a comedy of Molière's maturity. By his splitting the courtship and satiric actions and de-emphasizing the former, Betterton lets the cynicism of Brittle/Dandin overpower the possibilities more lightly and simply set forth in the courtship of Philadelphia and Cunningham. *Sir Salomon* controls its countermessage more successfully with the weight of a conventional moral conclusion; later comedies would control theirs with a rigorous balance of complementary relationships and deliberate manipulation of seemingly opposite terms like "play" and "sincerity."

The Nature of "Nature"

To assess the alteration of Carolean comedy between 1668 and 1672, one must first acknowledge that at least some of the changes seemingly introduced by borrowings from Molière's comedies were only speeding up developments already in progress; we would specifically point to pre-Molière plays like *She Would if She Could* and *Secret Love* which emphasized satiric over romantic actions and created more complex protagonists. Nonetheless, Molière's comedies did provide convenient models for changes in structure, focus, characterization, and tone which occurred during this phase of development. What was necessary, however, was that Carolean playwrights should ignore or alter certain elements of his comedies which were not congenial to English tastes: particularly his moral focus and conclusions but also his strong sense of caste and gender as social determiners. We note at the outset, then, the differences between Molière's structural impact on Carolean comedy and his lack of moral or thematic influence on those same plays.

In terms of plot, the potential for satire inherent in fletcherian comedy, which had already shown its ability to accommodate jonsonian humours characters, was further extended in terms of Molière's comic vision. To do so, the authors of plays like *Sir Martin Mar-all*, *Sir Salomon*, and *The Amorous Widow* amalgamated the elements of fletcherian courtship and French satire, either balancing them in separate actions or combining them through multi-functional characters. And while both these techniques had been used before—in plays like *The Committee* or *The Comical Revenge*—those previous plays had retained an essentially moral framework, establishing exemplary heroes and heroines in central roles to placate any parts of the audience likely to be offended by the libertine assumptions hidden behind the rest of the play's action.

During the 1668–72 seasons, for the first time, that moral base was seriously eroded. On the one hand, the plots of these new plays retained all the basic devices of the fletcherian mode—the "turns," surprises, climaxes and abrupt confrontations, mistaken identities, and deus ex machina rescues, conversions, and conclusions—and their staging also followed the English preference for numerous scene changes, full use of fore and rear stage areas, and multiple, simultaneous activity and business.[25] At the same time, French structural influences can be seen in the shifting of Fletcher's doubled or analogous lovers to make room for Molière's satiric noncourtship plots which supplied actions and characters operating in counterpoint to the courtship action rather than as its complement. Often resulting in solitary, uncoupled young male characters at the end of the play, this plot line temporarily produced a new approach to the fletcherian

---

[25]Molière followed the Italian model of single set design (usually a street scene), multiple exits and entrances with a good deal of the action occurring offstage to be narrated later, and single action blocking.

open ending: one which focused more on the tenuousness of traditional romantic solutions to the play's conflicts, the strong possibility of unstable marriages, embittered characters, and unanswered questions. Plays like *The Amorous Widow*, *Sir Salomon*, and *Marriage A-la-Mode* all end with at least two radically different ideologies coexisting uneasily or with an ambivalent solution which can be interpreted in two ways: as a conventional "happy ever after" ending or as a prediction of a future filled with doubts and infidelities.

But the greatest change in Carolean comedies with Molière borrowings was the displacement of the courtship hero from sole central position in comedy. Even in early plays like *Sir Martin Mar-all*, but more noticeably in plays like *The Amorous Widow* and *Sir Salomon*, this shift of attention was accompanied by a change in the rendering of comic character, a movement away from the broadly drawn versatile types of fletcherian comedy or the specific humours of jonsonian-based obstructors, rivals, and servants, where courtship heroes and heroines were personable and engaging, and simply motivated in the direction of marriage and money. Elevation of the fool or the blocking figure to central position in *Sir Martin Mar-all*, *The Amorous Widow*, and *Sir Salomon* changed this picture by inviting the audience's curiosity about behavior and motive in ways outside the scope of previous comedies. Drawing heavily on Molière sources for certain key characters—Sir Salomon, Barnaby Brittle—English Carolean dramatists were confirmed in the direction of more ambitious and also less easily interpreted characterizations, characters with the potential to arouse in the audience not just simple admiration or easy sympathy but empathy and familiarity, contempt and awareness. Instead of the distance built into the fletcherian mode by artificiality, extravagance, and Protean characters, Carolean borrowers from Molière follow the directions taken previously by Etherege and Sir Robert Howard and construct a society which closely resembles the one the audience inhabits, peopled not only with farcical exaggerations but also with realistic characters who behave like the audience and want what the audience does, not only Jordens and Sir Martins but Sir Peter Pride, Mrs. Brittle, and Sir Salomon.

In fact, the English versions of Molière's characters are in some respects more affective than their sources: adding romantic elements to satiric characters softens them; adding satiric functions to romantic heroes and blocking figures broadens them. Barnaby Brittle and Sir Salomon, for example, seem more psychologically complex than George Dandin and Arnolphe, and therefore more affective: one feels kinship for Brittle because he is surrounded by rogues and arrogant in-laws, for Sir Salomon because of his ingenuity and clear-sightedness. In any case, both characters because of their intricacy are likely to elicit more interest from an audience than the usual fletcherian or jonsonian hero, villain, or fool does, however charming or horrifying the latter might be.

Ultimately, of course, Molière's comedy and Carolean comedy are quite different: whereas Molière elaborates his central characters to criticize and warn the society which permits them to behave unnaturally, Carolean playwrights elaborate theirs in terms of agreed-upon assumptions about the nature of natural desires which motivate characters and audience alike. Almost all of the Molière-based Carolean comedies and those of the later 1670s use London settings to underwrite this linkage, thus providing a backdrop for characters and situations which, though sometimes exaggerated, are closely tied to the real world of the audience. Both the heroic and obstructive characters are drawn to resemble their analogues in the London society milieu, the fops aping current fashions, the gallants contemporary manners and speech patterns. Such verisimilitude was not merely cosmetic, but a step closer to constructing a universe wherein the audience might, if they wished, test and satisfy their own instincts and desires.

The changed tone of these new comedies shows up, again, in the areas of sexual behavior and generational conflicts. As previously discussed, fletcherian comedy is relatively frank about its characters' sexual mores and proclivities, and while extramarital liaisons do not exist in these comedies (though they do in the tragedies), they are often prevented only at the eleventh hour (*The Coxcomb*, *Rule a Wife and Have a Wife*), and are used mainly to heighten and titillate the audience's sensibilities. The French-influenced plays approach the subject of sexuality rather differently. It is not enough to say that these plays are racier than their predecessors, although they are. More importantly, their particular commingling of sexual conflict and social satire highlights varieties of human behavior which demonstrate natural and social drives in conflict (like adultery) or conflict between characters following their instincts toward the same goal (like love rivalry). In this respect, these plays are the link between the comedies of previous seasons, like *The Tempest*, *She Would if She Could*, and *Secret Love*, which tended to leave these questions somewhat open, and later plays like *Marriage A-la-Mode*, *The Man of Mode*, and *Epsom Wells*, which reveled in them.

The Amorous Widow and *Sir Salomon*, in particular, seem to reflect a feeling, discussed in chapter 2, that the social institution of marriage was breaking down. (We shall return to that issue in chapter 7.) Sir Salomon's absurd maneuverings to find a chaste wife and keep her so are based on his cynicism about marriage in modern society, a perception which the play doesn't deny. Another index to modern mores is seen in *The Amorous Widow*, where Barnaby Brittle's wish to marry above himself is aptly matched with his in-laws' desire to sell their daughter: the result is a marriage without understanding, compatibility, or respect, without even passion to hold it together temporarily. Previous plays like *The Country Captain* or *She Would if She Could* also present jaundiced views on marriage, but in both cases the play is firmly focused on young lovers who represent alternatives—who are wittier, more understanding, and better matched than the mismated couple. In *Sir Salomon* and *The Amorous Widow*, the focus and intensity have shifted.

Generational conflicts, too, have taken a new turn with the collapse of traditional distinctions between the forces motivating fathers and sons, mothers and daughters. While authority figures continue to assert, at least partially, their ancient prerogative of ordering their offsprings' lives, they have also chosen to compete with them sexually. Since they must, ultimately, be losers in the love game, their authority is discredited not, as Mr. Day's was, on moral grounds, but on those of inefficiency. In a comedy that chooses to assume that all its inhabitants respond to the same drives, competition becomes stiffer, and the game can only produce winners and losers. Variety is retained in the different characters' interpretations of how the game should be played and, to some extent, what the prize should be, but all acknowledge, generally speaking, that the game and the prize are worthwhile.

The altered nature of the relationship between audience and stage in the post-Molière plays can be seen in Wycherley's first play, *Love in a Wood or St. James Park* (1671). Though neither his best nor most popular comedy, *Love in a Wood* displays quite clearly several changes of emphasis in the genre we will begin to call London comedy.[26] The first is the displacement of the standard fletcherian courtship plot from center stage. There are courtships of a sort, to be sure, but the most central of them, those the comedy spends the most time on, involve characters who would, in a Fletcher play, be peripheral figures: a widow in desperate search of a second marriage, an "addleplot" determined to marry money, a would-be wit trying to outmaneuver his friend for the richer and younger of two prizes, a Puritan usurer seeking sexual entertainment as cheaply as possible, and a bawd and her daughter looking for a meal ticket. In accord with this shift of

---

[26]Some of these changes come from its Spanish source, Calderón's *Mañanas de abril y mayo* (see Rundle; Loftis 121–25).

emphasis, a marriage broker/bawd (Joyner) occupies an important pivotal role in all four schemes, juggling the often-conflicting desires of all the pseudocozeners while collecting a salary from each.

Those parts of the play which involve the love games of the three young heroes and two heroines are also transformed. For one thing, the numbers are off, suggesting at the outset the impossibility of neatly paired relationships. In proper fletcherian fashion, Wycherley produces a romantic couple—Valentine and Christina—and a "gay couple"—Ranger and Lydia—but Vincent is a lover only of drink, a hero solely by virtue of his friendship with Ranger and Valentine and his opposition in speech and person to the foppish Dapperwit. Jealousy is the motive and the mechanism by which errors and disguises occur in these love complications, though Valentine's jealousy of Christina is as unwarranted as Lydia's of Ranger is justified. Wycherley has some trouble with consistent characterization, particularly with Vincent who stops drinking midway through the play, and some difficulty juggling the multitude of subplots. Yet the play obviously intends and partly succeeds in achieving a balance between romance and satire, with the emphasis on the latter. The serious courtships take up less stage time and are less engrossing than the antics of the fools, wenches, and bawds.

One means Wycherley uses to distinguish his heroes and fools is in their respective attitudes towards love and money. Ranger, the roving young gentleman, is sorry to learn that Christina is an heiress "lest it should bring the scandal of interest, and design of lucre upon my Love" (II.iv; 49),[27] and the knowledgeable Mrs. Joyner confirms this: "'Tis as impossible for a man to love, and be a miser, as to love and be wise, as they say" (III.ii; 63). She is, however, quickly disabused of this universal truth by her encounter with Gripe, who manages to combine both lust and parsimoniousness: "I never knew any man so mortify'd a Miser, that he would deny his Letchery any thing" (III.ii; 63), she wails. The impecunious Addleplot and Dapperwit, though somewhat more liberal than Gripe, also temper lust with avarice; their main goal is Martha, Gripe's daughter and heiress, but they keep in reserve the (presumably) well-off widow. Appropriate punishments are meted out to all of the would-be avaricious lovers: Gripe is forced to part with five hundred pounds without enjoying Lucy and then

---

[27]In contradiction to this assertion, Lydia later accuses him of loving her only when he's out of funds: "When he has none, he has his desperate designs upon what little I have; for want of mony, makes as devout Lovers as Christians" (III.iii; 70). The play does not make clear whether his impassioned declaration or her denunciation is true; certainly, money is not Ranger's primary motivation, in any case.

marries her to get his money's worth, Addleplot has the felicity of delivering Martha into Dapperwit's hands and has to marry the impoverished widow, Dapperwit finds his new wife is six months pregnant with someone else's child.

Motive and wit together, then, serve to sort out characters while at the same time the play makes no particular effort to attach moral force to the heroes' side of the picture; it is sufficient that they are attractive, naturally witty, passably brave, and sexually active. Anyone in the audience with moral or romantic pretensions can see the Valentine/Christina marriage as normal and assume closure for the Ranger/Lydia one. A cynic can choose Vincent and Joyner as the clearsighted observers who serve their own appetites by knowing where the appetites of others will lead them, displaying acuity by their lack of involvement in the fantasies in which both lovers and fools believe.

Moraliste *Wit*

Most of our discussion thus far has slighted verbal wit, the trait of Restoration comedy that everyone remarks on, except as verbal behavior designed to accomplish something for the playwright and audience as well as the characters. But the styles of this wit, its formal requirements, as well as its usual "realism" and realpolitik about human nature, have their own life in cultural history. As with the push given to Carolean comedies by the plays of Molière, a French impetus lent force to a British practice.

In a highly consensual society—or, to be more exact, a highly consensual artistic idiom (for instance, real coterie entertainment or World War II patriotic movies)—characters and spectators see the world in the same way. Approved characters' speeches, then, can be studded with terse expressions of this bonding: in patriotic movies, slogans; in Elizabethan plays, old saws and proverbs. Shakespeare, writes Morris Tilley, had a "comprehensive knowledge of every kind of proverb. . . . And what is true of Shakespeare will be found to apply to two centuries of English literature." However, "as the seventeenth century drew to a close, there set in a reaction to the enthusiastic use of proverbs in literature" (viii). The "reaction" that Tilley rues did not snub the style of proverbs, as witness the snappy maxims in Dryden or Pope, some of Pope's having now achieved their own quasi-proverbial status. Proverbs were replaced, not banished, replaced because of the erosion of the old consensus, which required only a clever style to frame it. The same broadening of assumptions which we note in chapter 2 cast doubt on pithy folk wisdom and put its faith in empirical laws. Moreover, by the later seventeenth century this change of faith had a class bias to it, for who thought themselves upper-class were shying from "not just the language of ordinary people . . . but their whole culture," their "popular world-view" (Burke 272–73).

Thus, traditional proverbs in Carolean comedy usually come from the mouths of silly or out-of-date characters. The witty widow in Newcastle's *The Humorous Lovers* speaks for her peers when she exclaims, "I despise your old proverbial Saws" (II.iii; 17). For the functions served for Elizabethans by old saws, Carolean protagonists use what we will call "*moraliste* wit": they state a law or logic of human nature, based on observation of social habits or mores. The Carolean spectator, then, accepts the character as a specific observer—wit here is a matter of keen eyes and head, not merely a token of moral allegiance—with a bonding at once more individual and narrower (the character may speak the truth but not the whole truth, as the spectator would judge it) than in earlier plays.

Without any pretense to precise dates through tagging each instance of wit *moraliste* or not, we would place the vogue for reflective, empirically shrewd protagonists at about the same time that playwrights began making enthusiastic use of Molière. The vogue, as we have suggested, probably sprang from France, where from midcentury on the eagerness to make up maxims spread like an epidemic of colds, as La Rochefoucauld wrote Mme. de Sablé in 1660 (*Oeuvres* 2: 9). These "sentences" or "pensées" (Pascal) or "maximes" (La Rochefoucauld, Mme. de Sablé, l'Abbe d'Ailly, Mme. de la Sablière, Chevalier de Méré) and "réflexions" (La Rochefoucauld, Mme. Deshoulières) came from fashionable Parisian salons, and typically display an illusionless irony, a self-awareness, a devotion to laying down the law(s)—exactly the tones struck by Rhodophil, Dorimant, or Horner, though without their sardonic humor.

There may also have been direct French influence on English playwrights. Etherege, as it happens, was the son of the Purveyor to Queen Henrietta Maria; the elder Etherege died in France in 1650 and therefore had probably followed the Queen there in 1644, perhaps with his eldest son George. Since Etherege's letters prove he read and spoke French with ease, he may have spent time there with his father or his father's acquaintances before 1660 as the *Biographia Britannica* (1750) implies he did (Bracher xv–xvi). Wycherley spent the late 1650s in France and was admitted into salon society (McCarthy 24–27); in old age he himself wrote maxims in the manner of La Rochefoucauld, using the *Maximes* themselves and an English or Amelot de la Houssaie's French translation of Gracián's *Courtier* (1647) as bedtime books. Behn edited a *Miscellany* (1685) in which one section, "Seneca Unmasqued, or, Moral Reflections" is attributed to "the Duke of *Rushfaucave*" (sig. U7ᵛ). Within a theatrical culture in debt to prestigious French models for heroic and comic models, it is at very least historically plausible that the *moraliste* mode of Carolean wit in part derived from French *moralistes*, as has been suggested by Auffret.

But more to our point than elaborating the French connection are the powerful affinities between these two modes. The modes certainly look very similar:

—"This is a very blasting age to virtue, 'twill not thrive without a covering."
—" 'Tis the nature of all mankind: we love to get our mistresses, and purr over 'em, as cats do over mice, and then let 'em go a little way; and all the pleasure is, to pat 'em back again."
—"There's no sinner like a young saint."
—"Many an honest woman is weary of her trade."
—"Love can no more continue without a constant motion than fire can; and when once you take hope and fear away, you take from it its very life and being."
—"Love gilds us over and makes us show fine things to one another for a time, but soon the gold wears off, and then again the native brass appears."
—"New friends, like new mistresses, are got by disparaging old ones."
—"There are a great many men valued in the world who have nothing to recommend them but serviceable vices."

The sporting reader may want to pause here, before looking at the identificatory note, to decide which of these sentences, the accidentals of which we have modernized to avoid typographical clues, come from La Rochefoucauld's *Moral Maxims and Reflections* (the anonymous English translation of 1706) and which from plays by Crowne (*Sir Courtly Nice*), Dryden (*An Evening's Love*), Behn (*The Rover*), Etherege (*The Man of Mode*), and Wycherley (*The Plain-Dealer*) respectively and in that order.[28]

The affinity between Carolean playwrights and French *moralistes* allows a clearer view of the wit in "wit comedy." Maxim ll of "Mixed Thoughts" explains that "maxims are to the Mind, just what a Staff is to the Body, when a Man cannot support himself by his own Strength. Men of sound Sense, that see Things in their full and just Proportions, have no need of general Observations to help them out" (127). This view of maxims as prosthetic implies that they derive from

---

[28] The maxims by La Rochefoucauld are those about the honest woman, the constant motion, and the serviceable vices, numbers 365, 76, and 273 respectively of the "Moral Reflections" in the translation of 1706.

rather than shape "nature." Their aphoristic style, though, has the odor of dogma about it. And so, prefacing *Les Caractères, ou les moeurs de ce siècle*, La Bruyère refers to "maximes" as "comme des lois dans la morale," with their oracular, prescriptive brevity: "Ceux . . . qui font les maximes veulent être crus" (64)—"Maxim makers want to be believed." When examined, however, the moral laws set forth by La Rochefoucauld are largely descriptive, with room for exceptions. He no doubt did wish to be believed, as La Bruyère says, but believed from informed consent, not ex cathedra.

In counting La Rochefoucauld's qualifiers, Jean Rostand found in the later editions of the *Maximes* some forty-seven *often*s, sixteen uses of *sometimes*, and ten each of *ordinarily* and *almost always*, as against fifteen in toto of *always* and *never* (Hippeau 168). This habitual caution, as much as the aphoristic manner, makes La Rochefoucauld harder to refute. Unlike the makers of proverbs, he employs the new (for the mid-seventeenth century) rhetoric of probability. In keeping with the purview of this rhetoric, his subject matter is rational mastery over the irrational, the human passions whose seeming randomness he subjects to rough codification and whose unruliness, to syntactic balance. Unavoidably, too, his sardonic poker-faced aloofness and the force of his own principles call into question his motives in writing the maxims at all. La Rochefoucauld leaves little room for the credulity of supposing him, any more than anyone else, purely public-spirited. If his distant moral sociology holds, it demonstrates his own self-love, the wish to compel admiration for this duke as a keen-eyed, reasonable, stylish observer. Despite and because of their apparent withdrawal from the fray, then, the maxims form a self-subsuming, even self-ratifying, empirical appraisal of human nature. We have insisted in chapter 2 that the same sort of reflexivity marks the observant wit of the Carolean hero(ine).

Like La Rochefoucauld's, maxims in the comedies codify and to that extent master the irrational, while the characters who enunciate them also exemplify the egoistic springs of action that the maxims bring to light. Like his, theirs offer empirical generalizations as laws of behavior. The verbal tidiness of a maxim implicitly asserts that what it says is true and will continue to be, in "nature." Through style the speaker gains initial authority, and when the play sufficiently witnesses to the truth of the maxim (or to the truth of a world within which such a maxim might be presumed to be true), that authority solidifies. As with La Rochefoucauld's wit, one may consider the plays' wit moral (satirical), nonmoral (representing things as they are), and/ or maliciously amoral (delighted by the aesthetics of the studied quip, by the overturning of pieties, by *Schadenfreude*). Carolean playwrights staged the sour view of human nature held in the mid-seventeenth century by so many, from religious belief and social experience, but they left unclear how much the sourness might be sweet to the trained palate; just so La Rochefoucauld could be at one with the French equivalents of "Puritans" and cavaliers—Jansenists and *libertins*—alike.

But La Rochefoucauld forever stands on a catwalk above the theatre of human action; protagonists of Carolean comedies do not. Thus the plays still further complicate interpretation, a complication useful for their idiom, because the dramatic speaker and the author may have different beliefs which they have still different motives for expressing. And this difference between the personal and the "scientific" creates other differences between La Rochefoucauld's and the Caroleans' maxims, though they are of the same species. Stage hero(ine)s couch many of their maxims in the first person, as La Rochefoucauld rarely does, a practice that encourages identification with and of the individual speaker. The qualifying adverbs of the *Maximes* make explicit and "scientific" the limits of their use. (Folk proverbs presuppose such limits, because they accommodate what has happened rather than predict what will—blood is thicker than water only when someone has acted by that rule. La Rochefoucauld and Carolean comedies predict by describing probable behavior.) In the plays, the use of fallible speakers gives the implicit limits of proverbs a new, personal form.

Apart from its sophisticated view of the world or the cachet of a fashionable French practice, *moraliste* wit had several kinds of appeal for the playwrights. We have stressed its role in establishing hierarchies of character and value within comedies, but also important is that it is congenial with the plays' formal assumptions. Like any kind of aphorism it separates form and content: "What's sauce for the goose is sauce for the gander" has the same form as "A penny saved is a penny earned," but clearly the two expressions say different things and the "is" predicates differently in each (the first implies an "ought," the second specifies a set/subset relationship). Seventeenth-century drama loves the clever and the sententious, but aphoristic speech becomes a particular trademark of the fletcherian mode whose separation of form and content it echoes.

We hope to have made a case that in this mode Carolean comedies foster a high degree of abstract order based on analogy and contrast, which "masters" the subject matter of the play only by arranging it to be witnessed; the organization itself implies nothing, as with the sententious statement. Even more important for these plays is that from the aphorism's separation of form and content, *moraliste* wit creates a sort of rivalry. While balanced, rational form asserts the power of reason, the content of the maxims denies real, practical validity to reason in the world. The forms of wit and of plays alike are the apparatus whereby reason presents—and perhaps gratifies or justifies—the modalities of will and desire. Dryden's *Tempest* and *Marriage A-la-Mode* testify to this pleasant arrangement. By contrast, the content of the witty statement (for which the *moraliste* idiom is the Aristotelian "formal cause"), like the mimesis of the comedies, lays claim to what Gustave Lanson, in discusssing La Rochefoucauld, called "une probité scientifique" (471). The hero(in)es' wit when they speak and power when they act depend on their being able to infer what other people do under various stimuli. The hero(in)es' social graces lie in knowing what others want; their politeness and charm draw on the same faculty of psychological analysis which enables their wit to be devastating. Indeed, as that arbiter of such things the Chevalier de Méré announced (72), the first characteristic of the "honnête homme," the *libertin* ideal who is also arguably an ideal in the comedies, is his rare talent for intuiting others' thoughts ("genie bien rare et bien à rechercher . . . qui découvre par un discernement juste et subtil ce que pensent les personnes qu'on entretient.") This skill finds memorable codification in *moraliste* and related kinds of wit.

Our discussion of fletcherian dramaturgy has stressed hierarchy ("high" and "low" plots, or—a more complex hierarchical group— rakish and conventional, moral and amoral plots) and reversals in the narrative. Correspondingly, *moraliste* wit trades in comparisons and reversals of hierarchy, a leveling action calculated for surprise. The witty sentences given above, from five playwrights and La Rochefoucauld, exemplify what we mean. They claim, taken in order, that nature requires art ("a covering"); that man is animal and love is predation; that youth (i.e., innocence) and sanctity lead to sin; that honesty (chastity) is a kind of whoredom (a wearisome "trade"); that love (with its traditional ideal of fidelity) demands insecurity if it is to exist; that the base and the brazen are more real than what is "fine"; that alliances with others require fickleness; and that vices have value. The genre "aphorism" does not set this pattern: aphorisms may have the form of simple comparison (a watched pot never boils, a stitch in time saves nine) or simple empirical law (absence makes the heart grow fonder) rather than a combination of the two which includes a reversal of value. Nor does the genre "wit" by itself set the pattern— wordplay, for example, does not—which is aggressive, degrading the higher element in the comparison and flaunting the keenness as well as the ingenuity of the speaker.

We have focused on reflective, *moraliste* wit, though in these fast-moving, functional plays it occurs less frequently than other forms, because we believe it to be paradigmatic. Most of the other wit also aggressively creates comparisons that subvert standard categories. Such a belief is easier to assert than to prove, since people are bound to disagree about what statements count as wit. But it will make sense to anyone who thinks about the kind of situation that detonates wit: lovers or rivals vying, someone trying to extricate him- or herself from a jealous spouse, young women or men describing a fop who has not yet appeared. All of these involve a hierarchy, sometimes precarious, among characters, and the first two promise reversals in dominance. (The fop, as a witwould, is already an oxymoron.) The nature of the witty comment matches the demands that the plot puts upon it. We can illustrate, though not prove, what we mean with an example of each type.

Lovers vying. The famous proviso scene in *Secret Love* (1667) parodies and subverts the "higher" proviso scene in D'Urfé's romance *L'Astrée* (see CD 9: 343–44), and for those who do not catch the allusion, parodies and subverts the marriage contract. Florimell and Celadon "will be married by the more agreeable names of Mistress and Gallant" (V.i.551–52), and safeguard their privacy (and sexual freedom) by a series of threats, not promises. The scene moves by coupled statements, in which Celadon makes a stipulation and Florimell continues the subject, usually topping Celadon's demand or threat. This series ends when she cries out in triumph, "La ye now, is not such a marriage as good as wenching, *Celadon?*," and he reverses her string of victories by responding, "This is very good, but not so good, *Florimell*" (V.i.560–62). The passage, in other words, works within an environment of deliberate, parodic reversal, and engineers a sequence of reversals, ending with an upturning of the expectations of the sequence itself, as Celadon and Florimell discuss dominance in their married life by continuing to engage in a battle for immediate dominance.

Extrication. In the "wanton wife" plot (from *George Dandin*) of Betterton's *The Amorous Widow* (ca. 1669), Mrs. Brittle is rightly accused before her parents, Sir Peter and Lady Pride, of having an assignation with Lovemore, whose dimwitted man, Clodpole, has earlier blurted out the truth to Brittle. To Lovemore's covert plea for exculpation, "Did you, Madam, tell your Husband a strange Story, that I should make Love to you, and endeavour'd to corrupt your Honour?" she retorts, "I tell him! Why, when did you make Love to me, Sir? I assure you, had you let me know of your Passion, it shou'd not have gone unrewarded. . . . [S]ince he complains without any manner of Reason, I am resolv'd he shall have Cause. Therefore if you do love me, Sir, pray let me know it, and I do assure you, you shall not want Encouragement. He shall not use me at this rate for nothing" (III; 40).

The more knowing Mrs. Brittle's listeners are, the more they take her literally true statement literally. Lovemore understands an invitation, Brittle resents a shifty ploy for putting him down, and her parents hear a mere form of speech, an indignant denial of what their daughter scorns to deny explicitly. The ironically layered truth telling of Mrs. Brittle, self-aware and upper-class in its assumptions and skilled indirection, caps but also diverts a sequence that moves upward in class and rhetorical control: first, the servant Clodpole unwittingly spills the beans to the bourgeois Brittle who, second, announces it to his aristocratic parents-in-law. Part of the humor for the audience is the reversal in this sequence of (the prototypical) three elements—that is Betterton's, and Molière's, joke. Part is the reversal in social order, in that the tradesman is wiser than the aristocrats, the wife than the husband, the "immoral" than the guardians of established sanctions. And part is Mrs. Brittle's wittiness, which makes the "higher" values (honor, respect, the combativeness that Sir Peter boasts of in his ancestors) into the medium for the "lower" value, adultery. The implied comparison between these values reverses their real order. In fact, like the disguised protagonists whom we mentioned in chapter 2, Mrs. Brittle stoops to dependent status, reassuming the subordinate, accountable role of wife and daughter, so as to conquer with the attainment of more independent status.

Character description. The mode is one of lively, debasing images and tropes, like Ramble's complaint about his father-in-law-to-be, the first speech in act III of Crowne's *The Country Wit* (1675): "I must endure the humours of this old fellow, only because he club'd to the production of the fair Christina; as if a man were bound in civility to stand under the droppings of a conduit all days on's life, because once at a coronation it ran claret, and he was drunk with it" (54). A sequence of such witty comments is provided by the chorus of wits denouncing Sparkish in act I of *The Country-Wife* (1675) as "one of those nauseous offerers at wit, who like the worst Fidlers run themselves into all Companies," whose "Company is as troublesome to us, as a Cuckolds, when you have a mind to his Wife's," and who "will not let us enjoy one another, but ravishes our conversation" (I.i; 265). Indeed, the subject of Sparkish sparks a whole series of *moraliste* reversals, beginning with Harcourt's "Most Men are the contraries to what they wou'd seem; your bully you see, is a Coward with a long Sword; the little humbly fawning Physician with his Ebony cane, is he that destroys Men" (I.i; 265–66). The generalizations— Harcourt's, Dorilant's, Horner's—eddy from the individual pretentious ninny taken as an illustrative type; they conclude at Sparkish's entrance, which at once confirms them and, in the vividness of the fop's actual presence and the (feigned) respect he compels from his detractors, turns the play to something quite different in texture from wit. As with the proviso scene from *Secret Love* and Mrs. Brittle's self-extrication from *The Amorous Widow*, the fanfare of wit for Sparkish ends with a completion and also a reversal (or diversion) of a sequence. This need not be true for wit in Carolean comedy, but it is true often enough to remind one how ubiquitous at every level in these plays is the organizing principle of internal analogy.

The pleasures of wit, then, mirror the pleasures of structure in Carolean comedy. We can isolate four, beginning with the local delights of a well-turned phrase or volley of repartee, which is of course itself a structural element; a similar structural element is its nonwitty counterpart, the gag or stunt or lazzo. Comedy of all sorts tends to promote the local, but episodic structure in fletcherian drama gives it extra prominence. A second pleasure common to verbal wit and Carolean comedy, and much less typical of comedy as a genre, is that of formal patterning, again a fletcherian virtue. This wit and fletcherian comedy both involve a similarly well-marked style of thought, one so familiar from the unoriginal folk wit that *moraliste* aphorisms replaced as to make one wonder why people who ascribe pattern in these comedies to preciosity (or rampant Cartesianism or the artificiality of the Age of Reason) never scent the same factitious Zeitgeist in "Out of sight, out of mind." Be that as it may, in Carolean comedy the nature of verbal control is very like that of narrative control. A third pleasure, which we have discussed at length, is that of novelty: the rejection of the proverb, of the social order that is the donnée of the audience's everyday lives, in favor of individual achievement in word and act, and in favor of reversals. Here the formal patterning finds completion and, paradoxically perhaps, personal spontaneity finds its most admirable comic expression. The aphorism and the balanced plot prompt parallel construction, and novelty does too, since its principle of contrast logically depends on parallel constructions. Finally, a fourth pleasure returns to the hypothesis of chapter 2, for both the witty sentence and the play are "about" dominance, the creation of a time—a moment or longer—of being on top.

In the last analysis, wit and larger elements of dramatic construction show the same mentality at work. Some of the wit in Carolean comedies, like rochefoucauldian maxims or the description of ridiculous characters, remains essentially detached; some, like wit combats between lovers or clever attempts at slipping out of a jam, is more situational. These discriminable but often overlapping forms of wit correspond to the two principal kinds of scenes in the plays, those that deal with movement to or from a specific object of desire, movement that is at times free, at times thwarted or retrograde, and those that deal with the display of a character or characters who are cynosures, sympathetic or satiric. The verbal wit, whether detached so as to display character or situational so as to transact desires, exhibits an efficiency that is highly congenial to these plays of social accomplishment. Patterns of witty speech repeat their verbal economy in their economy of purpose: they spatialize time by so plainly binding seeming disparates in one syntactic unit. The scene in Carolean comedy—or, rather, the episode, which may be part of a scene on stage or may encompass more than one scene—has the same kind of single-mindedness. And, as we shall argue in the next chapter, dazzling and yet seemingly negligent, "easy" variations and cadenzas on this singleness, in action and words, create the glory of *Marriage A-la-Mode*, as of numerous major comedies of the 1670s.

Marriage A-la-Mode

As comparison with Shakespeare's *Tempest* clarifies Dryden and Davenant's, so comparison with Dryden's *Secret Love* (1667) clarifies his next two-plot tragicomedy, *Marriage A-la-Mode* (1671?). Dryden's *Tempest*, to be sure, shares thematic material with the heroic plot of *Marriage A-la-Mode*, such as the displaced court, the evocation of a state of nature, and the noble heirs in exile who display a brave innocence. But *Secret Love* and *Marriage A-la-Mode* share still more. Both plays, set in a mythical Sicily, take from romances of Mme. de Scudéry a heroic plot with the theme of morganatic marriage: in *Secret Love* the unhappy Queen of Sicily yields to her rival Candiope the man they both love, Philocles, who is "not of Royal bloud[,] . . . his fate unfit to be a King" (I.iii.257–58); and in *Marriage A-la-Mode* only one of the two heroic lovers (who knows which?) is the rightful heir, while the other is at least comparatively lowborn. Both plays involve characters of whom marriage is required, the Queen by her subjects, all the unmarried lovers in *Marriage A-la-Mode* by their fathers. Both plays portray rebellion against a sovereign and a favorite who remains unhappy and unwed. In both comic plots, the fickle man, the gay blade back from his travels, the witty lovers who court incognito, and the witty lady who uses male disguise also appear and both plays end with proviso scenes. In short, Dryden kept capitalizing on similar elements of dramatic construction and the thematic groupings on which they are built. At the end of both plays political order and marital order triumph, so that the brave get the fair whom they have deserved and vice versa. And yet, while *Secret Love*, like *The Tempest*, exemplifies the modified fletcherian mode of the mid-to-late 1660s, *Marriage A-la-Mode* strikes off in a somewhat different direction, that of the more daring, compromise-formation comedies of the 1670s.

From Secret Love *to* Marriage A-la-Mode

The "high" plot of *Secret Love* combines the "Spanish" codes and restrictions of early Carolean comedy (as in Tuke) with the political motif (as in Howard's *Committee*), where the figure of societal authority also serves as a blocking figure. In *Secret Love* the Queen of an island ruled by the Spanish in Dryden's lifetime, Sicily, agonizes over her silent passion for Philocles, a secret because he loves Candiope, he lacks "Royal bloud" (I.iii.257), and she must marry to beget an heir. Although she must stifle her love, she can and does manipulate, threaten, cajole, feign, rage, weep, try her best to thwart Philocles' marriage to Candiope, and politically outmaneuver the second male hero of the "high" plot, Prince Lysimantes, before she finally accepts defeat with great dignity and rededicates herself, a virgin queen, to her subjects. As a "natural" victim of social codes, she displays her own highest "nature"; as the abuser of political power to chain the movement of "nature" in others, her lowest. This queen has only her virginity, suffering, and noble renunciation in common with the exemplary females of Orrery's heroic plays or Racine's later *Bérénice* (1670), with their pure, unassailable virtue. Though Dryden converts the battlefields of *The Indian-Queen* and *The Indian Emperour* into a court of women and words, the Queen of Sicily is a sister under the skin to the Indian heroes of those plays, also torn by conflicting passions, desires, and obligations, also rigorously and repeatedly tested, and also victorious over her inner and outer enemies. This is a brilliant modified fletcherian plot, like those presented in chapter 3, with its powerful, complex affective turns proceeding from a consistent, motivated characterization.

Dryden's choice of a ruler who is female, therefore reliant on others for strong arms strongly armed, enables him to force the Queen's conflicts into her psyche. By so doing, he deepens and complicates the heroic ideology itself. Even the resolution, in which the Queen reasserts self-control to benefit her subjects, involves loss. Whereas the leading men in Dryden's heroic plays had found private and public fulfillment, this royal woman cannot, nor can her subjects Lysimantes (who loves her and vows to lead a single life) and Philocles (who gets his Candiope but laments his loss of the Queen). Much more crucially for the development of Carolean comedy, Dryden's feminizing of *Secret Love* puts women on an equal footing in nature with men: the Queen has a role of authority that she turns out to deserve, and she has a depth and breadth of sexuality like a man's. Her drives, just like men's, are the source of authority and sexuality both. Her love is a passion to possess a given object, not a clinging dependency on it; she is invested with full awareness not simply as a cognitive value but, far more significantly in Carolean comedy, as a requisite for the exercise of power. The loss she undergoes in her victory over herself, then, appears as the result of social constraints that bind women differently from men, rather than of a difference in nature. Through treating women as equal in nature, Dryden and most later Carolean playwrights make them as dangerous as men and (hence?) more valuable for the hero to acquire. They become better counters for demonstrating the hero's masculinity and male power—a relationship he has, that is, with other men—and also invert that function in fulfilling it, for women's equality in nature makes the hero the heroine's trophy as much as she is his.

Both the complication of an ideology and the equality of women also surface in the comic plot of *Secret Love*, in which the fickle, witty Celadon finds himself caught by the wittier, more flexible Florimell. Florimell and the Queen, two analogous heroines, are their plots' prime movers and most fully realized characters, authoritative, willful, single-minded, sometimes unscrupulous. Like the Queen, Florimell can act upon her jealousy to jab at her rivals and punish her errant suitor. Both women test their lovers without revealing their own feelings, keeping their "secrets" intact. And as the Queen is a woman in the typically male role of ruler, the clincher in the comic plot is Florimell's outmanning Celadon, when, disguised as "a very *janty* fellow," she quickly "get[s] both his [other] Mistresses from him" (V.i.8,2–3). Her triumph as a woman is to fascinate him, and her triumph as a male equivalent is to joust evenly with him in a highly entertaining proviso scene. She not only can dicker about that male matter, property, which is what provisos concern, she also can specify that after marriage, when by law she would become her husband's chattel, she intends to keep proprietorship of herself and thereby proprietorship of him, the hero who is the trophy of her charms, wit, and victorious ingenuity.

Her zest to have him hers is stoked by his being hard to get, or, rather, easy to get but hard to keep. As with Philocles in relation to the Queen, what makes Celadon the ideal lover to display Florimell's "greatness" is his failure in the role of ideal lover, his failure even to act the role convincingly. One can turn this paradox into a male's paradise: "Celadon can whore around as much as he likes and be all the sexier; so, then, can I." Freedom for women increases their willing availability for men. But, true to the principles of heterogeneity, the end of this plot yields another, less "masculine" reading too: to fix the affections of a rake demonstrates greater power than to fix those of a dying and sighing swain. Indeed, though marriage takes from the imperious virgin the power she has when courted, one tool for equality, it grants her equal sexual freedom, hence the power to humiliate through "the penalty of Cuckoldom" (V.i.556). Therefore, the courted Florimell, who enjoys little power from being able to withhold herself from one man, the negligent rake Celadon, can look forward to a large gain as a wife, when she will wield the threat of giving herself to many. Dryden adds a further twist to both these possible readings in that Florimell's ability to out-rake the rake, luring his mistresses from him, demotes him as it promotes her. Ruling Celadon with her wit, beauty, virtue, and élan, she achieves him as a person of less potency than her own, despite his getting the last word, just as the Queen shows Lysimantes and Philocles to be less potent than she.

From what we have said of the comic plot, one can see how Dryden complicates the ideology behind it. He thus complicates the kind of resolution that comic plots offer. Florimell and Celadon prepare to curb their natural freedom in a marriage based on rather elaborate judgments of self-interest. Although for the time they thus resolve their conflicts over obligation and license, the detailed provisos, at the least, suggest that a passionate marriage may be as ephemeral as passion itself: "[Let us] e'en love one another as long as we can; and confess the truth when we can love no longer," stipulates Florimell (V.i.534–35). The pair's famous last exchange, which we quoted in chapter 5, may be taken as competitive banter or something a bit sourer, when to Florimell's "La ye now, is not such a marriage as good as wenching, *Celadon*?," he replies, "This is very good, but not so good, *Florimell*" (V.i.560–62).

A curious convergence with the "high" plot takes place. The Queen, a heroic figure who must therefore follow her higher nature, sacrifices passion to role, and, hiding her solitude under the name of being wedded to her subjects (V.i.458–61), she maintains the continuing power of that role. But in choosing the opposite value, passion, Florimell also must depend upon her social role, not simply the passions she stirs in Celadon. However much she hides the social reality of marriage under "the more agreeable names of Mistress and Gallant" (V.i.551–52), her power now works through social rather than personal means, through provisos and fear of cuckoldry rather than wit, panache, and tempting beauty, all of which are likely to pall. Finally, one can ask, "If the pleasure of courtship has been in the (slightly but surely unequal) game of power, what will be the basis of pleasure and power in marriage?" We do not suggest that *Secret Love* is open-ended, that the marriage of Celadon and Florimell is suspect, but rather that a curious teasing of ideas and tones keeps the comedy, which ends very happily, from ending in happy repose. Desire has been caught in motion, as with a high-speed camera, so that the trajectory both does and does not stop with the final picture.

Because of the analogies between two compelling actions, *Secret Love* offers a variety of choices between them, as no earlier Carolean multi-plot play had done. Is a dedication to "glory" and high principles more important than a devotion to courtly or social standards? Does the heroic ideal falter under a kind of psychological scrutiny it cannot support? Do the magnetism of Florimell and Celadon, their vital licentiousness, and their wedding emphasize the sterility of the Queen's lofty abnegation and the unnaturalness of her martyrdom? Does the ephemeral dynamic of a given passion call into doubt a comic ideal set against the permanence of nobility? Though one does not need the "high" action to evaluate the comic or vice versa, in a nonfletcherian way, the juxtaposition may highlight such issues for some viewers, who will then weight the two actions differently. Surely, too, many Carolean playgoers could sustain enough double vision to admire the Queen and Florimell both, each within her own genre, identifying differently with each. Such viewers might see the issues of authority and sexuality fused so as to raise new questions, particularly for women.

Secret Love has no villains, for the main obstruction comes from the inner conflict between internal needs and external demands. The Queen reconfirms a political order and stability that might, by 1667, have seemed as alien to human experience as her sacrifice is to human needs. Similarly, in choosing the social stability of marriage, the lovers acknowledge the possibility of failure and the sacrifice of their infinite variety and freedom. In both plots, then, the compact between people and social institutions, endorsed for reasons of morality or exigency (and in this play, can one distinguish those?), invites skepticism. But the satisfying end to the generic expectations of both plots also allays that skepticism. In inviting and allaying, confirming and disconfirming, Dryden gives his play an up-to-date tartness and self-awareness that keep it from seeming too facile; he thus reaffirms what *Secret Love* says, that is, what each member of the audience projects upon it as its content.

This invitation to heterogeneity is among the many traits of *Secret Love* that recur in *Marriage A-la-Mode*. From the action of confirming and disconfirming, the later comedy develops a compromise formation: one can delight in and root for "immorality" while being protected from its moral consequences. *Marriage A-la-Mode* also repeats and elaborates the analogous plots of *Secret Love* with their different decorums and systems of motive behind them, one more morally rigorous (i.e., serious, "high") and the other more morally lax or indulgent (comical, "low"). Within the heroic plot of *Marriage A-la-Mode*, Leonidas, Palmyra, and the other figures from romance move under the secret, majestic eyes of a Nature with the aroma of Providence about her theatrical manifestations. In the other plot, Rhodophil, Melantha, Doralice, and Palamede act in accord with human nature, that is, with individual workings-out of shared human drives such as appear in the Dryden-Davenant *Tempest*. Lacking the equivalent of helpful fairies with vulnerary salves, the state of nature in this plot begins to look quite Hobbesian and requires a social contract. Since the play validates both the contradictory kinds of nature, neither plot produces loss such as the Queen and her noble lovers suffer. Desire in the comic plot of *Marriage A-la-Mode*, as in the wedding of Florimell and Celadon, has been caught on the move, as it were, but in the later play the conclusion is still more tenuous because the final pairings arise not from the characters' personal excellencies, like wit, charm, ingenuity, and sexiness (though these are in abundance), but from their social mediation as objects of desire: each man loves each woman because the other man does, and perhaps the same holds for the women's love of the men.

And all this works according to the mechanisms of nature that at once exalt freedom of choice and put it in question. In a remarkably probing essay on Dryden's playwriting, Alan Fisher describes the comic plot in *Marriage A-la-Mode* as having a consecutive logic, that of a maxim which runs its course until it renders itself inapplicable:

> Given that two fashionable, reasonable people who have some choice in the matter will fall out of love with one another, and quickly too, it follows that both will seek pleasure elsewhere. What now follows, however, is that each will notice that the other can *give* pleasure elsewhere. By the selfish principle of pleasure-seeking that ensures that they will fall out of love, each will desire that lost pleasure back again. Such mutual desires, however, are what we mean by "love." (44)

Since a logic of nature applies equally to all, men and women in this comic plot are on equal footing, like those in *Secret Love*.

The "high" plot returns the woman, Palmyra, to the tearful passivity of the traditional female in romance. Dryden has a reason for such backsliding: he wishes to take heroic and comic generic conventions to an extreme so that the two actions, reconciled as they are within one comedy, can display their irreconcilability. To compound the possibilities of interpretation, he gives more stage time to the comic than to the serious plot, so as to test the audience's moral boundaries more tantalizingly; and he also awarded it the extremely glamorous cast of Hart and Mohun, Boutell and Marshall, leaving only one star, Kynaston, for the serious plot. (Marshall and Mohun had played in the "high" plot of *Secret Love*.) We do not believe, however, that this casting shows where Dryden's true affections lay, for each plot goes beyond *Secret Love* in enacting the working out of desire, and accordingly reaffirms the worth of the characters in serious and comic plots alike. No torments of a lovelorn Queen, no hero's divided love perturb the directness of desire in the "high" plot of *Marriage A-la-Mode*, where the two lovers move with assurance, and the renunciation theme, embodied in Amalthea's sorrow, recedes. Whereas Candiope in *Secret Love* has no second lover and indeed does not appear until act III, every figure in *Marriage A-la-Mode* who is a suitable object of desire is confirmed as such by having two suitors. The lovers in the comic plot also bask in each other's glory, and Palmyra shares the glory of Leonidas, for she first appears with him like "two miracles! / Of different sexes, but of equal form" (I.i.330-31). More desired and therefore more desirable (to the other characters and to the audience), the principals of *Marriage A-la-Mode* enjoy a stature beyond that of their counterparts in *Secret Love*. And, by way of complement, the action of both plots is "higher" and more daring in the later play.

One reason that the principals of *Marriage A-la-Mode* rely on nature, personal force, and each other's endorsements for their stature is that this play lacks any social order to give them roles in which to fit. *Secret Love* and Dryden's *Tempest* both exhibit shakily ruled island states with some social order—the position of the Queen and Prospero—upon which, and contrary to which the natural order grows. *Marriage A-la-Mode* complicates this arrangement. In the public world, King Polydamas is no king but a usurper with a flattering, vengeful, self-seeking favorite, Argaleon. In the private world, marriage, which ought to be the seal of love and union among private persons, is out of vogue, at least for that purpose. Yet usurpation (Polydamas' quest for his heir), forced marriage for an heir (the bee in the rich old bonnets of Melantha's and Palamede's fathers), and the property interest in marriage, all of which the play condemns in one form or another, turn out to produce a happy and stable denouement. Both plots, then, avail themselves of the same setting of moral dislocation to execute a paradoxical reversal, in good fletcherian fashion. By linking disordered order and corrective nature, each plot develops an underlying rhythm in which a different nature, one "providential" and one "Hobbesian," rebukes but also authorizes culture, as society rallies around the approved monarchs and approved matrimonial pairs.

This rhythm begins in the comic plot when disaffected spouses, Doralice and Rhodophil, search for other lovers. By chance they hit respectively on Palamede and Melantha, strangers newly affianced by parental will, that is by raw authority and raw accident. The four weave through an obstacle course—fears of having one's rightful partner catch one with the partner of one's choice—till the spouses and fiancés are paired for reasons having to do with fascination, not love, if in fact *Marriage A-la-Mode* distinguishes the two. Even this pragmatic propriety comes only after the solution of a ménage à quatre ("Wife and Husband for the standing Dish, and Mistris and Gallant for the Desert" [V.i.353–54]) has also been rejected for practical, not moral reasons. Marriage in this plot is thus dishonored in both the breach, which sets the action on its way, and the observance with which the action ends.

The underlying rhythm in the serious plot ends with stability when the two pastoral lovers, Palmyra and Leonidas, not only wed but also ascend the throne to which he by birth and she by mutual love with him are entitled. Symbolically, the movement of their concord from the private and pastoral to the royal and public ought to extend ad exemplum regis to the kingdom, just as the disorder and absolutism of the court did at the beginning of *Marriage A-la-Mode*. Instead, while the heir and his faithful bride take the throne, their subjects, as we have said, continue in a Hobbesian state of nature, kept peaceful only by a Hobbesian contract. Though as loyal soldiers to a rightful king, Rhodophil and Palamede assist in restoring order to the monarchy (V.i.447–52), Melantha's and Palamede's subsequent comments (V.i.493–505) suggest that the principles of loyalty and right apply in a very different way to the comic plot, where appearances continue to reign. Thus at the beginning of the play, nature fills the vacuum left by the symbols and fact of proper order; although at the end, the symbols reappear, the fact of order really does not, except in the narrowest sense. Nature still fills the vacuum. In this too, *Marriage A-la-Mode* develops and transforms the material of *Secret Love* and the Dryden-Davenant *Tempest*.

The Parallel Modes of Marriage A-la-Mode

Marriage A-la-Mode, then, is itself a marriage a-la-mode: it weds two willful plots in a way that is as natural (formally elegant and apt in terms of roles) as the marriage of Palmyra and Leonidas, and as natural (wonderfully fractious and provisional) as the marriages of the comic lovers.[29] It validates two quite different ideas of nature, each with its own norms of desire. And through this conceptual opposition, as well as through making political and social misorder the fashion in the narrative, Dryden advertizes the starting point from which the two plots bifurcate, each tending to its own kind of restitution. With different significance for each plot, *Marriage A-la-Mode* takes place in a

---

[29]Three quite different readings of these plots are provided by Brown ("Divided"), who sees them as "neoclassically" ordained to disjunction; by Canfield, who sees them as chiming in to support sexual constancy; and by McKeon ("Marxist"), who sees them as in dialectical unity.

court that is not *the* court and that has most chance to be the court, the center of government, when dislocated, for its outward motion brings it toward "rightful" repose, serious in one plot and witty in the other.

Royalty and nobility have left Syracuse on a "progress" (I.i.100) designed so that Polydamas, the usurping "old King," can "search the farthest parts of *Sicily*, / In hope to find an Heir" (I.i.244–45), or rather, his fleshly and therefore public heir. He seeks to regain the child taken from him, its natural father, after his betrayal of another child, the true king's orphaned son. The absence of the anxious Polydamas from Syracuse, then, connotes a whole history of absences. His journey has been entailed upon him by misplaced trust, abducted children, wifely desertion, and the mysteriously found letter that tells him of death (his wife's) but is too "torn and sulli'd" (I.i.291) to tell him of life, the whereabouts or even the sex of his heir. For him the "progress" is to seek a different kind of progress, to secure his own and his kingdom's future by recovering his own past losses. Polydamas has created a peripatetic history through his own deeds, robbing the infant heir Theagenes of a realm and thus precipitating the flight of those on whom the succession should have fallen. Only through the peripeteias shown in the serious plot of *Marriage A-la-Mode* can this history work itself out, obscure to human minds but always directed towards a proper end. These characters, like those in the "high" plot of *The Tempest*, act not only within a certain framework of nature; they also act within a certain style of historical understanding, which exalts specific historical actions by individuals (unlike, for example, deterministic, fatalistic, or random notions of historical causation). This style of understanding relies on natural feelings, like parental love and solicitude, and on personal responsibility.

The underlying principle of the comic plot is quite the opposite. Rhodophil and Doralice, true courtiers in a usurped land where one's word is therefore merely a word, have created a limbo for themselves by doing their best to repeal their marriage vows. Their "progress" from court metaphorizes the loosened bonds of social stability. Seekers like Polydamas, they venture off without familial or proprietary constraints to direct them one way or another. Palamede and Melantha, their analogues, do have families but even less history, none at all together, and they start the play each interested in another lover. Palamede has been abroad, though unlike the characters in the "high" plot, he has traveled with no specific purpose, unencumbered with any past. Melantha's obsession with fashion—new courtiers and new expressions in franglais—carries the same motifs of transience, externality, and freedom from ties or purpose. For these two, the "progress" from court metaphorizes a spirit of holiday, albeit a holiday during which they both play hard. If one guesses from their companion couple, Doralice and Rhodophil, even the act of marriage in their future does not threaten to be a terribly deep, consequential commitment.

In this plot, then, the conclusion returns to history (one marriage refreshed, consent for a second), but the peripeteias derive from freedom, uncompelled and voluntary action. Each of the four young courtiers wants to secure the greatest personal advantage at each moment, regardless of previous ties, and to avoid an entrapment that might place limits on choice. Being caught poaching sexually on someone else's property would lead to such a limiting, but only because of a social convention about usurpation and infidelity in marriage, in which a spouse has property value (ownership, an index of credit). The peripeteias here, then, have to do with adaptive maneuvers and the deferring of responsibility, so that commitments beyond the shortest term need to be imposed or mediated by other characters' actions. So Rhodophil's renewed attraction to Doralice needs to be mediated through Palamede's attraction to her; Rhodophil's fancy for Melantha is contagious for Palamede; and Palamede and Melantha's marriage needs to be imposed by parental command. Although both serious and comic plots, then, operate through the peripeteias of the fletcherian mode, they do so with very different thematic rationales, and their similarities of structure make visible the disunity of norms and inconsistencies that fletcherian plays typically contain but usually conceal, or at least deflect attention from.

For this end, Dryden exaggerates the conventions of the genres that he joins. Crudely put, the characters create the narrative in the comic plot, and the narrative creates the characters in the serious one. This is concealed in that the exaltation of individual act occurs, paradoxically, in the heroic plot, and the arbitrariness of act and desire is a staple of the comic plot. But generally, heroic heroes of both sexes live out (and display to the audience) their fated careers through reacting to frequent shifts of circumstance; comic characters crystallize their environments around nuclei of their own needs, which they seek out ways to fulfill. Increasingly during the late 1660s and the 1670s, as we have said, those needs are framed in terms of drives or impulses that seize opportunities for realization. The action is essentially psychological, even though the comic characters lack developed psyches. One is meant to assume that they have an inner life sufficient to ground a plot based on motives that are natural, therefore shared with the audience. By contrast, heroic plays deploy fixed characters, and their drives express themselves as the narrative demands they do. Heroism, maybe paradoxically, involves less activity than reactivity. *Marriage A-la-Mode* capitalizes on this disparity between the two idioms.

The heroic and comic types appear in Dryden's directly previous play, *The Conquest of Granada*, first produced a year or so before *Marriage A-la-Mode*. Though "free as Nature first made man" (I.i.207) Almanzor must remain constant to one love and one code. He does not search for a situation in Granada (or elsewhere) where he can find proper objects for the strong passions with which he seethes. His ideological rival, the amusing though menacing libertine Lyndaraxa, is really left free to seek a way of doing or getting what her desires prompt. In repeating this polarity in *Marriage A-la-Mode*, Dryden exaggerates it. While the four comic lovers seek airily for opportunities to satisfy themselves, young women and men on the make, Palmyra and Leonidas seek only each other and right. More broadly, the serious plot of *Marriage A-la-Mode* takes to an extreme the generic traits of a heroic play with a pastoral scent. The material that provided the stuff for debate in other heroic plays, such as conflicts in duty between one's beloved and one's parent or king, remains active in the serious plot of *Marriage A-la-Mode*, but it no longer has the same force as in *The Conquest of Granada*, where weighing love and honor betokened a choice to be made. Here all the choices for the heroic figures are foregone conclusions. Leonidas and Palmyra are obviously meant for each other and meant to rule. Like characters in heroic plays, they exhibit virtues such as loyalty, steadfast passion, courage, and honor, but their success in the narrative has more to do with bloodlines rather than any of these.

In sharp contrast to Palmyra and Leonidas, the four comic lovers are paired in a most unlikely manner, an accidental chiasmus. Eminently substitutable, each exists for members of the opposite sex as a target of opportunity rather than a natural or logical partner. By the tightness of construction, Dryden counterpoints social bonds (of marriage or friendship; these would have a natural base in the "high" plot, but they are social here) with natural desires (for property or sexual adventure). He thus promotes the comic plot's standard of characters who crave socially defined objects that temporarily appease their natural needs, just as in the serious plot he embraces the idiom of fixed characters who live out their destiny through situations that exhibit that destiny to the audience. The Palmyra-Leonidas plot lacks any individuals who go deeper than acting out the roles expected in the genre of noble romance, and the Melantha-Palamede-Rhodophil-

Doralice plot dissolves such role expectations as the "gay couple"/ sober couple arrangement and the fast friendship of the two male leads. It even blemishes the attractiveness of the leading women. Melantha, "the greatest Gossip in Nature," displays an individualizing, incurable French flightiness and the "insufferable humour, of haunting the Court" (I.i.189,206). Doralice, unlike almost any of the comic heroines who precede her in Carolean comedy, has willingly married and therefore, as the play shows, must willfully renew her power—typical of the female lead—to fix male desire.

Marriage A-la-Mode assumes an audience aware enough to perceive typical generic actions, heroic or comic, as patterns. It then brings these recognized and, one might think, sharply different patterns into conjunction: similarities between what seemed sharply different have the same sort of witty effect as do some of Donne's or Cleveland's or Butler's or, for that matter, Dryden's similes in verbal wit. Such playing on similarity and difference produces the unexpected or sudden shifts in expectation, just as the fletcherian peripeteia does on the level of plot. Where one expects a certain train of events in a plot, difference is the mode of reversal; where one expects different patterns of convention in structure, comparison and likeness themselves are the modes of reversal. This effect is one that Dryden produces to some extent in earlier double-plot plays like *Secret Love*, but produces more fully here, through the close knitting of the two plots and, conversely, their normative independence from each other, each built on its own, socially validated conception of nature.

This effect of conjunction depends somewhat on actual plot links. For example, Dryden has Rhodophil usher in Hermogenes, Leonidas, and Palmyra, and he has their presentation to the king directly follow that of Palamede, whose father, like the father of Leonidas, was a fellow soldier of Polydamas "in the last Civil Wars" (I.i.319–20). We might remark that in the last scene of *Marriage A-la-Mode*, Dryden turns these connections to witty advantage, for by the rule of analogy the two friends shift their loyalties to Leonidas from Polydamas as they have just previously shifted their amorous allegiances. Mostly, however, the interlacing of the plots occurs through more oblique, though also deliberately visible, techniques. Both plots have the same general shape, in that they deal with questionable de facto authority, violated vows, usurpation, separation of husband and wife, and the return to love through novelty (Doralice's reunion with Rhodophil, Polydamas' finding the child he never knew). As Palamede's father had at least implicitly compelled his son to marry a stranger by threats of disinheritance, so Polydamas tries to compel Leonidas and Palmyra, "two miracles" (I.i.330) long pledged to one another by nature but allotted by royal and paternal authority to new claimants, Amalthea and Argaleon.

Beyond this, one has the tightness of construction pointed out by David Rodes, in his perceptive discussion of form in *Marriage A-la-Mode* for the California Dryden. He remarks that the two plots show

> careful planning, much attention to coordinating detail, and an almost obsessive mutual interest in themes and language. . . . The two worlds of *Marriage A-la-Mode* alternate with precise regularity between the comic and the heroic, each comic scene followed by a heroic scene of about equal length, until the fifth act, where the comic overbalances the heroic, taking more than twice the number of lines to bring the play to its general comic conclusion and diffusing into itself the tragic tendencies of the heroic plot. (11: 477-78)

He goes on to suggest that "each [of the five acts] has its individual keynote, expressed in the physical action and in the imagery and language of the act" (478). Thus the first act is an introduction at the conclusion of which rightful partners in each plot are divided from one another, only to be briefly reunited in a second act whose theme Rodes sees as "language—and how language defines the individual" (479). He treats the third and fourth acts as focused respectively on integrity versus subterfuge and on disguise and darkness, all matters that are resolved in the vigorous, celebratory final act. Whether or not one subscribes to Rodes' specifics, his general principle seems right. The plots produce parallel effects and within given areas of the play there is a massing of a given kind of thematic energy on which both plots draw. But these loci of thematic energy help produce unity, as we have argued, so as to define the discontinuities and disparities on which the formal pattern of *Marriage A-la-Mode* depends as much as it does on comings together.

In the action of *Marriage A-la-Mode*, Dryden follows the linear unfolding of parallels and reversals common to the fletcherian style, an obvious source of unity and disparities. We can simply list those between plots and within plots throughout act II, after the exposition of act I is complete. No sooner has Melantha set herself for her "amour" with Rhodophil, who has been courting her in the French fashion, than Palamede presents himself in a manner "extremely *French*" (II.i.41). Rhodophil finds out that Palamede is wooing his unwanted wife, Doralice (124), and is affianced to his mistress, Melantha (154), while Palamede finds that Rhodophil is married to *his* mistress, Doralice (135-36), and is wooing *his* unwanted fiancée, Melantha (160). Just after Rhodophil pledges his aid to keep the peace between the rivals

Leonidas and Argaleon (249–54), he declares his aim of breaking the peace, through betrayal, between himself and his rival Palamede, once his friend (255–60). As the serious plot is inaugurated in act II (261), Polydamas orders Leonidas to marry Amalthea just as Melantha's father (by letter) has ordered her to marry Palamede when the comic plot was inaugurated earlier in the act (21); but whereas in the comic plot the children are ready to obey their fathers, each by being no more than half-faithful to the intended spouse (101-5, 191), the serious plot shows Leonidas unwilling to obey his "parent" and faithful to his love. His rejection of Amalthea in this act is matched by Palmyra's of Argaleon. Polydamas' angry invocation of his rank to Leonidas—"You shall dispute no more; I am a King,/ And I will be obey'd" (312-13)—finds its echo in Leonidas' invoking his rank to Argaleon: "What? a disputing Subject? / Hence; or my sword shall do me justice, on thee" (402-3). Polydamas, as everyone knows, is no king, and Leonidas, who speaks like his son and takes his authority from Polydamas', is no prince—he is in fact, as a clever viewer can guess, the rightful king.

Finally, as in the comic plot the two young men had, by observation, discovered themselves doubly rivals in love, so here act II ends with Argaleon's spying on the long love duet between Palmyra and Leonidas. Dryden then improves on this analogizing by opening act III with another parallel and reversal involving observation: the husband and wife Rhodophil and Doralice behave lovingly when they know Artemis is watching them, but as soon as she steals away, *"they walk contrary ways on the Stage; he, with his hands in his pockets, whistling: she, singing a dull melancholly Tune"* (s.d.,37). In act II, then, one has a long series of fletcherian doublings, some in the same plot and some across plots, each of them turning on some term of concealment or discovery and most of them related to questions of identity, involving roles, desires, and expectations.

The rest of *Marriage A-la-Mode* dances the same minuet. Act III, scene i begins with the separation of Doralice and Rhodophil, each off to find a new lover, and ends with the separation of Palmyra and Leonidas, and Leonidas' speech (467–80) about his being alone. The previous dialogue had been about his accepting a humble state rather than a "large pension" at court (452), as the dialogue following Doralice's soliloquy on being alone (85–95) has been about the superiority of court to country (96–183). Melantha demonstrates her pretensions to French courtly elegance and receives a billet doux from Rhodophil, a scene that directly precedes Palmyra's being accused of pretensions in loving so far above her station—the angry Polydamas threatens to dress her with "a Player's painted Sceptre, / And, on her head, a gilded Pageant Crown" (301–2)—and then her receiving a letter that calls her a *"pledge of love."* This letter itself provides a reversal by showing her to be the daughter of Polydamas, and of course Polydamas' sentence upon her is a reversal or at least an irony in that he himself, a usurper, is a player king. The scene could hardly be more arranged.

Act III, scene ii finds the four comic lovers all having made assignations in the same grotto, just as act IV finds them having chosen the same device, male dress for the women, to promote their assignations at the time of the masquerade. Their comic disguise counterpoints the masked ball in the serious plot, meanwhile, for at the opening of act IV Palmyra's would-be rival, Amalthea, painfully disguises her love for Leonidas and counsels him about speaking to his beloved at the dance, while in IV.ii, his would-be rival, Argaleon, disguised as Leonidas, successfully deceives Palmyra there. Act IV ends with a near-duel between the women in the comic plot and then a summons to their male counterparts to report for military duty against a planned insurrection, thwarted in IV.iv; this pattern is repeated in act V, now with the men in the comic plot's being restrained from a duel and with the insurrection a success. The conquests in the comic plot of act V, with their provisos now refused (170–83), now accepted (359–68), therefore tally amusingly with the martial flurry and royal disposition with which the serious plot comes to its more conventionally political end. Melantha is overwhelmed by the fashionable words that Palamede spouts at her; the three other lovers yield before fear of fashionable, "natural" sexual depredations; and the usurpers are beaten by force of arms and virtue. And each of these parallel situations either embodies or leads to a peripeteia.

Of course the analogies between plots and within plots do not work the same way. Obviously the ideals of the two plots differ radically and so does the language. In act II, for instance, Leonidas and Palmyra even break into rhyme for a long duet of nostalgic lyricism, heightening the blank verse that itself contrasts with the prose of the comic plot. But more than lexicon, syntax, and rhythm are involved. The serious lovers' dwelling on the past, their musing about lost bucolic bliss, and their self-abnegatory love (407–502) all have counterparts in the comic plot designed to contrast with them: the old regretted obligations of the married couple, the French affectations and travel of the affianced couple, and the amorous attachments that imply a loosened hold on those to whom the lovers now are bound—these are the comic plot's versions of past time, pastoral distance, and uncertain possession. In the serious plot, these motifs appear in terms of absolute values. The imagined scenes of past and present, here and there, sharply demarcate what one has and what one does not. The characters know what is true or false in what they say, and the conventions of a romantic plot invite the audience to suppose that they too know. In the comic plot the shared motifs delineate only a broad area of meaning: past obligations retain a certain but indefinite grip on the present; France has its value because its non-Sicilian practices can be imported into Sicily; and neither of the two men actually wants to reject the woman whom in another sense he would like to be rid of. Tone is indefinite in meaning too, in that neither the audience nor the characters quite know how sincere any statement may be.

As with other plays in the fletcherian fashion, none of these analogies tell the audience anything they did not know: the character of Melantha does not comment on that of Doralice, Palamede, Rhodophil, or Palmyra. No doubt, as we have been repeating, someone of a romantic or moral turn of mind or a "realistic" and skeptical set of attitudes might choose to interpret the play as embodying her or his preferences, a freedom that *Marriage A-la-Mode* invites. But there is no textual or contextual evidence for subordinating one set of norms to another or for insisting that Dryden tried to strike some sort of golden mean between the two. The analogies, in fact, enhance this separation. Having the four comic lovers so interrelated, for example, presents a wry genealogy and exposé of moral behavior within a certain order of nature, and thus systematizes that behavior. Like the doubling of lovers in the rewritten *Tempest*, these comic analogies show that the way the lovers act and feel is universal. The interchangeability of the four lovers as objects of desire—not as people, for Dryden has given each his or her distinctive character—helps them serve as what in chapter 2 we called "specie," representatives of the socially valued. Their representative nature in the unpredictable comic plot is fixed by their doubling just as the representative nature of the heroic characters is fixed by the strict generic rules that dictate the outcome of strivings in the serious plot.

The analogies work differently too with regard to paralleled characters. In fletcherian style, Dryden has written a play in which either the "high" or the "low" plot could be staged, impoverished, without the other, while the narrative of both plots hangs on internal analogies that go beyond story line. To keep the paragons on a par, each of the two miraculous lovers needs a frustrated suitor. That these lovers are so much alike and that their suitors are brother and sister, Argaleon and Amalthea, may act as a false hint that Leonidas and Palmyra too will turn out to be siblings, a twist of plot that Dryden was later to use in *The Spanish Fryar* and *Don Sebastian*. But this whiff of guessworthy incest ends up doing nothing but enlivening the plot through suspense. It has narrative, not cognitive ends. Parity among characters in the comic plot has another narrative purpose. Dryden must allow for the switching of lovers at the end of this plot. On the principle that the more convertible the persons, the more convertible the lovers' fancies, he arranges the reciprocal discoveries in act II, the choice of the same dark grotto for assignations in act III, and the use of the same disguises in act IV. By compromising these lovers' absolute individuality, Dryden also establishes a kind of balance between the more highly particularized comic characters and the less particularized but more clearly extraordinary figures in the serious plot. The heroic figures, left undoubled, can plausibly shine in all the enraptured hyperbole about them. More important, as lonely figures they are driven and controlled by internalized duty, which in this plot lays claim to be part of nature. Along these lines, the comic figures are doubled precisely because in their plot nature is individualized and aggressive, and so requires external forces of equal strength, the other characters, to direct it and at the same time, by their example, to help glamorize it.

Correspondingly, Dryden separates the two plots in their style of self-awareness, the disposition of a character to stand aside from the action for a moment and to comment upon it. He thus proffers, ready-made, overtly different norms of evaluation, making it hard to read the plots in terms of each other. Leonidas, Doralice, Palamede, and Rhodophil all exhibit such reflectiveness, which is first of all a mode of social power, of asserting one's ability to comprehend a situation. In heroic actions, the usual although not universal style of reflectiveness is personal and either emotive or philosophically grave. For example, Leonidas generalizes, "How precious are the hours of Love in Courts" (II.i.406), which pretends to generality (and might appear, for example, in a didactic poem with a flavor of vanitas mundi) but which refers emotively to his own situation. In referring things to himself, he reveals himself to the audience as a heroic figure with the proper sentiments; Dryden gives him the grandeur of generality by making such an approved sentiment a principle of feeling to which Leonidas naturally adheres. Throughout the comic action, however, reflectiveness takes the *moraliste* form that we discussed in the previous chapter, that of stating an empirical law of nature about human behavior.

For instance, Doralice tells Palamede in the first moments of act I: "You travelling Monsieurs live upon the stock you have got abroad, for the first day or two: to repeat with a good memory, and apply with a good grace, is all your wit. And, commonly, your Gullets are sew'd up, like Cormorants: When you have regorg'd what you have taken in, you are the leanest things in Nature" (i.34–39). Doubling in the comic plot, so as to establish a small social group with its own analyzable dynamic, complements such a stress on social observation in the characters' language as well as in their calculations about how to act so as to get what they want. *Moraliste* wit usually refers to what underlies action, heroic reflectiveness to what underlies feeling. Sentences of both sorts enhance the characters who utter them and, differently, normalize behavior inside the plot to whose nature they apply.

Marriage A-la-Mode: *Desire, Freedom, Nature*

We should like to explore the ideals of *Marriage A-la-Mode* by tracing some of its repeatedly invoked ideas, in thematic pairs based on desire, freedom, and nature. The thematic pairs are the opposition play/sincerity as it relates to the expression of desire, the opposition choice/authority as it relates to personal freedom, and the opposition reason/passion as it relates to the logic of following the demands of nature. In each of these oppositions the first term—play, choice, reason—stresses the self as free agent and the second term—sincerity, authority, passion—stresses the self as an agent under constraint. Since no one can act significantly outside some defining system, "free agent" and "agent under constraint" are not objective distinctions. The terms mark only points of view towards an action. But as with the ambiguous norms of Dryden's *Tempest*, terms with loose meaning are all the more useful for organizing a heterogeneous comedy. Obviously these pairs might, and in *Marriage A-la-Mode* we would say they do, govern the sorts of "keynotes" that Rodes identifies: the way in which appropriate partners are separated and brought together, the social definition of the characters, the interplay between integrity and subterfuge, and the equivocal distinction between willed and unwilled behavior. Our terms are somewhat less specific than his "keynotes," but as compensation they allow for more discussion of continuity from event to event and of ingenious discontinuities from plot to plot.

In examining the pairs play/sincerity, choice/authority, and reason/passion, we are developing a point raised about Dryden's *Tempest*. Normative concepts of belief, we argued there, are strong but ambiguous: we remarked on two senses of "innocence," for example, and different ways of assessing "freedom." Similarly, as we have said, in *Marriage A-la-Mode* the strong, central ideal of nature differs in meaning from one plot to the other. Our argument here goes further: Dryden not only splinters apparently single terms, like "nature" or "innocence," to respond to the wishes of various constituencies, but he also breaks down apparent oppositions, like play and sincerity or choice and authority, so that they lose their distinguishing force. The norms to which they refer—play and sincerity to the expression of desire, for example—thereby become the more enigmatic, though the characters stoutly invoke them as if they were unproblematic, to defend behavior that is natural, freely chosen, or expressive of desire.

Dryden's sporting with ideas in this way, well beyond anything of the sort in the plays of the 1660s, amuses one as wit, like the witty parallels and disjunctions between the comic and heroic plots of *Marriage A-la-Mode*. But such collapsing of distinctions also undermines the rational basis for the characters' actions and thereby brings into prominence the willfulness that marks Carolean comedy of the 1670s and that invites members of the audience to respond to the action each in his or her own terms. With these issues in mind, we will look at the way in which the opening act of *Marriage A-la-Mode* establishes the implicit, sometimes explicit oppositions play/sincerity, choice/authority, and reason/passion, and then lets "play" melt into "sincerity," "choice" into "authority," "reason" into "passion," or is it the other way around for all three of these pairs?

The three thematic pairs begin where the play begins, with Doralice's opening speech, which sets up the principles on which the whole comic plot turns: "*Beliza*, bring the Lute into this Arbor, the Walks are empty: I would try the Song the Princess *Amalthea* bad me learn." She goes on to ask in the song that immediately follows why an old marriage vow should continue to oblige spouses whose "*Passion is decay'd.*" Since they cannot give or receive "*joys*" from each other, now that "*the Pleasure is fled,*" they should not hinder each other from giving and receiving joys with somebody else. The song suits Doralice perfectly; but why start with a song? and why have her bidden to learn it by the unmarried and virtuous Amalthea, whom it does not suit at all and who could hardly know how well it suits Doralice? Dryden could have kept just as well to the "A-la-Mode" part of his title by having Doralice quip about the decay of marriage or introduce the song as one in vogue around court. The gains from this opening, we believe, are thematic.[30]

The genre of song contributes to the pair play/sincerity, for a song

---

[30]This is a different issue from that of why the song is sung by a concealed singer, in an arbor. We find plausible Jocelyn Powell's suggestion (*Restoration* 50) that this is a contrivance so that someone else could perform for Rebecca Marshall, who was not a good singer; cf. *The Assignation* III.ii.6–7, where she as Lucretia says her talent is dancing, leaving Hippolita (Mary Knepp) to sing.

is a public form, stylized by meter and rhyme, and one does not know what personal meaning it has for its performer. Doralice herself has neither written nor as yet followed the advice of this song, nor has Amalthea. Because Doralice, a wife, immediately begins to flirt with Palamede, one suspects that she does subscribe to its sentiments. As yet, however, no one can tell how serious the flirtation may be or what the causal relationship may be between this court song and the courting that follows it. The "playful" act of singing becomes all the more intriguing and attractive because it may shelter the true feeling that is its apparent opposite. That Amalthea has commanded the song, then, brings up the pair authority/choice. Doralice here claims she is singing because she has been bidden to do so, but the song is so natural for her that the command is at once binding, or so Doralice says, and unnecessary. A *"foolish Marriage Vow,"* such as the song mentions, was once a choice but has become obligation or authority, and this obligation is promptly called into question by the obligated song (Amalthea's bidding) and the chosen flirtation that the song independently authorizes.

Finally, the logic of nature which the song celebrates raises our third pair of motifs, that of reason/passion, for the song is framed in terms of comprehensible causes and purposes. Marriage vows exist, says the song, only to serve a normally exhaustible resource: passion. Jealousy between those whose passion has decayed is therefore *"madness," "For all we can gain, is to give ourselves pain, / When neither can hinder the other."* This is cool and intelligent, giving precedence to an order based on the logical nature of things over, for example, a system based on social convention. Though the song presents the case for passion reasonably, not passionately, thus suggesting its intended addressee's scheme of values, it simultaneously asserts the priority of rationally approved passion (pleasure) and disapproved passion (jealousy). In the song passion is alive enough to decay or to flee; it embodies cause and purpose hidden from reason; it underlies the logic of human behavior. Moreover, passion, in its sense of something imposed, an unwilled motion of the will, becomes the criterion for action.

And so a song that argues for freedom and control—the right to discard empty vows—also argues for enslavement. This is a paradox that we discussed in Dryden's *Tempest*, where passion is a more profound ideal than reason, as it is here. The final twist here, however, is that the specific passion between Doralice and Rhodophil has fled and decayed not because of the workings of nature, as an application of the song would imply, but rather because of others' snickering, part of a system based on social convention. Since a rival's attentions to her rewhets Rhodophil's appetite for his wife, passion between the spouses returns because of the conventional possessiveness that the song decries in the interests of passion. Reason and passion both invoke the logic of nature, but in this case both return instead to the arbitrary formulas of convention.

The first dialogues following Doralice's song, those of Palamede with Doralice and then with Rhodophil, respond to the song in appropriately indeterminate ways. Palamede and Doralice engage for a two-day flirtation, stylized by rules on which the participants agree as well as by the elaborate forms of recognizable flattery. Because stylization conceals one's degree of sincerity, it is a flirtation open-ended as to intention and outcome. Although the pledge of two-days' ties is a calculated action, in tune with Doralice's rational song and the cool banter between her and him, the action emerges from or merges with passion, a compulsion so fatal that when Doralice leaves, Palamede comments, "Well, I'll say this for thee, thou art a very dextrous Executioner; thou hast done my business at one stroke: Yet I must marry another—and yet I must love this" (I.i.88–90). In the opening encounter of the play as in the preceding song, personal responsibility is lightly enough treated and hard enough to fix that a viewer is willing at least to defer judgment. Dryden continues, too, to keep choice and authority in question, for prior obligations are evaded only by substituting new ones. The rules of the flirtation game are for Palamede a commitment, an acceptance of authority, which runs counter to the commitments to his friend, to Doralice's husband, to his own father, and thus to his fiancée, whom he is commanded to marry.

In this opposition of interests, the relationship between Doralice and Palamede seems to stand for the freedom of nature as against the authoritative demands of society, like marriage vows or filial duty. Yet this neat opposition falls apart when Rhodophil enters with his duel between social obligation and the chosen object of his natural passions. In his fashion-fashioned ennui with Doralice and his would-be adventures with Melantha, the roles of nature and society get muddled. He has a social obligation vowed to his wife and a social obligation to tire of her ("the World began to laugh at me, and a certain shame of being out of fashion seiz'd me"); he is drawn by nature to a mistress, a "Cordial" to "patch up" his "disease" (I.i.158–60), but drawn to a fashionable, gossipy mistress, who passes up her assignations with him (and thus the restorative ends of nature) in favor of "haunting the Court" (206). Choice merges with authority, reason with passion. And though Rhodophil, like Doralice's song, claims that one naturally tires of a spouse, those who have not been able to tire of Doralice are likely to think his boredom unnatural: the audience have just seen her triply marked as an object of desire, through the hint of promiscuity in her song, through her wit, and through the eyes of Palamede. Palamede's trysting with her would thus seem all the more natural except that Dryden complicates things by introducing further criteria based on nature: he binds the two men in natural and social ties of friendship and pairs them so that they should share tastes, as of course they later do. The natural looks very much like the unnatural, the free like the unfree, since objects of desire are mediated, chosen because of another's choice, as Rhodophil allows: "If he loves you, there's something more in ye then I have found" (V.i.307).

Does the opposition play/sincerity in Rhodophil and Doralice's marriage also turn out to be no opposition at all? Of course. Their marital charades, in which he looks "infinite fond" of her "before company" (I.i.153), offer an element of social play that Rhodophil tries to undermine by claiming that their real relationship is simply the opposite of what they pretend. Yet since Rhodophil confesses that he "could have held out [loving Doralice] another quarter" of a year but for the world's derision (148–49), his behavior makes no sense. For if "the World" will mock a loving husband and if he is sensitive to the world's laughter, then the worst way to "set a good face upon the matter" should be to act as Rhodophil acts, in being "infinite fond of [his wife] before company" (152–53). He should love her sincerely in private and kowtow to critics by shunning her in public, rather than as he does, the opposite. Here is a paradox of behavior: in what acts or words is Rhodophil sincere? In some comedies, such a paradox would force a viewer to ferret out a concealed lie, and in some others, one might assume the writer inept. Neither solution fits here. Dryden simply explains a fact, that the spouses only seem happily married, with a bundle of rhetoric conventional for describing behavior as understood by both men and by the society in which they move. Within these explanatory conventions, the situation is open to two kinds of analysis. The marriage is aground because society has imposed on true feelings and/or because true feelings are naturally fleeting. "Ask those, who have smelt to a strong perfume two years together, what's the scent," snorts Rhodophil; "I lov'd her a whole half year, double the natural term of any Mistress" (137–38, 147–48). Dryden keeps the explanatory conventions operating as themes while he also keeps as an open question the validity and sincerity of the actual explanations. Although the situation looks fixed and capable of analysis, the truth may be that whatever one's real feelings may be, one by definition cloaks them or presents their opposite when in public.

If a person tries to comprehend his or her own feelings in publicly acceptable terms—and these characters could hardly conceive of any other—s/he may well thereby end up mystified. Play and sincerity become indistinguishable.

The last introduced and logically final figure in the quartet of lovers is Melantha, whose private self is largely a function of her public self. With her the three antinomies of play/sincerity, choice/authority, and reason/passion lose even the pretense to classify. Whereas the witty exchanges between Palamede and first Doralice, then Rhodophil, go by quickly and divertingly in actual performance, Melantha struts about on display for a long time, an embodiment of the themes and paradoxes already introduced, as Kalitzki notes. The quarry of both men, she nonetheless differs from them (and their other interest, Doralice) in acting from dominant humours rather than from universally "natural" needs and tastes. In this play, her fixed nature moves her upward toward the high characters on whom she fawns. Conversely, at the end Palamede plans to get her a place at court where she can introduce affectation—associated with the comic plot—into a royal establishment just reaffirmed as the home of frank, feeling nature. Indeed, her relation to the other "low"-plot lovers is a bit like that of the serious plot to the comic, in that she marks the bounds of a pattern of thematic dispersion: as the serious plot shows how certain elements of the comic plot might be extended and varied, so Melantha shows how certain elements of the other three lovers might be reinterpreted.

In their first dialogue, the two reasonable young men condemn Melantha's faults—haunting the court, gossiping, and hungering for new French words. Yet these faults echo Rhodophil's own submission to fashion and hunger for novelty, the "natural" tendencies that have put him out of love with Doralice. Like Rhodophil, Melantha prefers fashion to love, "for this insufferable humour, of haunting the Court, is so predominant," Rhodophil admits, "that she has hitherto broken all her assignations with me, for fear of missing her visits there" (I.i.206–8). Her motives in keeping distant from him thus appear as a version of his own. Melantha's foreign and court predilections give her ties to the traveler Palamede, too. He has learned no more from his travels, so far as one can tell from *Marriage A-la-Mode*, than how to fit himself to her at home. And in her relation to both men, she also relates to Doralice, who, like Melantha, is both connected and detached from Rhodophil and Palamede each by a shared rationale of fashion and nature. In short, Melantha's analogies with the other three comic lovers either vary themes that they introduce or muddle the distinctions that one might make—and that the characters, often overtly, rely on—between being sincere and insincere, free and constrained, and so forth.

Of course these analogies also let the play succeed on stage, for in performing the desires of the audience, the characters do best if they are both similar and various, if they evade classification while acting from "universal" motives, if they add glitter to what might elsewhere be slightly discreditable. The definition of all four lovers in terms of similar values also helps the denouement avoid seeming mechanical, with the men imposed on the women and vice versa; they are imposed, but at the same time they all seem to have been chosen, so that freedom—with all the ambiguities of freedom in this play—is thus asserted. One cannot praise enough Dryden's exquisite skill in making the women and men individuals while they also remain clearly substitutable for one another. Thematic definition such as we have been discussing makes his tour de force possible.

Dryden, then, confounds traditional antinomies, refusing to allot rights to reason and to passion, to create a polarity between authority and choice, or to draw the line between sincere and insincere, playful expressions of desire. The sophisticated ironies of the comic plot in *Marriage A-la-Mode* develop from his stretching the indeterminacy of play to include moments (or more than moments) of sincerity, from his giving social authority an allegiance that is both skeptical and genuine, from having the same person raisonneur and self-deceiver, or victim and willing victim of the compulsions of nature. A necessary theatrical condition for Dryden's writing this way is that it result in a comedy that is clever fun, intellectually tantalizing. But this is not a sufficient condition. *Secret Love* has a scene of tongue in cheek courtship between the masked Florimell and the newly arrived Celadon which resembles that between the newly arrived Palamede and the unmasked but to him unknown Doralice; but in the 1660s comedy the scene merely sets up a pattern of witty outwitting in a pure fletcherian manner, not a body of ambiguous themes to allure one through five acts. In *Marriage A-la-Mode* Dryden very early underscores these themes to bring into plain view issues that are common to *Secret Love* and to the revised *Tempest* as well as to this play, but only here provide visible ambiguity in values. He thus empowers members of the audience to respond in their own ways, as we have said, and he also forces them to lighten or to defer moral judgment until the denouement, by mystifying the characters' motives and thus throwing their personal responsibility into doubt. A third end in pitting rival claims on the same values against one another, let alone rival claims on different but equally venerable values (like the Love and Honour of heroic plays), is that Dryden can easily engineer peripeteias and multiple, partial resolutions in the fletcherian manner, while keeping the appearance of consistency in the characters' motives and goals. The consistency of the characters, as we have remarked, helps make them vehicles for mediating the desires of the audience.

But of course the comic plot only makes up half of *Marriage A-la-Mode*; of course, since Dryden builds in so many formal analogies between the two plots, he would build in thematic analogies as well; and of course, the way in which he transposes analogical elements from plot to plot follows a generic principle: what in the comic plot is a psychological issue becomes a function of events in the serious plot. Or, to rephrase this point in narrative terms, both plots have firm causal structures but differ in their conception of cause. In the comic plot, cause refers to efficacy, the way in which one event or psychological disposition brings about other events, but in the serious plot, cause refers to grounding, the overall design of virtue, roles, and inheritance which acts as the principle of coherence. To its fixities all events and modes of behavior at the court of Polydamas should be traced. Consequently, paradoxes of value which give the comic plot much of its tang and allow it to be read differently by different viewers, alert to different ironies, do not really appear in the serious plot. Dryden teases his audience with motives in terms of which events have individual meaning (the comic plot), and with events in terms of which motives get evaluated (the serious plot), and he makes the twain keep meeting on stage to keep them apart as ways of regarding and enacting desire in the world.

The simplest transposition of motifs from the comic to the serious plot is that the "play" in the pair play/sincerity becomes the equally role-oriented, equally difficult to penetrate, but much less psyche-determined motif of concealment and disguise ("playing a part"). Thus, in act I, old Hermogenes first represents Leonidas and Palmyra as his children, and then, when *"his Perruke falls off"* (s.d., i.357), says that Leonidas is the usurper Polydamas' son, Palmyra his own daughter. The audience may doubt this corrected version, since they know that the widowed Queen had had a son and had been accompanied in flight by Polydamas' pregnant wife (254–55); they can guess from the conventions of such plots that these children will reappear and that, like their mothers, the children will be virtuous and leagued. Here arises ironic energy when Leonidas acts like a prince—"You rather over-act your part, and are / Too soon a Prince," snaps the piqued court favorite Argaleon (I.i.423–24)—but which prince?, that of nature (the son of the rightful king Theagenes, "divinely born" in

Greek) or of force and authority (the son of Polydamas, "subduer of many" in Greek)?

By handling the motif of social authority equivocally, Dryden takes the heat off this question of lineage and makes it merely a narrative puzzle to solve. De jure, social authority here has no consistent support from ideas of natural right, of moral law, or of generic convention, but the ideology of the play also never makes it insupportable de facto. For example, as a usurper whose proud, ambitious, and revengeful favorite manipulates him, Polydamas ought to be a bad lot, in no way able to be Leonidas' father. Dryden does undercut his royal authority and put his paternal authority in question but otherwise impugns him as little as possible. The usurper of Sicily turns out to be affectionate, generous, and grateful, a possible father who would not disgrace Leonidas at all. In part, Polydamas benefits from Dryden's keeping him a suitable father for Palmyra, Leonidas's female double, but in part, too, from Dryden's resolution not to resolve the motifs of this comedy, or rather to resolve only the plot structure while keeping themes in complex motion. Dryden is so far from feeling duty bound to give social authority a moral basis that at the end of *Marriage A-la-Mode* he finesses the rewards and punishments in the serious plot. The noxious Argaleon winds up in precisely the same loveless position as his sweet sister Amalthea, he choosing to "be a prisoner always" and she to spend her life "with Vestals" (V.i.518,524). Here Dryden casts aside poetic justice or the easing of thematic tensions, while he carries through the theme of a limitation at once obligatory and chosen, an analogue to the resolution that the comic lovers find. Except for the necessary enthronement of Palmyra and Leonidas, this denouement seems adapted for the emotional convenience of the audience as much as that of the comic plot.

In the serious plot, then, play turns into a purely narrative issue, disguise (or concealment), as does choice, acting in tune with one's nature, that is, one's generic role. Sincerity becomes a function of story rather than, as in the comic plot, of a mixture of whim, wants, wit, and situation; and social authority turns into external compulsion, sometimes internalized as duty by the law abiding. Our point, again, is that one can and, for the sake of the play, should recognize the comic and serious forms of these motifs as akin. In neither plot does Dryden lend much moral backing to any norm for behavior. Usually he handles the serious plot by voiding it of thematic interest: the characters simply do what one expects them to do, no questions asked or worth asking. The same is true of the third motif we traced in the comic plot, that of the logic of nature (reason/passion). Characters in the serious plot have passions that move them but these passions remain the ones that the logic of nature at its least complicated would dictate. The lovers are instantly, intuitively worth loving. In them and in the action of which they are the centers of energy, what happens has a curious self-evidence about it. Reason coincides with passion, choice—when all the facts are known—with authority.

7

The *Moraliste* Comedy of the 1670s

The model of Carolean Comedy that we defined in chapter 2 best suits the comedies of the early-to-mid 1670s, such as *Marriage A-la-Mode*. Here one finds plays calculated to provide heterogeneity of response (different viewers, different morals) and compromise formation (vicarious sin with safety of conscience), and to offer the audience agents for their own desires. Playwrights working on this implicit model produced the Carolean plays most often studied and cited as Restoration comedy, even when that pigeonhole—or ostrich-hole, since it is so loose and general—also yawns for Congreve, Vanbrugh, and Farquhar. But just as the writers of the 1670s, despite their deserved reputation, did not necessarily produce the best Carolean comedies, so too they did not settle on some single mode from which the 1660s and the 1680s slope off into the transitional. Like the 1660s, like the 1680s, the 1670s were a period of change and experimentation. Therefore, having discussed how a specific Carolean comedy of the early 1670s, *Marriage A-la-Mode*, embodies and employs our model, Carolean Comedy, we should now like to stress the variety of ways in which that model appears in plays of high quality. As the model allows one to measure a diachronic pattern of differences (chapters 3–5, 8, 9), so it encourages specific distinctions among contemporaneous works, such as we pursue in this chapter.

We have chosen three comedies slightly later than *Marriage A-la-Mode*, comedies that differ markedly from Dryden's and, though all were produced within a year, from each other: *The Virtuoso* (May 1676), Part 1 of *The Rover* (March 1677), and *The Plain-Dealer* (December 1676). Each of the plays is among its author's best, which is very good indeed. Each was quite popular. *The Virtuoso*, Downes wrote, "got the Company great Reputation" (78); *The Rover* was repertory fare through the first half of the next century and prompted a sequel from Behn; *The Plain-Dealer* was to go through numerous editions by the end of the century. Each of these three comedies, moreover, exemplifies a different kind of source, in that Shadwell declared himself Jonson's follower, Behn adapted an earlier (pre-)Carolean play, Killigrew's *Thomaso, or, The Wanderer* (written 1654), and Wycherley borrowed from Molière's *Le Misanthrope*. Once again, we hope unnecessarily, we disclaim any notion that these plays of the 1670s are typical—unless one is ready to be very reductive, the "typical"

165

does not exist in literary history—but of course they do share a dramatic grammar within a shared, changing theatrical context.

The changes in context with which we are particularly concerned have to do with sources of authority, even to some extent the authority of established repertory. In the years 1672 to 1678, between *Marriage A-la-Mode* and the Exclusion Crisis, an unprecedented wave of new comedies washed the old out of the repertory (see appendix 2). Of the ninety-four comedies known or likely to have been performed then, seventy-five (about 80 percent) postdate 1660, and fifty-six of these (about 60 percent of the total) were brand-new. These plays also range widely in comic design and tone. Although comedies of the foreign, London, and multi-plot types continued to be produced, three new popular forms joined them: parody/burlesque, opera/pastoral, and provincial comedy. Each of these new forms, moreover, grows from and modifies the old, in elevating or parodying popular elements from previous comic modes. Song and scenery combine into opera; burlesque pokes fun at heroic drama and other extravagancies; London values are subjected to the fresh air of the country and found wanting. In each of these three instances, playwrights tinker with established dramatic norms and assumptions, a practice that again helps define repertory growth and activity during this fertile period.

Precisely because the companies, the Duke's in particular, hungered for new plays, older comedies in some form also returned to the stage. By 1674 more and more pre-War comedies began showing up revised—adaptations of Brome, Massinger, "T. B.," Ruggle, Fletcher, Middleton, Chamberlayne—after a period when Carolean writers had stolen pretty exclusively aux français. Behn's adapting Killigrew in *The Rover* fits with this trend. The change, we think, is significant, in that imitation of the French, even when the French themselves were imitating the Spanish, had the cachet of established fashion; but fashion could not have urged Caroleans to remake and, at least as important, to vie with the work of their literary grandfathers. Instead of following, as they had done with the French, playwrights now appropriated their sires' labors, rather as their heady protagonists were whisking the mantle of authority from the older generation of moneyed parents, proverb-mongering cits, wilted knights, and longingly lecherous matrons.

Most of the adapters, as one would expect, chose plays that could be made to speak to the audiences of the 1670s. Durfey, for example, eyed Fletcher's *Monsieur Thomas* for his own *Trick for Trick: or, The Debauch'd Hypocrite* (1678) because Fletcher not only combines jollity, intrigue, hypocrisy, and a frenchified servant, but also presents a father (Sebastian) who wants his son debauched; Durfey, a glutton for good things, had already offered variants of this familial plot device in *The Fool Turn'd Critick*, *Madam Fickle*, and *A Fond Husband*. For extra spice, he cuts Fletcher's marriages at the end of *Monsieur Thomas* in favor of a near-rape on stage in front of the lady's father. Four years earlier, the King's Company dusted off the anonymous *The Mistaken Husband*, perhaps adapted from Brome (Harbage-Schoenbaum 172); the edition of 1675 says that Dryden, in whose possession the text had long been, added a scene. In this comedy, a rich woman's father has used threats against his daughter to force her new husband, Manley, from her. Nine years later, Hazzard swindles from Manley (whom he resembles) a token from Mrs. Manley, and successfully impersonates her lost husband to get her eight thousand pounds. Hazzard then robs and abducts his supposed father-in-law for ransom and amnesty, and with the help of Mrs. Manley, who loves him but for whom his love is feigned, he manages to face down the real Manley, who reappears in act IV. Mrs. Manley, with a Carolean care for appearances, decides she "must abominate a real Vertue, / That unto Vulgar eyes I seem unspotted" (IV; 43). And "real Vertue" ends up abominated: Manley is paid off to disappear again and Mrs. Manley marries a wealthy, successful Hazzard. This is not the stuff that one would tailor for comedies in the early 1660s, but it seemed at least worth trying by the mid-1670s.

As these choices and changes suggest, the "sex comedy" of the 1670s served up fare whose unorthodoxy went well beyond sex. All these comedies in one form or another severely weaken the claims of traditional social authority, of parents over children, of men over women, of the demands of honor upon the individual, and of marriage. Such a development logically extends the sexual and generational conflicts seen in earlier comedies, but it differs in kind. Most 1670s' comedies show the young and privileged displaying their freedom, expanding their range of choices, purely to tickle their own desires rather than to respond to situations produced from without, as was more common in earlier plays. Unlike the disobedient children of *The Committee* or *The Tempest*, these heroines and heroes do not take on the legitimacy of young rebels. Rebel they do, but as a self-validating act of self-assertion, two sorts of self-assertion. Flouting authority and transgressing boundaries become ends, sheer willfulness, as well as means, serving the inner drives and outward rules by which these characters direct their energies. The protagonists' typical question, therefore, is not only practical but aesthetic: how to circumvent or conquer obstacles to their pleasure in the most self-gratifying way. Here one finds hero(in)es sporting in the ingenuity of their schemes and masquerades, just as the *moraliste* (often, in the comedies, the same person) enjoys the finish of language in the expression of observed truths. And for this aesthetic end the obstacles to pleasure become important largely as obstacles rather than as figures of real authority. Parents and guardians act as placeholders, even in fairly standard reworkings of the distressed lovers plot such as Otway's *The Cheats of Scapin* (taken quite directly from Molière) or Ravenscroft's *The English Lawyer* (from Ruggle's *Ignoramus*), where clever servants baffle silly old dads.

By the late 1670s, as we shall note in chapters 8 and 9, the delight in willfulness and boundary violations led to malicious rivalries between male friends, replacing previously solid conventions about honor with a situational ethics designed to serve the needs of a large ego at a critical moment. But a good deal earlier, the war between the sexes meant rivalries between women and men who were more nearly equal than had been true in the 1660s; again, we have traced stages of this development in previous chapters, including the discussion of *Marriage A-la-Mode*. Women in the 1670s more frequently take command over their own lives, sometimes over the action itself, whether as clever servants (*The French Conjurer, The Morning Ramble*) or as heiresses (*The Woman Turn'd Bully, The Triumphant Widow*). Such new authority accompanied new self-awareness about it. For example, Hillaria in Ravenscroft's *The Careless Lovers* (1673) announces to her uncle Muchworth that she will choose her own husband, for "it is not now as it was in your young dayes, Women then were poor sneaking sheepish Creatures. But in this Age, we know our own strength, and have wit enough to make use of our Talents. If I meet with a Husband makes my Heart ake, I'le make his Head ake I'le warrant him" (III; 33). When he stamps out, she continues, "I'le have Women say and do what They will: Have we not Rational Souls as well as Men; what made Women Mopes in former Ages, but being rul'd by a company of old Men and Women: Dotage then was counted Wisdom, and formerly call'd Gravity and good Behaviour."

Hillaria is no "Mope": she threatens Muchworth and a foreign fop, Don Boastado, with a bastinado, and later dons breeches (37, 50). Indeed, the increased activity and assertiveness of women often made them temporary males: breeches parts flourished in 1670s' comedies such as *The Counterfeits, The Debauchee, The Mall, The Amorous Old Woman, The Counterfeit Bridegroom, The Plain-Dealer, The Rover, The French Conjuror, The Morning Ramble,* and *The Woman Turn'd Bully*. These roles are defined and used differently from those in previous plays. Whereas in 1660s comedy a woman occasionally slipped into breeches to escape from her guardian (*The Rival Ladies*) or test her lover's constancy (*Secret Love*), sometimes making a fool of herself in the process, in 1670s comedy breeches more often lend her the freedom of a man. In *The Morning Ramble*, for example, after her betrothed takes her brother away for a "morning ramble," his mistress confides wistfully in her servant, "What I would give, *Rose*, to be a man but one Night, to see what pleasure there is in the inside of a Tavern; for sure, it must be something extraordinary to make Mr. *Merry* so continually delight in being there" (I.ii; 12). Both women don men's clothing to join in the fun.

Fears of the audience at the new roles for women are quieted because the plays value no traditionally female traits above their male counterparts. In fact the love plots derive from the central allegiances of the male code, virility, friendship, and power, and a heroine qualifies herself for that plot by her expression of those allegiances in her own person. Her wearing the pants may be a visual symbol for that, and we know of no breeches-wearer in Carolean comedy who, like Fletcher's Bellario in *Philaster*, fails to get her man. Apart from any ethos of the plays themselves, too, the Carolean woman in hose qualifies herself with a direct erotic appeal to the audience, supplementing the usual décolleté with long, tantalizing hints of what lay below the waist, the tightly encased legs and buttocks that women's costume hid (see Wilson, *Ladies* 73–85). Whereas the pre-War transvestite role was only a sexless pun, in which a boy played a woman playing a boy, without engaging the voyeurism of the audience, its Carolean successor allowed the woman in breeches to prove herself as a cynosure who must live up to her masculinity and her femininity within the play, and the audience's eager but critical imaginations. The erotic appeal to the eye then complements seductiveness that works through wit, gaiety, and panache. When successful, this being masculine at once challenges and caters to the male audience. It pays off their possible hostility by showing them two things that they want to see: the customarily hidden parts of the female body, and woman's real inability to be man (because for the audience her pretense calls attention to itself as pretense). Here is another sort of compromise formation, in which a main character's inability allows the audience to accept something that might otherwise threaten them.

Behaving variously in accord with male assumptions, the women in Edward Howard's *The Man of Newmarket* control all the action, setting up rivalries and tests of their suitors, whom they outwit at every turn; women also do the bulk of the wooing and cozening in *The Mock Duellist*, *The Counterfeit Bridegroom*, and *The Morning Ramble*. Together, these plays emphasize the increasingly accepted donnée of comedy that women respond to the same drives as men, acting upon those drives as nearly as possible the way men do, and that they may legitimately demand more freedom of movement and choice. One can see this refusal of the double standard even in so timid and inept a play as Edward Howard's *The Six Days' Adventure, or the New Utopia*, in which women run a commonwealth because they do not want to accept continued male rule. Though Howard, after some hints that women may after all be men's equals, hastens to "confirm the judgement and practice of the world in rendring [women] more properly the weaker Sex, than to authorize their government" (Preface, sig. A3^v), he shows the women's more absurd and obnoxious conduct as a mirror of that which is taken for granted among the men. In a variant of this mirroring, Wycherley's Horner not only communicates with women sexually through "losing" his masculinity, he also communicates with them in spirit by becoming friend and confidant to the "Virtuous Gang," who act like men and wits under cover, just as he does.

The increasing freedom for women in plays, coupled with a general social weakening of the norm of marriage, progressively strained what one might call the "ritual plan" of the plays, their standard reaffirmation of the social order, and thus their facility in presenting a compromise formation. During the first two-thirds of the decade, the enfeebling of marriage, at once encouraged and rebuked in *Marriage A-la-Mode*, usually affected only the rakish plot, as in *The Country-Wife* or *The Man of Mode*, where, as every modern commentator on the play remarks, Dorimant keeps Bellinda on the hook and his friend Bellair's Emilia in his eye, even as he traipses to the country after Harriet. Yet Alithea in Wycherley, Emilia in Etherege, seem safe enough within the tamer plots where they enjoy true love. Similarly, *The Careless Lovers* ends with the gay Careless, married to the gay Hilaria, advising whores in her hearing that he is still in circulation, to which she replies, "He has, as it were but one Mistress the more" (77). She may have her own daring in store, too, for she is the woman we cited above as exclaiming, "I'le have Women say and do what they will; Have not we Rational Souls as well as Men[?]" (III; 33). But elsewhere the same play sounds a moral tone. For instance, the soberer Lovell reproves Careless' wildness, claiming that the reformed rake makes the best husband because of having "experimented the Folly of that Lewd Course of Life" (V; 60).

Compromise formations, however, are sometimes uneasy or baldly improbable within comedies designed for audiences increasingly heterogeneous as new, unconventional social practices called for new efforts of tolerance. Joseph Arrowsmith's *The Reformation* (1672?) has, in its most recent editor's opinion, "a conservative stance on art, religion, and the relations between the sexes" (Payne, Introduction

v) and numbers of scholars have taken it, we think on very slim evidence, as a general rebuttal to the scandalous doings in *Marriage A-la-Mode*. The main plot does involve a wild quartet of lovers' settling down into traditional wedlock, with no behavior more antisocial than tying up an old virago and later doping her and a "heavy" father so that the lovers can sneak off to marry. While this plot exalts true love and wedlock, though, a more dour true lover who stands up for orthodox morality ends up humiliated and vengeful; a hypocritical and unfaithful husband is called "truly noble" (V; 78) for settling financially with his hypocritical and unfaithful wife so that each can enjoy an illicit affair; the wife's lover intends to repay her lavishness to him from the funds of a rich wife whom he seeks for himself; and the fool of the play marries "for love and Virtue" (V; 78) a witty woman who intends to profit from his folly and purse. "Conservative" values in 1672, then, mean a main plot in which the characters talk but do not act like libertines and two cynical subplots that turn on sex, money, and exploiting others' credulity. In its appeal to a heterogeneous audience, *The Reformation* develops compromise formation from the "reform" of its lip-service libertines and from demoting "immorality" into a subplot, but the emphasized innocence of the main plot allowed—or should we say, required?—more actual sexual liberty in that subplot than one finds in the less conservative *Marriage A-la-Mode*.

Not surprisingly, therefore, some of the less clever, up-to-date authors did not manage any compromise formation in their plays of the early-to-mid 1670s. Their easygoing, minor comedies relied mostly on happy amorality, a general call for tolerance. Speaking for the latitude we invoked in chapter 2, Townlove, one of the heroes of Nevil Payne's *The Morning Ramble, or, The Town-Humours* (1672), declares: "Since no Action, be it good or bad, but hath it's vouchees, I am for letting every one have his humour, and only beg that I may have mine, which terminates always in the consent of the parties I deal with, and the Devils in't if there can be harm in that, to which all Persons concern'd give their approbation" (I; 10). At the end of act V Townlove embraces the clever servant Rose as his mistress, declaring, "*Rose*, I'le warrant e'm thee and I will secure one anothers Reputations."

> For want of Custom wonders doth produce,
> And ills do lose that Name by frequent use.

At the end of J.D.'s *The Mall: or, The Modish Lovers* (1674), a play of elaborate, cynical sexual intrigue, all the characters take lovers if they can.

With authority so frail, normative standards multiply, depending on the occasion. Thus, though love as an ideal in these comedies makes licit whatever is needed to attack marriages of convenience (cf. Vernon), that other great social ideal, money, equally legitimates characters' actions toward such marriages. This is the case, as we have said, in *The Reformation*. When the disguised Camilla of *The Mall* asks Courtwell, grieving over her supposed death, if he can "talk of marrying any," he responds, "Why not, Sir, whilst there be woman and money to be had, and I suppose you will be of my mind too" (V; 64). In Caryll's *Sir Salomon*, the hero Peregreen Woodland promises his sister, sight unseen, to the rich ninny Sir Arthur Addle, as the hero Fairlove promises his, in her absence, to Sir Timothy Fop in Thomas Rawlins' *Tunbridge Wells: or a Days Courtship* (1678); indeed, another sister of Fairlove, the witty Courtwit, chooses to marry a lamebrained knight with two thousand pounds a year. Similarly, Flora in John Leanerd's *The Rambling Justice, or the Jealous Husbands*, first performed the month before Rawlins' play, marries Sir Geoffrey Jolt with the comment, "Those softheaded Husbands are the easiest Creatures to work upon; a Woman may doe what she pleases, keep a Gallant in Town, or maintain a comely Servant in the Country; who shall be as proud to effect my Will, as I desirous to command him" (V; 61). The relevant opposition in all the plays we have listed here is not love versus money but freedom versus compulsion, less an ideal of social benefit than a libertarian principle rooted in viewers' identification with individual characters. Woodland and Fairlove have their unengaged sisters' interests foremost, one is to suppose, and the sisters will freely ratify their brothers' pocketbook prudence.

What is reduced in these plays to a whisper, at most, is a positive image of marriage as a genuine mediator between societal order and those individual needs, like love and sexual desire, that can perpetuate community. Many of the plays seem to support this mediating role negatively, attacking mercenary and sexless (January-May) marriages with satire and the threat of sympathetic cuckoldry. But one should not blandly assume that the real foe of such comedies is the abuse of marriage—a thumpingly orthodox position—when the plays might just as well be read as sneering at any and all marriage except as a social convenience or convenience to wrap up a plot. Some contemporaries certainly did read them that way. In the conservative, anonymous *Mr. Turbulent: or, the Melanchollicks* (1682), written after the excitements of the Exclusion Crisis had made consensus and orthodoxy more respectable, the hero Fairlove responds to his comrade Friendly's saying that marriage "is grown as much out of Fashion as Trunk Breeches" with "Away, away, let's have no tilting against Marriage, the Theam is grown thred-bare, there is scarce a Comedy without it, the Poets and the Stage have laught at it so long, that they begin to be laught at themselves for it" (I; 4).

Those who saw the comedies as internally consistent would not have found defenses of marriage per se throughout many of them. Instead, if one applies a rule of consistency, the comedies endorse freedom and sexual pleasure, which could be won through a divorce—that is, a legal separation—rather than (or as well as) a marriage. Effectually that is what happens in the marital subplot of *The Reformation*, and it happens openly elsewhere. "The word *divorce* is heard in . . . John Dover's *Mall*, . . . Thomas Rawlins' *Tom Essence; or, The Modish Wife* (1676), and D'Urfey's *Fond Husband* (1677)," writes Susan Staves (160; on divorce law 145–55). Shadwell's *Epsom-Wells* (1672) ends with the Woodlys' divorce. In addition, the Manleys' marriage disappears in the course of *The Mistaken Husband*, and Behn's *The Town Fop, or Sir Timothy Tawdrey* (1676) ends with a promise to void a marriage. Some 1670s plays that support marriage, too, support it not as a social institution but as a matter of individual taste and pleasure. They also denature it from what Shadwell's parson Sneake names "the Mysterious Union of a Conjugal Knot, beyond the Gordian, too strong for the *Macedonian* Steel to rescind" (*The Humorists* V; 246). Marriage in the 1670s lacks the finality it has in earlier plays, where characters end up with each other for better or for worse, "better" being the presumption for unions promised at the ends of comedies even though "worse" fits better than "better" those unions actually depicted.

As one might expect, finally, numbers of 1670s' comedies, including all three of the plays on which we shall focus, present such male/female relations in settings where more general social authority loses meaning. These comedies may, for example, suspend social authority, as in the carnival time of *Love in the Dark* and *The Rover*, where rank and other sorts of social identity are at once insisted upon (a given of Spanish or Italian settings) and blurred. The plays may exhibit parodic authorities, such as mock astrologers and similar pretenders. This worn theatrical currency takes on in the 1670s a new value of counterfeit, showing representatives of more standard ethical or religious systems replaced by astute cozeners who set up their own false laws, as in *The French Conjuror* or Matthew Medbourne's version of *Tartuffe*. A similar vacuum of belief is filled by other trendy kinds of credulity, like that of Sir Nicholas Gimcrack in *The Virtuoso*, and even, in playwrights who deplore modern times, like the newfangled hedonism of Shadwell's Don John in *The Libertine* or of Edward Howard's Sir Ralph Nonsuch, "a Luxuriast" (Dramatis Personae) who rails against religion and the state in *The Man of Newmarket*. The fool and his tutor who enlist their self-interested friends to "reform" Venice on the English pattern in Arrowsmith's *The Reformation* are in the same camp. Broader yet, finally, is the collapse or compromising of authority which we have discussed in *Marriage A-la-Mode*. Another version of it occurs in *The Plain-Dealer*, where Manly, who has "procur'd the Command of a Ship, out of Honour, not Interest" (Dramatis Personae), has honorably sunk that ship in the face of a Dutch victory and the English court's indifference. This national weakness on the seas is matched by the red tape and red herrings that foul up the law at home. Such topsy-turvy communities allow the entrepreneurial heroines and heroes more scope to set out rules for behavior, whether through the apothegmatic laws of *moraliste* wit, the operatively defined laws of "nature" that they follow, or the social patterns that they enforce through what they do and what they satirize.

The Virtuoso

In a friendly critique of "hasty Shadwell" in "An Allusion to Horace," written within six months or so before *The Virtuoso*, Rochester remarks that

> Shadwell's unfinished works do yet impart
> Great proofs of force of nature, none of art:
> With just, bold strokes he dashes here and there,
> Showing great mastery, with little care. (44-47)

The force of art, though, is visible everywhere in the plot of *The Virtuoso*, which could serve as a textbook example of balanced construction. Two gentlemen, Bruce and Longvil, long for the Virtuoso's two nieces, Clarinda and Miranda respectively, but each niece loves the man who loves the other niece. The third lady in the house, the Virtuoso's wife Lady Gimcrack, lusts after both Bruce and Longvil. Each of the nieces has another suitor, the solemn orator Sir Formal Trifle, who flourishes in worn tropes, and the merry wisecracker Sir Samuel Hearty, who flourishes in "original" bywords, like "in the twinkling of a Bed-staff" (I; 112), and enjoys "hearty" roistering. Sir Formal is welcome in the Gimcrack house, Sir Samuel not. Sir Nicholas Gimcrack, the Virtuoso himself, cultivates the new (knowledge of contemporary science), and keeps a pert mistress, Flirt. His complement in the dramatic scheme is his houseguest Snarl, his uncle who decries the new (the manners and morals of others in the present age) and keeps a mistress, Figgup, who feagues him (flogs him) like a schoolboy. Sir Nicholas' mistress, Flirt, and Lady Gimcrack's kept man, Hazard, round things off by sleeping with each other.

Despite Shadwell's dogged loyalty to Jonson, this arrangement harks back to fletcherian practice, which it suits to a T. Jonson's comedies at all popular on the Restoration stage—*The Alchemist, Bartholomew Fair, Epicoene, Every Man In,* and *Volpone*—have no such elaborate balance among their dramatis personae. Shadwell's symmetrical lovers and symmetrical lusts, moreover, cannot function to suggest a cross section of a community of fools and knaves, as character diversity does in Jonson. Instead, the scheme of order in *The Virtuoso*, exercising its fletcherian powers, controls and classifies a full scheme of nature, the whole rerum natura rather than (as in Jonson) the part that needs chastening. Bruce and Longvil, according to the Dramatis Personae, are "Gentlemen of wit and sense," and Miranda and Clarinda are at least their equals. No wonder Bruce, when the play opens, is reading Lucretius about necessity and a distant, Epicurean nature: the busy experimenting and ogling virtuosi in their own idle way may simulate the role of emotionally unmoved mover, but that role really belongs to the hero as satiric raisonneur—the position Bruce and Longvil immediately assume in act I—and, beyond that, to the playwright. The emotionally unmoved movers, that is, are those who serve as the choric, reliable agents of the audience. (The lovers in more passionate moments, of course, also serve as the agents of other audience interests; Lucretian heights are necessary but insufficient locations in *The Virtuoso* as in the model, Carolean Comedy.)

Fletcherian construction also calls for symmetries and reversals in the action of the play. Dryden and Davenant's *Tempest* creates its main interplot symmetries and reversals between the "low" and love actions, *Marriage A-la-Mode* between "high" and "realistic" actions, but *The Virtuoso* between the love plot and fragmentary, parodic display scenes. One of the two unifying motifs for these display scenes, ironically, is concealment: all the sexual activity, of course, is hidden and also involves much hiding. Two of the three illicit couples hide together in a wood-hole (act IV); Sir Formal and Sir Samuel end up trapped in a dark vault together (acts III–IV); Sir Samuel disguises himself as a footman (act II), a woman (acts III–IV), and Scaramouch (act V), and after leaving a masquerade, he makes a final (non-)appearance in a "Chest of Goods" sent to Miranda; Sir Formal marries the masked maid Betty, whom he has taken for Clarinda. On the level above that of the buffoons come the trysts that Lady Gimcrack engineers with Bruce and Longvil in a grotto (act III) and—when she is disguised—a room during the masquerade (act V), in hopes of supplanting Clarinda and Miranda in their lovers' hearts (or lusts) or, failing that, at least of derailing their mutual happiness.

Wholly within the love plot is an analogue to these concealments, the two women's successful intimation that the gentlemen must switch the targets of their affection, with Bruce taking the woman Longvil loves and vice versa. This discovery for the men must be engineered by the women covertly, for social restrictions on their sex allow them to reveal only through concealing, by decorous indirection. "[U]njust Custom!" cries Miranda, "has made Women but passive in Love, as if Nature had intended us for Cyphers only, to make up the number of the Creation" (III; 143). But in this play, as in its opening quotation from Lucretius where "ev'ry deity must live in peace, / In undisturb'd, and everlasting ease" (trans. Creech 2: 606–7), the active and passive may merge. Act III, for example, presents three meaningful but cryptic ways of (not) talking about love. Clarinda and Miranda refuse to speak of love with their lovers (whom they want to exchange); Lady Gimcrack, in trying to take the place of each successively with these same lovers, protests her innocence and honor in a manner ostentatiously tongue in cheek; and then Miranda and Clarinda each takes the place of the other in agreed meetings with the surprised gentlemen whom they do love but who do not yet love them. Some of the concealments, then, are designed by the characters for discovery or partial discovery, as all the concealments are destined by Shadwell for discovery. These discoveries about people—theoretical and practical—counter Sir Nicholas' new insights into insects, air, and the like, just as the resolution of the plot counters the formulaic, deadly "healing" he practices.

Concealments and discoveries provide one plain source of fletcherian peripeteias. In *The Virtuoso*, they exist in the midst of other interrupted and reversed actions, like assignations begun and left dangling between the gentlemen and Lady Gimcrack, Snarl and Figgup (twice), Hazard and Lady Gimcrack, Sir Nicholas and Flirt. Sir Samuel's various disguises lead to his being "pumped," tossed in a blanket, dumped into the vault, kicked (as Scaramouch), and stood on his head inside a chest. Sir Formal falls through a trap door in midspeech about a trapped mouse. Sirs Formal and Nicholas are broken in upon by angry Luddites whom Bruce and Longvil disperse, as later in the same act (V) bullies break up the masquerade by inconclusive brawling (175) just before Bruce and Longvil's fight is broken up by the women; three successive shifts in advantage follow, as the men denounce the women, the women confound and break with the men, and the men in turn overhear the women confess their continuing love. At the end, the foolish characters who live by words,

Snarl with his satire and Sir Formal with his oratory, find themselves snared in the action of (degrading) marriage, while those who live by action, Sir Nicholas, the experimentalist, and Sir Samuel, the master of the "Intriguo," have no more than words of dismissal.

The second motif that unifies the farcical character scenes is that of transmutation and transfusion, a version of fletcherian analogy. It takes its note from the two heroines' interchangeability in the two heroes' affections, an interchangeability at once shallower and deeper than that in *Marriage A-la-Mode*, because at least on the page Shadwell—unlike Dryden—gives the leading men and women no individualizing mark, so robbing "love" of personal energy and making it merely in rerum natura. Lady Gimcrack generalizes this lateral interchangeability, since for her any lover except her husband will do. The other foolish characters exhibit lowering through interchangeability. Sir Nicholas thus equates insects and people. Ants have "a Republick resembling that of the States-General" (III; 140), tarantulas dance the pavane "with a kind of grave motion, much like the Benchers at the Revels" (142), and the spider who "misses its Prey . . . will retire, and keep its Chamber for grief, shame and anguish" (141); in fact one docile spider, Sir Nicholas', can be summoned by the name, Nick. An intercanine blood transfusion makes his mangy spaniel into a sound bulldog and vice versa (II; 128), but why maintain species lines? In the world of Gimcrackery, a madman transfused with sheep's blood "became wholly Ovine or Sheepish; he bleated perpetually . . . and a . . . Sheeps Tail did soon emerge or arise from his Anus or humane Fundament" (II; 130).

Sir Nicholas, who learns swimming from a frog, gives the cue for many characters to be named—hardly slandered—as animals during the course of *The Virtuoso*: mad dog (I; 113; and "dog" repeatedly throughout the play), monkey and puppy and drone (I; 115), toad (II; 122), owl (II; 123), mouse (III; 145), goat (IV; 149), insect and drone and dormouse and cuckoo (IV; 150), stallion (IV; 152), baboon (V; 180)—we do not pretend that the list is complete. In another way, this motif of interchange comprises Sir Samuel's self-transmutations through disguise and the other ridiculous characters' lechery and hypocrisy, so that all are something mindlessly instinctive or predatory that they pretend not to be. This is not wholly affectation: Sir Nicholas is a real as well as a mock virtuoso, and Snarl proves his love of the old days by reverting to schoolboyhood and cherishing the birch rod. But both have a lower nature (whether the one they show or the one they hide need not be clear) into which they effortlessly transmute themselves. All these interchanges, we should add, are elements of stability, not flux, in *The Virtuoso*.

Despite their common relation to fletcherian peripeteias and analogies, then, concealments and interchangeability occur differently in the love and the satiric plots. The same is true of other structural analogies. For example, Bruce begins the play with Latinity, reading Lucretius; very shortly afterward Longvil describes Sir Formal as "the most *Ciceronian* Coxcomb" (107); and the first scene ends with Longvil's comment about the Stoicism of noisy, "original" Sir Samuel, "Pox on him, he has read *Seneca*: he cares not for kicking; he never scap'd kicking in any disguise he ever put on" (113). Or again, after the "unwilling" Lady Gimcrack has her interrupted rendezvous in the grotto with Bruce and Longvil successively (III; 135–37), Sir Formal attempts sexual assault on the protesting Sir Samuel, dressed as a woman, when both are in the dark vault (IV; 147–49). Don R. Kunz brings up a third example, noting that when Bruce and Longvil must switch their hearts' allegiances (V; 177), "they continue to speak of their affections in reductive pseudo-scientific terms of transplanted vegetation, reflected sun beams, and bent metal" (201). "Reductive pseudo-scientific terms" are not only those of virtuoso-dom; they are also, of course, those of the real rerum natura, and one can read this analogy, like the others, as setting up an opposition between yielding properly to nature as one understands it (like the gentlemen in each of these three instances) and a wild oscillation between imposing upon it and not understanding it at all (like the satirized characters). None of the analogies demands to be read as casting a shadow on Longvil and Bruce, though of course we do not want to gainsay such a reading, which some members of the heterogeneous audience might prefer.

We would point out, however, that in accord with fletcherian style these analogies have no cognitive function. No one needs to learn through Longvil and Bruce about the nature or faults of Sirs Formal, Nicholas, and Samuel, or Lady Gimcrack. No one needs, either, to learn through the fools about the rakes. Those whom Shadwell proclaims "Gentlemen of wit and sense" (Dramatis Personae) appear in the opening scene, accurately, as rakish men-about-town who might be expected to have hangovers ("your Head-ake, and your Morning-Qualms," as Longvil puts it, 105), who "have run together into all the Vices of Men and Wit" and go to church only as "a fine Curiosity" (107). Both would cuckold Sir Nicholas in act III and do so in act V. The young ladies, too, accept the gentlemen as "Men of Wit and Pleasure" (I; 114; V; 176). Analogies, then, are broadly formal, in that they domesticate the extravagancies of the action. At their simplest, they exhibit events as rephrasings of other events, a technique for order and happy surprise, as when Sir Nicholas' practice swimming, thrashing about like a frog (II; 125-26), is immediately followed by Sir Samuel's being "soundly pump'd and toss'd in a Blanket" (II; 129). More generally, as we have said, analogies define a realm of nature in *The Virtuoso*.

Nature does not have much to do with Christian morality here. The only squabble among lovers arises not out of the gentlemen's infidelity or moral faults but their suspecting the ladies' faith and morals; one penitential sentence from each man clears the way for reconciliation, as Clarinda recognizes that "I love *Longvil* to that height, . . . I can forgive him anything" and Miranda, "I love *Bruce* too almost to distraction" (V; 176-77). Yet wedding bells do not ring for the quartette at the end of this comedy, not yet. Critics have hit on moral reasons why not. For Kunz, "There is just a hope that the guardians may graduate to husbands after further study compels them to regard their wards as other than fair game or property" (202), and Alssid explains "the girls'" caution from their knowledge "that lust dominates the rakes" (74). Our model, however, predicts that such interpretations will find favor only as part of a compromise formation to satisfy the most conservative members of the audience—in the repertory of the mid-1670s Bruce and Longvil are pretty tame, and for very few viewers do they need to be taken down a peg. Take Shadwell as sour on rakery and see the gentlemen punished by delay for their flightiness; but take Shadwell as in tune with the Carolean comedy mode in which male libido must be fixed in order to satisfy the woman who must look to the future, and see the marriages delayed in a way that asserts female power.

This alternative explanation for the denouement, that it allows the heroines to fix the affections of the heroes, follows from conditions specific to *The Virtuoso*, where the gentlemen have just shifted affections between heroines who are not well discriminated from each other, and this when in real life marriage was felt to be less final than it had been. For reasons of idiom, not ethics, by this reading, Shadwell could not easily patch up two weddings on such unstable grounds. So, since the young women are presumably between fourteen (the age after which one could choose a new guardian) and twenty-one (the age after which no guardian was needed), they make provisional tender of their goods and their hands, a kind of premarriage appropriate for the climate of the 1670s.[31] "You must have time to leave off

---

[31] Shadwell relies on a version of the law of guardianship revoked a few years earlier; by 12 Car.II c.24, a father who bequeathed guardianship of minors, as here, would thereby bind them till the age of twenty-one (Blackstone 1: 462).

your old Love, before you put on new," says Miranda at the end of the play (180), to which the sanguine Bruce responds with a *moraliste* generalization in a closing couplet: "*If Love can once a Lady's Out-works win, / It soon will master all that is within.*" Each reinforces the idiom of Carolean Comedy: she stresses the fixing of affection upon the heroine, he the compelling force of female desire for the hero.

The love plot of *The Virtuoso* tallies further with the model we proposed in chapters 1 and 2. It depicts its four characters' actions as both autonomous and driven, with the driving force being natural, all-powerful love. As in the model, Bruce and Longvil lower themselves in pretense, here by impersonating the "natural philosophers" whom Sir Nicholas approves, so as to win their subversive freedom to court his well-guarded nieces. Shadwell, moreover, bonds the susceptible audience to the young men in three familiar ways. First, he makes them clever, vital, and independent, leaving them almost wholly out of the blighting power of any character except the young women. The mutual passion of the lovers—circularly? cybernetically?—further marks them all as desirable because desired by those who are themselves desirable. Second, Shadwell gives his four young lovers verbal control and reflectiveness, which sometimes produce *moraliste* wit; our examples come from act II: "Old Fools always envy young Fools" (Longvil, 131); "A Man often parts with his honesty, but never with his opinion for a Bribe" (Miranda, 123); "There was the same Wenching [in the last Age]: only they dissembled it. They added Hypocrasie to Fornication, and so made two Sins of what we make but one" (Bruce, 132); "Most Men are apt to break [that is, default] in Womens debts" (Clarinda, 120). Their epigrams come as close as Shadwell's prose speakers may to the Lucretian ideal of penetrating sententiousness which Bruce praises in the play's opening speech. And third, by acting as commentators upon and manipulators of the foolish characters, the lovers become agents for the audience's amusement and the authentication of the audience's values and self-esteem. Shadwell intensifies this effect by making humours characters like Sirs Nicholas and Formal so exotic that they trigger no recognition from everyday life, unlike the exaggerations of everyday types in Jonson. Nothing is at stake when the audience laughs at the virtuoso, the Ciceronian coxcomb, or the noisy fool who "has never made Love where he was not refus'd, nor wag'd War where he was not beaten" (I; 108); the laughter is that of simple superiority, with the lovers as ushers, if not barkers for this sideshow.

The Virtuoso veers furthest from our model in offering so narrow a range of possible appraisals. Only one plot puts forth values that anyone could approve, and those values, moreover, are made norms for judging the deviant, though often accurate satirist (Snarl), the deviant, never accurate observer (Sir Nicholas), the deviant speakers (Sirs Formal and Samuel), the deviant rake (Sir Samuel), and the deviant contriver of plots (Lady Gimcrack). Each deviant element in these fools—satire, observation, elaborated speech, rakery, plotting—corresponds to a normative element within the type of the acid, aloof, witty, rakish, scheming protagonist. Shadwell approximates that type in Bruce and Longvil, and, except for the sexual zest, Miranda and Clarinda. This arrangement makes the "comedy of manners" central to the functioning of the "comedy of humours" but restricts the heterogeneity of value to one issue, whether one should see Longvil and Bruce as reformed rakes or as rakes in monogamous repose, converted by love and virtue or by the promise of Epicurean delights with a brisk, bouncing, and bountiful bride. That issue, admittedly, underlies compromise formation in many Carolean comedies, and like other playwrights Shadwell does leave it suitably unresolved. An orthodox moralist would hardly have done so, but few of them were in the business of writing Carolean comedies. Once Bruce and Longvil, "Men of the Town," learn faith in Miranda and Clarinda, who are very "little Women of the Town" (I; 114), and once the men declare that they do not want unwilling spouses (V; 177), they need and get no other overt purgation in *The Virtuoso*. And Lady Gimcrack escapes thwarted but otherwise pretty well unscathed.

Shadwell here subscribes to the principle that a Carolean comic playwright of the early-to-mid 1670s should do as much—in other words, as little—as necessary in order to send the audience out untroubled and smiling. If the hero shows himself dangerous, like Dorimant or Horner, then he must get a good measure of comeuppance before he triumphs. If the hero threatens to turn social contradictions into an excuse for profligate delight, like the quartet of lovers in the comic plot of *Marriage A-la-Mode*, self-love and social must ingeniously work out to be the same, so the threat dies away. If the hero follows a conventional love pattern, like Bruce and Longvil, he can with near impunity violate most other conventional values: he can be a rake, an Epicurean, a devotee of "private pleasure" who is amazed to be "caught any way in a Church" (I; 107), a man who would cuckold his host, and even, although the creature of a playwright who once claimed to write "for the reformation of Fopps and Knaves" (Preface, *The Humorists* 1: 184), a man who sneers philosophically, "say what we can, the Beastly, Restive World will go its way; and there is not so foolish a Creature as a Reformer" (107).

The Rover

The Virtuoso, with its relatively gentlemanly heroes, tests the limits of our paradigm. Not so Part I of *The Rover*, which one might choose as a prototypical Restoration comedy, with its "gay" and sober couples, its tyrannical brother and English country fool, its half-teasing devotion to love and honor, its moral muddles, its wit, trickery, masking, and bravado, and its multiple debts to pre-War comedies. Tucked by Allardyce Nicoll under the rubric "Comedy of Intrigue" (*History* 222–23), *The Rover* of course displays the episodic, peripatetic, cunningly plotted structure that we have called fletcherian. Willmore the rake bobs back and forth between the courtesan Angellica and Hellena the nun-to-be, with little detours after Valeria and Florinda; characters trot about disguised and battle in the dark; and the tug-of-war between the English and the Spanish Neapolitans, men and women, has a resolution only when the play itself does. The main action also embodies an ideology familiar in the Carolean Comedy model, for it ends with the courtesan Angellica, who offers mere love, unable to fix the desires of Willmore, while the wealthy virgin Hellena can bring him to marriage, "the accommodating of male inconstancy to the natural feminine desire for stability" (Musser 24).

As usual in fletcherian style, too, the "high" and comic (or sober and "gay") plots keep cognitive independence. They do not express the same morality. Belvile is admirably constant to Florinda and Willmore admirably—or so it seems—inconstant to every woman. They do not express the same counsels of prudence. Willmore has a whore fall in love with him and give him money in her house, and Blunt has a whore pretend to fall in love with him and steal all his portable possessions in her house, from which he is dumped into a sewer. In fact, *The Rover* has no counsel of prudence because no kind of action has a probable consequence, so engrossed is Behn in fletcherian reversals. For success, skill in ad hoc maneuvers matters a lot but, until the end, promises nothing, for too much is random. At last, fate rewards the best players under each set of rules, for want of any other mode of closure.

Inconsistent treatment of moral issues like honor and prudence in *The Rover* insures that they appear only as materials for enlivening the plot or for offering a compromise formation. Underlying them is a more consistent, familiar code: men bind themselves by promises or implied obligations (for example, sticking by a friend, defending the outnumbered) to other men. Still more power inheres in the call of nature, love and, to some extent, lust. Thus love would allow Belvile, the man of honor, to seize upon a mistake and take Florinda in marriage though her brother gives her to him believing him to be the viceroy's son Antonio, whose clothes he is wearing (IV.ii). Men certainly do not bind themselves by promises to women—"I never heard of mortal Man, that has not broke a thousand Vows," says Willmore (V; 95). Nor do they have natural obligations to women in sexual matters: at the low end of the scale, Frederick and Blunt decide not to rape Florinda only because "'twou'd anger us vilely to be truss'd up for a Rape upon a Maid of Quality, when we only believe we ruffle a Harlot" (IV.iii; 85). These are not admired characters, especially Blunt, but Frederick at least is the friend of Belvile and Willmore. The lack of obligation to women is also a free-market condition, not, so to speak, a feudal condition in which dominance implies responsibility. Thus Englishmen treat as possessions even women whom they neither love nor have married, nor for whom they have assumed guardianship in the manner of Spanish brothers (here, Don Pedro). For example, Willmore, who has deceived Angellica and longs to sleep with another woman, can still be up in arms at the arrival of Antonio, who has paid Angellica for her services: "How is this, a Piccaroon going to board my Frigate! here's one Chase-Gun for you" (III.iv; 61). Behn makes these conditions between men and women quite clear; it is not so clear that she objects to them. If they imperil women, they also offer the chance for freedom and power, in the Carolean Comedy way.

As in other foreign comedies that succeeded *The Adventures of Five Hours*, *The Rover* celebrates English freedom over Latin strictness (and Catholicism): "I am of a Nation," Willmore boasts, "that are of opinion a Woman's Honour is not worth guarding when she has a mind to part with it" (V; 103). In practice such freedom raises the risks as well as benefits for women, since "has a mind" means "can be wheedled or swindled." "Freedom," whatever its connotations of airiness, gaiety, and choice, implies not freedom from society but contractual engagement within it, the resolution of a Hobbesian state of nature, where sexual interchanges are likely to be predatory, impoverishing, nasty (if taken seriously), brutish, and fickle. *The Rover* shows this state skirted by the sober couple, the constant Belvile and Florinda and dealt with contractually by the "gay couple," Willmore and Hellena. The Hobbesian battle brings a third couple, Willmore and Angellica, to sorrow for her (from his fraudulent protestations) and potential death for him (from her will to use force, a gun), for "Force, and Fraud, are in warre the two Cardinall vertues" (*Leviathan* I: 13).

Behn creates a Hobbesian state of nature by plunging her audience into near anarchy, the comic anarchy of an exotic city, Naples, at carnival time. At the Neapolitan carnival everyone is still more at sea, still more divorced from "normal" behavior, still more apt to conceal and change identity (and to expect the same from others) than is usual in comedy. The setting also shields the characters' adaptive behavior from serious challenge. Within this anarchic context, no nature stands behind moral options as in the serious plot of *Marriage A-la-Mode*. Some characters opt to be moral, like Florinda and Belvile, others not. In any event, the play, with both kinds of characters and both kinds of members of the audience, turns moral issues into rhetorical instruments. For example, when Willmore seduces Angellica's hitherto virgin heart (II.ii), he claims to scorn her mind, for poor as he is he would not sell himself as she does (38); she responds that men practice "the same mercenary Crime" in asking of a prospective wife not "how fair, discreet, or virtuous she is; but what's her Fortune—which if but small, you . . . basely leave her, tho she languish for you" (40). Willmore wins her with his answer, no doubt truthful, "It is a barbarous Custom, which I will scorn to defend in our Sex, and do despise in yours." Not too long after this concord on lack of mercenary motives, fairness, discretion, and virtue, however, Angellica wishes Willmore mercenary, so that she can believe that he has courted Hellena for her 200,000 crowns (IV.ii; 71), and indeed the sum makes him slaver ("Ha, my Gipsy worth two hundred thousand crowns!—oh, how I long to be with her—pox, I knew she was of Quality."). Of course he knows nothing of her virtue and nothing creditable about her discretion. When he agrees to marry Hellena, however, he invokes no social standards (virtue, discretion, money), but exults in a match of like spirits ("I adore thy Humour and will marry thee, and we are so of one Humour, it must be a Bargain") and claims that he "lov'd her before [he] either knew her Birth or Name" (V; 101, 103). In motivating Willmore this way, the play evokes different schemes of moral and social value—those in which baseness and scorn have meaning, in which money and birth rouse desire, in which birds of a feather soar together—and commits itself to none of them.

The rest of the play, too, bears several similar traces of a moral typology it does not really mean. Thus the lustful Blunt, stripped of finery, must crawl through a sewer; the woman who sells herself loses any chance for true love; the loyal cavaliers who, the play implies, have lost by following the exiled court (I.ii; 17), anticipate by their own good fortune the restoration of their princely master. None of these is developed, let alone developed consistently. The disparate moralities that are staged and given equal weight in *Marriage A-la-Mode* reappear in *The Rover*, weighted unequally through a process of allusion, to enliven and variegate the comedy and to enhance its capacity to placate those who might otherwise find it wholly amoral.

Flurries of emotion, suggesting depth and responsibility in the characters, such as Angellica, give the illusion of moral intensity and thereby encourage a compromise formation for those who wish one. At the same time, Willmore's charming naturalness casts a light of innocence on even his most dubious activities, so that the moral intensity has no central object of praise or blame, and for most viewers, we suspect, expresses itself as an invitation to empathic emotions, like pathos or sympathetic delight.

In the absence of more than these bare traces of moral standards, however, *The Rover* presents only patterns for achieving desires. The Rover himself plainly enacts the wishes of many men in the audience, for he epitomizes male success in fighting, drinking, taking risks, maintaining gaiety and wit, and attracting women. By use of analogy, Behn at once makes this embodiment of natural desire dominate the play and normalizes his extravagance: Willmore is the play's focal character by drawing into himself the wishes and strengths of all the others. Like Angellica, he has an irresistible image used for conquest. "Thou hast a Power too strong to be resisted," she sighs, because that image—his appearance, his demeanor, his words—gives her what she wants. As she satisfies male lust and fantasy for a price, so he converts her from merchandise to angel, rapt in a delusion of regained purity, of true, nonvenal love (II.ii; 42). His really promiscuous but seemingly constant ardor traps Angellica, the whore with a long-term rental service, while he in a sense takes over her role as prostitute, receiving money from her that anticipates, of course, the enormous portion that comes with Hellena. If he wins Angellica by both being and serving a type of Angellica, his ardent promiscuity enchants a Hellena whose temper would lead her the same way. She after all is the "little Rover," as Blunt calls her (V; 104), who has tempted her sister to ramble with her into the carnal carnival of Naples.

As Willmore doubles the women in *The Rover*, so he doubles the men: Belvile, whose goal is Don Pedro's sister Florinda, with whom he trysts and who is to be saved from forced marriage; and Ned Blunt, who successively wants to whore (with Lucetta), to be revenged on womankind, and at the end, when he enters dressed like a Spaniard, to be at once included within and excluded from the group of Spaniards in Naples. Like Belvile, Willmore trysts with and weds one of Don Pedro's sisters, this one snatched from another threat to Latin life and love, confinement in a nunnery. He enacts Blunt's frustrated desires by whoring and making his whore miserable, and by being both Spaniard (as Hellena's husband) and Englishman at last. Even part of the compromise formation, much of which is rendered unnecessary because Willmore's high-spirited, extraverted recklessness keep him from threatening the audience, comes from his resembling Blunt in some blunders. First, in act III, just after Blunt's mishap with someone else's mistress, Lucetta, the drunken Willmore enrages his friend Belvile by trying to whore a woman who turns out to be Florinda, whom Blunt shortly thereafter (IV.iii) threatens with rape. More vaguely, Willmore's untimely openness and brawling (IV.ii) suggest Blunt's country modes of proceeding. Attached in these ways to every major character in *The Rover*, the Rover dominates not only the action but also the expression of a variety of moods and tastes. He thus appears so normal, so according to nature, that Behn needs no further compromise formation beyond the obvious moral ending, Willmore's agreeing to marry shortly after denouncing the idea (V; 100–103).

Willmore, then, gains a firm representative status by being so variously interchangeable with the other characters. Fletcherian style, with its analogies, its disguisings, its uniform human nature (in the Carolean theatre), and its treatment of characters as placeholders within elaborate plots, of course encourages interchangeability, which is even more pronounced in this play than in *Marriage A-la-Mode* and *The Virtuoso*. Not only Willmore's flitting from wench to wench but the whoring of Blunt and Frederick, the concealment of Belvile, Florinda, Hellena, and Willmore in vizards or disguises or darkness, the substitution of Willmore for Belvile (III.iii) and Belvile for Antonio (IV.i–ii), Florinda's being taken for a slut first by Willmore, who "consider'd her as mere a Woman as I could wish" (III.iv; 60), and later by Frederick and Blunt—all these stock situations of intrigue plays, embodied in this play by vivid, individualized characters, bring to the fore two rival claims. One is that of distinction, the hero and heroine as skillful, attractive, flamboyant; the other, that of interchangeability, the hero and the heroine as types who meet certain standard needs of the other characters and of the audience. We argued in chapter 2, on the analogy of star athletes in team sports (or other kinds of star performers in various kinds of repertoire), that central characters in Carolean comedy had to meet both these rival claims so as to create and enact the desires of a composite public. The idiom of *The Rover* makes that dual capacity quite visible.

Interchangeability applies to women as it does to men, with added complications because women more typically represent substitutable objects of desire for male characters than vice versa. As Willmore rhymes it: "For tho to worse we change, yet still we find / New Joys, New Charms, in a new Miss that's kind" (IV.ii; 77). Like the female leads in *Marriage A-la-Mode* and *The Man of Mode*, Hellena performs the heroine's necessary labor, mending the hero's inconstancy with the homeopathic medicine of captivation and noncommitment. As to a lesser extent in the 1660s, women do best in the comedies of the 1670s by emulating men and using freedom as a weapon for procurement. And among the narrative ends served by the abundant breeches parts in 1670s' comedies, as we have noted earlier, is the raising of a woman through her daring to assimilate herself to a man. Since Carolean comedies normally suppose women equal to men, mentally, emotionally, and in human nature, and also stress their inequality before law and custom, the ruse of breeches makes narrative sense. Thus in *The Plain-Dealer* Fidelia must display manly love and courage, even to being wounded, before Wycherley awards her Manly to her, and she, like Hellena and the two heroines in the comic plot of *Marriage A-la-Mode*, dresses as a male. (Miranda and Clarinda in *The Virtuoso* do not, but they do take the male role of choosing lovers.) To be a woman with whom the audience bond, then, Hellena must be effectively a man acting under a set of special constraints. "Egad," cries Willmore to Hellena with his last bachelor's gasp in the closing speech of *The Rover*, "thou'rt a brave Girl, and I admire thy Love and Courage." Her success allows her to prescribe with Willmore a contract of Hobbesian origin: it is based upon fear of loss caused by someone relatively equal in strength who follows a law of nature common to both parties. Even afterward, she has the implied need of keeping him fixed by keeping him fearful, meeting his strength with her own in a kind of perpetual isometric exercise of the will, in the manner of Florimell, Doralice, or Harriet (in *The Man of Mode*). Her power, still more than the virginity that she is about to lose and that she exploits for every bit of its exchange value, is what really distinguishes her from Angellica.

Hellena, then, gets and holds the inconstant Rover by displaying her wares enticingly and by letting Willmore purchase them only for an equal offering, himself. Similarly, she gets and holds the audience through display and compromise. She shows them her wares, which are superior to their own, and, simultaneously by appearing before them in tight breeches, submits to their (nonendangering) desires. Women's bodies, the locus of attraction in which they differ from men, are—by Willmore's apothegm about finding new charms in a new, kind miss even if she is "worse" than the familiar, kind miss (IV.ii; 77)—that in which they are essentially interchangeable, however much the men exclaim that their beauty is incomparable. Women's minds, the locus of attraction in which they resemble men, are that by which they are individuated. This ratio helps bring together Willmore's relations with Angellica and Hellena. Angellica appears in the play first as an erotically enticing image on public display, when her picture is hung outside her house to advertise her. She prices her power at a thousand crowns a month, social counters for respect, physical pleasures, and freedom. Since exactly those benefits are pledged by Willmore's own display, his freely (in every sense) given and richly gilded rhetoric of love, her surrender of her power to him has an obvious logic to it. She has put herself forth as a social image only, therefore an interchangeable one, and she gets paid in common, transferable coin. Willmore creates "money" or exchange value according to social practice, as he says, the practice that the semblance of individual feeling facilitates and masks. Of course Angellica has more to offer than her body: genuine and pleasing honesty, shrewd social observation, and real emotion. One feels sorry that she loses Willmore, because she has become a person by the time that happens. But Behn has given Hellena a sprightlier version of each of these appealing qualities, and so, in the Neapolitan marketplace, Hellena wins the man.

Of course Hellena, with whom *The Rover* opens, prices herself differently. She advertises herself not as an image of desirable woman but as a type of desirable person who refuses to surrender power, comradeship, and sexuality by going into a nunnery, forever off display: "Have not I a world of Youth? a Humour gay? a Beauty passable? a Vigour desirable? well shap'd? clean limb'd? sweet breath'd? and Sense enough to know how all these ought to be employ'd to the best Advantage: yes, I do and will" (I.i; 11). As mere image of woman or body of woman she is interchangeable with others, so could not in that way force constancy upon Willmore, though she can lure him in the first place by an Angellica-like display of her face (III.i; 48), a token (as with Angellica) of the interchangeable body though (as not with Angellica) of a virgin's body. Hellena then makes the most of what she has shown him by becoming one of the boys, one of the very best of the boys, and forcing him to accept her self-image, as her rival does only after the prize has been lost. Angellica graduates from being merely another mad cast mistress, like Loveit in *The Man of Mode*, when she too proves manly in presenting the pistol to Willmore's breast and then granting him life "to show my utmost of Contempt" (V; 98). Her stature here, and Willmore's amazement, suggests again that Behn had less interest in moral points about whores, not a common theme in Carolean comedy, than in what is perhaps the most insistent theme of Carolean comedy, the self-creation of personal value, hence of personal power.

The interplay between social image and personal image that Behn thematizes with Hellena and Angellica usually appears in satire throughout Carolean comedy, as it does here when Blunt is on display.

Moraliste Comedy

Since he is the only dolt in *The Rover*, she makes the most of him. Thus the audience see him creeping from the sewer (III.ii; 55); then Frederick announces his plight to their friends and visits him (IV.iii; 79-80, 83), until in act V all the men come, and when "Blunt *looks simply, they all laugh at him*" (s.d., 87). He makes his appearance at the end "*in a* Spanish Habit, *looking very ridiculously*" (s.d., 104), the more so because he had departed the stage earlier in act V dressed only in shirt and drawers. As the only dolt in *The Rover*, too, Blunt needs to have a kind of comprehensiveness, and so in the first two scenes where he appears he sounds most of the themes in the play, as witness his "Joy [in] a cheap Whore" [I.ii; 17] (what rake would think of paying at all? and if paying, would look for bargains?), his lack of Stuart loyalty, his vanity about his image ("I have Beauties which my false Glass at home did not discover" [I.ii; 23]), his self-advertising ("[his] Humour is rather to have a proclaim'd Clap, than a secret Amour"[II.i;28]), his folly at exchange, and his gullibility about appearances. As in *The Virtuoso*, though, rather than as in *Marriage A-la-Mode*, the effect of the analogy is to isolate the palpable fool from the other characters and thereby to normalize their conduct. Blunt has what amounts to his own plot line, and he is the only major character in the play who is always seen as who and for what he is, the self-explanatory image understood by all save its possessor. Amusing but uninteresting, he neither marries nor is coupled with anyone, and in a Spanish habit, "the Mode of a Nation [he] abominate[s]" (V; 104), he ends the play as a man of no country rather than, like the lovers, of two.

We can indicate *The Rover*'s place as a comedy of the 1670s, finally, by glancing ahead to the years with which our two concluding chapters deal. The sequel to this play, *The Rover; or the Banish'd Cavaliers, Part II* (1681), strongly resembles it in plot and themes, such as nature, the sexual interchangeability of women, the enslavement of women by marriage, and the contest between love and money. Roles are similar too, for besides the Rover and fools, one has the friend (here, Beaumond), the sprightly "masculine" girl avoiding a socially imposed fate (here, Ariadne, designed for forced marriage), and the passionate, loving, gorgeous whore (here, La Nuche—cf. the slang term "nugging" for sexual intercourse). Yet, although the now dead Hellena's role in *Rover I* has devolved on Ariadne, she does not end up married to Willmore, whom she loves. Instead she renounces him in anger at his falseness (V.iii; 207) and turns to the fiancé whom she has spent five acts trying to escape, Beaumond. He in turn surrenders his paid rights to the whore La Nuche, whom he has pursued throughout the play, and settles for Ariadne, "the dull Property" of whom he earlier has wished to be "handsomly rid" (II.ii; 150; III.i; 153). Willmore goes off to live with La Nuche, an arrangement that he manages to equate with marriage: "You have a hankering after Marriage still, but I am for Love and Gallantry."

> So tho by several ways we gain our End,
> Love still, like Death, does to one Center tend. (V.iii; 211)

Obviously no compromise formation exists and marriage gets no due. True love calls for social consent but thrives outside social institutions (see Gewirtz 105). Behn lightens the whole enterprise by adding farce, through a plot in which Blunt and a new ninny, Fetherfool, decide to marry Jewish sisters, one a dwarf and one a giant, for their money; Willmore impersonates a mountebank, a Harlequin does tricks, and Fetherfool pretends to be a clock (V.iii; 202) and later is dragged off for an enema (211). Despite all the similarities between the two parts of *The Rover*, then, they are two quite different plays. In 1677 Behn wrote very much within the model of Carolean Comedy we sketched in chapters 1 and 2; by 1681, she was doing something different. What that was we will try to specify in chapters 8 and 9 through some modification of the hypotheses that we have been developing.

The Plain-Dealer

The Virtuoso, with its ladies and gentlemen really ladies and gentlemen, distant from its fools, arouses very little cognitive dissonance and therefore poses very limited interpretive problems. *The Rover* poses more. And to judge by modern reactions, *The Plain-Dealer* perhaps troubles critics above any other Carolean comedy: it is, writes Hume in a critical survey of Wycherley studies, "genuinely complex and problematical, a work we cannot respond to with assurance" ("Wycherley" 412). A "lack of internal norms," Hume goes on, "leaves the texts wide open to the importation of the reader's own standards and prejudices. . . . Wycherley is disconcerting because in *The Country-Wife* and *The Plain-Dealer* no definite attitude is established towards the protagonists" (414–15). We would add that in this, Wycherley deals plainly with the "lack"—or contradictory plethora—"of internal norms" that the inherited idiom of Carolean comedy usually masks. His plain dealing about the world (that it cannot be plainly dealt with) becomes visible because his comedies, and particularly *The Plain-Dealer*, are so energetically satiric as to warm into unusual life one's zeal for making judgments. By "satiric" we mean that he gives his protagonists a great deal of *moraliste* wit, so as to generalize laws of behavior from real or likely plot situations, and that he freely employs the display scene. (The same recipe, with less *moraliste* wit, creates so-called comedy of humours, for example in so differently configured a play as *The Virtuoso*.) One is made to want to make judgments but is given scant basis to do so, at least about the central figures. Some critics have projected this axiological problem of theirs into epistemological problems of Wycherley, as in Peter Holland's ingenious reading of *The Plain-Dealer*. We do not intend to offer a counterreading of this knotty comedy, since we have throughout balked at the univocal terms of judgment that readings often elicit. Nor can we take up all the issues that arise in it. But we will try to frame its issues through the idiom and problematic that we have been describing, to develop the description further and, we hope, to cast some light on the play.

Comparison with *The Virtuoso* suggests how common Wycherley's materials are. In both plays, main male characters open the play denouncing the modern world of noise and flattery; old-fashioned and newfangled fools (Snarl, Oldfox; Sir Samuel, Novel) and "Ceremonious[,] Supple, Commending Coxcomb[s]" (Sir Formal; Lord Plausible—so described in the Dramatis Personae to *The Plain-Dealer*) document the satire; chaste heroines suffer because their action involves both passion and passivity, while wives (Lady Gimcrack; Olivia) are lecherous; and obsessive, jargon-bound older figures lose their guardianship by their wards' free choice (Sir Nicholas; the Widow Blackacre). The plays also share, as does *The Rover*, stock thematic concerns having to do with various senses of nature: nature (the desire for sex, money, and approval, or even for love) served by hypocrisy (deceits, sometimes innocent ones); nature (truth of feeling) opposed by hypocrisy (affectation, prudent reticence, prudery); and nature (the world as it "really" is, a social environment within one must maintain a certain status) assuming and subsuming hypocrisy as characteristic of most human behavior in a sophisticated society.

If the materials for so much of *The Plain-Dealer* are common, one might expect common roles to contextualize Manly's. Wycherley has composed Manly of two sets of expectations, both also associated with gay blades like Bruce and Longvil or Willmore: the cynicism and apartness of the rake (marked almost allegorically by Manly's association with the exploitative, egoistic Vernish and Olivia, to whom at the start of the play he offers integrity and loyalty) and the integrity and loyalty of the true lover and friend (marked by his association with the generous Fidelia and Freeman, to whom during most of the play he offers cynicism and apartness). As the protagonist of the main plot, Manly flanks on both sides the self-serving cynicism and friend's honor of the other plot's protagonist, Freeman. His troubling abuse of Fidelia and bed tricking of Olivia are part of a rake's repertoire, just like his penetrating view of the world's follies. His capacity for faith is requisite for the true lover of Carolean comedies, except in the most darkly Hobbesian plots. As a composite figure, Manly has an unusual openness to ridicule by his own standards, allowing some equivalent of a compromise formation, before such a formation occurs in his simultaneous reward and chastening at the end.

To look at Manly as a partial variant of the rake is to focus upon a degree of social engagement often overlooked but quite clearly developed in the text. Manly has "many a Female acquaintance, whom [he] has been liberal to"; he "know[s] half the Town, ha[s] so many Friends, and ha[s] oblig'd so many" (V; 496; see also III; 456, where a "young Fellow" wants to marry "a Wench, that . . . [Manly] had lay'n with"). Notwithstanding his rough temper, his sailors feel free to rag him (I; 395), the Alderman knows him well enough—perhaps they have feasted together at "a Reader's dinner" (III; 452)—to greet him with "Captain, noble Sir, I am yours heartily d'ye see: Why shou'd you avoid your old Friends?" (III; 460), and the fops come to visit him in act I and later importune him to join them in drinking. "Gad," Novel declares, "all the fine things one says, in their company, are lost, without thee" (V; 503). Manly's skill at manipulating the bevy of acquaintances in Westminster Hall (III; 456–61) shows the keen, practiced observation of the rake in many Carolean comedies (P. Holland 196–97), and the same observation underlies his *moraliste* wit, crisp and balanced in its form as it enunciates empirical laws, albeit suffused with "the language of feeling" (Berman 467). Although as a plain dealer, not a grave appraiser, he relishes hyperbole, he characteristically wields it with deadly control. The text does not support a reading of Manly as a railing hermit, an aging ingenu who needs to be educated, or a pure idealist whose hands are dirty only with mariner's tar.

Manly also centers around himself the "ethical emphases" that Ben Ross Schneider finds central to the "finished gentleman" admired and rewarded in Restoration comedy: "Liberality, Courage, Plain-dealing, and Love" (22). These are, of course, also the mainstays of that rather raw gentleman, Willmore. Plain-dealing and love need not be documented for Manly, nor perhaps need his courage, social or physical; "Cowardice and I," he tells Fidelia sternly, "cannot dwell together" (I; 400), and cowardice is one of the most cutting charges he makes against anyone, from the boy Fidelia who cringes at battle to the foppish Novel with his useless dress sword. As to liberality, he offers Fidelia half his money when he dismisses her for her fear (I; 400); he has "sunk the value of five or six thousand pound of his own" to keep his ship from the Dutch and the courtiers (I; 392) and left an equal amount, the rest of his fortune, for Olivia (I; 407), from whom he no sooner recovers it than he offers it to Fidelia (V; 513–14). The last twenty pounds he has in the world he gives to his crew, asking Freeman "Wou'd you have the poor, honest, brave Fellows want?" (III; 462).

These "ethical emphases" of Schneider are reinforced by being shared among the characters who love Manly and truly stick by him. For all Freeman's being blamed for complaisance, he shows himself aptly named ("free" as "plainspoken"). He is frank to Manly (I; 397) and to others, even beginning his suit to the Widow by telling her he wants her money (II; 432). He is also courageous. The other two motifs, love and liberality, are Fidelia's, who has left "the present possession of Two thousand pounds a Year . . . to follow" Manly (V; 514). In bald contrast, Vernish and Olivia display avarice, falseness, and hypocrisy, and Vernish at least, who runs at Manly "*with a dark Lanthorn and a Sword*" before Manly has drawn (V; 511), a despicable cowardice. The contrast between Olivia and Fidelia, Vernish and Freeman, then, is not that between interested and disinterested motives, for the good and bad alike act to get what they want for themselves. Wycherley's comedies, like Carolean comedies in general, assume that, as the philosophical rector Joseph Glanvill put it in 1661, "every man is naturally a *Narcissus*, and each *passion* in us, no other but *self-love* sweetened by milder Epithets" (*Vanity of Dogmatizing*, qtd. in Kaye 1: lxxix n; cf. *Plain-Dealer* I; 398). But in the pursuit of what they want, Freeman and Fidelia risk themselves while Vernish and Olivia remain sordidly close. With such illuminating analogies and contrasts, Wycherley creates a plain-dealer who embodies admired values, indeed who carries them to an extreme such that some modern critics have seen in him an allusion to "high" or heroic plots, which Wycherley sardonically or quizzically or tongue in cheek brings into contact with gritty reality (Rogers 83, 96).

We assume that Wycherley did not expect everyone to find Manly overwhelmingly sympathetic, since he supplies the materials for a compromise formation by having the play first direct satire against Manly and then divert it. How seriously one takes that satire depends, as in any Carolean comedy, on how benign one feels toward the Manly we have described. The range of plausible response in *The Plain-Dealer* is exceptionally wide for Carolean comedies, as that in *The Virtuoso* is unusually narrow, but then this idiom has a great deal of tolerance within it. We note, however, that the drift of Wycherley's borrowings from *Le Misanthrope* suggests that he did intend a largely sympathetic Manly. Alceste loves a woman whom he knows to be egregiously flawed in just the ways he detests; Manly, by contrast, has been deceived by vows and tears from Olivia. Alceste declares a frightful hate ("une effroyable haine") against human nature and all people (I.i.114–18); Manly assumes without rage that in a state of nature "men devour one another like generous hungry Lyons and Tygers" (I; 408), a sentiment transferred to him from the *honnête homme* Philinte, not Alceste (*Misanthrope*, I.i.173–78), and he admits a "few good men in the World" (I; 390). Alceste engages in no satire or wit, unlike Manly, who provides witty satire throughout the act in which his character is established, nor is Alceste set off against a coxcomb and blunt sailors, for he disputes with the disinterested Philinte. Whereas Alceste rejects, till it is too late, the "solide et sincère" (I.i.245) heart of Eliante, Manly rejects Fidelia only as a cowardly boy, her disguise being good enough to fool everyone in the play. And unlike Molière, Wycherley does not offer a more socially attuned couple, for the sensible Eliza never even meets the sensible Freeman; in *Le Misanthrope* Eliante accepts the love of Philinte. Whether or not Wycherley was among those who found Alceste a noble, dignified figure of empathy to start with (Molière 1: 812), he consistently alters borrowed material in Manly's favor.

At the end of *The Plain-Dealer*, Manly is engaged to marry Fidelia and engaged in male friendship with Freeman. In his embrace of both, he—and the play—accepts and reconciles two ideologies that seem far apart. While Freeman embroils himself in pettifogging and wheedling the Blackacres, Fidelia, with her blank verse and her talk of love and honor, has the flavor of women in "high" plots, like "Bellario" in Beaumont and Fletcher's *Philaster*, a lord's daughter who follows her beloved Philaster disguised as a page, who sues for him with his mistress, with whom she is accused of adultery, and who is wounded like Fidelia. (Because Fidelia's creator, Elizabeth Boutell, specialized in breeches parts, she may have played "Bellario" late the previous season, May 1676; *LS* 244.) Wycherley mutes the fletcherian reversal in action—in *Philaster*, the climactic discovery that "Bellario" is a woman—by letting Fidelia reveal herself to the audience early (I; 406), and he substitutes a conceptual reversal: Fidelia's truth resides precisely in her willing disguise, in her way of not being a plain-dealer. This reversal brings her closer to Freeman than first appears.

One may explore this point through the contrast between Fidelia and Olivia, for Wycherley quite exactly defines Fidelia's way of oblique dealing by setting her actions against the feigning of the other actress with designs on Manly: Fidelia's virtue, voyage, surrender of Manly's money, and desertion of "her multitudes of Pretenders" in the North

(V; 514) correspond to Olivia's mouthing virtue, her false promise to voyage across the seas with Manly, her greed for Manly's money, and her hushing her marriage so as to bilk more suitors. At one level the difference between the women is that Fidelia acts from love, a socially approved passion, and Olivia from disapproved ones. At another level, the difference refers to the senses of nature which we mentioned as we began to discuss *The Plain-Dealer*. Fidelia's motives are natural in one sense of the term (immediate and naive), while Olivia's superimpose on a second sense (desire for sex and power) something that is natural in still a third sense (love of praise and fear of blame, a natural "approbativeness" as A. O. Lovejoy calls it). Typically, Carolean "high" and "low" plots endorse the first two kinds of the natural, whether the love of Palmyra and Leonidas or the healthy lust of Palamede and friends, but register ambivalence about approbative motives, like Rhodophil's shame at loving a wife even if she is Doralice. Olivia's approbativeness, then, calls attention to Fidelia's spontaneity, with its freedom to invoke standards other than the social mode.

This pairing of Fidelia and Olivia helps one understand the relation between the honorable friends, Fidelia and Freeman, who stand for analogous values—those we have mentioned—but in different modes. Roughly speaking, she is a rigorist and he a utilitarian in ethics. "High" plot protagonists in Carolean plays, all rigorists, measure acts as Fidelia does, against criteria of a priori value, embodied in notions like honor, love, truth, and courage. "There is nothing certain in the World, Sir," says Fidelia to Manly, "but my Truth, and your Courage" (IV; 469). "Low" plot characters, like Freeman, are most often utilitarians who measure acts against criteria of efficacy in fulfilling needs. As in *Marriage A-la-Mode* Dryden exaggerates the differences between parallel genres, so Wycherley here exaggerates those between ethical measures. He provides a romance ending for the absolutists, Fidelia and Manly; for the pragmatist, Freeman, he avoids even so conventional a romantic staple of fletcherian courtship plots as marriage. Specifically, he does not bring Freeman and Eliza together, giving Freeman needs that involve not sexual love but money, the prize most fungible for all situations. The compromise formation, letting the audience enjoy Freeman's conniving without feeling guilty about doing so, works because the Widow is so egregious and dishonest, a true cousin of Olivia, not because Freeman veers from his principle of utility.

Critics have found *The Plain-Dealer* puzzling in part because the two plots are taken to such generic extremes, one wholly eschewing courtship and the other drawing so heavily and perhaps so incongruously on romance. We suggest that each plot concludes with the decorum that its internal structure of values establishes. Nor do we see that Wycherley pushes one to prefer this set of norms to that, despite their sharp difference and the surprise of finding them both in the same comedy. Both rigorism and utilitarianism as methods of making ethical decisions have historically had strong philosophical backing, and indeed both retain their persuasive force nowadays, as witness John Rawls' influential *A Theory of Justice*, which challenges "the predominant systematic theory" of modern times, "some form of utilitarianism" (vii) with a Kantian rigorist system, deriving from the myth of original equality in social contract theory. Both methods were used to satirize hypocrisy in Wycherley's time. Pascal's *Lettres provinciales* (1656–57), for example, adopts Fidelia's rigorist criteria to flay Jesuit pragmatism; Rochester's "A Satyr against Reason and Mankind," essentially contemporary with *The Plain-Dealer*, assaults false reason and pride with utilitarian criteria like Freeman's. Neither seventeenth-century nor modern standards force a choice between Fidelia and Freeman in this play, which after all ends with Manly's giving his heart to Fidelia, whose inner truth rectifies Olivia's inner falsehood, and his hand of friendship to Freeman, whose free, frank nature shows up Vernish's opaque varnishes. Freeman's motives, in his financial straits, are as natural as Fidelia's, and might be thought as honorable as hers, if one can draw any inferences from Wycherley's own statements about his marriage to the Countess of Drogheda (McCarthy 141–42). To decide between Freeman and Fidelia, then, is as idle as deciding between the "high" and "low" lovers in *Marriage A-la-Mode*, though much more plausible, for as Dryden had brilliantly kept his two systems running in parallel, Wycherley has brilliantly kept them rubbing against one another, with Manly at the interface.

With the rigorist/utilitarian distinction, we can now bring together the roles of Fidelia and Freeman with that of Manly as male lead in Carolean comedy, including his satiric, *moraliste* wit and his involvement in a cuckolding plot. In tracing behavior to self-love and snatching the mask of altruism from the virtues, the French *moralistes* empowered a rigorist argument against utilitarianism: that no action, whatever its consequences, is virtuous if it redounds to self-love, as all moral actions do. Thus Jacques Esprit wrote, "depuis que l'amour propre s'est rendu l[e] maitre & le tyran de l'homme, il ne souffre en luy aucune vertu ni aucune action vertueuse qui ne luy soit utile" (1678; qtd. in Kaye, 1: lxxxviii–ix)—the self-love that is man's master and tyrant permits him only those virtues that are useful to him. Jansenists, strong Christians among the *moralistes* who believed in general human depravity, took the ubiquity of self-interest as evidence of that depravity. Not as a Christian but as a man of honor, Manly shares this attitude and puts into action the kind of rigorist principles Fidelia stands for, humiliating the fops and thwarting the crowd at Westminster Hall by his contemptuous manipulation of their self-serving humours. His satire again and again bites deep, and like other satiric heroes in Carolean comedy, he voices the contempt of the audience for empty vanity (the fops), an oppressive Establishment (the law), and cringing opportunism (the courtiers). S/he who attacks these standard comic butts is the audience's agent.

Manly unites this positive function with the positive attributes that we have mentioned—liberality, courage, plain-dealing, and love—and, moreover, does what he does from inner promptings, naturally, not from approbativeness as the fops do (V; 503, 507). His *saeva indignatio* is therefore an effect of his own freedom. Even Olivia, who despises him and who alone pronounces any serious criticism of him, attributes his behavior to a natural humour, "his own singular moroseness" (IV; 482). As Norman Holland usefully oversimplifies, Manly is not "a moralist. What he objects to in society is not wrongdoing, but the unwillingness to admit it—pretense and affectation" (98). A man of courage, Manly accepts, perhaps even stands for the revelation of nature and detests its concealment, Olivia and Vernish's element.

Manly's position, nonetheless, has three drawbacks for him. First, as a rigorist position, it involves a moral or aesthetic judgment as well as simply an observation about self-interest. Outraged as he is by behavior that Freeman finds a joke or an opportunity, Manly lacks the insouciance that wipes away all blame from 1670s heroes such as, most magically, Willmore. Second, when Manly makes exceptions to his indictments, like La Rochefoucauld, he has to go a step further than maxim makers and decide on specific exceptions in the normal course of life. He thus must violate what Moore calls "respect for the mystery of motive" in La Rochefoucauld, whose epistemological position was based on probability, a means for knowing humankind but rarely individual humans (34). Since in sifting virtue from vice Manly is likely to count as vice whatever looks like vice (which he labels brazenness or ethical blindness) and also whatever looks like virtue (which he labels hypocrisy), he has no way of testing such a principle of discrimination. Hence he relies on his intuition and ends up the prey of Vernish and Olivia. Third, he deludes himself into thinking that he is exempt from the self-delusion he sees everywhere around him; his amour propre takes the impossible form of denying his amour propre. He thus exemplifies his own keen observations. In this matter, Wycherley follows the rule that the more powerful the hero and the more s/he threatens the amour propre of the audience, the more s/he must undergo chastening in order to succeed, as Manly does, at the end of the comedy. Wycherley also follows the rule that the fools in the comedy have their own power, that of contamination. Their desire for flattery and, with Novel and Oldfox, for originality visibly infects Manly.

An overview of the play's structure, then, might look like the following. Wycherley satirizes the world at large, mostly through Manly, by elaborating the sense of the old proverb, "Plain dealing is a jewel but they that use it die beggars" (Tilley P382). He even literalizes the proverb in a stage prop, Manly's filched, then restored casket of jewels. However, Wycherley's fletcherian style calls for reversals and his *moraliste* style calls for undercutting disinterested motives. Manly and Freeman, therefore, can achieve plain dealing (display scenes of Olivia's and the Widow's dishonesty) only through self-interest and deviousness, in each case by using a "boy" (the disguised Fidelia, Jerry) as a pawn. The initial pattern here has been set by Fidelia, who facilitates her self-interested, passionate truth through the deviousness of disguise, using the image of a boy. As Fidelia's desires cause her simply to pursue Manly, true even as far as to pimp (after a fashion) for him, Manly and Freeman pursue their desires without knowing exactly where they will lead, and all three characters end with acts of restitution. As usual in Carolean comedy, the ideological basis of the plot relies on an assumption about nature, that motives are naturally so interested that the notion of plain dealing deconstructs. This assumption serves a romantic conclusion (the marriage of two like characters, Manly and Fidelia) and an amoral one (Freeman's blackmail) equally well.

Although the assimilation of Manly to other heroes of Carolean comedy admits the differences between *The Plain-Dealer* and other plays, it suggests that those differences can be understood within a common idiom. We return, then, to the questions that this study has consistently asked: how does Manly enact the audience's desires? how are they and he bonded? does the play follow fletcherian construction, and if so, how does that affect the relation between the two plots and their schemes of value? We have already given partial answers to all of these. Manly enacts the audience's desires by acting as impresario for the display of their enemies' folly and by scourging with impunity those to whom the audience in daily life might have to truckle. When Vernish and Olivia breach their promises toward him, he takes proper revenge by cuckolding the one, bed-tricking the other, and publishing their dishonor. Now acting rather than railing, he not only discharges his lust and takes a benefit (Olivia's body) which its owner deceitfully promised him (I; 407), but he also transfers his disabling temper to his enemies, for Olivia storms off and Vernish exits *"doggedly,"* that is, in an ill-tempered, surly manner. Manly thus also wreaks poetic justice upon two would-be adulterers. By the standards of Carolean comedy, Manly's bed trick is no rape, for as it involves no force, it falls under the civil law principle that punishes no one "for violating the chastity of her, who hath indeed no chastity at all, or at least hath no regard to it" (Blackstone 4: 213). But thoroughly to exculpate Manly's act, Wycherley juxtaposes it to real rape: Vernish plans to rape Fidelia and implies his having raped others, for he rages at his servant, "How durst you come in, when you heard a Woman squeak? that shou'd have been your Cue to shut the door" (IV; 488). Despite Manly's weak judgment about his seeming friends and himself, then, his acts help bond him and the audience, as do his values, his virtues, and the love he gets from the most obviously favorable characters (if any are), Freeman and Fidelia. It is not surprising that, as Milhous and Hume note, "for nearly three hundred years critics assumed that Manly was the 'hero' and that he served as a spokesman for the author" (23), or that, as Peter Holland says, "Wycherley's friends called him Manly and the Plain-Dealer with utter seriousness" (173), or that Pope used "gen'rous Manly" who "raves" "at half mankind" as a type character of virtuous discernment as well as indignation (*Epistle to Cobham* 115–16).

The Plain-Dealer collapses "high" and "low" ideals into a relatively "low" plot, though not very low, given the presence of Fidelia, Vernish's attempted rape and attempted murder (of Manly), and the personal force of Manly and Olivia, as played by the creators of Aureng-Zebe and Nourmahal a year earlier (November 1675). Wycherley treats it as a "high" plot in that he gives it moral charge and complements it with the morally lax plot involving Freeman and the Widow. Freeman, of course, is sufficiently important in the Manly/Olivia/Fidelia plot that he can offer an alternative to its moral rigorism, and Manly dominates so much of act III in Westminster Hall, the Widow's bailiwick, that the "lax" plot extends and broadens the satire of the action in which he is more centrally involved. Nonetheless, in fletcherian style the two plots remain distinct, for no character plays an active role in both of them till Freeman and others, with their plot complete, burst in with lights to reveal Vernish vanquished, Olivia lavishing blind care on Manly, and Fidelia a wounded woman. Until the denouement, Freeman only comments on Manly and his world, and Manly only comments on the world of the law courts. Nor do the two plots, for all the obvious thematic analogies between them— hypocrisy with its jargon, self-serving relations, unrendered services paid for—tell one much, if anything, about each other. Though the

Blackacre plot does not admit of moral seriousness as the Manly plot does, the world looks the same in both. On the other hand, Wycherley keeps plying formal analogies: the two virginal, threatened youths who come into their own (Fidelia, Jerry); the planned rape that is interrupted by money matters (Fidelia's rape by Vernish, the Widow's by Oldfox, "through the ear . . . with my well-pen'd Acrostics" [V; 507]); the fiction-tainted clandestine sex (Olivia's sleeping with Manly/Fidelia, which Manly intends to make public; the Widow's intention to make public the claimed bastardy of her son Jerry); the detention of goods (Manly's cabinet of jewels and his purse, the Widow's legal "Writings"); and at the ends of each plot, a discovery by witnesses of illicit dealings, a transfer of money from the woman to the man, and the foundering of a venal marriage (presumably the legal one of Vernish and Olivia, certainly the contemplated one of Freeman and the Widow).

In other ways, too, Wycherley follows fletcherian style, such as the symmetry of the play. Manly has two male friends and two female, one of each sex true and one false. Olivia has two fops as suitors, one cringing and conservative (Plausible, whose name means "ingratiating," "winning public approval") and the other, Novel, strutting and original. The Widow has an overage Major (Oldfox) and an overage minor (Jerry). The adversarial sense of "suit" in "lawsuit" carries over to all suitors, Manly and the two fops who follow Olivia, and Freeman and the one fop who follow the Widow. In fletcherian style, the lesser plot involves a series of reversals, with Freeman, rejected by both Blackacres in act II, winning Jerry but losing his mother in two successive plots (acts III and IV), and finally winning her body (which he rejects) and a bribe from her—payment of his debts plus an annuity—in act V. Unlike these reversals, which result from action toward a set goal or suit of Freeman's, the main plot turns on reversals that involve knowledge of hidden truths. Each scene reverses the audience's or a character's expectations with a successive discovery: Olivia's infidelity, her hypocritical virtue and so her lust for Fidelia, her marriage to Vernish, her infidelity to him, the sex and identity of Fidelia. The pattern here, once more, resembles that of *Marriage A-la-Mode*, in which the whole comic plot grows from the four lovers' pursuit of their desires but in which much of the serious plot pivots on revelations of true identity.

At the end of *The Plain-Dealer* Manly says he has not reformed. He tells Fidelia that "this ill World of ours" is "odious to me," and takes Freeman's hand for some *moraliste* plain dealing about dubious motives. From Manly's constancy and what she has seen, the lovestruck Fidelia, like the breezy Freeman, has continued to admire him, thus

Moraliste *Comedy* 201

puzzling some modern critics of the play and leading others to nod knowingly about Wycherley's irony. As we have remarked, Manly's embrace of both of them indicates his reconciliation with their two versions of nature. Yet this rapprochement remains unexplained by the play. Freeman claims that "most of our quarrels to the World, are just such as we have to a handsom Woman: only because we cannot enjoy her, as we wou'd do" (V, 515), but Manly's surliness was in full growl when he could "enjoy her": he had ten to twelve thousand pounds before the play began, and he was as sure of Olivia and Vernish as he now is of Fidelia and Freeman. In the matter of being sure, Manly inconsistently ends the play by recommending an empirical test, *"let no one e're confide / In Tears, or Oaths, in Love, or Friend untry'd,"* but in fact empirical tests fail before *moraliste* analysis, which treats deeds like words, as surfaces that hide motives. Such analysis calls in question any predictive reading of other people. (In what does one "confide" to judge love? How does one "try" a friend for a future reliance?) Though these factitious wrappings-up might vitiate or render ironic a comedy in another idiom, in the fletcherian style they do not. The play comes to a formal close with the three representatives of frank nature rewarded (and even the natural booby, Jerry, rewarded and freed), each of them consistently her- or himself. Within this ample structure of values, familiar from *Marriage A-la-Mode, The Virtuoso,* and *The Rover,* the play comes to as much ideological closure as the individual member of the audience sees. We suspect, however, that the unusual combination of rake and hero in Manly, and the double edge to the evaluation of his excess, made that closure harder to accomplish for many in the audience. If we may judge by much modern reaction to him, Manly causes uneasiness by following the logic of the hero (in his zeal) and of the rake (in his *moralisme*) too far. As we shall elaborate in the next chapter, a number of his approximate contemporaries, such as the heroes of Durfey's plays, also carried the logic of the rake to extremes and led away from the model of Carolean Comedy through being so faithful to some of its governing impulses.

Durfeyan Comedy and *The Spanish Fryar*

Though *The Spanish Fryar* (first performed shortly before November 1680?) is another of those double-plot plays that Dryden found congenial, it differs from and revamps its predecessors. To clarify how it does so, we shall go back to a strain of Carolean comedy during the later 1670s, particularly visible in the plays of Durfey and in Dryden's durfeyan *The Kind Keeper; or Mr. Limberham* (March 1678). These plays emerge and depart from the mode of heterogeneous, compromise-formation comedy that we have been discussing. Because they are so much more single-minded, uncompromising, and licentious, they illustrate very well how the internal dynamic of Carolean comedy both served and endangered it. We say "dynamic" because any comedy of wish fulfillment almost by definition incites characters to transgress bounds, to convert limits into a challenge and test. Like champions in highly competitive sports, the protagonists thus can stay where they are, so to speak, only by doing more, seeking more, refusing stasis.

In Carolean comedy these transgressions are authorized, and hence gain their capacity to draw the audience in, by the imperatives of nature. The characters openly or implicitly appeal to nature when they wish to defy or coopt society, rules, or whatever is "arbitrary" or "artificial." This affects the plays both as plays and as representations of action. Natural characters, "realistic" in portrayal and emphatic as standard-bearers for nature, always threaten to distend the necessarily unnatural, contrived, literary genre that creates and empowers them. As *Marriage A-la-Mode* suggests, even circa 1670 Carolean comedy is filled with self-consciousness about its conventions, which both reaffirms it as intelligent and self-aware and drives it toward more fidelity to a presumed ideal of nature. This tendency increases during the 1670s. In addition, the more natural the protagonists are, governed by appetite rather than by social rules, the more liable they are to violate social norms in the represented action. As we have argued, the identification of the natural with violation served some members of the Carolean audience, who came to the theatre to see their stand-ins romp precisely where they themselves dared not. Audiences need not have craved to see certain specific acts of violation performed (i.e., to perform such acts vicariously themselves) in order to have longed for the excitement and liberty betokened by the flouting of arbitrary social norms. Protagonists whom one admired for being natural in this sense might show their allegiance to nature in all sorts of dismaying ways.

A system in semi-independent motion, like the new Carolean repertory we have just described, undergoes strain when keyed to another system moving at a different rate, like Carolean society. By the later 1670s, repertory growth itself, with its demand for change and violation of norms, helped increase the strain. Perhaps this might have been less true if the idiom of Carolean comedy had had built into it a countervailing urge to social restraint, like flossy wish-fulfilling Hollywood films before World War II, with their mass, provincial audiences and their docility before the Hays Code. But the roar of manly Wycherley was less friendly to the status quo than that of the MGM (or the Cowardly) lion. The logic of Wycherley's and his competitors' styles kept pushing outward the bounds of willful behavior, shows of power, and sexual hopes. We have provided part of this logic just above, and the conditions of the theatre fill in the rest of it. Anything less than expansion would have been tame, because all sorts of behavior that had been outré had now become familiar in the repertory from previous years' comedies.

Social attitudes changed slowly and the comic repertory changed fast. As the 1670s moved on and the violation of bounds became progressively more daring, playwrights had to take their protagonists' behavior either more or less seriously than before, because an increasing percentage of the audience was likely to be made uncomfortable by investing themselves in the kind of agents that the comedies were in some sense obliged to provide. When the characters' increased outrageousness hit close to real social taboos, like helping one's discarded whore marry one's best friend, writers could refuse to harmonize it as it is harmonized in *Marriage A-la-Mode* and *The Man of Mode*. Then one gets black comedies like Otway's and hostile satire, as in Lee's *The Princess of Cleve*, where people who came to see "the most polish'd Hero" were wrenched from their expectations of engagement by Lee's showing them "a Ruffian reeking from Whetstone's-Park" (2: 153). Or writers could dilute moral judgment by concocting satirical or farcical comedies where adultery, betrayal, and humiliation could be laughed away. The master here was Edward Ravenscroft. A writer as ingenious, adaptable, and up-to-date as Dryden could provide such farce and light satire, weight the play with some of the brazen ruthlessness of a Durfey, and make claims of moral satire: this smorgasbord, we believe, is what he served up in *Limberham*.

Implied in this account of late 1670s comedy is a jostling not only of the audience's moral expectations in the represented action but their generic expectations in the literary artifact as well. Black comedy and the sort of drama that may be taken as either amoral farce or moral satire plainly elude the bounds of the classical genres. The number of such plays increased as the 1670s wore on. Non-Drydenian examples are Shadwell's *The Libertine* (1675) and, perhaps in the season after *The Spanish Fryar*, Lee's *The Princess of Cleve* (see Hume, *Rakish* 113–18). Shadwell called his play a "tragedy"; Hume (*Rakish* 174) better describes it as "a sardonic mock-tragedy," "a diverting travesty of the libertine philosophy"; but it is not "mock" like *The Rehearsal* or Duffett's travesties of *The Tempest* and *The Empress of Morocco*. It has real emotion, real libertine arguments, and real deaths. In his dedication to *The Princess of Cleve*, Lee himself described it best: a "Farce, Comedy, Tragedy or meer Play" (2: 153). As we have noted, even comedies of the sort discussed in chapter 7—satirical plays, like *The Plain-Dealer*, or light plays that deepen with the emotion of romance, like *The Rover*—had called generic decorum into question. From the time of the Greeks and the Romans, satire and romance have in practice straddled narrative forms with happy and unhappy outcomes, the amusing and the serious. So they do in these plays.

If the standard genres had had the iron grip one might expect from studying the scholars' talk about "(neo)classicism," perhaps the dynamic of Carolean comedy might have been curbed. But pragma, not dogma, ruled the playwrights. Just as most of the writers let their dashing protagonists exploit the forms of social conduct and indeed just as these playwrights wrote plays with an ambiguity of moral stance, thus exploiting the range of social attitudes, so they wrote comedies that exploited formal principles rather than accepted them as imperatives. The genres had their uses in helping the dramatists attain commercial success and their peers' respect. Nonetheless, a great fund of pragmatic energy makes Carolean comedy a restless endeavor. In moving from the chaste drama of Tuke to the witty plays and Shadwellian humours of the mid-to-late 1660s to the sexy, disruptive comedies of the mid-1670s to the kind of play discussed in this chapter, playwrights resembled their adventurous ancestors at the end of the sixteenth century and the start of the seventeenth (as opposed, for instance, to later Jacobean and Caroline writers or to comic playwrights between the Licensing Act and the 1890s). Precisely because critics of the time called attention to the genres in an attempt to codify them, playwrights could turn the critics' yardsticks into levers for raising their comedies in dignity or into kindling that fueled their anarchic energies. Self-consciousness invited subversion as an act of freedom for the writer just as a consciousness of bounds, we earlier argued, invited subversion as an act of freedom for the rake in the later 1670s.

By any accounting, Dryden's two plays before *The Spanish Fryar* fitted in with the shifts we have been describing, though *Limberham* boasted Charles II as "parcell poet with [Dryden] in the plott" (*LS* 259) and *Troilus and Cressida* (April 1679) boasted Shakespeare in the same role, an odd couple. Though *Limberham* is a comedy and *Troilus* a tragedy in Dryden's version, as perhaps in Shakespeare's ("tragedy" for the First Folio but not the 1609 Quarto), each is what Shakespeare's *Troilus* has long been called, a "problem play." While Dryden's *Troilus* lies outside a book on comedy, then, we would note its erosion of generic distinctions. Its chief comic characters resemble those that mark the contemporary acid comedies of Otway, like *The Souldiers Fortune* (June 1680). The railing Thersites represents the type of cynical satirist whom one finds in Otway's Courtine or Wycherley's Manly, an embittered outsider; the cooing Pandarus represents the cynical voyeur, a lustful outsider who thrives on vicarious indulgence, like Otway's Sir Jolly Jumble or Dryden's own Aldo in *Limberham*. These types, which seem to epitomize the charges of licentious ridicule and sexual display made against Carolean comedy itself, appear in a play that Dryden thought reasonable to preface with an essay on "The Grounds of Criticism in Tragedy." He does dignify Shakespeare's action by cutting Achilles' onstage murder of the unarmed Hector and by ending the play with heroic additions, Cressida's suicide, a battle royal in which Troilus is slain, and some political saws from Ulysses. Making the action thus tragic widens Shakespeare's tonal gulf between heroics and gritty comedy. But Dryden does not counterpoint the two idioms, in accord with the technique of his double-plot plays of the 1660s or *Marriage A-la-Mode*. Rather, he sandwiches them together so that they say the "same" thing. In his *Troilus*, comedy and tragedy both comment on a web of complots, deceits, losses, and the overwhelming of royal brothers (Hector and Troilus in the play), all of which refer to English politics in 1679 (Novak, *CD* 13: 497–500, 518–19). As we shall suggest, similar handling of genres recurs in *The Spanish Fryar*.

The notorious *Limberham*, a year earlier than *Troilus*, touches not the meeting of comedy and tragedy, but comedy and farce. Its single action breaks into a series of concealments and discoveries as Woodall tries to arrange and juggle simultaneous secret affairs with three women, all living in the same house. As often with farce, fletcherian reversals here are carried to a reductio ad absurdissimum. In public, Dryden protested that *Limberham* was "intended for an honest *Satyre* against our crying sin of *Keeping*" and prognosticated for it: "This *Comedy* is of the first Rank of those which I have written, and . . . Posterity will be of my Opinion" (Dedication 4: 271). Posterity by and large has not been, about the quality of the play or its intention. As to the latter, one can hardly avoid asking—and thereby implicitly answering—the question of whether, with Charles II as "parcell poet," *Limberham* was likely to be a satire on "keepers." Nor does the text of *Limberham* itself, which Dryden says was cut and cleaned up for publication, support very well a claim of satire on keeping. Most of this comedy has to do with ruses and near-discoveries, not with mockery of Limberham, the sexually incompetent "keeper" of Tricksy. He is only one of two cuckolds, the other being the swaggering husband Mr. Brainsick, and Tricksy is only one of three hypocritical women who fornicate during the play and one of four women whom the dashing young Woodall conquers. Nor does Dryden satirize anything that might be thought inherent in keeping. A jealous or doting husband could, and in Carolean comedy often did, suffer the same way Limberham does. In fact, because Limberham's doting and lack of "masculinity" balance Brainsick's bombast and despotism, the form of the play implicitly equates whoremaster and jealous husband, as the uxorious Sir Jaspar and the suspicious, menacing Pinchwife are implicitly equated in *The Country-Wife*, for example. When Dryden's denouement then transforms the whoremaster into a husband by having him marry his mistress, he does not thereby seem more or less silly and contemptible.

Most interesting about Dryden's claim of satire is that he evidently thought it plausible. He must have thought, that is, that one might read *Limberham* as affirming a general social good over natural, private pleasures, and therefore as targeting a vice absolutely, not relative to the merits of the characters. The "vice" of keeping, after all, runs afoul of social ethics rather than personal desire. Such a comedy would in these respects veer from the pattern that, we have argued, typifies Dryden's earlier comedies. To be taken seriously, his claim of satire would have to be squared with a letter of his (July 1677; *LS* 259) where he says he is writing "almost such another piece of businesse as" Durfey's roaring success *A Fond Husband*. A moral apologist for Dryden might assert that his debt to Durfey was to some extent parodic, that Dryden produced a comedy that took over Durfey's amoral swagger but, unlike Durfey's, could be read as satire. Dryden's alleged satire would also follow Durfey's plays in discarding any real compromise formation and any complex drawing on heterogeneity of audience response. But we do not see any reason to take Dryden's adaptation of Durfey's mode as parodic. On the contrary, one might guess that he was drawn to these fashionable changes, at least in part, by the powerful lodestone of Durfey's ample gate receipts. The most probable assessment of his motives and achievement remains Novak's: "Until D'Urfey's *A Fond Husband* . . . Dryden was the master of smutty comedy, and once D'Urfey had shown the way to write a completely amoral sexual farce, Dryden was equal to the challenge and produced *The Kind Keeper*" ("Margery" 3).

What Durfey had done in *A Fond Husband* was to develop the logic inherent in the comic form this chapter has been discussing: the play ends with a resolution by one of its protagonists, Ranger, to be fashionably amoral, and it emphasizes chance, not (even for lip service) Providence, as the agent of discovery. One can see how this sort of conclusion follows from what Durfey had done in two comedies of 1676, *Madam Fickle* and *The Fool Turn's Critick*. Fickle, having been deserted by her husband, vengefully strings along and deceives three men, including the protagonists Lord Bellamore and Manley. Although at the end of the play her husband returns and the protagonists marry others, so that compromise formation may be maintained, Durfey's next play, *The Fool Turn'd Critick*, serves up only mock marriages for the male leads, Frank Amorous and his friend Bernard. Frank not only steals Bernard's love, Penelope, but he plots to injure him further: "I'gad the hopes of beguiling him of [a] second Mistress is so sweet, that I am not able to resist it" (IV.ii; 38 [misnumbered 36]). With this practice to help perfect his hand, Durfey involves the characters of *A Fond Husband* in malice and mutual betrayal among friends, false clandestine marriage as in *Fickle* and *Fool*, adultery and the threat of divorce, and association with one of the most brazen "heroes" in Carolean comedy. Rashly tells Bubble, whom he has been cuckolding, "Well, Sir—if I have injur'd you, I wear a Sword, Sir,—and so— Farewell" (V; 57). However much fun this sort of play may be, and Durfey is moderate fun, we suspect that it ceases to trace for the audience trajectories of desire that large numbers would be comfortable to identify as their own. Nor does it allow them easily to own and disown the action through compromise formation. Instead, it lets them enjoy the action—the maneuvers of the energetic and unpalatable cast—as something from which they are disengaged, as one is disengaged from farce or spectacle. Short of the audiences' staying home, only such disengagement makes possible this degree of violation on stage.

Of course Durfey was not alone. Other comedies of the later 1670s also illustrate this trend that clarifies Dryden's aims and claims in writing *Limberham*. For instance, take two other comedies of the 1677– 78 season, both of which adapt or borrow heavily from Middleton.

In John Leanerd's *The Rambling Justice, or the Jealous Husbands*, first played at the other theatre two or three weeks before *Limberham*, not only does Sir Generall Amorous cuckold with impunity a brace of old fools, Sir Arthur Twilight and Sir Contentious Surly, but Sir Arthur must also beg for his life and pardon his wife and cuckolder. Sir Generall sums up his own morality with typical generosity: "What will Sir Arthur say when he shall miss his Wife? he can but vex or perhaps hang himself, let him do either, all's one to me so I but enjoy his Wife" (III; 31). Sir Arthur's daughter Emilia, whom Sir Generall marries, does not expect fidelity, and we have already cited the comment of his other daughter, Flora, who says she fancies (what she gets) a witless husband so as to do "what she pleases, keep a Gallant in Town, or maintain a comely Servant in the Country; who shall be as proud to effect my Will, as I desirous to command him" (V; 61).

Similarly, at the start of this same season (*LS* 263) one finds Behn's(?) *The Counterfeit Bridegroom: or the Defeated Widow*. In *The Counterfeit Bridegroom* and its source, Middleton's *No Wit, No Help Like a Womans*, a young man steals the money his father gives him to ransom his abducted mother and brings home a wife instead, whom he fobs off on his father as his abducted sister; the father is told that the wife is dead. Middleton treats this with some pathos and seriousness, as for example when the young man reacts with cries of horror and deep misery to his apparent incest when his wife seems really to be his sister. But in the Carolean version sin vanishes as the young man fumes in rake fashion, "Must all my Courtship, Expence and Constancy, ay, Constancy, *Sam*. be jilted by the resurrection of a long lost Sister?" (III.i; 36–37). The other plot of *The Counterfeit Bridegroom* involves the applauded bed-tricking of a widow so that she must marry a man to avoid being thought a whore. Neither this play nor Leanerd's makes more than a gesture toward compromise formation.

Limberham follows along the same lines. Though his sexual adventures and concealments with his lovers Tricksy and Mrs. Brainsick weary him, Woodall never has his amorous schemes curtailed, nor does he suffer in any way for them. We cannot quite accept Baker's ingenious suggestion (378) that Woodall's being spent with his sexual exploits and therefore being unequal to bedding Saintly in act IV and his bride Pleasance at the end of the play (or so she jibes at him) suggests that he will shrink his way into an impotent old age, like his father; Horner does not meet with scorn for running out of china. Pleasance in fact has "a grudge to" her husband-to-be, "for the Priviledge of his Sex" in whoring two or three women (III.i; 298). Bouts of illicit sex benefit these two or three women, moreover. The hypocritical Saintly marries sturdy Gervase, Tricksy gets marriage with four hundred pounds a year for separate maintenance, and Mrs. Brainsick "earns" her husband's (less substantial) promise that "hereafter, *Memphis* shall not boast a Monument more firm, than my affection" (V; 341). The only conventionally honest figure in the play is a servant, Giles, whom Woodall discharges and who ends unrewarded. As the other, less scrupulous servant, Gervase, says as he leads in his new, well-to-do wife Saintly, "When will *Giles*, with his honesty, come to this?" (V; 340).

Equally unpunished, wholly impenitent, and, as far as one can tell, blameless is the impotent "Father" Aldo, who pats and purrs over the "Ladies of Pleasure" he counsels, consoles, and assists with his purse (I.i; 280). Though Aldo is more promiscuous, decayed, and open in egging on all kinds of sexual high jinks than Limberham, the sexually tame but lavish "keeper," they are obvious moral equivalents, and if *Limberham* were the satire Dryden claimed, they would be treated as such. In fact, Aldo acts the agreeable role of the anti-Oedipal father, who does not vie with his son in matters of sex or (because he cannot recognize his son) of authority, but forwards the freest expression of desire as "role model," financier, pimp, and eventual provider of the rich, unblushing bride: "Be you the *Lyon*, to devour the Prey, I am your *Jack-Call* to provide it for you: there will be a Bone for me to pick" (I.i; 280–81). Behind him frowns the spectre of the socially orthodox Father, guardian of his son's good faith and morals, for Aldo impersonates that Father when his sense of his paternal role urges him to do so. Woodall is thus leery of being discovered by Aldo as his son. But Aldo's concession to social expectations is this venture into hypocrisy, nothing more substantial. Dryden's final joke is that at the end of *Limberham* Aldo can join the roles of father and pimp by revealing Pleasance's real, distinguished lineage: as he takes over a stock paternal role, the Father as trustee of the social order, he also sends the only chaste woman in the house off to bed with his son Woodall, the house's favorite libertine.

Despite ending with Woodall's wedding Pleasance, in short, *Limberham* does not defer to social standards enough to have a compromise formation or encourage much heterogeneity of response in the manner of *Marriage A-la-Mode*. It may elicit different responses, as any play may, but they are not guided by value systems that compete within the play itself. The single rather than multiple plot of *Limberham* would have hampered such competition of values even if Dryden had desired it. Nor do the main characters correspond to the types of the earlier 1670s. Woodall shows his masculine prowess by sexual mastery over four women (one vicariously, through sending Gervase in his stead; one after the play ends), but female desire is not fulfilled here as in "high" Carolean comedy, by creating a woman on whom the audience's interests and desires can focus. For the first time in Dryden's career, the comic hero's match has neither intrigue nor bouts of witty repartee with him; in fact the voluble, acid-tongued Pleasance does not appear till act III. Woodall does profess that Pleasance will "find me so much [sexual] imployment in my own Family, that I shall have little need to look out for Journey-work" (V; 339), but however sexy the actress may have been, Dryden does not try to make her otherwise vivid, fascinating, and glamorous enough to fix the male. As generally in comedy after the very early 1660s, not to fulfill female desire involves not creating a desirable female, and that in turn implies not really fulfilling male desire either.

A comedy that debased desire by representing it as mere, unglamorous animal impulse might be thoroughly cynical and amoral, what one finds in the nineteenth and twentieth centuries as "naturalism." Or it might be a spiritual and moral comedy. Opting for this second, more generally flattering possibility, Dryden's claim that *Limberham* satirizes vice attempts to *re*claim the play by making it moral. Behind that line of "timeless" argument, we suggest, was Dryden's timely urge to be seen as a socially responsible, right-thinking citizen. Only a few months after the first performances in 1678 came the onset of the Popish Plot furor, bringing fears, then the reality of political and religious violence. By late 1679 or early 1680, when Dryden made his moral assertion in the published version, a combination of social instability and patriotic fervor must have made the role of benevolent tutor suddenly appealing. By insisting that *Limberham* "decry'd" the vice it so amply "express'd" (Dedication 4: 271), Dryden maneuvered his text, now bowdlerized so that no one could detect whatever had led to the play's being banned, closer to an ideal that he was to embody in his new comedy, *The Spanish Fryar*, finished in the late autumn of 1680.

About *The Spanish Fryar* Milhous and Hume write, "No one doubts that Dryden was in favor of the legal succession and against libertinism" (141). Our argument, following from our comments above, might fliply be put that Dryden is, uncharacteristically, against libertinism in this play *because* he is in favor of the legal succession. Social cohesion marks both plots, and both plots, unlike those in other, earlier comedies of Dryden, work against the fulfillment of desire for the characters and against the audience's investing the characters with the role of agents. Legitimacy is doubly enforced in the plots, and then reinforced by blocking the action from the creation and service of the audience's wishes. This pattern, used rather bitterly in Dryden's *Troilus*, makes *The Spanish Fryar* differ from *Secret Love*, *The Tempest*, and

Marriage A-la-Mode in that its two plots say the same thing in more or less the same way. By this means, *The Spanish Fryar* makes the scheme it takes from *Limberham* unproblematic. There is no contradiction between Aldo's two roles, the socially good and bad fathers, when they reappear in two people, one in each plot, the kindly, imprisoned King Sancho who is as invisible as is the moral side of Aldo, and the shrewd, exploitive friar who cheerfully pimps away. There is no contradiction between moral and amoral views of sexual licence either, when a passionate, overdevoted good character, Torrismond, who gets what he wants at the end, can be balanced against a bad romping rake, Lorenzo, who ends up with nothing much.

The similarity between what the two plots say in *The Spanish Fryar* has some parallel in the way in which the two plots are conducted. Dryden's earlier plays, of course, exploited generic decorum. As we suggested in chapter 3, the double-plot scheme invites playwrights to distinguish the two actions through assigning each a different decorum, sometimes a different genre. The most striking Carolean instance of this device is *Marriage A-la-Mode*. A less striking one, *The Man of Mode*, still plainly divides its plots along an axis of decorum: Bellair and Emilia cannot do what Dorimant can, and, perhaps more clearly to the point, vice versa. By the later 1670s, we have noted, Dryden and Etherege's slight juniors, then Dryden himself, increasingly wrote plays that challenged assumptions of decorum based directly or obliquely on genre. In *The Spanish Fryar* Dryden follows decorum in the serious and comic plots so as to show its limits: to be as constant as a Torrismond or as libertine as a Lorenzo is no longer heroic. And so when Dryden congratulates himself modestly on "*the management of two Plots, so very different from each other, that it was not perhaps the Tallent of every Writer, to have made them of a piece*" (Dedication 5: 119), he has in mind new sources of similarity and difference here from those in his earlier plays.

Comparison with Dryden's previous practice is the more striking in that *The Spanish Fryar* reworks plot devices from his own earlier plays and follows a fletcherian pattern of construction. The serious plot deals with a Queen, daughter of a usurper, who has been bequeathed by her late father to one of his princely subalterns, Bertran, but who falls in love with a brilliant, passionate young general, Torrismond. Although he seems to be a high-placed commoner when the play begins, Torrismond turns out at last to be the rightful crown prince. The Queen who conquers her conquering general but dreads to stoop, and the jilted prince of the blood come from *Secret Love*. The usurper's daughter and the royal heir reappear from *Marriage A-la-Mode*, where another prince, Argaleon, is jilted and much is made of the difference in rank between Palmyra and Leonidas. That play also has sudden revelations from pretended fathers about the real bloodline of their "children," as in *The Spanish Fryar*.

The "low" plot of *The Spanish Fryar*, in which Elvira has been married to an impotent banker of sixty (played by James Nokes in 1680) and prefers a young rakish colonel (played by William Smith), has an initial parallel in *Limberham*, in which the cast is hypothesized by Summers (4: 267)—following Genest—to have had Nokes (Limberham) and Smith (Woodall) playing closely analogous roles, and in *Limberham*'s model, *A Fond Husband*, in which Emilia is married to Nokes' character (Bubble) and sleeps with Smith's (Rashly). The pimping Spanish friar himself was a role for Anthony Leigh, who created Old Fumble, a nearly blind and deaf lecherous dotard in *A Fond Husband*, probably the pimping, impotent father Aldo in *Limberham*, and Pandarus in *Troilus*. Dominic is what we called "the anti-Oedipal father," noncompetitive in matters of sex or authority with his "son" (III; 152) Lorenzo and "daughter" Elvira, whose desires he promotes. We need not pile up more parallels to indicate how Dryden stuck to familiar ground in contriving this unprecedented (for him) play. And even older familiar ground: the first interview between banker and colonel, Gomez and Lorenzo, follows one in Dryden and Newcastle's *Sir Martin Mar-all* (August 1667; reprinted and perhaps revived on stage in 1678), between Mar-all (Nokes) and Swallow (Smith?; see LS 111, 263). The more familiar the ground, the simpler for Dryden, of course, but also the more chance for him to trade on audience expectations that he had himself in part created.

One thing Dryden, like Durfey and the others, did not change was a continuing allegiance to fletcherian serialism and reversals. In the high plot of *The Spanish Fryar*, the defenders of Saragossa expect (i) defeat but get (ii) victory through Torrismond, who then appears (i) triumphant but (ii) imperils himself by braving Bertran, who (i) reports his audacity to the hostile Queen, Bertran's betrothed. In an about-face (ii) she then falls in love with the awed suppliant, Torrismond. Their bliss in marriage is reversed, and she becomes the suppliant, when Torrismond discovers that he is the true king, son of Sancho, whom she has had murdered—or so it is believed, for this too will be reversed—by Bertran, whose roles as her betrothed and her agent are also each reversed.

The comic plot works the same way. First, Elvira and Lorenzo (i) meet and flirt, but (ii) by inadvertently letting her husband in on the secret, Lorenzo pushes them apart. Then Dominic, the eponymous friar, (i) delivers a letter and, later, delivers Lorenzo to Elvira; (ii) Lorenzo's disguise, as another Dominican, gapes so that he is discovered by her husband, Gomez. In a third episode, Lorenzo (i) uses the help of the specious father, Dominic, to have Gomez carried off by soldiers as a political conspirator, only (ii) to learn that Alfonso, Lorenzo's real father, has rescued Gomez. And, finally, when Lorenzo (i) menaces Gomez into self-contradictions in court, he (ii) discovers that his own wishes contradict themselves, for Elvira is his sister, who coyly remarks, "You see, Brother, I had a natural affection to you" (V; 199). The comic plot moves back and forth with these reversals, like both plots of *Marriage A-la-Mode*; the serious plot spirals toward increasing emotional complexity and passion, like the love plot of Dryden and Davenant's *Tempest*.

What do the two plots share with one another? Lorenzo the rake first comes on stage to announce his cousin Torrismond's victory over the Moors, and in the last act the two men fight side by side to defeat the rebellious elders—Lorenzo's father, Alfonso, and Torrismond's foster-father, Raymond—who raised them. This linkage of rakish to noble figures at the beginning and end of a play may seem reminiscent of Rhodophil and Palamede. The relation between comic and courtly figures, however, remains consistent throughout *Marriage A-la-Mode*. By contrast, Lorenzo and Torrismond begin poles apart, one the whoremonger in heat for whatever flesh is to be found—"Fair, Black, Tall, Low: / Let her but have a Nose" (I; 131)—the other awed to the point of dumbness before the inaccessible glories of the Queen. By the last act, each finds himself saved by Providence from an Oedipal crime, Lorenzo from incest (with his sister Elvira), Torrismond from parricide (by proxy in his union as one flesh with the guilty Leonora); the allusion to *Oedipus* may be intended, since Dryden and Lee's redramatization of the story had "[taken] prodigiously" (*LS* 273) in the autumn of 1678. As *The Spanish Fryar* develops, its two plots to some extent converge. Torrismond increasingly takes on new social responsibility as lover, then husband of the Queen, then as king in disguise. Also in disguise (as "Hernando") Lorenzo fixes his attention on one woman, Elvira, seemingly as "inaccessible" and really as virginal as the Queen, Leonora. He woos her and wins her in an increasingly societal plot which is set first indoors, then outside, finally at the court. When the social order is divinely restored, his stolen Elvira must return to old Gomez just as the usurped kingdom reverts to old Sancho.

In the fletcherian manner, the two plots have close formal connections but, again in the fletcherian manner, they draw little cognitive substance from one another. This is not, as in *Marriage A-la-Mode*, because they get to their different resolutions by such different paths. In *The Spanish Fryar*, as in *Troilus*, paired plots say the same thing and do not need each other for commentary. They even end with the same sort of arbitrariness, unlike *Marriage A-la-Mode*, where both plots have a recuperative logic. The rectifying love of Leonidas and Palmyra leads to the raising of first one lover, then the other, then the one again, and then both to a proper state, so as to keep recouping losses for themselves and their kingdom. Jealousy and emulation bring the comic lovers, satisfied for the moment, to the point at which they started, unsatisfied. But the double denouement in *The Spanish Fryar*, by contrast, rejects any consecutive logic. Sancho is saved from prison and Lorenzo from incest by accident or Providence or one masquerading as the other.

The deliberate alogic of accident or Providence solves both actions with a surprising familial reunion, father, son, and daughter (-in-law). Although familial ties are precisely what each plot has thrown into question, Dryden reinvokes them, implausibly and rapidly, at the end. By doing so he not only affirms a watchful albeit sluggish Providence, he also insists, as throughout these plots, that reasoning is sham and willfulness therefore should win the day. But it is divine willfulness and not, as in earlier comedies by Dryden, the characters': the jilted Bertran does good with no good intentions, as does Lorenzo when he chooses to bear arms against his father not for the right reason, defense of the crown, but because, as his rather nasty irony— the irony of the late 1670s rake—puts the matter, "'Tis policy for Son and Father to take different sides: / For then, Lands and Tenements commit no Treason" (V; 189). Equally paradoxically, Raymond's fierce loyalty to the king detours through vengefulness and thus revolt against the king, ostensibly in the king's own name.

Reasoning in *The Spanish Fryar*, then, ought not to be taken at face value, and yet the play includes a good bit of reasoning, in particular about political duty. With the Exclusion Crisis at its peak, as Milhous and Hume point out (147), Dryden was eager to proselytize. Understandably, scholars have rummaged through tracts and treatises to find out how he might have done so. Bruce King, for example, has linked some of Torrismond's pronouncements to the policy of nonresistance endorsed by the Anglican Church and the writings of Sir Robert Filmer (154–55). We agree that the audience in 1680 had to recognize the arguments as familiar from the debates of the day, for through these arguments, Dryden distinguishes his characters and points his audience toward applying the events in Saragossa to those in England. We very much doubt, though, that Dryden could count on an audience impressionable enough to accept his side of highly agitated issues from the mouths of actors spouting controversial doctrine as part of stage debates. In addition, he would have been foolish to proselytize on a basis so easily challenged and so partisan. Dryden's political strategy, we suggest, follows that which he was to use at the end of *Absalom and Achitophel* one year later: end dispute through divine fiat. People may sling reasons back and forth, but when all is said and done, what they have done may not be what they have said. It is in God, that partyless Tory, that everyone had better trust, because he and the royal agent who acts through his power make society cohere. To understand that crucial point, Dryden maintained, "the things we *must* believe, are *few*, and *plain*"—or so he was to write in a section of *Religio Laici* (1681) where he attacks Catholics and commonwealth's-men, the very foes of legitimacy in *The Spanish Fryar* (CD 2: 122, 1.432).

Because in the tenor of this play reasoning must bulk so large, and at the same time be ineffectual, Dryden supplies his characters with a great deal of special pleading. In order to excuse the real or intended taking of a false liberty, they repeatedly invoke a false authority through reasoning. And in this play the substance of special pleading preempts action or, at any rate, voluntary action by insisting on an amoral driving force, just the sort of passion that reason properly serves and is confounded with in *Marriage A-la-Mode*. For instance, Torrismond's love for the Queen deprives him of reason: "Madmen ought not to be mad: / But who can help his frenzy?" (I; 134; see 142, 144). In raging at Sancho's supposed murder, he calls upon "The Power that guards the Sacred Lives of Kings" but insists that "She be spar'd / That hindred not the Deed" (III; 165). Beaten by Raymond from an argument which would excuse any act of usurpation, he pleads a complacent, fated blindness: "I see no Crime in her whom I adore, / Or if I do, her Beauty makes it none" (IV; 181). The Queen in turn begins with a partial excuse when she consents to the murder—"If then I break divine and humane Laws, / No Bribe but Love cou'd gain so bad a Cause" (III; 162)—and immediately exculpates herself completely:

> I wou'd not doe this Crime,
> And yet, like Heaven, permit it to be done.
> The Priesthood grossly cheat us with Free-will:
> Will to doe what, but what Heaven first decreed?
> Our Actions then are neither good nor ill,
> Since from eternal Causes they proceed;
> Our Passions, Fear and Anger, Love and Hate,
> Meer sensless Engines that are mov'd by Fate;
> Like Ships on stormy Seas, without a Guide,
> Tost by the Winds, and driven by the Tyde.

As we have said, Dryden had a polemic interest in showing arguments and zeal treacherous, while putting no one (except the scapegrace scapegoat Dominic) beyond the pale, and—in keeping with much comic practice by 1680—preventing any character from being a consistent agent of the audience's asocial desires. The characters who appear on stage in *The Spanish Fryar*, except for Pedro, always find some tempting passion to prefer to virtue (Fisher 44–50); sympathetic but virtuous, Dryden always calls the passions into question and the passionate back to order.

If one hypothesizes for Dryden a strategy in which man proposes, faintly or falsely, and God disposes by the end of act V, one can see a political reason why *The Spanish Fryar* should disempower any human desires, whether the libertine's or the uncritical lover's, that do not meet the test of moral orthodoxy. One can also see why intentions, which are the test for purity of spirit in Dryden's earlier heroic plots, make so little difference in this divinely governed world. Desires and intentions are typically corrupted and this world has the strength of grace. A. W. Ward wrote that "the serious plot . . . has the great blemish of representing the heroine (Leonora) as morally guilty of a crime and thus unworthy of sympathy." Torrismond, he thought, "should have erroneously supposed Leonora to have sanctioned the order for his father's death, instead of her actually sanctioning it" (3: 377). But, after all, for self-serving reasons Queen Leonora—unimpeded by her Torrismond—has from before the play opens kept the good old Sancho locked in a sunless dungeon "where Joy ne'er enters," bound, grieving, "upon the unwholesom Earth" amid "gloomy Vapors" (III; 163). Both she and Torrismond might be judged "morally guilty of a crime" even if the regicide took place through sickness, privation, and despair rather than by a dagger blow. Pedro, Alfonso, and Raymond obviously think so, and blame Torrismond's "dotage to th'usurping Queen" (II; 140). Torrismond perhaps thinks so too, for, fresh from his visit to Sancho, he tells the Queen that she is so beautiful, "you justifie Rebellion: / As if that faultless Face could make no Sin" (III; 164).

He and she do sin, however, and briefly but intensely suffer for it; human behavior in this play carries a bad though cleansable odor about it. In fact Dryden underlines this moral point and the importance of pardon by having Torrismond welcome the surprised Bertran as "no more my Foe, but, Brother," when he discovers that Bertran has not in fact killed the king. "Bad men, when 'tis their Interest, may doe good," says Bertran bluntly, and "plead[s] no Merit, but a bare Forgiveness." Torrismond will have none of this. He grants "Favour" to the man who preserved "*Sancho*'s Life, / Whether by Vertue or Design" (V; 200–201). Raymond and his associates, who have at the end rebelled against Torrismond's own regal authority, are also pardoned. Whereas in "high" Carolean comedy, the equivalent of pardon—the rake's being rewarded with the choice lady—is an element in the compromise formation, as we argued in chapter 2, here pardon univocally signals that there is no compromise of values, no ambiguity of values, just that severe judgment is too harsh for a world where humans are naturally so self-deluded and their desires so errant. One might say that Dryden adapts a principle of compromise formation, in which the end cancels out or largely conceals the previous action, but gives this principle a new meaning. His conception here resembles those cited from Mary Douglas in chapter 2, where purification rituals have "the status of a rite of annulment" (*Purity* 136).

Even from generous or loving characters in *The Spanish Fryar*, pardon can be as suspect as reasoning; human motives corrupt it. Supposedly a vicar of divine love and grace, the comic lovers' advisor, Dominic, pardons for pay. The second facilitating character, Leonora's advisor Bertran, pardons Sancho to serve his own personal interests, when like the moor Abdalla (her father the usurper's other old ally) he battles against the refusal of his love. Tangential to the play itself, though not to its political application in 1680, is the strong hint that too much goodness and generosity in pardon may lead to disaster. King Sancho, Bertran sneers, was a "patient Saint," an "Anvil of Affronts," whose royal "Lenity" was "supinely good" and unwise (III; 162). Dryden would hardly have wanted to look as if he were urging passivity on Charles II or to make pardon so easy that right and wrong lost definition. By obliquely warning against excessive clemency, he controls these dangers. Nonetheless, he does not expatiate on this warning: Sancho's acts should not seem faulty and thereby explain, even in some degree excuse, revolt. Bertran alone criticizes the old king, and then only in an attempt—part of the recurrent special pleading in this casuist's delight of a play—to get Leonora's consent to murder. His special pleading, of course, promotes cruelty, and he follows it, for self-interest, with "pardon" in only simulating Sancho's death. Analogously, Torrismond's special pleading on behalf of the Queen works against pardon in that his arguments accept Sancho's continued imprisonment. For a time Torrismond also sullies pardon by granting it to the Queen in advance, while he pretends that no wrongdoing is taking place.

But true pardon, with its emphasis on outcome rather than the stream of preliminary acts, gives *The Spanish Fryar* a special stamp. Sancho embodies this value, as Torrismond says in his closing speech:

Oh! fear not him! Pity and he are one;

> So mercifull a King did never live;
> Loth to revenge, and easie to forgive.   (201)

In keeping with such graciousness, Dryden extends the olive branch to those who have not supported Charles II in the past. This is a play, as we have said, of social cohesion. For that very reason, however, the audience of *The Spanish Fryar*, unlike the audiences of Dryden's early comedies, cannot have it both ways, relish the illicit conduct and also relish their righteousness. The pardon is public recognition of sin, not an invitation to go out and do or fantasize likewise in the assurance that the slate can always be washed clean. In the terms we used earlier for "high" Carolean comedy, the actions of this play's protagonists are not meant to seem easily forgivable and limited in their consequences. One does not find the ubiquitous tone, the undertone, the overtone of playfulness that marks the expression of desire in acts and words throughout *Marriage A-la-Mode*. Rather, faced with the protagonists' violation of bounds in *The Spanish Fryar*, Dryden takes their behavior more and less seriously than before, more seriously in that he marks it as sinful, less seriously in that he annuls it so fully through situating it in an overruling, divine context.

As we said earlier, this play also differs from Dryden's earlier work in that each of the plots, with its plainly dubious behavior and "providential" ending, disempowers human desires, those of the characters and those of the audience. Alan Fisher points out that though the serious plot of *The Spanish Fryar* looks like standard heroic fare, it runs afoul of passion, which makes Leonora try to frame Bertran and Torrismond marry the woman who consented to Sancho's murder. When Torrismond finds himself the crown prince, "what he does is heroic, but in an odd new way. He puts down his supporters, [the rebels headed by Raymond and Alfonso,] but tries to preserve their lives; he maintains his wife's life, but without returning her love; he maintains his legitimate kingship, but protects his father's murderer. . . . Torrismond's balancing act must deny both the absoluteness of his passion and the perfection of his virtue, in order to preserve any semblance of either; he strikes a balance which is also a mess" (49).

In the "low" plot, correspondingly, Gomez, who ought to be a booby like other characters created by Nokes—Limberham, Behn's Sir Credulous Easy (*Sir Patient Fancy*), Peregrine Bubble (*A Fond Husband*), Durfey's eponymous Squire Oldsapp—"nonetheless understands things, can engage in repartee, has some status as a person, not merely as a victim" (Fisher 51). Lorenzo increasingly resorts to force, not wiles, as a way of dealing with the shrewd Gomez, and thus rakery loses a good deal of its panache. It turns instead into the unstylish bullying that marks Durfey's rowdy, raunchy, raw comedy. In a play that opens in a kingdom besieged by Moors and usurped from Sancho, we would add, mere force seems less appetizing than usual. Fisher concludes that Dryden is challenging the genre itself: "If we rejoice in the maxims of a cuckolding comedy, this [plot] tells us, we will have to bid farewell to civilized living" (53). Maybe so; more likely, perhaps, is that Dryden separates the audience from the traditional enactments of their desire, here as in the serious plot, for purposes local to *The Spanish Fryar* though in keeping with late Carolean comedy.

Obviously *The Spanish Fryar* makes radical changes in the central themes from *Marriage A-la-Mode* and *The Tempest* it reworks. Though the lovers' desires are absorbing, they do not serve to express the desires of the audience. Though in this play the central, invisible metaphor is the absent Sancho, an emphasis on pardon redefines the meanings of authority and freedom, which an imprisoned, paternal king evokes. Though reasoning crams the play, a divine hand casts it into doubt. In *Marriage A-la-Mode*, Dryden had knotted authority with freedom, sincerity with play, reason with passion so as to make enigmatic the evaluation of actions and to let willfulness serve to justify them. Sincerity and play do not cause problems in *The Spanish Fryar* because they are not an issue, but at first glance the other two pairs look as hard to untie here as in *Marriage A-la-Mode*. Yet in the end Dryden arrives at a different conundrum from that in *Marriage A-la-Mode*: freedom and authority, reason and passion do not have their center of gravity in the lovers. The serious plot offers its lovers a political complement to these pairs, in that the freeing of true authority, Sancho, achieves both freedom and authority, both reason and passion for Torrismond and Leonora; nothing else could do so. The comic plot, with its libertine notions of nature, exerts the voice of nature unexpectedly, in the discovery that Elvira and Lorenzo are siblings, so as to deny reason, passion, freedom, and the importance of authority in the lovers, in their father, in Elvira's husband, or in social institutions like the state and the church. These are the institutions the spiritual enfeeblement of which is represented in one plot by Sancho's imprisonment and in the other plot by the subversion of church and state so that both serve the rake. Dryden makes this subversion visible in that Lorenzo wears a uniform, the trappings of the state, and his Dominican accomplice displays the trappings of the Catholic church.

Dryden's handling of Lorenzo, of course, also subverts the familiar subversiveness that had been enjoyed by so many playgoers watching so many rakes. Again, Dryden makes the point visible through Lorenzo's consistent partnership with the friar. The two dress alike in act III, and in act IV plot together in an abuse of power which may have salted some wounds in 1680: Dominic advocates having the soldiers kill Gomez; Lorenzo has them "secure [Gomez] as a Traitor" (170). Dominic's gourmandise and avarice analogically establish Lorenzo's appetite for Gomez' wife and wealth as lust and greed rather than—or better, as well as—enviable traits of the licenced rake. Furthermore, in a play with so much reference to Heaven, the stage image of this *"Jacobin"* (II; 145) has a sinister force. Anthony Leigh, who created Dominic, was a bulky man; as a Dominican, he was dressed in black. The stage picture with him and the slender Smith in red as Lorenzo (see III; 155) would have been striking, the more so because a number of contemporary comedies featured devils, who we suppose were dressed in black, or characters with blacked faces whom other characters mistake for the devil. Black-faced characters who cause a devil scare (in plays after 1675) occur in Francis Fane's *Love in the Dark*, Thomas Rawlins' *Tom Essence*, John Leanerd's *The Rambling Justice*, and Durfey's *Squire Oldsapp*; Shadwell has devils on stage in *The Libertine* and *The Lancashire Witches*, of course, but also in *A True Widow*, performed (with prologue by Dryden) in 1678, like the comedies by Leanerd and Durfey. Even after the "revelations" of the Popish Plot, one finds joking about black devils: when Ramble's face is blacked in *The London Cuckolds* (III.ii), Townly identifies him with "the Prince of Darkness" and the chimney sweep Guiliom is called "Devil" when he appears black-faced in Behn's *The False Count* (V.i).

Such a connection strengthens the hypothesis that Dryden's black friar appeals to a visual convention of the diabolic. At the very opening of the play, shortly before he describes the friar (128–29), Pedro reminds Alfonso that the usurper, Leonora's father, stole the kingdom with moorish troops, black infidels.[32] And at the very end of the play, just before the miracle of Sancho's being found alive, Dominic himself, in his last speech, couples himself with the forces of darkness: "May your Sisters, Wives, and Daughters be so naturally lewd, that they may have no occasions for a Devil to tempt, or a Fryar to pimp for 'em" (200). We need hardly add what everyone can guess, that the pamphleteers of the day repeatedly linked the Devil and the Popish Plot. (For pictures, see, e.g., *POAS* 2: prints facing 370, 372; Mack 6.)

Dominic does more than wow the crowds diabolically and let Dry-

---

[32]For black moors on the Restoration stage, see the drawing of "the moorish dance" done for the 1673 Quarto of Settle's *The Empress of Morocco* and the portrait of the actor William Harris as the Empress of Morocco in Duffett's farce of that name, plates 19 and 9 respectively in Powell, *Restoration*.

den flaunt an antipapist royalism. He also serves to hold the two plots together by combining three major themes that we have discussed—power, special pleading, and pardon—with one we have not, paternity. Through excommunication Dominic can exclude those who do not truckle to him, in a play whose central concern is usurpation of power and consequent acts of exclusion: the jailing of Sancho, the framing of Bertran, the attempt by Raymond and his band to make Torrismond exile his wife the Queen, and, obviously, Gomez' jealous bondage of Elvira and Lorenzo's attempts to pry Elvira from Gomez by force and by locking him up. Dominic, the special pleader, is at home in a play filled with deceit and casuistry. His right to pardon, as a confessor, stands in analogy with Bertran's (selfish) decision not to follow the Queen's tacit order to kill Sancho, and with the disposition to pardon shared by Torrismond and Sancho themselves. And as priest, Dominic is a father, so addressed repeatedly by Elvira and Lorenzo, in a play which launches its political force from notions of patriarchal authority. The legitimacy of this authority, kept in question by Dominic, is repeatedly both accepted and rejected through the Queen's father's usurpation and his betrothal of his daughter to Bertran, Torrismond's relation to his two fathers Raymond and Sancho, Lorenzo's jolly defiance of his father, and Alfonso's forcing his daughter, fresh from the convent, to marry a grasping, jealous, impotent old despot.

This last, politically charged issue, paternity, remains complex in *The Spanish Fryar*, and Dryden gives a deft turn to the ideology that encased it, which he affirms and also attenuates. In the year of *The Spanish Fryar*, 1680, loyalists to the throne printed a first edition of Filmer's *Patriarcha*, for its eloquence in favor of the thesis that Scripture, Aristotle, and history agree in the absolute power of kings and fathers. During the same year, others of Filmer's tracts, also written before the Civil Wars, had been grouped in a volume "bundled through the press . . . so hastily that its pages were wrongly numbered and its title page did not tally with its contents," then reprinted once more, as Laslett recounts in his introduction to *Patriarcha*. The loyalists' haste to broadcast Filmer's thought, which "formed the *ipsissima verba* of the established order" (34), was matched by their opponents' haste to demolish it. Of the several Shaftesburians who rushed to their quills, Locke, of course, was the most eminent and successful in the attack on Filmer, through his *Two Treatises of Government*, begun in 1679–80 and published ten years later. Laslett's edition of *Two Treatises* notes, however, that in July 1678, when Locke was in France and had no political occasion for attacking Filmer, he wrote his own "abbreviated sketch of a complete theory, relating man to God, father to son, the individual to society, in familial, patriarchal terms" (48). If Locke's notions of natural law in 1678 were patriarchal, one can see why Filmer's patriarchal ideas were recognized as heavy artillery in 1680: they based their declaration for absolutism on beliefs extremely widely held in the seventeenth century even by those who found themselves siding with (or even, Locke proves, with the deepest intellectual debts to) the Whig Earl of Shaftesbury. Presumably, then, Dryden would not have had to argue for the natural (as opposed to contractual) basis of kingship in 1680, certainly not in a popular comedy, although his easy, cautious acceptance of that patriarchal ideology would have helped to reinforce it as a natural assumption.

In making Torrismond the son of Sancho and in having a man replace a woman as true heir to the throne, *The Spanish Fryar* adheres to this ideology. Of course such plot structures recur in many plays, but that was all the better for letting the patriarchal ideology seem natural when new political debates turned it into a visible alternative, a choice rather than an unseen given. Sancho owes his rights to natural law, not a contract or consent of the governed. He does not appear on stage, we surmise, so that he can embody kingship in the abstract, paternity in the abstract, the better for Dryden to generalize the political point. But the better too for Dryden to blunt the political point. As an absent character, Sancho does not carry much affective weight with the audience, who know him only in what others say of him and in his relation to the hero Torrismond. While he does not need the consent of the people of Saragossa to qualify him as king, he does need that of the people in Dorset Garden to qualify him as a persuasive figure, and both his "real" and stage thrones come from his son's valor and passion. The child is father to the man by embodying him: only a worthy person could father Torrismond, biologically and as a man of feeling, patriotism, endurance, and popular favor. This sort of character bonding lets Dryden use the patriarchal metaphor but also disavow any extremism in his use of it.

The Spanish Fryar thus can assume for the position "Father" a reverence that the actual human fathers in the play must earn and rarely do. After all, Torrismond is right to put down his "father" Raymond's rebellion, Leonora to disregard her father's bequeathing her to Bertran, Lorenzo to join forces against his father Alfonso; and, however one feels about Elvira's hopes to rob and cuckold her odious husband, Gomez, no objections to her doing so spring from her having been married to him by her father. Sir Robert Filmer would have hated this comedy. No more respectful of the fathers who appear than Carolean comedies generally are, *The Spanish Fryar* deploys Filmerism as an affective, limited, logically inconsistent, historically ungrounded proof of kingship, and so negotiates between Tory and Whig politics by acknowledging both parties. Father Dominic, inimical to most Whigs and Tories alike, and a man whose split between his position and his personal abuse of it is wholly indisputable, acts as a lightning rod for the energy generated by Dryden's politically shrewd, ideologically inconsistent procedure.

The Filmerite argument, and Dominic's role, have another fillip to them, too. One must assume that Sancho and Torrismond, rightful, deserving kings, are Catholics, like the Duke of York, who had been sent to sit out the Exclusion Crises in Brussels, seat of the Spanish governor of the Netherlands. The play, however, has numerous (and for Dryden, typical) anticlerical comments directed at Catholics, as well as the presence of the egregious friar. Of course the open purpose of these comments is to ally Dryden with other right-thinking Englishmen in decrying plots and popery. We suggest that a more covert purpose is the defense of royal patriarchy against enemies from both Catholic and Protestant sides. At the very opening of *Patriarcha*, as Filmer maintains the absolute power of kings, he blames "Schoolmen" for hatching and "succeeding Papists" for fostering the dangerous tenets of contract or consent theory. His first attack, right after the introductory section of the book, is against Bellarmine, whom, however, he has previously linked to Calvin and "zealous favourers of the Geneva discipline" (53). In short, Filmer believes, Catholic kings are rightful, but Catholic clerics are as disruptive of proper order as Calvinists (for which, in 1680, read "commonwealth's-men"). As Swift says in the penultimate section of *A Tale of a Tub*, the "Humour and Dispositions [of *Jack* and his Brother *Peter*] were not only the same, but there was a close Analogy in their Shape, and Size and their Mien" (199). Filmer and Swift's arguments, like Dryden's toward the end of *Religio Laici*, couple false domination and false liberty. So does Dryden's in this play: the defective fathers—Leonora's, Raymond, and Alfonso—all use illegitimate force upon their children (the usurper, upon his subjects too) and all take part in rebellion.

To make the appropriate politico-religious analogy for the Exclusion Crisis, Dominic needs to repeat and parody these fathers, to embody the churchman as disordering rebel whose authority subverts authority. Elvira's "Ghostly Father" (II; 149) is vested with institutional power to bind and release like her real father, a judge. Moreover, Dominic's clerical function makes him a kind of extension of the convent in which Elvira was kept before being handed over to Gomez, and he, fatherlike, arranges her near union with Lorenzo. He also tries to destroy her marriage with Gomez just as Raymond tries to destroy Torrismond's with Leonora. Once again, these parodies do not comment on Alfonso's, Raymond's, or the usurper's behavior, which is in each case quite clear by itself. They do throw that behavior into relief, and they at once point to its applicability to contemporary politics and also remove some of the onus of that parallel on to the papist Dominic. By both likeness and contrast with these fathers, Dominic sharpens and delimits the accusation against them; since at the end of the play he is expelled by the rabble (whom they have led and who are the rebellious analogues to Catholic casuists in Filmer's terms), he becomes the condign scapegoat so that other fatherly rebels and usurpers can be pardoned.

This scapegoat function for Dominic explains why Dryden locates him in the comic plot. Carolean libertines, we have argued, fulfill desires by rebellion against the patriarchal law of society: tradition, authority, female chastity. Lorenzo is such a libertine par excellence. He refuses to worry about the state or his family, represented by the beleaguered Torrismond, at the beginning of the play, and he accepts no one's authority. The woman with whom he plans to elope is both someone else's wife and, wonderfully enough, a virgin to deflower. He is eager to supplant a man his father's age in the bed of that man's wife, and to this end he beats the older man and threatens him with soldiers (first a threat of billeting soldiers upon him, then an attempted kidnapping) in a way that anticipates his using his soldiers against his own father. Gomez, as a father surrogate, is humiliated by Lorenzo in public, in front of Lorenzo's own father (with Lorenzo standing behind him), and must testify to Lorenzo's physical and moral virtues and his innocence. Down to the (averted) incest from supplanting the surrogate father, a displacement from Dryden's *Oedipus*, this plot acts out the libertine attack on patriarchy. As false father, Dominic serves both the attack and its rebuttal. He typifies its subversive strength, gives a quasi-paternal sanction to Lorenzo's pranks (like Aldo to Woodall's), and in so doing, in being both libertine and father, he qualifies himself to act as scapegoat for an action at once so typical of Carolean comedy and so charged with symbolic force in this political play.

Dominic's clerical status, moreover, parodies the union of sacredness and paternity in the royal person of the one good and true father in *The Spanish Fryar*, King Sancho. "Heaven makes Princes its peculiar Care," as Torrismond pronounces in the last line of the play. Earlier, however, people are less sure: "Heav'n must not be Heav'n," says Pedro in the opening dialogue, speaking of the usurpation (127), and Raymond insists:

> Marriage with *Torrismond!* it must not be;

> By Heaven, it must not be; or, if it be;
> Law, Justice, Honour, bid farwell to Earth;
> For Heaven leaves all to Tyrants. (IV; 180)

Dominic embodies these doubts about divine justice in that he images religion in the world as hypocrisy. He displaces the danger of atheism—a rejection of the Father in Heaven because he vacations instead of supervising—from God to priests.

The denouement assures the audience that as human activity blunders helplessly in the rest of the play, so here. God needs no holy intermediaries, and the attacks on priests can safely be divorced from the acts of blasphemy they may have seemed to resemble. Without Dominic, the audience know that Providence will intervene, because Heaven has been so often invoked during the play that not to have divine intervention would be to encourage atheism. With him as a focus, though, their skepticism or cynicism can have full swing and still not impair their faith. Again, something adapted from a compromise formation is at work here, in offering the audience a comic plot and a targeted character as a place where their impieties can sport about. The play's recognition of scepticism and the audience's exercise (or discharge) of it permit them all to collaborate at last, when by Heaven's judgment, Sancho rises from his dungeon on the arms of the noble and Dominic hustles into the wings with pushes of the mob.

We have dwelt much more on unity in *The Spanish Fryar* than in *The Tempest* or in *Marriage A-la-Mode*, where formal coherences allowed for a controlled dispersion of effects, for variety, not unity. Eventually in the 1680s and 1690s, the fletcherian configuration was to be modified under the pressures for unity. Though that has not yet happened in *The Spanish Fryar*, a cursory chart of the way the two plots intermesh will show how differently Dryden develops them from the pendular movement and return of *Marriage A-la-Mode*. He establishes a focus in act I, with the rivalries of Torrismond and Bertran for the Queen (the advantage temporarily Bertran's) and of Lorenzo and Gomez for Elvira (the advantage temporarily Gomez'), and then, in act II, presents a first reversal of both advantages. After that, however, he divorces the plot actions to a more marked degree than in the earlier plays we have discussed, focusing first on the comic plot, next on the serious one for long stretches. The only real interplay from the entrance of Dominic (II.iii) to the double denouement comes in the first scene of act IV, where the soldiers' planned imprisonment of Gomez, the lovers' near-elopement, the advice of Dominic to have Gomez killed, and the rescue of Gomez by Lorenzo's father, Alfonso, echo the events of the serious plot: Sancho's imprisonment by force and the advice of Bertran to kill him, the readying of the marriage between Torrismond and Leonora, and the attempt by Alfonso's brother Raymond, Torrismond's supposed father, to rescue Sancho and prevent or annul the marriage. This interplay, as we have suggested, represents not only a formal but also a conceptual convergence of the plots, of a sort that one does not find in *The Tempest* or *Marriage A-la-Mode* as we read them.

Convergence, of course, does not mean that one plot comments cognitively or affectively on the other in a nonfletcherian way. Thus Lorenzo's fleshliness does not, in our reading of this idiom, cast Torrismond's heroics in doubt or vice versa. (Of course a good sense of dramatic form allows the audience to guess future events in one plot from past events in the other, but that is something else.) In respect to this mode of construction, however, *The Spanish Fryar* does differ slightly from Dryden's earlier plays. That is in the role of Dominic, who appears in the comic plot but who, during the Exclusion Crisis, presumably evoked intense political feelings, the sort of feelings proper to the serious plot. Given this special sort of linkage, he can epitomize the gap between hierarchical position and human person, between God's watchfulness and human faith, between true and false authority and liberty. We have suggested that Dryden takes advantage of this, using Dominic to highlight certain themes in both plots and to apply these themes to the political situation of 1680. Once the audience have been alerted to the implications of the themes in this way, each plot develops them under the kind of scrutiny appropriate to it.

More generally, the devices of Dryden's earlier comedies reappear in this, but adapted for different ends, political ends that matched well with what was dramaturgically up-to-date in 1680. Heterogeneity of response becomes mixed response within each of the two plots. The rakish comedies' emphasis on drives turns into, on the one hand, excuses for characters who jump to the tune of their passions, and on the other hand, a divine fiat that puts a moral end to both plots. We do not believe that Carolean comedies often rely on Providence or stagger beneath the well-intentioned weight of doctrine, though for the occasion on which this one was written, Providence proved useful as an affective maneuver. Still, to invoke Heaven fits with an increased interest in arriving at social consensus, during a political crisis that challenged consensus and made people reflect on their social values. These became more immediate, at least on the public stage, than the individual satisfactions hunted for during the past ten years or more. With the next wave of consensual instead of heterogeneous comedy, and even with some of the plays slightly later than *The Spanish*

Fryar, reliance on other emotions besides that of religious awe becomes standard. One can see the beginnings of the process in Otway and Durfey, and to some extent in Dryden's last and greatest comedy, *Amphitryon* (1690), second in popularity only to *The Spanish Fryar* during the following century.

9

The Last Years of Carolean Comedy

As we have explained in chapters 7 and 8, we locate the history of Carolean comedy up to 1678 along an axis of decreasing social cohesion, while satire took sharp shots at the constraints of the status quo and also at certain foppish and bourgeois alternatives to them. When the imagined and real horrors of the Popish Plot burst upon the public, the dramatic satire rapidly began to serve a new purpose. Refocused, it catered to a sudden upsurge of need for social cohesion. We do not mean that all beliefs must have become more alike in time of political crisis but that the public flaunting and relishing of egocentrism became less palatable. The first break in the history of Carolean comedy occurred; the next was to come at the next upsurge of need for cohesion, the Revolution of 1688. In some sense, playwrights of the late 1670s and early 1680s found themselves in the same state as those writing comedy just after the Glorious Restoration had given God's viceroy Charles his throne and his community of Britons. These early Carolean comedies, such as we discussed in chapter 3, were largely in tune with social values: John Wilson's *The Cheats*, Tuke's *The Adventures of Five Hours*, Howard's *The Committee*. By the time of the Exclusion Crisis, Carolean comedies had lost the innocence of those distant plays, for the anarchic mode of *A Fond Husband* and *Limberham* had left its imprint. Still, through insisting on satire or farce if they depicted amoral or immoral behavior, or diverging still further from the patterns of wish fulfillment, compromise formation, and heterogeneous response that we have discussed, they could pay tribute to a need for social consensus and cleansing the body politic's bad blood. *The Spanish Fryar*, with its profound awareness of the generic expectations it flouts, beautifully exemplifies this new mode. If one takes it and *Limberham* as models—not as poles marking extremes but as models exemplifying ways of proceeding—the confusions and achievements of late Carolean comedy, 1678–85, become easier to comprehend. There is more strategic continuity among these remarkably various plays than even sympathetic critics have made clear, and infinitely more imaginative understanding of the theatre and its demands than scoffers have supposed.

Shadwell and Otway, 1678–85

We can illustrate what we mean, perhaps, by looking at the relation between love and authority in three plays produced after 1678 by each of Dryden's two most distinguished fellows, Shadwell and Otway. Our earlier discussion has set the background for the comparisons. In chapter 3 we pointed out that comedy of the early 1660s adapted its inherited fletcherian structure by keeping the courtship plot central but realizing the characters more fully and consistently than Fletcher and his disciples had done. An added premium thereby accrued to the vividness, or sense of presence that a character conveyed, and some of the plays of the later 1660s, like the Dryden-Davenant *Tempest* or a few comedies derived from Molière, went so far as to demote the young lovers as foci of interest in favor of vivid characters who wielded authority. By the early-to-mid 1670s, the rake combined the roles of lover and figure of authority, with rival authorities, if any, localized in ridiculed humours characters, a configuration rare in the 1660s: compare the Days of *The Committee* or Don Henrique of *The Adventures of Five Hours* with the parents in *The Man of Mode* or the cuckolded husbands in *The Country-Wife*.

Because the rake became more and more outrageous in the later 1670s, however, his exercise of authority (personal power with at least tacit social backing, such as Horner or Dorimant exercises) increasingly threatened to make him, more rarely her, unsympathetic to the audience. The demand for consensus at the time of the Exclusion Crisis operated predictably upon this dynamic. By the 1680s, playwrights were once again disrupting the alliance of rakishness and authority. Some returned to the fletcherian model of the early 1660s, as in Crowne's *Sir Courtly Nice*; some demythified the vivid, powerful lover by challenging the dramatic formulas from which he derived authority in the eyes of many, maybe most members of the audience, as in *The Spanish Fryar*. Alternatively, Lee's *The Princess of Cleve* continues allying rakery and authority, but with tools honed by the *moralistes* and the anarchic mode of *Limberham*, it devalues these allies. The rake Nemours is powerful, triumphant in love, and thoroughly odious, a man who "if he were dying . . . with his Veins cut, he wou'd call for Wine, Fiddles, and Whores, and laugh himself into the other World" (V.ii.31–33).

Shadwell and Otway each produced a comedy in the spring of 1678, before the Popish Plot furor: *A True Widow* and *Friendship in Fashion*. Shadwell's *The Woman-Captain* and Otway's *The Souldiers Fortune* graced the beginning (September) and end (June) of the 1679–80 theatrical season. Then, at the beginning of the 1681-82 season, Shadwell offered *The Lancashire Witches*, and the end of the next one, 1682-83, Otway closed his dramatic career with *The Atheist*. All six comedies were staged by the Duke's Company, and though the full casts of Shadwell's are not extant (the Otway casts are), one can reasonably presume that by and large the same actors, certainly Barry and Leigh, appeared in them all. The plays are not much alike, but they do follow a certain pattern: those of 1678 adapt the anarchic Durfeyan model; those of the 1679-80 season retreat into reworkings of old repertory (Shadwell) or a more conventional courtship plot (Otway); and the last pair disrupts (Shadwell) or devalues (Otway) the alliance of libertine love and authority, in the manner respectively of *The Spanish Fryar* and *The Princess of Cleve*.

We may begin with Shadwell's fine, though in 1678 unappreciated *A True Widow*, which in the manner of Durfeyan comedy keeps a courtship plot or plots at the center, thinning the compromise formation and representing a world of malice and betrayal on all sides. *A True Widow* is a remarkably dense comedy. It resembles Shadwell's earlier plays, and Carolean comedy generally, in its fletcherian peripeteias, facilitated and also formally repeated by an arrangement of interlocked, contrasting characters. The more rigid a play's characters, of course, the more the movement of the play devolves upon turns in plot. An elaborate system of defining characters in terms of each other, as in this play, tends to increase the dramatic value of rigidity. Thus here the humours characters include two gossips, one male and one female (Old Maggot, Lady Busy) versus one man who can think and talk only of himself (Selfish); the artistic type (Young Maggot, a would-be poet and playwright) versus the sportsman and gamester (Prigg); the adaptive worldly conniver who writes her bonds and legal papers in slow-vanishing ink (Lady Cheatley) versus the religious man of method who has his routines set down for the next half century (her brother, Lump). Shadwell then uses the narrative to link these characters across these pairings: Old Maggot, an enemy to wit, stops funding Young Maggot's endeavors of art; Lady Cheatley inveigles Prigg into dressing as a parson to conduct a mock-marriage for her; Lady Busy acts as a bawd for Selfish.

In the courtship plots, the same pattern holds. Stout Carlos woos an imperious tease, "cruel" Theodosia, while Bellamour tries to seduce—and ends up loving and marrying—the indignantly virtuous Isabella, and Stanmore successfully seduces Isabella's ninny sister, Gartrude. Again, the narrative interconnects these characters. Bellamour, who watches Selfish deflower Gartrude in the backstage of a theatre, thinks he is watching Isabella betray him; Stanmore meanwhile pursues her as Gartrude. More broadly, in a classic statement of the mediated, competitive desire we discussed theoretically in chapter 2 and practically in chapters 6 and 7, Theodosia requires her lover Carlos to rival his friends: "I must have my Servant all Wit, all Gaiety, and the Ladies of the Town run mad for him: I would not only triumph over him, but over my whole Sex in him. . . . Make *Isabella* slight *Bellamour*, little *Gartrude* sacrifice *Selfish*: Be the third word in every Ladies mouth, from fifteen to five and thirty; and you shall find what I'l say to you" (II; 311).

As a result of this density, *A True Widow* enjoys, as Hume says, "genuine complexity of perspective" (*Development* 332), and the more so because a major motif, perhaps the major motif of this comedy, is deceit and betrayal. Here Shadwell responds to the atmosphere of the late 1670s. We have already mentioned some of the betrayals, real and suspected, in the courtship plots; a particularly Durfeyan one that we have not mentioned is the betrayal of friends—the third man-about-town, Stanmore, tells the ladies that "*Carlos* has an ill breath, and takes Physick of a *French* Surgeon; and that *Bellamore* keeps a Player, and will run out his Estate," for in keeping with the fashion, "*Stanmore* . . . speaks well of no man" (III; 326). As to the Lady Cheatley plot, brother and sister, mistress and servant, lady and suitors, creditors and debtor, mother and daughters all betray each other. Even the silly Gartrude, infatuated and on the marriage market, follows her backstage coitus with Selfish (who betrays her by boasting of it) by immediately doing the same thing with Stanmore: she thus completes the abridged play the group has just been watching on this very stage. By "Prickett," it has dwelt on a wife and her two lovers. (Shadwell perhaps recognized how Durfeyan a climate he had created and meant Prickett's play to parody *A Fond Husband* [Hume, *Development* 333].) Thus betraying Selfish, she betrays herself, behaving in a way just exposed in public. In Shadwell's own play, the most idiotic characters of course betray themselves. Selfish, for example, who claims to slay all the ladies with his charms, gets into a preening match with Young Maggot which reduces the fop and the poetaster to bawling the monosyllable "I" at each other (II; 312).

The moral criterion of *A True Widow*, if any, appears to be social efficiency, since the three gentlemen of the town all get what they want, Carlos his "cruel Mistress," Bellamour his virtuous lady (once he accepts marriage), and Stanmore his Gartrude's young body. With none is there a compromise formation, in which the audience enjoy both "immoral" behavior and exculpation for their having enjoyed it. The audience are invited to enjoy the swindles of Lady Cheatley, who not only ends up victorious but also can promise "a good Estate"—

which "belongs of right to other People"—to her new, duped husband, Old Maggot, if he "will go on and maintain what [she has] done" (V; 361). As one of the conjurers we mentioned in chapter 7, she does by and large impose on people one is pleased to see imposed upon, and Shadwell softens her guilt by having her explain that "my Husband was cheated on his Estate by my Brother, and other Rascals" (III; 323). Still, there is no exculpatory action near the end of the play, and rewards and punishments go indifferently to the undeserving, harmless fools and real knaves. One may have the feeling that justice has been done, an affective state that lets the comedy end in Carolean fashion, with cognitive dissonance very low, but that state is not to be confused with the sort of moral vision that critics divine in Shadwell's alleged master, Ben Jonson.

At first, *The Woman-Captain* looks more morally coherent because it is so much more cautious. In a little note to the reader of *A True Widow*, published in early 1679, Shadwell staunchly insisted, "I had rather suffer, by venturing to bring new things upon the Stage, than go on like a Mill-Horse in the same Round" (3: 288). But mill-horse he became, to grind out *The Woman-Captain*, in which the main plot takes its grist from two previous successes of Shadwell, *The Libertine* (1675) and *Timon of Athens* (early 1678). Sir Humphry Scattergood, "A Prodigal, Extravagant, and Luxurious Knight" (Dramatis Personae), feasts and whores, scorning his old, hand-wringing steward, till his fortune is gone and his friends desert him. He does not die, like Don John and Timon before him, but with the bravado of the first and the willfulness of the second, he undergoes the comic equivalent of death, marriage to his "she-pyrat" (V; 83) of a whore, Phyllis, to regain what she has robbed from him. In the other, more amusing plot, Mrs. Gripe disguises herself as her brother, a soldier, to get her own back from her excruciatingly mean and miserly husband, whom she can "enlist" because he cannot resist her recruiting shilling. He and a number of the foolish debauchees are humiliated and beaten as infantrymen. Mrs. Gripe ends up freed from her marriage, the whores either married or guaranteed incomes—the play is "about" female authority's inheriting the force proper to absent love and to absent male authority. Sir Humphrey impoverishes himself by dispersal, Gripe impoverishes himself by balking at disbursement, and Mrs. Gripe's military brother, who represents the authority of the state, never appears.

No doubt the void of authority and its ersatz expression through distorted social institutions—a marriage to a proud, rich, thieving whore, acts of discipline enforced by a specious show of the army—represented to Shadwell the state of England in 1679. And yet, like *A True Widow*, *The Woman-Captain* makes no moral point. Its satire is diluted by a stream of (rather poor) farce. Its attack on Sir Humphrey's behavior flags when he turns out to be the most intelligent and decisive of the dissolute men. Its point about authority, seemingly enforced by Sir Humphrey's having to marry the distasteful Phyllis, is undermined by the joyful sympathy one has for Mrs. Gripe, who deserves her borrowed clout. In fact this play carries to an extreme the Carolean principle of being all things to all viewers as much as possible. The figures satirized are so grotesque as to admit of no divided opinion among the audience; Shadwell flatters women by showing them in charge, and men by showing that women are in charge only when men default; the end is moral in the debauchees and the miser's suffering, but amoral in the whores' triumph; and the farce—"*Plenty of Noise, and scarcity of Wit*," says the honest epilogue—makes sure no one will take anything too seriously. The same epilogue attributes the feebleness of the play to Shadwell's contempt for an audience who could not appreciate *A True Widow*, but the characteristics of *The Woman-Captain* have as much to do with the state of the theatres during the early Exclusion Crisis as with the smarting of an unappreciated artist. The bold mode of the earlier play now sneaks on, recognizable but barely so.

If *A True Widow* represents Shadwell's appropriation of the late 1670s themes of betrayal and moral anarchy, and *The Woman-Captain* the pale consensus seeking of the early Exclusion Crisis years, *The Lancashire Witches* tries to achieve consensus while devaluing, more seriously than *The Woman-Captain*, both the old allies, wild love and authority. Thus Shadwell for the first time puts on stage a favorably drawn parent, Sir Edward Hartfort, whose firm Protestantism and sensible doubts about witches are echoed by the two exemplary young men, Bellfort and Doubty, who come courting his daughter and destined daughter-in-law. Yet Sir Edward would have his witty, beautiful, strong-minded daughter marry a pert Oxonian who is heir to the neighboring estate, and would have the neighbor's witty, beautiful, and strong-minded daughter marry his sottish son. He ends up treated like the heavy Carolean fathers before him, as Isabella, "a free English woman," resolves to "stand up for my Liberty, and property of Choice," and Theodosia declares, "I hate the imposition of a Husband, 'tis as bad as Popery" (I; 111–12), strong and perhaps surprising language in 1681, especially for so great a foe of popery as Shadwell, and especially in a play with a popish priest named Tegue O Divelly. Confronted with the heroines' clandestine marriages to Doubty and Bellfort, Sir Edward does bless the fait accompli, and with these two well-bred beaux, he certainly deplores witch-hunting, in contrast to all the stupid, clownish, and knavish bigots in the play. But then, the bigots are right and the men of sense wrong about the witches. Mother Demdike and her crew flit about on their brooms, talking bloody tragedy—about "glewy Stuff" from dead men's eyeballs and the like (II; 132)—and acting conjurer's farce on stage. In an incident that, though isolated, still seems to epitomize the confused state of authority in *The Lancashire Witches*, Sir Edward and the beaux rhapsodize over the "Golden days of Queen *Elizabeth*" and true Englishmen, scorning the "poyson" of "Forreign Vanities" and gentry who are "grown servile Apes to foreign customes"; then, contented Britons, they call for music and admire "*An Italian Song*" (III; 136–37).

In *The Woman-Captain*, we argued, the strenuous exercise of authority by women marked for Shadwell the absence of proper male authority. The whores' triumph is a meaningful analogue of Mrs. Gripe's. Here, despite two exemplary male lovers and, supposedly, an exemplary father, the exploits of the witches are similarly analogous to the heroines', though both groups of women must submit to social (male) authority at the end, when the witches are jailed in Lancaster and the new brides must beg Sir Edward's blessing. During the play, though, the role of Sir Edward's daughter seems to have let Elizabeth Barry repeat the display of martial arts she had made as Mrs. Gripe, for Isabella boxes the oafish Sir Timothy's ear (I; 111; IV; 156), threatens to tear his eyes out (II; 129), and stones him (III; 142). She behaves, in short, like those other subversive female authorities, the witches, who maul the men. Shortly after Isabella last boxes Tim's ears and pulls him by them, Mother Demdike's potion causes "a Million of Needles" to prick the "Bowels" of the contemptible Chaplain Smerk (IV; 161), and then the witch enters in propria persona, but invisible, to cuff and kick O Divilly (163). Isabella's laying strong hands on Tim precedes her giving her loving hand to Bellfort; just so, after Mother Dickenson and O Divilly battle with witch's staff and rosary beads as weapons, and she wins in her violent "male" role, she wins again in her female role by bed-tricking him. During the latter part of this play, too, the heroines pretend now and again to be witches (V; 173, 181, in particular).

The epilogue to *The Lancashire Witches* compares it to *The Spanish Fryar*: "You had a Spanish Fryer *of Intrigue,* / *And now we have presented you a* Tegue." We would like to pursue the comparison in four points beyond Dryden's and Shadwell's similar casting of Anthony Leigh as a corrupt, alien Papist. First, both comedies undermine socially constituted authority in the state—Dryden's female usurper, glassy-eyed male lover, and paternal rebels; Shadwell's unwise fathers and justices of the peace—and the church, where Dryden exhibits only Dominic, and Shadwell adds a sniveling Anglican, Smerk, to the Papist O

Divilly. Under these circumstances, both plays agree on what Sir Edward says in the closing couplet of *The Lancashire Witches*:

How shallow is our foresight and our prudence!
Be ne're so wise, design what e'er we will,
There is a Fate that over-rules us still.

One is back to the ruefulness of the Carolean Prospero, trapped in the timid 1660s, but now without the compensatory animal buoyancy of Hippolito and Dorinda. Second, neither comedy presents libertine behavior or a compromise formation, and neither allows much room for heterogeneity of response. Third, both Dryden's "Tory" and Shadwell's "Whig" comedies treat the supposedly dangerous Papist as a character of farce, somewhat less sinister in 1681 (Shadwell) than in 1680 (Dryden), since "by the autumn of 1681, the Popish Plot could at last be seen in its gaunt perspective, and the nation was now rallying to the throne after the assaults of the exclusionists" (Ogg 2: 630). The two comedies strive to be within the range of consensus, though in the ten months that had elapsed between them, that range had shifted. Fourth, because Shadwell's priest ("Father") and witches ("Mothers") appear in the "low" plot, the theme of parental authority and its assumption by the lovers—a theme that occurs, quite differently treated, in *The Spanish Fryar* and *The Lancashire Witches*—can be modified obliquely, by analogy, to have both private and communal overtones. Like Bertran, an influential figure of false pardon and passion who echoes Dominic in the "high" plot of *The Spanish Fryar*, Theodosia's mother, Lady Shacklehead, represents the lust, domination, and disorder of the witches in the love plot of Shadwell's play. Like Dominic in the "low" plot, the witches set forth an image of power and passion and will serve as unexcused scapegoats while the lovers are pardoned by the comprehending father. Weber points out that the rake's erotic energy took a place in the popular imagination that had earlier been filled by the demonic sexuality of witches (20–26): Shadwell's lecherous witches reverse this process and, with the heroes exemplary, represent the outlet for the debauchery earlier located in his libertines, Don John and Sir Humphrey.

The same kind of movement we have been discussing, from a comedy of betrayal and moral anarchy to one of caution, and thence to one that saps the alliance between rakish love and authority, appears in Otway's comedies, *Friendship in Fashion*, *The Souldiers Fortune*, and the latter's sequel, *The Atheist* (1678, 1680, 1683). *Friendship in Fashion*, produced about a month after *Limberham*, resembles it in following Durfey's lead. Goodvile, the male lead whose role was taken by Betterton, strikes the Durfeyan note by declaring, "I would on a good occasion lose my life for my Friend; but not my pleasure" (III; 382). As this cool maxim suggests, Otway gives him and some of the other schemers a capacity for wit, including *moraliste* wit: "[Modesty] is a quality which though [women] hate never so much in a Gallant, they are apt for many reasons to value in a Husband: Fear not, Dissimulation is the natural adjunct of their Sex; and I would no more despair of a woman, though she swore she hated me, then I would believe her though she swore she lov'd me" (III; 376). The value given to wit in this play resembles that in *A True Widow*: the fools decry it but the lovers practice it to a degree not found in *The Woman-Captain* or *The Lancashire Witches*. Thus, marriage "Is to Love, as the *Jesuit*'s Powder to an Ague, it stops the Fit, and in a little time wears it quite off"; or "Jealousie, like the Small-Pox; if it comes out kindly, is never mortal" (V; 352, 358).

Friendship in Fashion proves Goodvile's cynicism to be on the mark, except for his implied distinction between the sexes. For both sexes, malice and vengefulness are as endemic (and natural) as lust; and gall, not frankness, prompts Goodvile to blurt to his wife of a year, "*Victoria* has been my Mistress, is my Mistress, and shall be my Mistress, and what a Pox would you have more? and so God b'ye to you" (IV; 399). During the course of the play, Goodvile tries to marry Victoria to his friend Truman so that he himself can seduce Camilla, fiancée of his other friend Valentine; Truman, in revenge, cuckolds Goodvile whom Victoria also betrays to Mrs. Goodvile, her cousin and "Friend" (II; 356), whom she has of course been betraying. Not only do these characters feign friendship and virtue as the action develops, but at the end Goodvile, by his own wish, is left in the dark or at least in the gloaming: "*Truman*, if thou hast enjoyed [my wife], I beg thee keep it close, and if it be possible let us yet be friends" (V; 430). In Durfeyan manner, *Friendship in Fashion* combines a good many displays of emotion with more standard comic fixtures, like several fools and lecherous elders, and with musical diversions as ironic tokens of cheer, an unusually large number of the dances and songs praised by the fools (I; 349). Whereas Durfey mixes in such matter to lighten the action, however, Otway uses these fashionable, superficial amusements to call attention to what they hide, an action forever proceeding in the darkness of seamy motives and of mistrust.

The vestigia of compromise formation remain in the play's structure: as in *A True Widow*, there is a rake plot/moral plot pair, with both heroes successful (Truman cuckolds Goodvile, Camilla and Valentine marry), and there is a rake plot doubly moralized in that Goodvile deserves cuckolding and also in that his wife's affair with Truman can hardly keep going on. But also as in *A True Widow*, though for other reasons, the audience get no model of rakery to carry out their desires. Here, by his early love for Victoria, Truman, the cuckolder, in fact endorses the ethic of the conventional love plot before Mrs. Goodvile, for her own sexual purposes, tells him that Victoria is Goodvile's whore. *Friendship in Fashion* does not hold up ways of life, virtuous or rakish, to be tenanted by the audience, but rather legitimates a variety of behaviors within—and only within—the context of the play, where they serve as punishments for violations of a code of male solidarity. (Victoria ceases violating *female* solidarity with Mrs. Goodvile and becomes Lady Noble Clumsey.)

The logic of this reading would predict a minor role for the virtuous love plot, which must be attractive enough for the audience to resent characters who intend to spoil it but not so attractive as to draw attention from the action in which those spoilsports get their comeuppance. The Valentine/Camilla love plot fits this description exactly, and therefore fails to ensnare the audience in the romance it depicts. As to "immoral" doings, the audience can enjoy them in Otway just as in Etherege and Wycherley but cannot comfortably situate these doings in some imagined form of their own lives. For the ecstasy of sleeping with a glamorous, seemingly inaccessible woman, here embodied in one's best friend's wife, one must choose between unpalatable alternatives: either one must be treacherous like Goodvile and thus of course dissociate oneself from the moral indignation of his cuckolder, the very person who serves as the audience's agent on stage; or, like Truman, one must have best friends whose treachery justifies treachery in return. With an elegant comedy like *Marriage A-la-Mode*, where sincerity and play are always in question, this dilemma hardly poses itself, but Otway's grim tone forbids that escape. Without being a clone of *Limberham* or *A True Widow*, then, *Friendship in Fashion* emerges from very similar generative principles.

In *The Souldiers Fortune*, two years later, Otway loyally responds to the politics of the time, making his two heroes, Beaugard and Courtine, impoverished soldiers whom parliamentary order has forced to disband, just as Otway himself had been. Beaugard's duped cuckold, too, Sir Davy Dunce, dabbles in Whiggish treasons for his own ends, so that he merits dishonor as a seditious hypocrite, not only as a jealous old fool whose wife has been pushed into his "rank surfeiting arms" by "the perswasion of Friends [i.e., family] and the Authority of Parents" (V; 182). Combining self-seeking and luck, the ethos of politics redefines "soldier" and "fortune" so as to empower free, aggressive action on the domestic front just as the disloyal libertinism of Goodvile had empowered such action in *Friendship in Fashion*. Still, the demands for social cohesion at the time of the Exclusion Crisis, not to mention the increased demand to please customers now only too ready to desert "our abandon'd Stage" (as the prologue puts it), keep Otway's satire here less savage than in his earlier comedy. The friends who betray each other are not Courtine and Beaugard but Sir Davy and an impotent, sexually polymorphous pimp and voyeur, Sir Jolly Jumble. The scenes between these two, furthermore, are funny: as Cibber writes of Leigh, "in Sir *Jolly* he was all Life, and laughing Humour; and when *Nokes* acted with him in the same Play [as Sir Davy], they return'd the Ball . . . dexterously upon one another" (86). Sir Davy too is not only the old fool we have described and the employer of a servant named "Vermin;" he is also the husband of Beaugard's once betrothed and a would-be murderer (of Beaugard). As in *The Woman-Captain*, where Sir Humphrey Scattergood is betrayed by debauched friends and whore, so here there is no courtship plot with admired figures in which a more shocking betrayal can occur, nor is there bitterness.

One would expect the rakish plot of *The Souldiers Fortune*, thus legitimated, to end with some promise of a permanent liaison, and indeed the love affair—"limited Fornication" marked by some real feeling, as opposed to "arbitrary Whoring" (IV; 153)—between Beaugard and his Clarinda seems likely to continue. Correspondingly, the marriage plot displays Sylvia and Courtine as witty, tough-minded, well-suited, with two of the proviso scenes (II; 120–21; V; 175–76) that mark a shrewd equality between the sexes in Carolean comedy. Here Otway underlines these scenes not only by contrasting this equality with the compulsion once exercised on Lady Dunce (I; 109) but also by thematizing the use of political instruments, starting with the debentures with which the former soldiers have been paid (I; 101). Later, Sir Davy pays one hundred pounds for what one would now call a "contract" on Beaugard (IV; 162) and he contracts for his own cuckolding along with his niece Sylvia's marriage (V; 192–93). In 1680, then, Otway's oblique handling of political themes makes *The Souldiers Fortune* a good deal closer to the plays of the mid-1670s than its bitter predecessor, with scenes of rakery milder than in Etherege, Wycherley, or Behn because of the old true love between Beaugard and Clarinda. His retreat does not involve reworking earlier plays, as Shadwell does in the Scattergood plot of *The Woman-Captain*, but retreat it is.

The Atheist; or, The Second Part of the Souldiers Fortune is another story, one of Otway's comedies that worked the same lodes as his tragedies. In 1680, *The Orphan*, with its central theme of distrust among those bound together and with its dark treatment of the rake's code, generalized the concerns of *Friendship in Fashion*; in 1682, with the multiple perfidies of the Exclusion Crisis clearer, *Venice Preserv'd* anticipated the nihilism of the next season's *The Atheist*. *Venice Preserv'd* not only puts Jaffeir in a complex version of the double bind characteristic of later 1670s tragedy, where the protagonist is damned if s/he does and damned if s/he doesn't, but also displays every seemingly positive value—love, friendship, patriotism—as intrinsically tainted in Otway's Venice. These values serve the audience merely as nostalgic, inevitably ironic points of reference rather than as ideals that might be possible but are unfortunately denied or mutually contradictory, like those, for instance, in *All for Love*. And these values are both interconnected and political: the patriarchal scheme of politics, as invoked in the Exclusion Crisis, makes much of the alignment of proper order in religion, in marriage, and in social relations, so that the dissembling and disassemblage of that alignment in *Venice Preserv'd* and then in *The Atheist* becomes politically specific. We are not insisting that Otway despised the politics of the Filmerites or of Dryden, that he was anti-Whig in belief and anti-Tory in his plague-on-both-your-houses disgust. Our argument is that his two last plays curiously rework the previous decade's principle of comic heterogeneity in terms of the 1680s' desire for cohesion. In both *Venice Preserv'd* and *The Atheist*, Otway offers a single, black vision meant for all the audience to accept, unlike the plays of the 1670s. The interpretation of this vision, however, depends (as in much twentieth-century drama) on the audience's taking it as satire, nihilism, or both, whether in support of an implicit moral and political order, in despair of establishing such an order, or in disdain of the credulity needed to legitimate one.

Daredevil, the titular atheist, gets short shrift from the play that bears his name: terror makes him contemptibly devout. But this standard reversal does not reinforce the theistic argument typically implied by such turnabouts, from Faust to Rochester to Robinson Crusoe to the new nonatheists whom World War II chaplains supposedly found in foxholes. Daredevil is simply self-serving, overturning values by his apparent subscription to them as much as by his boastful denials. As a figure who empties values and their language, he gives *The Atheist* its key. Courtine declares to him that "'Tis certainly the fear of Hell, and hopes of Happiness, that makes People live in Honesty, Peace, and Union one towards another" (II; 324), but of course people in *The Atheist* do not live in honesty, peace, and mutual union. For this is a comedy in which the hero Beaugard—announcedly a nominal Christian and a rake—finds Daredevil "a Companion pleasant enough" and, after a rhapsody on an epicurean life, asks: "What sayst thou to this, *Daredevil*? Is not this coming as near thy Doctrine as a young

Sinner can conveniently?" (I; 309; III; 328). His penultimate speech is a paean to the powers not of Providence but of chance (V; 398).

In this play, paternity, family, friendship, and patriotism are boobytrapped values. A scapegrace father invokes paternal rights to milk guineas from his wealthy son; the family begun so smartly between Sylvia and Courtine in *The Souldiers Fortune* (a play also in the 1682–83 Dorset Garden repertoire) has rotted into sullen disgust; supposed friends of both sexes can never trust each other; and a soldier learns "the Liberal Arts of Murder, Whoredom, Burning, Ravishing, and a few other necessary Accomplishments for a young Gentlemen to set up a Livelihood withal, in this Civil Government, where, Heav'n be prais'd, none of those Vertues need grow rusty" (I; 300). As in *Venice Preserv'd*, Otway joins a melodramatic plot, in this case that of Spanish comedy, with farce, and intersperses both with naturalistic, gritty scenes, here those between Courtine and Sylvia. The "Enchanted Castle" (II; 316) of Courtine's house in the country, where he is plagued with his jealous, overloving wife, has its parallel in the city house, the "Castle" (V; 389) where the widow Porcia is locked up by her covetous brother-in-law and her unwanted suitor, both with holy names—Theodoret (*theios*, "divine" + *doretes*, "benefactor") and Gratian. In this house Daredevil is "converted" (by fear) and Beaugard's father fraudulently dresses as a chaplain; blackamoors serve and nothing is what it seems. Otway combines a stock farce situation and a comment on the Devil's realm by having much of the action take place in darkness.

In discussing *The Lancashire Witches*, we argued for inconsistencies in apparent values, so that Shadwell effectually disrupts their old alignments. Otway's inconsistencies call the values themselves into question. An example is Daredevil's ostensible conversion, ethically undercut as we have pointed out and visibly undercut by an analogous conversion, the Father's disguise as a chaplain. Other socially accepted values find similar treatment, as for instance, marriage and liberty. Otway begins the play with Beaugard's cry, "Sir, I say, and say again, No Matrimony; I'll not be noos'd," only to end it with his marriage to Porcia impending, as in the usual socialization of the rake. But in *The Atheist*, simply "by the Vertue of Matrimony, and long Cohabitation" (I; 305), Beaugard's twin rake Courtine has learned to detest his marriage to a loving, clever wife, a wife who is Porcia's cousin. Though marriage concludes the play, then, one suspects it does not end the action. Otway has Porcia "transported . . . With hopes of Liberty . . . : it is an English Woman's natural Right" (V; 379), a usual paramount value in comedy, expressed in almost the exact words of Isabella in *The Lancashire Witches*. Yet Porcia's cry of liberty, too, has a can tied to its tail, for in defense of the "natural Right" she continues: "Do not our Fathers, Brothers and Kinsmen often, upon pretence of it, bid fair for Rebellion against their Soveraign; And why ought not we, by their Example, to rebel as plausibly against them?" However Barry interpreted this line—Sylvia's response to it, "Most edifying Doctrine this is, truly," sheds no light on that—Porcia offers an argument that undercuts taking "natural Right" seriously as stated.

Clarification about liberty and authority might come from the interweaving of the Beaugard and Courtine plots, for such interweaving unifies *The Atheist*; these plots, unlike those of compromise-formation comedy, comment upon each other, the more so because Beaugard and Courtine are so similar. Yet as with Beaugard and Porcia's marriage, so with their liberty: what liberty means to Sylvia and Courtine, in a marriage that began as freedom but turned into compulsion, is not only a dissolution of bonds but moral dissolution, farcically implied in Sylvia's being well wooed by another woman (Lucrece in men's clothing, V; 369–70) and Courtine's getting ready to fornicate with another man (Daredevil in the dark, V; 388).

In *The Atheist*, then, one sees most of the characteristics frequent in 1680s comedy: the increased unification of the play; the development of an intrigue plot with a wide generic range from farce to melodrama (in *The Lancashire Witches*, "operatic" special effects); the dropping of a compromise-formation structure; the use of themes suggested by the nation's recent political crisis with commitment to only those political positions held consensually by the audience; the disappearance of the commanding, *moraliste* rake; and the disallowing of some of the assumptions about value which had typically marked the comedy of the 1670s. *The Atheist* works out these characteristics very differently from *The Lancashire Witches* or other plays of its own time, just as Dryden, Etherege, Wycherley, Shadwell, and Behn had worked out the characteristics of 1670s comedy very differently. We want to stress, not minimize, those differences, which embody shared rules of procedure.

Modes of 1680s Comedy

The strategic continuity among 1680s' comedies, as we have indicated, operated under theatrical conditions of turmoil, bafflement, and return to consensus. In the last seven seasons of Carolean comedy, as in the first few seasons, "old," pre-War plays, foreign comedy (like *The Adventures of Five Hours* and Behn's *The False Count*), and political plays (like *The Committee* and Crowne's *City Politiques*) dominated the repertory (see appendix 2). Affairs seemed to have come full circle, too, in the companies' financial return to rocky times. The King's Company, which had led the way into the early-to-mid 1670s, in fact eddied to an end in 1682, after ten years of internal squabbling, defection, and lawsuits. The Duke's Company swallowed it into a United Company, and gratefully so, for during the anti-Catholic excitements, a good theatregoer was hard to find. Even *"the Idle Youth forsake our Plays,"* complains the prologue to *The Woman-Captain*. And healthy crowds surprised the beleaguered managers. "How! the House full! and at a *Royal Play!*," begins the prologue to Durfey's *The Royalist*, "That's strange! I never hop'd to see this day" (Wiley 50). The United Company, sudden monopolists, quickly moved to the tried and true, reviving "the several old and Modern Plays, that were the Propriety of Mr. Killigrew" and his King's Company. These revivals allowed the audience to watch familiar, favorite plays performed by favorite actors never before seen together on the public stage, a distraction from the content of the plays. For some time this practice "so ingrost the study of the House, that the Poets lay dorment; and a new Play cou'd hardly get admittance, amongst the more precious pieces of Antiquity, that then waited to walk the Stage" (*LS* 316). In the three seasons after the United Company was formed in the summer of 1682, only eight new comedies were put on, all but one—Southerne's *The Disappointment*—by repeatedly proven playwrights, Crowne, Otway, Ravenscroft, Durfey, and Tate.

Even before the merger, danger signs of change appeared in the repertory. Between 1678 and 1685 are recorded only ninety performances of thirty-two new comedies and twenty-eight from the earlier repertory. Though these figures seem to present a comfortable balance of old and new, "new" here may be a misnomer, given that playwrights were scurrying back to rewarm used plots, like Shadwell in *The Woman-Captain*, even adapting pre-War plays. The prolific Behn in 1680 and 1681 made use of Marston's *The Dutch Courtesan*, Tatham's *The Rump*, and Killigrew's *Thomaso*, respectively, for *The Revenge*, *The Roundheads*, and the second part of *The Rover*. *The City Heiress* (1682) borrows heavily from Massinger's *The Guardian* and Middleton's *A Mad World, My Masters* (Bentley 4: 790). Other writers retreated a bit later. Ravenscroft bustled back to his usual French sources for *Dame Dobson* (1683), "the Poets *Recantation* Play" (Prologue) after the farcical bawdry of *The London Cuckolds*. This gulling comedy of the mock-astrologer sort was borrowed, according to its epilogue, from "the *French Divineress*," the hugely successful *La Divineresse ou les faux enchantements* (1679) by Donneau de Visé and Thomas Corneille (cf. Lancaster, pt. 4, 2: 290).

Even Durfey's last two contributions to Carolean comedy—the second of them actually produced after James' accession—are as far from *A Fond Husband* as *Dame Dobson* is from *The London Cuckolds*. Ever with an ear to the ground, the once and future king of moral chaos set to adapting innocuous romances by Shakespeare and Fletcher, *The Injur'd Princess* (1682) from *Cymbeline* and *A Commonwealth of Women* (1685) from *The Sea Voyage* (1622). Another example of a different kind: after the Duke of Monmouth had been pitted against the Duke of York, the title of Nahum Tate's *A Duke and No Duke* (1684) might have raised political expectations, the more so when Fletcher's *A King and No King* was current. But Tate's play itself is pure farce, reworked from Sir Aston Cokain's *Trappolin Suppos'd a Prince* (1658), in which a roguish parasite is transformed into the spitting image of his enemy, the tyrannical duke of Florence, and the two men vie in giving and countermanding orders, imprisoning and releasing each other's allies, at an increasingly frantic pace. Perhaps bold with success (Hume, *Development* 373), Tate a year later leapt stoutly backward to adapt *Cuckolds-Haven* from *Eastward Ho*, a play then eighty years old. A final indication of the Parthian mood of the theatres is the posthumous first production of *Sir Hercules Buffoon* (1684) by John Lacy (1615?–81), all three of whose other plays date from the later 1660s; in style and technique, this one gives no sign of having been written later.

Within the field defined by the eight plays we have discussed in chapter 8 and just above, two by Dryden and three each by Shadwell and Otway, we can survey the range of new repertory in the last Carolean years. In particular, we would like to look more closely at one tragicomedy by a new, important playwright, Southerne's *The Disappointment*, and at the two 1680s' comedies most popular for the next hundred years, Ravenscroft's spicy *The London Cuckolds* (obviously a member of our category London comedy) and Crowne's chaste *Sir Courtly Nice*, a foreign comedy whose Spanish source was suggested to Crowne by King Charles. *Sir Courtly Nice*, in fact, qualifies as the last Carolean comedy, for the king died while it was in rehearsal, and it also reminds one of the first Carolean comedies, for it derives from Agustín Moreto's *No puede ser*, used nearly twenty years before by Sydserf for *Tarugo's Wiles* (1667).

If in the 1660s Sydserf's comedy was, as its prologue admits, "like all others of the time; *viz.* A new Toot out of an old Horn" (sig. A3), what shall one say of Crowne's in the 1680s? A crucial likeness between the early 1660s' and early 1680s' sounding of old horns, rather than the new (cuckolds') horns of the 1670s, is their similar moral stance. The epilogue to *Sir Courtly Nice* ends with the supposition that dirty plays attract dirty crowds, in which "roosting Masques s[i]t cackling for a Mate" and audiences give up the communal activity of play watching for the private activity of "get[ting] a Shot at Whores." However, "this Comedy throws all that lewdness down" and "Promotes the Stage to th'Ends at first design'd, / As well to profit, as delight the Mind." In short, common submission to a public spectacle leads to common improvement. Of course when playwrights play at being their siblings' keepers, the role above all denied them by heterogeneous, compromise-formation comedy, they must speak from a single, privileged stance, their right to which the action on stage ratifies. For the last years of Carolean comedy, certainly, we regard this author/play/audience relationship as more important than various questions we think it subsumes, such as how bawdy the play is. We have noted this hierarchy of questions in examining how the work of Dryden, Shadwell, and Otway narrowed potential responses from the audience during these years.

The cleanness of *Sir Courtly Nice*, which is nearly as "nice" as its namesake fop, therefore accompanies several other traits. Although the plot involves two pairs of lovers, Violante and Lord Bellguard, and his sister Leonora and his enemy Farewel, no compromise formation exists. When the fraternal patriarch Bellguard accepts women's freedom, recognizing that only her virtue can guard a belle, he joins in opinion with the other three lovers and ipso facto wins Violante. In keeping with this mode of consensus comedy in action, the expression of heterodox values too is hedged in *Sir Courtly Nice*. Only plainly deluded characters spout cynical wit. For example, Bellguard, apart from his (disproven) sneers at women, announces that "none but Fools will marry.... Fortune is as fond of those Bits of Men, as Bigots are of Reliques; wraps 'em in Silver" (II.ii; 307). Yet he, a rich lord, and Farewel, "a young Man of Quality and Fortune," both want to marry, not to whore. A rake's voice is given to the morose, boozy Surly: "the word Love is a Fig-Leaf to cover the naked Sense, a Fashion brought up by *Eve*, the Mother o' Jilts; she cuckolded her husband with the *Serpent*, then pretended to modesty, and fell a making Plackets presently. And her Daughters take up the Trade" (II.i; 299). But not only does this view of love find no warrant in the play, it also does not inform Surly's own actions, any more than Bellguard's view of marriage informs his. Nor does anyone offer *moraliste* wit. One may compare Horner's speech opening *The Country-Wife*, "A Quack is as fit for a Pimp, as a Midwife for a Bawd; they are still but in their way, both helpers of Nature," with an early quip by Crack, who engineers the lovers' plots, "A Pimp is as much above a Doctor, as a Cook is above a Scullion; when a Pimp has foul'd a Dish, a Doctor scours it" (II.i; 295). Horner's comment keynotes *The Country-Wife* and defines "nature" for it, but Crack simply marks his own character with this joke—Violante's immediate response to it is, "This is an arch Blade." In fact, Crack negates anything subversive in the comments by his own role in the plotting. He serves as a kind of wholly innocent pimp, who fouls no dishes but maneuvers so that two chaste lovers can get together and marry.

As in many earlier plays, for instance *The Virtuoso, Sir Courtly Nice* sets humours characters in opposition to one another so as to show them effectually the same. A boor like Surly balances off a fastidious fop like Sir Courtly; Crowne gets much fun from clashes between them and also employs them equally in the plot, each of them having been assigned as unworthy suitor to one of the young women. Two twists on this technique of satiric equivalence seem worth noting in an examination of the play as consensus comedy. First, the technique is doubled, in that the two political factions that had so recently been at each other's throats are also equated. Testimony, a stock Tartuffean fanatic who hides lust under cant, and his counterpart, Hothead, an angry loyalist zealot, are the two enemies of liberty whom Bellguard trusts to watch over Leonora. Their squabbles provide Crowne with more fun but virtually no plot action, unlike Sir Courtly and Surly. Instead, as Bellguard's agents, they comment upon him through their set animosity, like his to Farewel, and their coerciveness, like his to women.

The second twist to the handling of humours characters comes in the stunts of Crack, who pretends to be a rich madman effectually billeted upon Bellguard. His "madness" then repeats characteristics shared by Hothead, Testimony, and his jealous and self-confident host, Bellguard. To begin with, Crack (as "Sir Thomas Calico") is absolutely fixed in his exotic, delusory ways, just as Bellguard "has put the whole Force of his Wit into this [repressive] Form of Government . . . a Dream fit for nothing but *Utopia*" (I.i; 289–90). "Calico" requires a retinue to "serve him as his Slaves" (III.iii; 321); Leonora is kept by Bellguard in "eternal Slavery" (I.i; 282). "Calico's" "Loathing in me of Females" (322) obviously refers to Bellguard's attitude toward women. And his "pimping"—though no sexual contact ever takes place—responds to Bellguard's venal matchmaking between Leonora and the nonsensical Sir Courtly Nice. Crack's other traits recall those of his fellow male guests at Bellguard's, the agents of Bellguard's repressive policy: Crack expresses his fixity like Testimony in strange, hypocritical cant and his rages (V.i.346; V.ii.350) resemble Hothead's.

Through these analogies, public ideological issues turn into a general mockery of extremism. Crowne presents a consensus position, in favor of "Virtuous Liberty," as the epilogue puts it; people should do as they like, as long as what they like is what society likes ("Virtue"). Favored characters end up localized, then, in no place: they speak for no principle though they must appear principled; they have no striking character traits, though they must be likeable and vivacious; above all, they violate no bounds. In one grouping of characters, the opinionated Bellguard sets the bounds for ideologues he hires, in that they implicitly comment upon him. In another grouping, the humours characters—Surly, Sir Courtly, and the chaperoning Aunt—establish the arena in which the rest of the lovers operate pragmatically. The Aunt is at once an envious prude and a would-be lecher, imaging Bellguard's hopes and fears for woman. (She is, of course, another of his guardian guests.) By contrast, the lovers have their own, better versions of restraint and passion, based on possibility, not on frustrated appetites like the Aunt's. Surly and Sir Courtly respectively caricature bold action and delicacy, while the lovers display decent versions of both. In short, this comedy essentially defines its positive figures, the lovers, through their negation of others, balking the others' actions and rejecting what they stand for. One may contrast the lovers' characterization here with the far more specific, involved treatment of the lovers in *The Virtuoso*, a 1670s play with a superficially similar structure (guardianship; a watchful, lecherous older woman; paired-off boobies around a love plot) which we discussed in chapter 7. Crowne here much more closely resembles the later Shadwell who stages exemplary lovers in *The Lancashire Witches*, again a play with guardianship, a watchful and lecherous older woman (Lady Shacklehead, one heroine's mother and the other's intended mother-in-law), and paired boobies. As we have argued above, the male lovers in *The Virtuoso* combine at least a mildly rakish love and authority, the lovers of whatever sex in *The Lancashire Witches* do not; and similarly, in *Sir Courtly Nice*, Bellguard's use of authority is the very blockage of his power to be a lover at all, rakishness here being out of the question.

Sir Courtly Nice, as a Spanish play, shares a number of traits with the foreign-comedy mode that replaced the Spanish during the 1670s. Behn's *The Rover, Part II*, and *The False Count*, both produced in 1681, and Southerne's *The Disappointment* (1684) follow some earlier comedies of Behn as well as Lewis Maidwell's *The Loving Enemies* in this mode. All involve a restrictive moral code followed by some characters and broken by others, love/honor and freedom/captivity conflicts, multiple love pairs, and heavy dependence on disguise (often exotic or grotesque) and trickery (often by a clever, manipulative servant) to move the plot. As we have remarked, the mode has an enormous tonal range, often even within individual comedies. At the dark end of this mode's emotional spectrum, as far as can be from *Sir Courtly Nice*, is Southerne's play, which perpetually threatens to become tragedy: it is about as funny as *Othello*, which it to some degree resembles, though it ends well and features some bluff buffoonery from Rogero, a part written for Anthony Leigh. In keeping with the disruption of genres in the later 1670s and 1680s, such as we noted in the previous chapter, the title page of *The Disappointment* calls it simply "a Play," not even "tragicomedy." In it, the debauchery of a gay libertine, Alberto, triggers the destructive jealousies of a husband and a lover, so as to provide fletcherian peripeteias of emotion, in scenes of distress, rage, melting passion, and penitence. All told, *The Disappointment* is so distant in tone from *Sir Courtly Nice* as to make certain affinities between the two plays more striking.

One such affinity, obviously, is the separation of rakish love and authority, since the powerful rake brings misery upon the sympathetic characters. He must be blocked in his exercise of authority and reclaimed for love, as in *Sir Courtly Nice*. Southerne's young women, innocents here as in *Sir Courtly Nice*, resist Alberto's advances, one in each plot. They do so unbeknownst to him, for his previous victim, Juliana, takes the place of each of them in a pair of bed tricks, and eventually reclaims Alberto for marriage; the maid Clara in one plot and the ingenue Angelline in the other serve, like Crowne's Crack, as innocent pimps. *The Disappointment* professes only one moral standard, so that there is no compromise formation, and the abundance of cynical, *moraliste* wit comes from the mouths only of the self-serving and deceived: jealous misogyny fares no better here than in Crowne. Precisely because these women cleave to social law, they are allowed to bemoan in song their fate at the hands of "Tyrant Man, whose arbitrary Reign / Scarce gives us Will, or Power, to Complain" (II.i.76–77). In this context, the jealous husband, another figure of authority, becomes a tyrant indeed in his obsession with his wife's imagined lusts and his own imagined (dis)honor, on the model of Othello. By act V he is brandishing a dagger to kill his Erminia, whose name presumably betokens her true whiteness.

Again like Crowne in *Sir Courtly* and Dryden in *The Spanish Fryar*, Southerne aims for unity beyond the familiar level of parallels between plots. Here one seduced woman's bed tricks thwart one seducer's attempts on the two ingenues, falsely accused and eventually cleared; here the husband's confidant in one plot serves as the lover in the other, willing to gauge the probable success of his marriage on the success of his friend's; here the vengeful husband, disguised as a simpleton, actually witnesses the tricking of the rake by the veiled

Juliana in one plot, a close parallel to what has happened in the other plot about which he is vengeful. The play thus reinforces its singleness of values.

At the third point of a triangle with *Sir Courtly Nice* and *The Disappointment* at the other two, one might think, stands that great tour de farce *The London Cuckolds*, certainly not in the Spanish (or Italian) mode, though it too adopts a conflict between freedom and captivity, multiplies its lovers to three pairs, and revels in elaborate disguise and trickery. Ravenscroft's plots again harmonize as variations on a theme, for the joke of the play is that one will become a London cuckold no matter whether one weds "a meer Infant in her intellects," "a woman with wit," or a "Church zealot" (I.i; 147, 150, 152). Though this singleness of values does not allow innocence in the manner of Crowne and Southerne, it cultivates an analogous simplicity. That is why it differs so radically in tone from *The Country-Wife* a mere six years earlier, the women of which offered the same configuration that Ravenscroft's assume: the rustic booby (Margery; in Ravenscroft the same name, Peggy), the lady of wit and fashion (the Fidget crew; Ravenscroft's Arabella), and the lady of conscience (Alithea; Eugenia). The rage of Pinchwife, the sophisticates' aggressive cynicism, the authority wielded by Horner and Harcourt, the country wife's regret over her "musty Husband," and of course the *moraliste* wit all vanish. In fact, even the cuckolding serves largely as rough comeuppance for foolish men who plume themselves on their shrewdness in avoiding it and who are still doing so (with somewhat wilted plumes) at the end of the play: Wiseacres is "ne'er a whit" convinced of his folly; Dashwell "woul'd not yet change [his] Wives Virtue for [Doodle's] Wives Wit"; and Doodle still thinks, "*Consideratis Considerandis*, the witty wife is the best of the three" (V.v; 266–67).

When ordinary guys like Townly, Ramble, and Loveday appear, the enviable, insinuating superiority of Horner and Harcourt correspondingly disappears. Ravenscroft thus lessens the audience's wish to be like such commanding males, who exemplify style, mind, and menace in the process of fulfilling the much simpler desire they share with the audience, the desire for cleverly stolen sex. While the heroes of *The London Cuckolds* share that desire too, they fulfill it only on the audience's own level of power and achievement. Ramble, like some endearing jerk who hits it lucky in a Hollywood film, begins "unfortunate": "I always meet with occasions, but never bring 'em to perfection; . . . for either my Mistress jilts me, fortune jilts me, or the Devil prevents me, I can never bring it to a home push" (I.ii; 156). On his escapades in this play, he is stuck "fast in a window, there to be burnt with a Link, drown'd with a Chamber-pot, Rob'd of [his]

Cloths, taken by the Watch, suspected to be a thief," and "jear[ed] by his intended lover and his friend" (IV.i; 212). Loveday and Eugenia are actually in love and speak the language of tenderness: at one time betrothed, they were separated by a venal parental ruse (IV.ii), like Beaugard and Lady Dunce in *The Souldiers Fortune*. Unlike any earlier Carolean rake-hero, Loveday is marked with smallpox. And Townly, though attractive and opportunistic, does not plot but simply accepts Arabella when she puts herself in his way, "muffled up in her hoods" and well endowed with wiles (V.iv; 253).

No doubt, as Harwood points out in his acute analysis of this play, the old elements of heterogeneity remain. The "plot suggests a rather traditional moral vision" but the couples "do not represent or endorse any values except those associated with sensual pleasure," "the libertine's moral assumptions." While in the play "the essence of sexual politics is the revolt of women against their economic and sexual enslavement" and the young Cavaliers cuckold cits in accord with "a political, if not a moral, imperative," yet the characters show no such awareness and "to perceive [this comedy generically,] as farce[,] forestalls further aesthetic and moral considerations" (91, 92, 95, 96, 97). Our argument suggests how the heterogeneity got there and why, in the 1680s, Ravenscroft reduced it as he did. For in contrast to the plays of the 1670s, *The London Cuckolds* neutralizes "vice" with frivolity and extenuations from the start rather than letting it have its full run before interposing what some might construe as a moralized denouement. As a permissible saturnalia, of course, this play held the stage for apprentices' delight on the Lord Mayor's Day till halfway through the eighteenth century; and perhaps that offers some prima facie evidence that Ravenscroft's farce might have been thought to have some socially beneficial effect other than those that Harwood mentions and discards. By lightening the "vice" of a Dorimant or Horner into naughtiness, *The London Cuckolds* altered the expression of the appetites it helped the audience vent. Thus, one might argue, although some starchier moralists (like Richard Steele in *Tatler* 8) might sputter, society could wisely approve an annual fling for young men, safely kept to a stage performance. It is rather like Belle Epoque fathers' taking their pubescent sons to the Folies Bergères, to initiate them into the rites of passage and prepare them for becoming bourgeois patresfamilias.

Ravenscroft himself could hardly have had these beneficent motives and obviously did not trust others to attribute them to him, for as we have mentioned, he quickly "recanted" *The London Cuckolds* with the chaste *Dame Dobson*. That play, with its return to the popular conjurer plot, comes no closer to challenging social proprieties than in a request for "any thing that will cause an Abortion" and, differently, in the Dame's comment that "such a secret as that to transform a Man to a Woman or a Woman to a Man wou'd make me a rich Woman indeed" (III.viii.37; V.ii.57), a theme, we might note, that recurs intriguingly in these plays, especially when men long to be women (cf. *The Rover, II*, V.iii; 199). But we should also note that Ravenscroft's later comedy does for swindling something of what his earlier one does for illicit sex, that is, makes it acceptable as a marginal social practice if—and, implicitly, only if—its results are sufficiently benign. This position, as embodied in both plays, again suggests their role in fixing the limits of consensus.

Still one more strain of comedy flourished in the 1680s, a strain that dwells on the issue of authority and seems to call into question our argument that comedy after the Exclusion Crisis typically moved toward consensus, not conflict. We are, of course, thinking of politics in plays, and not necessarily plays wholly devoted to politics, either. The audience in the early 1680s probably smelled the remnants of triumphant royalist bonfires when the cits were gulled in *The London Cuckolds*. They certainly could do so with the more exotic, romance-based plays, where the genre itself turns on usurpers, Machiavellian courtiers, lost or stolen heirs, and the like. In the wake of Otway's bewhigging his Sir Davy Dunce in *The Souldiers Fortune* (June 1680), some city and some romance comedies invested traditional character types—the usurper, the old fumbler, the fop—with Whiggish attributes. That was the ploy of Tories like the fertile Durfey in *Sir Barnaby Whigg* (late 1681?) and *The Royalist* (early 1682?), Behn in *The Roundheads* (late 1681) and *The City Heiress* (April 1682?), and whoever wrote *Mr. Turbulent* (early 1682), all plays that opened at about the same time as *The London Cuckolds*. Politics here is a thin varnish to make old stuff shine.

Durfey's *Sir Barnaby* bears witness to the strength of this general argument, since even in this openly, noisily loyalist play his political bravado is tamer than it might seem. In the dedication to *Sir Barnaby*, he snorts that "in this Age 'tis not a Poets Merit, but his Party that must do his business," and in the prologue he gets that business done: the poet, Durfey says, "shall know both Parties, now he Glories; / By Hisses th'*Whiggs*, and by their Claps the *Tories*." But outside of Sir Barnaby, "one of *Oliver's* Knights" (Dramatis Personae) who is prepared to turn Papist or Muslim for a rich wife, the usual cast and the usual love intrigues reign supreme: the occupational humourist, Captain Porpuss, who uses nautical cant; a jolly foolish cuckold, Sir Walter Wiseacre, who likes to make others drunk or cuckolds; a misogynist, railing beau and a modishly inconstant one; and the expectable bevy of unfaithful, misandrist, and/or hypocritical women. Similarly, although *The Royalist* has a first act set at Boscobel during the Civil Wars, and recalls *The Committee* in its plot about sequestration, the commonwealth's-men exhibit the same greed, vulgarity, lack of principle, and love of legal jargon that typify Durfey's nonpolitical butts in other plays, and the satire on the age is very much of a piece with that in comedies that predate the Popish Plot. One has the sense with such plays that Durfey is lifting himself by his own bootstraps, using tested devices to forward his political satire so that he can use this political satire in turn to boost his new (or renovated) comic offerings.

To do this in a theatre where a controversial play could so easily be hooted down, as Shadwell says was attempted with *The Lancashire Witches* (4: 99–100), presumably involves caution, not daring. However emphatic the political attacks may seem to be, they must remain within the bounds that the great bulk of the audience accepts as reasonable for a patriot, bounds that themselves depend on consensual values, even if the specific expression of those values might not meet with the same consensus. This supposition gains strength in that every one of the politically cued comedies of the period, save for *The Lancashire Witches*, shows a royalist bias, which the audience must therefore have shared to a degree. But playwrights learned the hard way when bounds were overstepped, as when the harsh ridicule and personal lampoons of *The City Politiques* were forbidden in 1682. Acted in 1683, this play drew upon Crowne so much "Resentment of . . . numerous Enemies" that he appealed for a nontheatrical sinecure from Charles II, at whose behest he then wrote the innocuous *Sir Courtly Nice* (Dennis 2: 405). And *The City Politiques* itself strives for consensus along the path already cleared by the Poet Laureate: Crowne's play ends like *Absalom and Achitophel*, a poem his poetaster Craffy attacks, with the voice of absolute viceregal authority asserting itself over a batch of posturing, disloyal, self-serving frauds who temporarily hold political power.

Some other politically spiced comedies present a more complex pattern, but still one that aims at consensus or at the muting of antagonistic partisanship. Two examples, from different positions, are *The Lancashire Witches*, once again, and the anonymous *Mr. Turbulent*. Shadwell's witches at the end of act II cannibalize babies and "*kiss the Devil's Arse*" (131), behavior associated not only with witches but, more significantly, with Irish Papists. For instance, the "Teagues" in the Whig satire "Popish Politics Unmasked" (late 1680, *POAS* 2: 380–90) stew babies in their own blood, and Tories in "Strange's Case, Strangely Altered" (1680; *POAS* 2: 367–73) associate with the devil. Yet the political application remains oblique. Admirable men who believe in the Popish Plot disbelieve in witches. These witches plague only characters whom the audience scorn and who believe in them, counter to all literary convention for works that assert the reality of supernatural creatures. On the other side of the aisle, *Mr. Turbulent* connects political uproar with madness rather than sorcery. Although the heroes Fairlove and Friendly must deal with a crew of factious hypocrites, as they successfully, expectably do, the play also makes a point of locating the honest practice of marriage—social stability rather than madness and faction—at "this end of the Town even to *Moor-fields*, where . . . Men and their Wives ordinarily walk . . . together very lovingly" (I.i; 4). The city, which is the breeding ground for avarice, zeal, and fraud, also fosters the basic moral values of marriage and family. To join love and authority, the heroes have to socialize love to marriage and join purged versions of court and city, a procedure that would have been unthinkable in the 1670s and that is irenic rather than politically contentious here.

Still less thinkable in the 1670s would have been the disruptive handling of love, rakery, and authority in Behn's *The City Heiress*. From this Tory comedy one would expect all the usual laurels for Sir Charles Meriwell, who ends the play with loyal sententiousness about "due Order," "the Kingdom's Care and Love" for "*Caesar*," and a concord of "all honest Hearts . . . / To bless the King." But in this very scene Sir Charles marries a woman who gives him her hand while "Sighing and looking on *Wilding*" (V.v; 298), with whom she has earlier slept. A hero's wife who has neither maidenhead nor her dead husband's bulging coffers? and who loves another man? As to the Tory Wilding, Sir Charles's friend and premarital cuckolder, he cares so little for politics that he declares:

> Let Politicians plot, let Rogues go on
> In the old beaten Path of Forty one;
> Let City Knaves delight in Mutiny,
> The Rabble bow to old Presbytery;
> Let petty States be to confusion hurl'd,
> Give me but Woman, I'll despise the World.   (III.i; 258)

Though as a character Wilding is barely capable of fidelity, like his predecessor Willmore, his role as Tory hero commits Behn to dubbing him a faithful gallant at the end. He therefore must take seriously the affairs of the heart that Willmore could treat as fun. Behn secures the right tone by giving all four lovers passionate speeches, but she pays for this by having to whitewash the generic contradictions in the action of the play and therefore to sickly o'er its political momentum with the pale cast of nonthought. She could hardly have reconciled the conflicting energies of *The City Heiress* even if she had been able to employ a compromise formation. In fact, the striving for consensus (for loyalty to king and spouse) would not have allowed such an option.

The political plays of the 1680s are a great deal less divisive, less partisan than they might seem, and they do not contradict our general theses about 1680s' comedies. That is hardly surprising, since political changes were not the only reason for the movement from compromise-formation comedy to the kinds of plays we have described in this chapter. As we argued earlier, within the everyday context of beliefs and attitudes there were crises developing in the Carolean repertory. The need to produce new, bolder comedies, to push the limits of acceptability outward, to outdo the current or the previous seasons' hits, even those written by oneself—these set in motion a system that outran the sort of public tolerance needed for heterogeneous, compromise-formation structures. We would guess, then, that even if Titus Oates and his troupe had not seized the stage of England, even if the King's Company had not succumbed to its own worst enemy, Carolean comedy would have moved in the direction it did, though perhaps not at the same pace.

But if this direction was overdetermined, the playwrights' specific ways of accommodating it were not. What happened, we believe, happened largely because theatrical monopoly stifled the sort of energetic, inventive experimentation that had kept producing comedy of great value for twenty years or so. The United Company, Milhous notes, was "expertly run and highly profitable" till the Revolution and its aftermath (1688–92), and used its monopoly to lower by 80 percent or so the number of new plays per year (*Thomas Betterton* 42). Few new writers developed, therefore, and comedy stagnated. More clearly, perhaps, than earlier years in the history of Carolean comedy, the 1680s illustrate what is, or ought to be, a commonplace: that at any moment the drama is a joint production of generic expectations, ideology, box office assumptions, and combinatorial resources on hand (e.g., authors, actors, accoutrements of the theatres). Each of these assorted cohabitants, in a familiar cant phrase, has a life of its own.

10

Retrospect

Our history of Carolean comedy has had what seems like a natural beginning, the reopening of the theatres after the King's return, followed by a flourishing of new plays and then a waning during the near-Exclusion of the King's brother, the collapse of the King's Company, and the death of the King himself. These royal events had plain financial consequences for popular entertainment that depended on cash flow from the box office. Neither so visibly nor so fully the result of these external, material events is the course of our narrative about the logical and ideological development of a repertory. It has described what may look like a parabola, as a certain style rose with the new monarch, peaked, and fell into decadence and decay in his last years. A historical "period" and a narrative content for it, then, match; but as we suggested at the end of chapter 9, this match very likely has a large element of accident. The siren song of Exclusion politics, seducing the audience from the theatres, just happened to coincide with a high tide of Durfeyan cynicism inside those theatres, though the same social erosion of normative authority no doubt underlies both. We would also balk at making the starting point of our linear, parabolic narrative a beginning, moreover, for we have emphasized the lack of beginning (the essential continuity of fletcherian style from pre- to post-War stages) and of linearity (the density with which old and new plays were woven together to make a repertory). We do not, therefore, claim that we have isolated a natural period and gladly agree that one could step further back than we have done to write an equally continuous history of seventeenth-century comedy or comedy from 1660 to 1714, or could step closer, as we in fact have done in chapters 3 and 5, for example. To create "the Carolean period" for analytic purposes is to display how accidental, unbounded, and various any so-called period really is, even one that seems this clear.

We should mention, with furtive hope, a point that we obviously cannot develop. In regard to the role of accident, the absence of clear beginning, and the variousness of repertory, the visible course of Carolean comedy resembles those of other genres. Our historically grounded model in chapters 2 and 3 shows, we hope, why at least the larger particulars we discuss happened as they did in this genre, at a time when copious new repertory was needed for audiences with the values of the 1660s and when a fletcherian dramatic formula was at hand. But we also see the way Carolean comedy altered as offering clues to the ways in which other literary genres may alter, though these other genres do not so obviously exist as parts of a competitively formed repertory, catering to desire (as measured by the box office) at a time when previously settled ideologies were in flux. For this comparative purpose, the ideological tolerance of the Restoration, the political upheavals, the economic pinch, the need for lots of new repertory, and the elaborate, productive logic of desire that we have traced throughout this book all make Carolean comedy an especially promising specimen of generic development, in that what may well be common processes of change were highly motivated, explicable, and simplified.

We will, regretfully, not even hint at demonstrating this point, seeing that the method we have used in this one relatively simple case has demanded a complicated model with complex applications. Our "demanded" reflects the imperative to deal with the four essential pulls on Carolean comedy to which we referred at the end of chapter 9: the needs that the comedies filled for a diverse audience, the logic of the dramatic idiom, the external restraints on the role of this idiom in filling needs, and the resources of the theatres. Each of these pulls is itself divisible. The needs that the comedies filled included the sort of wish fulfillment that we detailed in chapter 2, leading to the mode of heterogeneity and, in the 1670s, often of compromise formation; but these needs also included, for example, anglicizing Parisian favorites so that the English stage could be "in" with the up-to-date and also outdo the foreigners at their own game. The dramatic idiom, as we argued in chapters 8 and 9, had multiple demands of value constitutive of it, and as these diverged, the idiom disintegrated. External constraints varied. When the theatres opened and again at times during the Exclusion Crisis, but not anywhere nearly so much between the time of the Plague and the Exclusion Crisis, the combination of events and public temper outside the public theatres imposed sharp restraints on the available range of expression inside them, as was to be true, of course, during the eighteenth century after the Licensing Act. Tuke's, Farquhar's, and Goldsmith's plays kept fulfilling wishes, for a light evening, for a society in consensus, for ethical reassurance, but the expression of these wishes differed in range from that in any of Dryden's comedies that we have discussed. No one, finally, should slight or simplify the multiply compromised power of the fourth "pull" we listed, the resources of the theatres, their money, their arsenal of stage effects, their authors, and their actors. Carolean comedies do not make for a cosy evening at hearthside (or the modern equivalent, TV-side): their appeal to a watcher as an individual and also, necessarily, a social animal requires the ambiance of other watchers and the contingency of live performance, actors and theatre management putting themselves out to give the audience what it desires.

Change, in our version of dramatic history, came about through the workings of these four, internally divisible vectors. Starting in the early 1660s, an idiom was at hand that could accommodate a various audience and such fancy imports as Spanish comedy and Molière, and that could alter easily to keep renewing itself as a current repertory raised new expectations and wishes among the audience. Few restraints were levied from the outside upon this idiom, and the introduction of actresses into ever more splendid, splendidly equipped, and fashionable theatres enlarged the resources of the companies as needed, prompting a rush of playwrights to try their hands at comedy. In its heyday, Carolean comedy reflects the wonderful energy of a mode in rapid change that the writers met with answerable ingenuity. They kept doing so even when, in the very late 1670s and 1680s, the mode was drawn not in one general direction but in several. But by the start of James II's reign, when opportunities in the theatre had shrunk with the King's Company's default and when the public and political temper was more uncertain, the authors could not keep dazzling the crowd. Needs, the logic of the idiom, restraints, and resources had all changed. The finest playwrights during the rest of the Stuart period—Dryden, Southerne, Congreve, Vanbrugh, Farquhar—slowly evolved principles variously different from those that we have been discussing, principles that place individual prowess in the context of larger schemes of interconnection, such as also mark other artistic forms in the 1690s and well into the eighteenth century. We should quickly add that one can easily trace these principles of interconnection back to work by Otway, Shadwell, and Dryden himself (*The Spanish Fryar*) which we have considered: we are not here proposing a history of continuities demarcated by fissures but one of always-fissured continuities, sometimes more plainly plane and sometimes increasingly creased.

This way of visualizing literary history has urged us throughout this book to focus, first, on playwrights' practice rather than on conceptual explanation and, second, on the close linkage between aesthetic value and innovative power in the Carolean theatre. We would insist on such linkage although in retrospect a few uninfluential plays (mostly written at times of public uncertainty) seem aesthetically better and a few influential ones (mostly performed with star actors) seem worse than they did in the days of Barry and Betterton. More typically, at any given time the best playwrights were creating a dominant mode by way of their admired practice, tacitly understood and used by others as a body of flexible, generative rules. Practice thus altered but not through conceptual breaks, Kuhnian "paradigms" whose emergence implies dissatisfaction with available ways of conceiving major problems in a discipline. Embodying but updating the current mode of Carolean comedy—its form of change—was much more like conversing in a contemporary language or the practice of a creative technology, say that of special effects in films or of restaurant cuisine, which defines what services it can render and how. Both aesthetic judgments about the comedies and the history of their generic development depend on understanding this point. We would reject a history of Carolean comedy based on changes in its cognitive focus just as earlier we rejected a measure of its aesthetic value which depends upon a disparity between what the audience hunger for and what the work serves up (Jauss 25). The aesthetic value of a Carolean comedy hangs on its being able to make what it serves up seem vital and spontaneous, becoming a source of energy (like the food of elegant cuisine) by being so eagerly swallowed. A given play's place in the history of Carolean comedy hangs on the frequency with which it exercised these charms over the public, thus altering or enlarging or reinforcing a dramatic idiom (a matter of noncognitive expectations). This principle underlies our choice of studying a whole repertory, old and new plays alike, when the extant records make that possible.

Aesthetic value and innovative power differ too from the personal, expressive value of a comedy, the criterion put forth, for example, in a pronouncement by the Marxist Ernest Mandel, writing about crime stories: "Real literature . . . reflects society as through the 'broken mirror' of the author's subjectivity" whereas "in *Trivialliteratur* that subjectivity is absent, and society is 'reflected' only in order to cater, for commercial purposes, to some supposed needs of the readers" (26). At one level this dogma is obvious, for if art works have little distinction from one another, they are likely to have little distinction, period. And distinguishing marks must in some sense arise from the author's individuating style, her or his "broken mirror" of "subjectivity." Etherege reads like Wycherley no more than one "subjective," "Romantic" poet reads like another. At a deeper level, however, we hope to have shown that the opposition between "real literature" and literature that "caters, for commercial purposes, to some supposed needs of the readers" is false and facile, apart from its unappealing snobbery. An author's subjectivity is configured like those of his or her readers because readers (or audience) and authors are products of and producers of the same society. "Desire is part of the infrastructure," as Gilles Deleuze, glancing at both Marx and Nietzsche, aptly puts it (qtd. in Descombes 174). Etherege, Wycherley, Dryden, Shadwell, Behn, Durfey, and Otway catered to their audiences and also induced a taste in their audiences for the dishes that each of these writers cared to cater. If these plays are subversive (and they are), that is because Carolean society was itself subvertible, because the playwright's dark, cynical, or worldly-wise vision was always already there, though maybe inchoate and timid, in her or his audiences.

We would wager that in this respect, the history of Carolean comedy resembles the history of almost every other art in almost every other "period." What may be striking for some Marxists, though, is that the triumphs of Carolean comedy originate not only from their expressing their "age's" ethos of entrepreneurial capitalism, competitive and exploitive, but also from their own production within that ethos. Do the witty heroines and heroes jockey for power and for turning others into agents of their own pleasure? Do they turn their own apparent autonomy into a means for wooing those whom they desire? Well, so do the playwrights, ogling the purses and needs of their audiences. Carolean plays were commodities for a shrewd, arrogant, and fickle public whose appetites imposed a multiplicity of contradictory demands on the theatre. As such public demands multiply, the individual author's "subjectivity" presumably has less space for itself, especially given Carolean Comedy's adroitness at removing any "distinction between the logic of the work and that of the social system" (Horkheimer and Adorno 121). By any one of the Marxist dogmas, indeed by almost any of the dogmas that have set out the "oughts" of artistic value in the twentieth century (or earlier), these plays surely should not be what they are, among the greatest glories and continuing delights of the English-speaking stage. *Something* needs to be rethought.

Appendixes

Bibliography

Index

Appendix 1:
Formation of the Repertory and Use of Repertory Data

The earliest developments in Restoration drama were very much a function of the peculiar conditions of the time. The climate for theatrical enterprises was hardly ideal in 1659–60.

> With the restoration of Charles I early in 1660, an opportunity arose for the theatrical world to begin anew and the player, manager, playwright, and spectator to restore the drama to its former position in England's culture. By 1660 the principal actors of the days of James I and Charles I had died or had so drifted out of touch with dramatic enterprise that the continuity of acting had been impaired, though certainly not lost. Furthermore, most of the pre-Commonwealth theatres had been closed, destroyed, or converted to purposes other than theatrical. In addition, the playwrights of the old regime no longer were productive. And a new generation had appeared in London, one which had little intimate knowledge of acting, the drama, or the playhouse.   (*LS* xxi–xxii)

The situation altered very rapidly and, as Robert D. Hume puts it, "within a very few years after 1660 we find ourselves in a new and distinctive world" (*London Theatre* xii), a world which had acquired the solidity of permanent companies and playhouses, a repertory of new and old plays, and an increasingly sophisticated audience. But these changes did not occur overnight or without strain. A brief overview should serve to isolate the more significant theatrical facts of the years 1659–85.

By 9 July 1660, Sir William Davenant and Thomas Killigrew had secured patents from the king entitling them to a monopoly of all professional theatrical enterprises in London.[1] And by November 1660,

---

[1] In theory, these patents enabled the two to suppress legally any other theatre company; in practice, as John Freehafer points out, it was a continuous battle, joined immediately: "Although the King threw his full authority behind a grant that the patentees expected to give them prompt and absolute control of the London stage, Killigrew and Davenant had to struggle for four full months before they could impose their authority upon the London actors" ("Formation" 6). (See also Milhous, "Company" 1–34; Hume, "Securing.")

both the Duke's (Davenant's) and the King's (Killigrew's) companies had hired actors, rented playhouses, and amassed sufficient scenes and costumes to begin production. Davenant and then Killigrew began experimenting with scenic effects in the next few years, and both companies moved to new or newly converted quarters to accommodate such effects. During the same time period, actors and actresses became popular drawing cards for the companies, and plays were chosen or written to display their special talents in typical roles.

It took somewhat longer to achieve a stable repertory, owing to a number of factors. The most important initially was play ownership; production rights in the older drama were often contested during the early years. Originally, production rights belonged to the company that had commissioned and paid the dramatist for the script. But even before the Interregnum, companies changed managements, disbanded and reformed, and production rights were subject to litigation (Freehafer, "Contention"). When the Civil War broke out, the players scattered, but many returned to London afterwards and reformed into a single company which played sporadically (see Hotson). Under such conditions, it was unlikely that much thought was given to play ownership, but at the beginning of the Restoration, managers found it necessary to establish such rights almost immediately.

By February or March of 1660, there were three companies performing in London: "the 'Old Actors' at the Red Bull, Rhodes's young company at the Cockpit in Drury Lane, and Beeston's troupe at Salisbury Court" (Freehafer, "Formation" 13). When Killigrew took charge of the "Old Actors," who claimed descent from the pre-Commonwealth King's Men through the actors Burt, Hart, Clun, and Mohun, he also claimed the old King's Company repertory of plays (see Freehafer, "Formation" 7-8; Murray 170-72, tables ff.).[2] This included, among others, almost all the plays of Beaumont and Fletcher and all of Jonson's (Sorelius, "Rights" 184).

Meanwhile, Davenant took over Rhodes's Company of actors, except for Kynaston and Betterton who went to Killigrew, and Beeston's Company also continued to be active for a time (Freehafer, "Formation" 25-26). This meant, as Freehafer points out, that Davenant essentially had third choice of actors: "If Beeston's troupe still contained Beeston himself, Bird, and Jolly, then it was a stronger group, even after the loss of Lacy, than Rhodes's company, especially after

---

[2] Another basis for Killigrew's claim was a letter (dated 8/30/60) from Humphrey Moseley, the play publisher, ceding production rights in all of Moseley's plays to Mohun (see Freehafer, "Formation" 17-18; Hume, "Securing" 157-61).

Formation of Repertory 263

the removal of Kynaston and Betterton" ("Formation" 25).³ More to the point, Davenant had difficulty obtaining plays for his actors to perform.

> Of the thirteen plays that his players are known to have acted before coming under his management, only *The Changeling* and *The Bondman* now remained available to them without time limit. Obviously, Davenant could not launch his company in public with a repertory of but two plays. In order to keep his actors going, on December 12 he had to obtain the special permission of the Lord Chamberlain to continue to present six plays from their old repertory for "two months' time." This slim two months' allowance evidently proved insufficient, however, for Davenant's company acted at least four of these six plays after the grace period had expired. . . . *The Spanish Curate* . . . *Rule a Wife and Have a Wife* [along with] . . . *The Mad Lover* and *The Maid in the Mill* (both "two months' plays") remained permanently in the repertory of the Duke's Men, instead of reverting to the King's Men, as the remaining four plays evidently did in 1661. Besides granting Davenant two months' rights in six plays that his company badly needed to retain, the Lord Chamberlain on December 12 also granted Davenant exclusive rights in his own plays (covering the ten he had written prior to 1642), in nine plays by Shakespeare, and in one each by Denham and Webster.⁴   (Freehafer, "Formation" 26–27)

Despite all these difficulties, Davenant coped so well that by the time of his death in the spring of 1668, his was the superior company in all measurable ways. Once the initial handicaps were overcome, a theatre company's success was largely a matter of skilled management, experience, and attitude, and Davenant surpassed Killigrew in

---

³By January of 1660, Davenant had induced Betterton to return to the Duke's Company.

⁴In an earlier study, Allardyce Nicoll, puzzling over why Davenant was granted Shakespeare plays which in some cases "belonged" to the King's Company, suggested that Davenant might have possessed some pre-Commonwealth promptbooks with which he could have made a case for his right to produce them ("Rights"). But Hazelton Spencer refuted this theory by pointing out that in almost all cases the "source of the adopter is regularly the latest pre-Wars quarto" ("Restoration" 443–44).

We should also note that Davenant's rights in the Shakespeare plays were restricted by the terms of the Lord Chamberlain's agreement: "Davenant was not permitted to stage the stipulated plays by Shakespeare, Denham, and Webster until he had first reformed and adapted them—a process not completed, in the case of Shakespeare, until seven years later. Among the numerous commentators who have denounced Davenant for 'improving' Shakespeare, not one seems to have noted the crucial fact that Davenant was legally obliged to 'reform' these plays, as a prescribed condition for obtaining the right to perform them" (Freehafer, "Formation" 27).

all these areas.[5] After 1668 external and internal factors continued to affect the Restoration repertory, though not as much as during the early years. After Davenant's death, management of the Duke's Company was turned over to actors Betterton and Henry Harris, and the summer of 1670 saw the Duke's Company begin construction of a new theatre in Dorset Garden, which they occupied on 9 November 1671 (*LS* 143, 165, 185). In January 1672, the King's Company's theatre in Bridges Street, Drury Lane burned down; they did not apparently act again until 26 February when they occupied the Duke's Company's old theatre in Lincoln's Inn Fields. Not until late in the 1673–74 season (March 26) did they finally move into a newly-built theatre in Drury Lane (*LS* 185, 209).

In 1676–77 both companies underwent changes in management. Harris was replaced by William Smith as comanager of the Duke's Company, and dissentions within the King's Company between Killigrew and his son Charles caused the Lord Chamberlain, in September 1676, to appoint as actor-managers Charles Hart, Michael Mohun, Edward Kynaston, and William Cartwright. In late February of 1677, Hart was given full authority over the others, and in July, the players achieved self-governing powers. Serious disagreements continued within the King's Company throughout the next five seasons, and Drury Lane was closed for a time in 1678 or 1679 (*LS* 247, 261, 271, 279, 289).[6]

Following the Popish Plot in October 1678, the theatrical world suffered from the tensions of the general populace: audiences were scarce, and the 1678–79 season was, at best, fitful; conditions improved only slightly in 1679–80 and sagged again in 1680–81 (*LS* 299). Negotiations to combine the two companies were begun in April 1682, and the 1682–83 season began with a United Company. Afterwards, the

---

[5]Davenant, who exercised daily control over his company, set up and ran a successful business. When he died in 1668, his immediate subordinates Thomas Betterton and Henry Harris, had the training and experience to take over, and they managed successfully on behalf of the sharing actors and Davenant's heirs. Killigrew, in contrast, took only a desultory interest in his company. He made grandiose plans, but did not carry them out, leaving daily operation to a committee of senior actors. His company quickly ran into censorship difficulties; discipline was slack, recruitment erratic, and money tight. Although the stockholders pulled together and rebuilt after fire destroyed their theatre in 1672, the King's Company never altogether recuperated from that disaster.   (Milhous, "Company" 3)

[6]"The last ten years the company existed were spent bickering over control, first among the actors, then between Killigrew and his son Charles. Though Charles won a court suit for possession of the patent in 1677, the actors refused to work with or for him" (Milhous, "Company" 3).

players alternated between Drury Lane for dramas and Dorset Garden for more spectacular productions (*LS* 299, 313). "In addition, the new company for some time relied more heavily upon revivals than upon new plays, for the number of premieres in the 1682-83 season fell below the combined total of new productions in most of the preceding seasons" (*LS* 313). In 1683–84, the company again produced relatively few new plays. Finally, in the 1684–85 season, the death of Charles II closed the playhouses for about ten weeks (*LS* 321, 331).

In themselves, these theatrical conditions give us little basis for analysis, merely the parameters within which such analysis must take place. Davenant's initial lack of old plays, as has been pointed out, was no doubt responsible for his company's innovations in spectacle, while his poor relation's share of actors probably offered youngsters like Betterton a fuller opportunity to develop their talents. Similarly, the management problems of the King's Company may eventually have taken the edge off the competition necessary for growth within both companies; as has been suggested, for example, by Robert D. Hume (*Development* 340), such stagnation seems to have accompanied merger and perhaps preceded it. Thus, the realities of production are a necessary backdrop to a study of repertory development, but only that. In order to chart the course of Carolean comedy, we need to create a methodology which absorbs the data that we know and accounts plausibly for what we don't.

Within the last few years, since the production of the first *London Stage* volume in 1965, use of the repertory evidence to discuss Restoration and eighteenth-century drama has become critically acceptable. Despite the acknowledged inadequacies of the data, recent writers such as Robert D. Hume (*Development*) and George Winchester Stone, Jr. join with pre-*London Stage* writers James W. Tupper, John Harold Wilson (*Influence*), and Gunnar Sorelius (*"Giant"*) in attempting to find order, continuity, and influence in the mass of plays which jockeyed for position over a given span of time during the Restoration.

Instead of treating all plays in the 1660s as essentially equivalent, we are actively seeking out the most popular and ignoring the rest, with certain exceptions, up through the 1668–69 season when the loss of Pepys' evidence makes the records so skimpy as to make such distinctions impossible. After 1668 when Pepys' diary ends, even relative popularity will be ignored; plays either exist or do not exist and are treated as equivalent unless additional information, from Downes for example, is available. Although we know a good deal about the circumstances under which plays were produced during the Restoration, other necessary information is limited or of questionable accuracy. Our most felt lack is in the performance figures themselves.

Although the *London Stage* makes the existing records readily accessible, the data, on the face of it, seem seriously inadequate. Numbers of recorded performances for the first twenty-five seasons range, for example, from lows of 13 in the 1678–79 season, 15 in the 1669–70 season, 19 in the 1683–84 season, and 25 in the 1664–65 season to a high of 151 in the 1667–68 season;[7] while the number of possible performances seems to be about 468 for two companies in any given year (*LS* lxvii).[8] Initially, then, it would appear ill advised to use a sample of only 4 percent to 37 percent (using a compromise number of 400) in determining relative popularity.[9]

We believe, however, the performance figures can be used to provide a criterion of selectivity. The discrepancy between actual and recorded performances in the first three seasons is probably the lowest. The 1659–60 "season" is mostly pre-Restoration and prepatents. External political turmoil, arrests of players, and suppression of performances all combined to make production sporadic in 1659–60 and 1660–61 (Freehafer, "Formation" 6–13). Even after the patents were granted and enforced, it was some time before Davenant's company, at least, was ready to perform regularly.[10] Other seasons with low figures coincide with the Popish Plot (1678–79), post-Union (1683–84), and Plague years (1664–65), and were also undoubtedly low performance years. Hence, the data obtainable for these years may well be proportionally equivalent to those from years with more generous performance figures.

What we can and have done is to adjust our use of the data to fit what we know about how they were collected. By far the greatest amount of information comes from Pepys and other observers recording performances they attended and heard about. And because

---

[7] Performance figures for the 25 seasons are as follows: 1659–60: 30; 1660–61: 116; 1661–62: 118; 1662–63: 70; 1663–64: 51; 1664–65: 25; 1666–67: 87; 1667–68: 151; 1668–69: 95; 1669–70: 15; 1670–71: 35; 1671–72: 40; 1672–73: 24; 1673–74: 22; 1674–75: 71; 1675–76: 50; 1676–77: 55; 1677–78: 30; 1678–79: 13; 1679–80: 27; 1680–81: 24; 1681–82: 42; 1682–83: 22; 1683–84: 19; 1684–85: 31.

[8] Milhous posits a slightly lower figure of 210 performances per company during a slightly later period ("Company" 17). Stone (184) suggests 180.

[9] Hume states in his review of volume 5 of *The London Stage*: "For the earlier years, performance records are drastically incomplete, and so the actual number of recorded performances for a play is essentially meaningless" (390).

[10] "Evidently Davenant's company did not at first act on a daily basis. Contemporary observers have recorded few performances by them before July 1661. Pepys attended thirteen performances by the King's Men before he saw the Duke's Men act, and Herbert indicates that Betterton appeared in only 110 performances between November 1660 and May 1662—a period of time during which a London company might have acted four times that often" (Freehafer, "Formation" 27).

Pepys, for one, followed the crowd, going again and again to a hit play, attending well-publicized premieres, approving of what the court seemed to like, we can assume that the plays mentioned most often in the *Diary* are likely to have been the most popular plays in a given season. A play which isn't mentioned at all was likely either not to have been performed or not to have been noteworthy. Between these two extremes, there is no way of determining relative popularity, and we will not attempt to make such distinctions. In all cases, we have followed the *London Stage* data except when additional information suggests their alteration, as for example, when the *London Stage* editors have indicated when new editions of old plays have been printed and suggested that this probably indicates a new revival. After 1669, we have consistently added such information to our performance numbers. Also the information from "Browne's List" has been added to the 1660–61 season.[11]

---

[11]This list, printed by W.W. Greg in his "Theatrical Repertories of 1662," contains plays Browne saw. Although formerly believed to have belonged to the 1661–62 season or later (*LS* 35–36), John Freehafer argues convincingly that two of the lists are from 1660–61 (see "Formation" 10, 21–22, 26). (Mr. Freehafer further clarified this information in a letter of 28 July 1973.)

Appendix 2:
The Carolean Comic Repertory

1659-65

Plays Written before 1660	Number of Performances
The Alchemist (Jonson)	7
Bartholomew Fair (Jonson)	7
Beggar's Bush (Fletcher-Massinger)	6
The Chances (Fletcher)	4
The Country Captain (Newcastle)	3
The Dancing Master (Newcastle)	3
The Elder Brother (Fletcher)	4
Epicoene (Jonson)	9
Father's Own Son (Fletcher)	3
The Humorous Lieutenant (Fletcher)	16
A Jovial Crew (Brome)	5
A King and No King (Beaumont-Fletcher)	5
The Little Thief (Fletcher-Shirley)	5
Love in a Maze (Shirley)	4
Love Lies A'Bleeding [Philaster] (Beaumont-Fletcher)	4
The Loyal Subject (Fletcher)	3
The Mad Lover (Fletcher)	3
The Maid in the Mill (Fletcher-Rowley)	6
The Merry Wives of Windsor (Shakespeare)	4
The Queen's Masque (Heywood)	4
Rule a Wife and Have a Wife (Fletcher)	5
The Scornful Lady (Beaumont-Fletcher)	6
The Spanish Curate (Fletcher-Massinger)	5
The Tamer Tamed (Fletcher)	6
Volpone (Jonson)	3
The Widow (Middleton)	6
Wit Without Money (Beaumont-Fletcher)	5

Plays Written before 1660	Number of Performances
The Wits (Davenant)	8

Plays Written after 1660	Number of Performances
The Adventures of Five Hours (Tuke)	14
The Comical Revenge (Etherege)	3
The Committee (R. Howard)	3
Cutter of Coleman Street (Cowley)	6
The Law Against Lovers (Davenant)	4
The Rivals (Davenant)	3
The Slighted Maid (Stapylton)	3
The Stepmother (Stapylton)	3
The Surprisal (R. Howard)	3

1666–68

Plays Written before 1660	Number of Performances
Bartholomew Fair (Jonson)	2
The Custom of the Country (Fletcher-Massinger)	2*
The Country Captain (Newcastle)	3
Epicoene (Jonson)	2
The Goblins (Suckling)	3*
The Humorous Lieutenant (Fletcher)	2
Hyde Park (Shirley)	2*
Love in a Maze (Shirley)	3
Love Lies A'Bleeding [Philaster] (Beaumont-Fletcher)	2
The School of Complement (Shirley)	3*
The Scornful Lady (Beaumont-Fletcher)	4
The Storm [The Sea Voyage] (Fletcher-Massinger)	5*
The Wits (Davenant)	3

*first recorded Restoration performance after 1665–66

Plays Written after 1660	Company	Number of Performances
Spanish Comedy:		
An Evening's Love (Dryden)	King's	9*
The Man's the Master (Davenant)	Duke's	4*
Tarugo's Wiles (Sydserf)	King's	4*
Multi-Plot Comedy:		
All Mistaken (J. Howard)	King's	3
The Comical Revenge (Etherege)	Duke's	5
Flora's Vagaries (Rhodes)	King's	3
The Mulberry Garden (Sedley)	King's	3*
Secret Love (Dryden)	King's	12*
The Surprisal (R. Howard)	King's	5
The Tempest (Dryden-Davenant)	Duke's	15*
English Comedy:		
The Committee (R. Howard)	King's	4
The English Monsieur (J. Howard)	King's	3
The Humorous Lovers (Newcastle)	Duke's	3*
The Old Troop (Lacy)	King's	2
Sauny the Scot (Lacy)	King's	2*
She Would if She Could (Etherege)	Duke's	5*
Sir Martin Mar-all (Dryden-Newcastle)	Duke's	16*
The Sullen Lovers (Shadwell)	Duke's	6*
Tu Quoque (Davenant)	Duke's	3*

*first recorded Restoration performance after 1665–66

Carolean Comic Repertory 1668–72

Plays Written before 1660	Number of Performances
The Alchemist (Jonson)	1
Bartholomew Fair (Jonson)	1
The City Match (Mayne)	1*
The Coxcomb (Beaumont-Fletcher)	2*
Epicoene (Jonson)	1
Every Man in His Humour (Jonson)	1*
The Faithful Shepherdess (Fletcher)	4
The Gamester (Shirley)	1*
The Gentleman of Venice (Shirley)	1*
The Grateful Servant (Shirley)	1
The Heiress (Newcastle) [lost]	2*
The Island Princess (Fletcher)	4*
A Jovial Crew (Brome)	1
A King and No King (Beaumont-Fletcher)	1
Lady Errant [Romantic Lady] (Cartwright)	2*
The Lady's Trial (Ford)	1*
The Little French Lawyer (Fletcher-Massinger)	1*
Love Lies A'Bleeding [Philaster] (Beaumont-Fletcher)	1
The Mad Lover (Fletcher)	1
The Maid in the Mill (Fletcher-Rowley)	1
The Pilgrim (Fletcher)	1*
The Queen of Arragon (Habington)	2*
The Queen's Masque (Heywood)	1
The School of Complement (Shirley)	1
The Scornful Lady (Beaumont-Fletcher)	1
The Sisters (Shirley)	1
The Spanish Curate (Fletcher-Massinger)	2
The Tamer Tamed (Fletcher)	1
Twelfth Night (Shakespeare)	1

*first recorded Restoration performance after 1667–68

Plays Written before 1660		Number of Performances
Wit A la Mode [Wit at Several Weapons] (Fletcher)		1*
Wit Without Money (Beaumont-Fletcher)		1
The Wits (Davenant)		2
Women Pleased (Fletcher)		2*

Plays Written after 1660	Company	Number of Performances
Molière-based Comedy:		
The Amorous Widow (Betterton)	Duke's	2*
The Citizen Turn'd Gentleman (Ravenscroft)	Duke's	5*
Damoiselles A la Mode (Flecknoe)	King's	2*
The Dumb Lady (Lacy)	King's	1*
The Hypocrite (Shadwell) [lost]	Duke's	1*
The Miser (Shadwell)	King's	1*
Sir Martin Mar-all (Dryden-Newcastle)	Duke's	7
Sir Salomon (Caryll)	Duke's	4*
The Sullen Lovers (Shadwell)	Duke's	4
Tartuffe (Medbourne)	King's	2
Other Foreign Comedy:		
The Adventures of Five Hours (Tuke)	Duke's	4
The Amorous Prince (Behn)	Duke's	1*
An Evening's Love (Dryden)	King's	2
The Feign'd Astrologer (anon. from Corneille)	?	1*
The Forc'd Marriage (Behn)	Duke's	2*
The Generous Enemies (Corye)	King's	1*
The Gentleman Dancing-Master (Wycherley)	Duke's	1*
Guzman (Orrery)	Duke's	2*
Juliana, Princess of Poland (Crowne)	Duke's	1*
The Reformation (Arrowsmith)	Duke's	1*

*first recorded Restoration performance after 1667–68

Carolean Comic Repertory

Plays Written after 1660	Company	Number of Performances
The Royal Shepherdess (Shadwell)	Duke's	6*
The Six Days' Adventure (E. Howard)	Duke's	1*
The Women's Conquest (E. Howard)	Duke's	1*
Multi-Plot Comedy:		
The Comical Revenge (Etherege)	Duke's	6
Flora's Vagaries (Rhodes)	King's	1
Marcelia (Boothby)	?	1*
Marriage A-la-Mode (Dryden)	King's	1*
Secret Love (Dryden)	King's	3
The Tempest (Dryden-Davenant)	Duke's	3
Parody/Burlesque:		
The Rehearsal (Buckingham)	King's	2*
English Comedy:		
The Cheats (Wilson)	King's	1
The Committee (R. Howard)	King's	2
Cutter of Coleman Street (Cowley)	Duke's	2
The Humorists (Shadwell)	Duke's	7*
Love in a Wood (Wycherley)	King's	1*
Mr. Anthony (Orrery)	Duke's	1*
The Parson's Wedding (Killigrew)	King's	1
She Would if She Could (Etherege)	Duke's	2
The Town-Shifts (Revet)	Duke's	1*
The Wild Gallant (Dryden)	King's	1

*first recorded Restoration performance after 1667–68
(This list does not include the following lost plays: The Recovery [anon.], She's Jealous of Herself [anon.], and The Woman Made a Justice [Betterton].)

1672–78

Plays Written before 1660	Number of Performances
The Alchemist (Jonson)	2
Arviragus and Philicia (Carlell)	1*
Bartholomew Fair (Jonson)	1
Beggar's Bush (Fletcher-Massinger)	1
The Captain (Fletcher)	1*
The Elder Brother (Fletcher)	1
Every Man Out of His Humour (Jonson)	1*
The Island Princess (Fletcher)	2
A King and No King (Beaumont-Fletcher)	1
Love in a Maze (Shirley)	2
Love Lies A'Bleeding [Philaster] (Beaumont-Fletcher)	3
The Mad Lover (Fletcher)	1
The Merry Wives of Windsor (Shakespeare)	1
The Ordinary (Cartwright)	1*
The Scornful Lady (Beaumont-Fletcher)	2
The Spanish Curate (Fletcher-Massinger)	1
The Tamer Tamed (Fletcher)	1
Volpone (Jonson)	1
The Widow (Middleton)	1

Plays Written after 1660	Company	Number of Performances
Foreign Comedy:		
The Adventures of Five Hours (Tuke)	Duke's	2
The Amorous Old Woman (Duffett)	King's	1*
Amorous Orontus (Bulteel)	?	1
The Assignation (Dryden)	King's	2*
The Counterfeits (Leanerd)	Duke's	1*
The Dutch Lover (Behn)	Duke's	1*
The English Lawyer (Ravenscroft)	King's	1*
An Evening's Love (Dryden)	King's	1

*first recorded Restoration performance after 1671–72

Carolean Comic Repertory

Plays Written after 1660	Company	Number of Performances
The French Conjuror (Porter)	Duke's	1*
King Edgar and Alfreda (Ravenscroft)	King's	1*
Love in the Dark (Fane)	King's	1*
The Man's the Master (Davenant)	Duke's	1
The Rival Ladies (Dryden)	King's	1
The Rover (Behn)	Duke's	1*
Scaramouch (Ravenscroft)	King's	1*
The Spanish Rogue (Duffett)	King's	1*
The Wrangling Lovers (Ravenscroft)	Duke's	1*
Multi-Plot Comedy:		
Flora's Vagaries (Rhodes)	King's	1
The Mulberry Garden (Sedley)	King's	1
Secret Love (Dryden)	King's	1
Wits Led by the Nose (Chamberlayne)	King's	1*
London Comedy:		
The Amorous Widow (Betterton)	Duke's	3
The Careless Lovers (Ravenscroft)	Duke's	1*
The Cheats of Scapin (Otway)	Duke's	1*
The Citizen Turn'd Gentleman (Ravenscroft)	Duke's	3
The Committee (R. Howard)	King's	1
The Counterfeit Bridegroom (Behn)	Duke's	2*
The Country-Wife (Wycherley)	King's	3*
The Country Wit (Crowne)	Duke's	3*
Cutter of Coleman Street (Cowley)	Duke's	3
The Debauchee (Behn)	Duke's	1*
The English Monsieur (J. Howard)	King's	1
Epsom Wells (Shadwell)	Duke's	6*

*first recorded Restoration performance after 1671–72

Plays Written after 1660	Company	Number of Performances
A Fond Husband (Durfey)	Duke's	3*
The Fool Turn'd Critick (Durfey)	King's	1*
Friendship in Fashion (Otway)	Duke's	1*
The Humorous Lovers (Newcastle)	Duke's	1
Mr. Limberham (Dryden)	Duke's	1*
Madam Fickle (Durfey)	Duke's	1*
The Mall (J.D.)	King's	1*
The Man of Mode (Etherege)	Duke's	3*
The Man of Newmarket (E. Howard)	King's	1*
The Mistaken Husband (anon.)	King's	1*
The Mock Duellist (Belon?)	King's	1*
The Morning Ramble (Payne)	Duke's	1*
The Plain-Dealer (Wycherley)	King's	3*
The Rambling Justice (Leanerd)	King's	1*
She Would if She Could (Etherege)	Duke's	2
Sir Martin Mar-all (Dryden-Newcastle)	Duke's	4
Sir Patient Fancy (Behn)	Duke's	1*
Squire Oldsapp (Durfey)	Duke's	1*
The Sullen Lovers (Shadwell)	Duke's	2
Tom Essence (Rawlins)	Duke's	1*
The Town Fop (Behn)	Duke's	2*
Trick for Trick (Durfey)	King's	1*
A True Widow (Shadwell)	Duke's	1*
Tunbridge Wells (Rawlins?)	Duke's	1*
The Virtuoso (Shadwell)	Duke's	2*
The Woman Turn'd Bully (anon.)	Duke's	1*
Provincial Comedy:		
Country Innocence (Leanerd)	King's	1*

*first recorded Restoration performance after 1671–72

Carolean Comic Repertory

Plays Written after 1660	Company	Number of Performances
The Triumphant Widow (Newcastle)	Duke's	1*
Parody/Burlesque:		
The Empress of Morocco (Duffett)	King's	1*
The Mock-Tempest (Duffett)	King's	1*
Psyche Debauched (Duffett)	King's	2*
The Rehearsal (Buckingham)	King's	2
Opera/Pastoral:		
Calisto (Crowne)	Court	3*
The Constant Nymph (anon.)	Duke's	1*
Cytheria (Smith)	?	1*
Love's Kingdom (Flecknoe)	Duke's	1
Pastor Fido (Settle)	Duke's	1*
The Tempest (Shadwell)	Duke's	12*

*first recorded Restoration performance after 1671–72
(This list does not include the following lost plays: *No Fool Like Ye Old Fool* [anon.], *The Sea Captains* [anon.], and *Sir Popular Wisdom* [anon.].)

1678-85

Plays Written before 1660	Number of Performances
Epicoene (Jonson)	1
The Humorous Lieutenant (Fletcher)	1
A Jovial Crew (Brome)	1
A King and No King (Beaumont-Fletcher)	1
The Loyal Subject (Fletcher)	1
The Maid in the Mill (Fletcher-Rowley)	1
The Northern Lass [Castle] (Brome)	1
Rule a Wife and Have a Wife (Fletcher)	2
The Scornful Lady (Beaumont-Fletcher)	1

*first recorded Restoration performance after 1677–78

Plays Written after 1660	Company	Number of Performances
Foreign Comedy:		
The Chances	United	2
The City Politiques (Crowne)	United	1*
A Commonwealth of Women (Durfey)	United	1*
The Disappointment (Southerne)	United	2*
A Duke and No Duke (Tate)	United	2*
The English Lawyer (Ravenscroft)	United	1
The False Count (Behn)	Duke's	1*
The Feign'd Courtezans (Behn)	Duke's	2*
The Injur'd Princess (Durfey)	King's	1*
The Loving Enemies (Maidwell)	Duke's	1*
Mistaken Beauty (anon.)	United	1
The Rover (Behn)	Duke's	2
The Rover, II (Behn)	Duke's	2*
The Young King (Behn)	Duke's	1*
Multi-Plot Comedy:		
Marriage A-la-Mode (Dryden)	United	1
Secret Love (Dryden)	King's	1
The Spanish Fryar (Dryden)	Duke's	3*
London Comedy:		
The Amorous Widow (Betterton)	Duke's	2
The Atheist (Otway)	United	1*
The Cheats (Wilson)	United	1
The Cheats of Scapin (Otway)	United	1
The City Heiress (Behn)	Duke's	2*
The Country-Wife (Wycherley)	United	1
Cuckolds-Haven (Tate)	United	1*
Dame Dobson (Ravenscroft)	United	1*
Epsom Wells (Shadwell)	Duke's	2

*first recorded Restoration performance after 1677–78

Carolean Comic Repertory

Plays Written after 1660	Company	Number of Performances
A Fond Husband (Durfey)	Duke's	1
The London Cuckolds (Ravenscroft)	Duke's	4*
Madam Fickle (Durfey)	Duke's	1
The Man of Mode (Etherege)	Duke's	2
Mr. Turbulent (anon.)	Duke's	2*
The Plain-Dealer (Wycherley)	King's	3
The Revenge (Behn)	Duke's	1*
The Roundheads (Behn)	Duke's	1*
She Would if She Could (Etherege)	Duke's	2
Sir Barnaby Whigg (Durfey)	Duke's	1*
Sir Courtly Nice (Crowne)	United	2*
Sir Hercules Buffoon (Lacy)	United	1*
The Souldiers Fortune (Otway)	Duke's	4*
The Virtuous Wife (Durfey)	Duke's	1*
The Wild Gallant (Dryden)	United	1
The Woman-Captain (Shadwell)	Duke's	1*
Provincial Comedy:		
The Lancashire Witches (Shadwell)	Duke's	1*
The Old Troop (Lacy)	King's	1
The Royalist (Durfey)	Duke's	3*
Parody/Burlesque:		
The Mock-Tempest (Duffett)	King's	1
The Rehearsal (Buckingham)	United	1
Opera/Pastoral:		
The Tempest (Shadwell)	Duke's	2
The Unfortunate Shepherd (Tutchin)	United	1*

*first recorded Restoration performance after 1677–78
(This list does not include the following lost plays: Fools Have Fortune [anon.], Like Father, Like Son [Behn], Pair-Royal of Coxcombs [Philips], and The Restoration [Buckingham].)

Bibliography

Play Texts

For texts of plays we have used first editions except for the plays and playwrights listed below; we have preferred modern editions to old when we had that choice, so that our citations would be from more widely available texts, and we have preferred old-spelling texts to modernized ones, in order to give our citations from Carolean drama a uniform appearance and to express distaste for needless editorial tampering. When possible, we have given line numbers for citations within plays, using a period to separate them from act and scene references: I.i.207. When we did not have line numbers, we have given page numbers, separating them with a semicolon from act and, where available, scene references: I.i; 12.

The abbreviation *CD* stands for the California Dryden, i.e., *The Works of John Dryden* (Berkeley: U of California P, 1962–84). Textual citations are to plays in the following volumes: vol. 8, *The Wild Gallant, The Rival Ladies, The Indian-Queen*, ed. John Harrington Smith and Dougald MacMillan, textual ed. Vinton A. Dearing, vol. 9; *The Indian Emperour, Secret Love, Sir Martin Mar-all*, ed. John Loftis, textual ed. Vinton A. Dearing; vol. 10, *The Tempest, Tyrannick Love, An Evening's Love*, ed. Maximillian E. Novak, textual ed. George Robert Guffey; vol. 11, *The Conquest of Granada, Marriage A-la-Mode, The Assignation*, ed. John Loftis and David Stuart Rodes, textual ed. Vinton A. Dearing; vol. 13, *All for Love, Oedipus, Troilus and Cressida*, ed. Maximillian E. Novak, textual ed. George Robert Guffey.

We have also used *Dryden, The Dramatic Works*, ed. Montague Summers, 6 vols. (London: Nonesuch, 1931–32). Volumes 4 and 5 contain texts for *Mr. Limberham* and *The Spanish Fryar*, not yet published in the California Dryden cited above.

Arrowsmith, Joseph. *The Reformation*. Intro. Deborah C. Payne. Augustan Reprint Society, Nos. 237–38. Los Angeles: William Andrews Clark Memorial Library, 1986.

Beaumont, Francis, and John Fletcher. *The Dramatic Works in the Beaumont and Fletcher Canon*. Ed. Fredson Bowers. 2 vols. Cambridge: Cambridge UP, 1970.

———. *The Works of Beaumont and Fletcher*. Ed. Arnold Glover and A. R. Waller. 10 vols. Cambridge: Cambridge UP, 1905–12.

———. *The Works of Francis Beaumont and John Fletcher, Variorum Edition*. Ed. A. H. Bullen. 4 vols. London: George Bell, 1904–12.

Behn, Aphra. *The Works of Aphra Behn*. Ed. Montague Summers. 1915. 6 vols. New York: Phaeton, 1967.

Betterton, Thomas. *The Amorous Widow: or, The Wanton Wife. The Life of Thomas Betterton, the Late Eminent Tragedian*. Charles Gildon. 1710. London: Frank Cass, 1970.

Cowley, Abraham. *Essays, Plays and Sundry Verses of Abraham Cowley*. Ed. A. R. Waller. Cambridge: Cambridge UP, 1906.

Crowne, John. *The Dramatic Works of John Crowne*. Ed. James Maidment and W. H. Logan. 1874. 4 vols. New York: Benjamin Blom, 1967.

———. *Sir Courtly Nice. Restoration Comedies*. Ed. Montague Summers. Boston: Small, Maynard, 1922. 271–400.

Durfey, Thomas. *Two Comedies by Thomas D'Urfey: "Madam Fickle; or, The Witty False One" and "A Fond Husband; or, The Plotting Sisters."* Ed. Jack A. Vaughn. Rutherford: Fairleigh Dickinson UP, 1976.

Etherege, Sir George. *The Dramatic Works of Sir George Etherege*. Ed. H. F. B. Brett-Smith. 2 vols. Oxford: Blackwell, 1927.

Howard, Sir Robert. *Sir Robert Howard's Comedy "The Committee."* Ed. Carryl Nelson Thurber. *University of Illinois Studies in Language and Literature*. 7 (1921).

Lacy, John. *The Dramatic Works of John Lacy, Comedian*. Ed. James Maidment and W. H. Logan. 1875. New York: Benjamin Blom, 1967.

Lee, Nathaniel. *The Works of Nathaniel Lee*. Ed. Thomas B. Stroup and Arthur L. Cooke. 2 vols. New Brunswick: Scarecrow, 1954–55.

Molière [Jean-Baptiste Poquelin]. *Théâtre complet*. Ed. Robert Jouanny. 2 vols. Paris: Garnier, 1962.

Otway, Thomas. *The Works of Thomas Otway*. Ed. J. C. Ghosh. 2 vols. Oxford: Clarendon, 1932.

Ravenscroft, Edward. *The London Cuckolds. Restoration Comedies*. Ed. Montague Summers. Boston: Small, Maynard, 1922. 143–270.

Shadwell, Thomas. *The Complete Works of Thomas Shadwell*. Ed. Montague Summers. 1927. 5 vols. New York: Benjamin Blom, 1968.

Shakespeare, William. *The Complete Works*. Ed. Hardin Craig. Chicago: Scott, 1951.

Wycherley, William. *The Complete Plays of William Wycherley*. Ed. Gerald Weales. New York: Doubleday, 1966.

Scholarly Sources

The abbreviations *LS* and *POAS* respectively stand for: *The London Stage, 1660–1800: Part 1: 1660–1700*, ed. William Van Lennep (Carbondale: Southern Illinois UP, 1965) and *Poems on Affairs of State: Augustan Satirical Verse, 1660–1714*, ed. George deF. Lord, Elias F. Mengel, Jr., and Howard H. Schless, 3 vols. (New Haven: Yale UP, 1963–68).

We can hardly express our indebtedness to—and gratitude for—the text and notes of the California Dryden and the repertory compilations in *The London Stage*. We have relied on both wherever possible.

Allen, Ned Bliss. *The Sources of John Dryden's Comedies*. Ann Arbor: U of Michigan P, 1935.

Allestree, Richard. *Works*. Oxford, 1695.

Alssid, Michael. *Thomas Shadwell*. New York: Twayne, 1967.

Auffret, J. "Wycherley et ses maîtres les moralistes." *Etudes anglaises* 15 (1962): 375–88.

The Bachelor's Directory: Being a Treatise of the Excellency of Marriage. London, 1694.

Baker, Van R. "Heroic Posturing Satirized: Dryden's *Mr. Limberham*." *PLL* 8 (1972): 370–79.

Behn, Aphra, ed. *Miscellany, Being a Collection of Poems*. 1685.

Bentley, Gerald Eades. *The Jacobean and Caroline Stage*. 7 vols. Oxford: Clarendon, 1941–68.

Berman, Ronald. "Wycherley's Unheroic Society." *ELH* 51 (1984): 465–78.

Blackstone, William. *Commentaries on the Laws of England*. 11th ed. 4 vols. London, 1791.

Bracher, Frederick, ed. *Letters of Sir George Etherege*. Berkeley: U of California P, 1974.

Brown, Laura S. "The Divided Plot: Tragicomic Form in the Restoration."*ELH* 47 (1980): 67–79.

———. *English Dramatic Form, 1660–1760*. New Haven: Yale UP, 1981.

Burke, Peter. *Popular Culture in Early Modern Europe*. New York: Harper, 1978.

Canfield, J. Douglas. "The Ideology of Restoration Tragicomedy." *ELH* 51 (1984): 447–64.

Capp, Bernard. *English Almanacs 1500–1800: Astrology and the Popular Press*. Ithaca: Cornell UP, 1979.

Cawelti, John G. *Adventure, Mystery, and Romance: Formula Stories as Art and Popular Culture*. Chicago: U of Chicago P, 1976.

Cibber, Colley. *An Apology for the Life of Colley Cibber.* Ed. B. R. S. Fone. Ann Arbor: U of Michigan P, 1968.

Clark, J. C. D. *Revolution and Rebellion: State and Society in England in the Seventeenth and Eighteenth Centuries.* Cambridge: Cambridge UP, 1986.

Corman, Brian. "Interpreting and Misinterpreting *The Man of Mode.*" *PLL* 13 (1977): 34–53.

De Lauretis, Teresa. *Alice Doesn't: Feminism, Semiotics, Cinema.* Bloomington: Indiana UP, 1984.

Dennis, John. *Critical Works.* Ed. Edward Niles Hooker. 2 vols. Baltimore: Johns Hopkins UP, 1939–43.

Descombes, Vincent. *Modern French Philosophy.* Trans. L. Scott-Fox and J. M. Harding. Cambridge: Cambridge UP, 1980.

Donahue, Joseph W., Jr. *Dramatic Character in the English Romantic Age.* Princeton: Princeton UP, 1970.

Douglas, Mary. *Natural Symbols: Explorations in Cosmology.* 1970. New York: Pantheon, 1982.

———. *Purity and Danger.* 1966. London: Routledge, 1980.

Downes, John. *Roscius Anglicanus.* Ed. Judith Milhous and Robert D. Hume. London: Society for Theatre Research, 1987.

Filmer, Sir Robert. *Patriarcha and Other Political Works.* Ed. Peter Laslett. Oxford: Blackwell, 1949.

Fiore, Robert L. *Drama and Ethos: Natural-Law Ethics in Spanish Golden Age Theatre.* Lexington: U of Kentucky P, 1975.

Fisher, Alan. "What Does It Take to Be in Dryden's Audience?" *New Homage to John Dryden.* Los Angeles: William Andrews Clark Memorial Library, 1983. 31–57.

Freehafer, John. "The Contention for *Bussy D'Ambois,* 1622–41." *Theatre Notebook* 23 (Winter 1968/69): 61–69.

———. "The Formation of the London Patent Companies in 1660." *Theatre Notebook* 20 (Autumn 1965): 6–30.

Freud, Sigmund. *Inhibitions, Symptoms and Anxiety.* 1926. Trans. Alix Strachey. Rev. and ed. James Strachey. New York: Norton, 1959.

Fujimura, Thomas H. *The Restoration Comedy of Wit.* Princeton: Princeton UP, 1952.

Geertz, Clifford. *The Interpretation of Cultures.* New York: Basic, 1973.

Gewirtz, Arthur. *Restoration Adaptations of Early 17th Century Comedies.* Washington, DC: UP of America, 1982.

Gilder, Rosamund. *Enter the Actress: The First Women in the Theatre.* London: George G. Harrap, 1931.

Gildon, Charles. *The Life of Mr. Thomas Betterton, the Late Eminent Tragedian.* 1710. London: Frank Cass, 1970.

Girard, René. *Violence and the Sacred.* Trans. Patrick Gregory. Baltimore: Johns Hopkins UP, 1977.
God's Revenge Against Punning. The Prose Works of Alexander Pope. The Earlier Works, 1711–1729. Ed. Norman Ault. Oxford: Blackwell, 1936.
Greg, W. W. "Theatrical Repertories of 1662." *Collected Papers.* Ed.J. C. Maxwell. Oxford: Clarendon, 1966. 44–47.
Grene, Nicholas. *Shakespeare, Jonson, Molière: The Comic Contract.* Totawa, NJ: Barnes, 1980.
The Guardian's Instruction, or, The Gentleman's Romance. London, 1688.
Harbage, Alfred. *Annals of English Drama, 975–1700.* Rev. S. Schoenbaum. London: Methuen, 1964.
Harth, Phillip. *Contexts of Dryden's Thought.* Chicago: U of Chicago P, 1968.
Harwood, John T. *Critics, Values, and Restoration Comedy.* Carbondale: Southern Illinois UP, 1982.
Hawkins, Harriett. "The 'Example Theory' and the Providentialist Approach to Restoration Drama: Some Questions of Validity and Applicability. *The Eighteenth Century: Theory and Interpretation* 24 (1983): 103–14.

———. *Likenesses of Truth in Elizabethan and Restoration Drama.* Oxford: Clarendon P, 1972.
Highfill, Philip H., Kalman A. Burnim, and Edward A. Langhans. *A Biographical Dictionary of Actors, Actresses, Musicians, Dancers, Managers & Other Stage Personnel in London, 1660–1800.* 10 vols to date. Carbondale: Southern Illinois UP, 1973–.
Hill, Christopher. *The World Turned Upside Down: Radical Ideas during the English Revolution.* 1972. Harmondsworth, Eng.: Penguin, 1975.
Hippeau, Louis. *Essai sur le morale de La Rochefoucauld.* Paris: A. -G. Nizet, 1967.
Hobbes, Thomas. *Leviathan, or the Matter, Forme & Power of a Commonwealth Ecclesiasticall and Civil.* 1651. Oxford: Clarendon, 1909.
Holland, Norman. *The First Modern Comedies: The Significance of Etherege, Wycherley and Congreve.* 1959. Bloomington: Indiana UP, 1967.
Holland, Peter. *The Ornament of Action: Texts and Performance in Restoration Comedy.* Cambridge: Cambridge UP, 1979.
Horkheimer, Max, and Theodor W. Adorno. *Dialectic of Enlightenment.* 1944. Trans. John Cumming. New York: Continuum, 1982.
Hotson, Leslie. *The Commonwealth and Restoration Stage.* Cambridge: Harvard UP, 1928.
Hughes, Leo. *A Century of English Farce.* Princeton: Princeton UP, 1956.
Hume, Robert D. *The Development of English Drama in the Late Seventeenth Century.* Oxford: Clarendon, 1976.

———, ed. Preface. *The London Theatre World, 1660–1800.* Carbondale: Southern Illinois UP, 1980. xi–xiii.

———. *The Rakish Stage: Studies in English Drama, 1660–1800.* Carbondale: Southern Illinois UP, 1983.

———. Rev. of Part 5 of *The London Stage*, ed. C. B. Hogan. *Philological Quarterly* 50 (July 1971): 390.

———. "Securing a Repertory: Plays on the London Stage 1660–5." *Poetry and Drama, 1570–1700: Essays in Honour of Harold F. Brooks.* Eds. Antony Coleman and Antony Hammond. London: Methuen, 1981. 156–72.

———. "William Wycherley: Text, Life, Interpretation." *MP* 78 (1981): 399–415.

[Hunt, Thomas ?]. *Mr. Emmertons Marriage with Mrs. Bridget Hyde Considered.* London, 1682.

Jauss, Hans Robert. "Literary History as a Challenge to Literary Theory." *Toward an Aesthetic of Reception.* Trans. Timothy Bahti. Brighton, Eng.: Harvester, 1982. 3–45.

Kalitzki, Judith. "Versions of Truth: *Marriage à la Mode.*" *Restoration* 4 (1980): 65–70.

Kaye, F. B., ed. *The Fable of the Bees: or, Private Vices, Publick Benefits.* By Bernard Mandeville. 2 vols. Oxford: Clarendon, 1924.

King, Bruce. *Dryden's Major Plays.* New York: Barnes, 1966.

Kirsch, Arthur C. *Dryden's Heroic Drama.* Princeton: Princeton UP, 1965.

———. *Jacobean Dramatic Perspectives.* Charlottesville: UP of Virginia, 1972.

Knight, David M. *Ordering the World: A History of Classifying Man.* London: Burnett, 1981.

Kracauer, Siegfried. *Theory of Film: The Redemption of Physical Reality.* New York: Oxford UP, 1960.

Kunz, Don R. *The Drama of Thomas Shadwell. Salzburg Studies in English Literature.* Salzburg, 1972.

La Bruyère, Jean de. *Oeuvres complètes.* Ed. Julien Benda. Paris: Gallimard, 1951.

La Rochefoucauld, François, duc de. *Moral Maxims and Reflections.* 2nd ed. London, 1706.

———. *Oeuvres complètes.* Ed. A. Chassang. 2 vols. Paris: Garnier, 1883–84.

Lancaster, Henry Carrington. *A History of French Dramatic Literature in the Seventeenth Century.* 5 parts. Baltimore: Johns Hopkins UP, 1929–42.

Lanson, Gustave. *Histoire de la littérature française.* 7th ed. Paris: Hachette, 1902.

Lewis, Philip E. "La Rochefoucauld: The Rationality of Play." *Game, Play, Literature*. Ed. Jacques Ehrmann. Boston: Beacon, 1968. 133–47.

Lindenberger, Herbert. *Opera: The Extravagant Art*. Ithaca: Cornell UP, 1984.

Locke, John. *Two Treatises of Government*. Ed. Peter Laslett. Rev. ed. Cambridge: Cambridge UP, 1963.

Loftis, John. *The Spanish Plays of Neoclassical England*. New Haven: Yale UP, 1973.

Lovejoy, Arthur O. *Reflections on Human Nature*. Johns Hopkins UP, 1961.

McCarthy, B. Eugene. *William Wycherley: A Biography*. Athens: Ohio UP, 1979.

Mack, Maynard. *Alexander Pope: A Life*. New York: Norton, 1985.

McKeon, Michael. "Marxist Criticism and *Marriage à la Mode*." *The Eighteenth Century: Theory and Interpretation* 24 (1983): 141–62.

———. *The Origins of the English Novel 1600–1740*. Baltimore: Johns Hopkins UP, 1987.

Macpherson, C. B. *The Political Theory of Possessive Individualism: Hobbes to Locke*. London: Oxford UP, 1962.

Mandel, Ernest. *Delightful Murder: A Social History of the Crime Story*. U of Minnesota P, 1984.

Marriage Promoted in a Discourse of Its Ancient and Modern Practice. London, 1690.

Maus, Katharine Eisaman. "Arcadia Lost: Politics and Revision in the Restoration *Tempest*." *Renaissance Drama* ns 13 (1982): 189–209.

———. "'Playhouse Flesh and Blood': Sexual Ideology and the Restoration Actress." *ELH* 46 (1979): 595–617.

Méré, Antoine Gombaud, Chevalier de. "De la vraie Honnêteté. *Oeuvres posthumes*. 1700. Ed. Charles-H. Boudhors. Paris: Roche, 1930.

Mignon, Elizabeth. *Crabbed Age and Youth*. Durham: Duke UP, 1947.

Milhous, Judith. "Company Management." *The London Theatre World: 1660–1800*. Ed. Robert D. Hume. Carbondale: Southern Illinois UP, 1980. 1–34.

———. *Thomas Betterton and the Management of Lincoln's Inn Fields, 1695–1708*. Carbondale: Southern Illinois UP, 1979.

Milhous, Judith, and Robert D. Hume. *Producible Interpretation: Eight English Plays, 1675–1707*. Carbondale: Southern Illinois UP, 1985.

Mizener, Arthur. "The High Design of *A King and No King*." *Modern Philology* 38 (1940): 133–54.

Moore, W. G. *La Rochefoucauld: His Mind and Art*. Oxford: Oxford UP, 1969.

Morris, Herbert. *On Guilt and Innocence: Essays in Legal Philosophy and Moral Psychology*. Berkeley: U of California P, 1976.

Murray, John Tucker. *English Dramatic Companies, 1558–1642. Volume 1: London Companies*. London: Constable, 1910.

Musser, Joseph F., Jr. " 'Imposing Nought But Constancy in Love': Aphra Behn Snares *The Rover*." *Restoration* 3 (1979): 17–25.
Nagel, Thomas. *Mortal Questions*. New York: Cambridge UP, 1979.
Nicoll, Allardyce. *A History of English Drama, 1660–1900. Volume I: Restoration Drama, 1660–1700*. 4th ed. Cambridge: Cambridge UP, 1952.
———. "The Rights of Beeston and D'Avenant in Elizabethan Plays." *Review of English Studies* 1 (Jan. 1925): 84–91.
Novak, Maximillian E. "Margery Pinchwife's 'London Disease': Restoration Comedy and the Libertine Offensive of the 1670s." *Studies in the Literary Imagination* 10.1 (Spring 1977): 1–23.
Ogg, David. *England in the Reign of Charles II*. 2 vols. 2nd ed. Oxford: Clarendon, 1955–56.
Ornstein, Robert. "Shakespearean and Jonsonian Comedy." *Shakespeare Survey* 22 (1969): 43–46.
Pechter, Edward. "The New Historicism and Its Discontents: Politicizing Renaissance Drama." *PMLA* 102 (1987): 292–303.
Pepys, Samuel. *Diary*. Ed. Robert Latham and William Matthews. 11 vols. Berkeley: U of California P, 1970–76.
Powell, Jocelyn. "George Etherege and the Form of a Comedy." *Restoration Theatre*. Ed. John Russell Brown and Bernard Harris. London: Edward Arnold, 1965. 42–69.
———. *Restoration Theatre Production*. London: Routledge, 1984.
Rawls, John. *A Theory of Justice*. Cambridge: Harvard UP, 1971.
Rochester, John Wilmot, Earl of. *Complete Poems*. Ed. David M. Vieth. New Haven: Yale UP, 1968.
Rogers, Katharine M. *William Wycherley*. New York: Twayne, 1971.
Rollins, Hyder Edward, ed. *The Pack of Autolycus*. Cambridge: Harvard UP, 1927.
Rundle, James Urvin. "Wycherley and Calderón: A Source for *Love in a Wood*." *PMLA* 64 (1949): 701–7.
Rymer, Thomas. *The Tragedies of the Last Age*. London, 1678.
Sahlins, Marshall. *Culture and Practical Reason*. Chicago: U of Chicago P, 1976.
Schneider, Ben Ross. *The Ethos of Restoration Comedy*. Urbana: U of Illinois P, 1971.
Scouten, Arthur H. "Recent Interpretations of Restoration Comedy of Manners." *Du Verbe au geste*. Nancy, 1986. 99–107.
Scouten, Arthur H. and Robert D. Hume. " 'Restoration Comedy' and its Audiences, 1660–1776." *The Rakish Stage: Studies in English Drama, 1660–1800*. Robert D. Hume. Carbondale: Southern Illinois UP, 1983. 46–81.
Sedgwick, Eve Kosofsky. "Sexualism and the Citizen of the World: Wycherley, Sterne, and Male Homosocial Desire." *CI* 11 (1984): 226–45.

Smith, John Harrington. *The Gay Couple in Restoration Comedy.* Cambridge: Harvard UP, 1948.

Sorelius, Gunnar. *"The Giant Race Before the Flood": Pre-Restoration Drama on the Stage and in the Criticism of the Restoration.* Acta Universitatis Uppsaliensis, Studia Anglistica Uppsaliensia, 4. Uppsala: Uppsala UP, 1966.

———. "The Rights of the Restoration Theatrical Companies in the Older Drama." *Studia Neophilologica* 37 (1965): 174–89.

Spencer, Hazelton. "The Restoration Play Lists." *Review of English Studies* 1 (Oct. 1925): 443–44.

———. *Shakespeare Improved: the Restoration Versions in Quarto and on the Stage.* 1927. New York: Frederick Ungar, 1963.

Spufford, Margaret. *Small Books and Pleasant Histories: Popular Fiction and Its Readership in Seventeenth-Century England.* Athens: U of Georgia P, 1982.

Staves, Susan. *Players' Scepters: Fictions of Authority in the Restoration.* Lincoln: U of Nebraska P, 1979.

Stone, George Winchester, Jr. "The Making of the Repertory." *The London Theatre World: 1660–1800.* Ed. Robert D. Hume. Carbondale: Southern Illinois UP, 1980. 181–209.

Stone, Lawrence. *The Family, Sex and Marriage in England 1500–1800.* New York: Harper, 1977.

Swift, Jonathan. *A Tale of a Tub.* Eds. A. C. Guthkelch and D. Nichol Smith. Oxford: Clarendon, 1920.

Symons, Donald. *The Evolution of Human Sexuality.* Oxford: Oxford UP, 1979.

Taylor, Richard C. "The Originality of John Caryll's *Sir Salomon.*" *Comparative Drama* 20 (Fall 1986): 261–69.

Teague, Frances. "Ben Jonson's Stagecraft in *Epicoene.*" *Renaissance Drama* ns 9 (1978): 175–92.

Thomas, Keith. *Man and the Natural World: A History of the Modern Sensibility.* New York: Pantheon, 1983.

Thompson, James. "Ideology and Dramatic Form: The Case of Wycherley." *Studies in the Literary Imagination* 17 (1984): 49–62.

Tilley, Morris Palmer. *A Dictionary of the Proverbs in England in the Sixteenth and Seventeenth Centuries.* Ann Arbor: U of Michigan P, 1950.

Traugott, John. "The Rake's Progress from Court to Comedy: A Study in Comic Form." *SEL* 6 (1966): 381–407.

Tupper, James W. "The Relationship of the Heroic Play to the Romances of Beaumont and Fletcher." *PMLA* 20 (Sept. 1905): 584–621.

Underwood, Dale. *Etherege and the Seventeenth Century Comedy of Manners.* New Haven: Yale UP, 1957.

Vernon, P. F. "Marriage of Convenience and the Moral Code of Restoration Comedy." *Essays in Criticism* 12 (1962): 370–87.

Vieth, David M. "Entrapment in Restoration and Early Eighteenth-Century Literature." *PLL* 18 (1982): 227–33.
Visser, Colin. "The Anatomy of the Early Restoration Stage: *The Adventures of Five Hours* and John Dryden's 'Spanish' Comedies." *Theatre Notebook* 29 (1975): 56–69, 114–19.
Wadsworth, Philip A. *Molière and the Italian Theatrical Tradition*. Birmingham, AL: Summa Publications, 1977.
Waith, Eugene M. *The Pattern of Tragicomedy in Beaumont and Fletcher*. New Haven: Yale UP, 1952.
Ward, Adolphus William. *A History of English Dramatic Literature to the Death of Queen Anne*. Rev. ed. 3 vols. London: Macmillan, 1899.
Weber, Harold M. *The Restoration Rake-Hero: Transformations in Sexual Understanding in Seventeenth-Century England*. Madison: U of Wisconsin P, 1986.
Wilcox, John. *The Relation of Molière to Restoration Comedy*. New York: Columbia UP, 1938.
Wiley, Autrey Nell. *Rare Prologues and Epilogues, 1642–1700*. 1940. Port Washington, NY: Kennikat, 1970.
Wilson, John Harold. *All the King's Ladies: Actresses of the Restoration*. Chicago: U of Chicago P, 1958.
———. *The Influence of Beaumont and Fletcher on Restoration Drama*. Ohio State University Studies in Language and Literature, 4. Columbus: Ohio State UP, 1928.
Zimbardo, Rose. *A Mirror to Nature: Transformations in Drama and Aesthetics, 1660–1732*. Lexington: U of Kentucky P, 1986.

Index

Actors/Actresses, 59–61, 63, 76, 113
"Adjectival" characters, 46–47, 50, 58, 59
Ailly, l'Abbe d', 129
Allen, Ned Bliss, 66
Allestree, Richard, 17
Alssid, Michael, 179
Aristotle, 99
Arrowsmith, Joseph: *The Reformation*, 109, 170–73
Auffret, J., 130

"B., T.," 166
Bachelor's Directory, The, 19
Ballads, Restoration, 15–19
Barbieri, Niccolò: *L'Inavvertito*, 116n
Barry, Elizabeth, 230, 234
Beeston, (William?): as actor, 262; as company manager, 262–63
Behn, Aphra, 35, 108, 242. Works: —*Amorous Prince, The*, 109–10; —*City Heiress, The*, 242, 250, 252; —*Counterfeit Bridegroom, The*, 168–169, 208; —*Debauchee, The*, 168; —*False Count, The*, 220, 241, 246; —*Miscellany*, 129–30; —*Revenge, The*, 242; —*Roundheads, The*, 242, 250; —*Rover, The*, 4, 130, 165–66, 168, 173, 182–91, 197, 201, 204; —*Rover, The, Part II*, 189–90, 242, 246, 250; —*Sir Patient Fancy*, 218; —*Town Fop, The*, 173
Belon, Peter (?): *Mock Duellist, The*, 169
Bentley, Gerald Eades, 86
Berman, Ronald, 192
Betterton, Thomas: as actor, 38, 46, 119, 235, 262–63, 263n, 265, 266n; as manager, 20, 264, 264n; as playwright, 108; —*Amorous Widow, The*, 111, 114–15, 118, 120–26, 134–36
Bird, Theophilus, Jr., 262
Blackstone, William, 179n, 199
Boisrobert, L'Abbé François de, 111
Boutell, Elizabeth, 143, 194
Bowne, Tobias, 19
Boyle, Roger, Earl of Orrery, 108, 139; —*Mustapha*, 96

Bracher, Frederick, 129
Brecht, Bertold, 44
Brome, Richard, 166–67
Brown, Laura, 1, 10, 14, 145n
Browne's List, 267, 267n
Bruyère, La: *Les Caractères, ou les moeurs de ce siècle*, 131
Buckingham, George Villiers, Duke of: —*Rehearsal, The*, 11
Burke, Peter, 129
Burt, Nicholas, 262

Calderón de la Barca, Pedro: *Mañanas de abril y mayo*, 126n
Canfield, J. Douglas, 145n
Carolean Comedy, 26n, 43, 45, 81, 95, 165, 175, 180, 183, 190, 201; defined, 41–84 passim
Cartwright, William: as actor, 61; as manager, 264
Cartwright, William (playwright), 108n
Caryll, John: —*English Princess, The*, 96; —*Sir Salomon*, 16, 113, 115, 118–20, 119n, 122–26, 172
Cawelti, John G., 31
Chamberlayne, William, 166
Cibber, Colley, 238
Clark, J. C. D., 12, 13
Clun, Walter, 262
Coello, Antonio: *Los empeños de seis horas*, 65n
Cokain, Sir Aston: *Trappolin Suppos'd a Prince*, 243
Collier, Jeremy, 24
Compromise formation, 45, 67, 95, 121–22, 124, 128, 165, 169–70, 181–82, 185, 187, 190, 192, 195, 217, 231; defined, 8–9, 41–84 passim
Congreve, William, 165
Corey, Katherine Mitchell, 61
Corman, Brian, 10
Corneille, Thomas, 110
Cowley, Abraham: *Cutter of Coleman Street*, 43, 56, 60, 61–64, 68–69, 75

290

Crowne, John, 108, 242. Works: —*City Politiques*, 241, 251; —*Country Wit, The*, 135; —*Juliana, Princess of Poland*, 109; —*Sir Courtly Nice*, 130, 229, 243–48, 251

D., J.: *Mall, The*, 16–17, 168, 171–72
Davenant, Sir William: as manager, 261–65. Works: —*Law Against Lovers, The*, 43, 52n; —*Man's the Master, The*, 71; —*Rivals, The*, 43, 52n; —*Tempest, The. See under* Dryden, John; —*Wits, The*, 78
Davis, Moll, 59
de la Houssaire, Amelot: translation of Graciàn's *Courtier*, 129
de Lauretis, Teresa, 29
Deleuze, Gilles, 257
Denham, Sir John, 263, 264n
Dennis, John, 24, 28
Deshoulières, Antoinette Ligier de la Garde, Mme., 129
Donahue, Joseph W., Jr., 41
Douglas, Mary, 8, 14, 217
Downes, John, 165, 265
Dryden, John, 3–5, 20, 35, 38, 65n, 108, 128. Works: —*Absalom and Achitophel*, 96, 215, 251; —*All For Love*, 239; —*Amphitryon*, 227; —*Assignation, The*, 156n; —*Aureng-Zebe*, 199; —*Conquest of Granada, The*, 67, 80, 148; —*Don Sebastian*, 153; —*Evening's Love, An*, 54–55, 71–73, 82, 109, 111n, 130; —*Indian Emperor, The*, 84, 96, 139; —*Indian-Queen, The* (with Sir Robert Howard), 80, 96, 139; —*Marriage A-la-Mode*, 4, 13, 27, 37, 73, 95, 124–25, 129, 133, 137, 138n, 142–66, 168, 170–71, 174–75, 177, 181, 184, 186–87, 189, 195–96, 200–203, 205, 209, 211, 213–15, 218–19, 225–26, 237; —*Mistaken Husband, The*, 167; —*Mr. Limberham*, 202, 205–12, 218, 224, 235, 237; *Oedipus* (with Nathaniel Lee), 213, 224; —*Religio Laici*, 215, 223; —*Rival Ladies, The*, 56–58, 57n, 64–65, 67–69, 168; —*Secret Love*, 2, 74, 82, 84, 89, 95–96, 100, 123, 125, 134, 136, 138–45, 161, 168, 187, 210–11; —*Sir Martin Mar-all*, 16, 78, 79n, 100, 111, 113–14, 119–20, 123–24, 212; compiled with *L'Etourdi*, 115–18; —*Spanish Fryar, The*, 4, 153, 210–30, 234–35; —*Tempest, The* (with Sir William Davenant), 4, 57n, 74, 84–107, 118, 120, 125, 133, 138, 142, 144–46, 153, 155, 157, 161, 167, 175, 210, 213, 219, 225–26, 229, 235; —*Troilus and Cressida*, 205, 210, 212–13; —*Tyrannick Love*, 96; —*Wild Gallant, The*, 56–57, 61, 64–67, 66n, 72, 74
Duffett, Thomas: —*Amorous Old Woman, The*, 168; —*Empress of Morocco, The*, 220n
Duke's Company, 56, 61, 70, 108n, 262–66
Durfey, Thomas, 17, 201, 242. Works: —*Commonwealth of Women, A*, 243; —*Fond Husband, A*, 167, 173, 206–7, 212, 218, 231, 243; —*Fool Turn'd Critick, The*, 16, 167, 207; —*Injur'd Princess, The*, 243; —*Madam Fickle*, 16, 167, 207; —*Royalist, The*, 16, 242, 250–51; —*Sir Barnaby Whigg*, 250–51; —*Squire Oldsapp*, 218, 220; —*Trick for Trick*, 166
Durfeyan comedy, 230–31, 236

English comedy, 71, 75–84, 108–9, 111
Esprit, Jacques, 196
Etherege, Sir George, 3, 35, 38, 75, 124, 129. Works: —*Comical Revenge, The*, 23, 73–75, 78–79, 79n, 81, 82n, 84, 87, 95–96, 123; —*Man of Mode, The*, 7, 9–11, 13, 20, 24–25, 27–28, 30, 34, 37, 66n, 67, 73, 82, 95, 125, 129–30, 170, 181, 186–88, 203, 211; —*She Would if She Could*, 66n, 76–84, 79n, 80n, 81n, 82n, 118, 120, 122–23, 125

Fane, Sir Francis: *Love in the Dark*, 173, 220
Farquhar, George, 165
Fielding, Henry, 92
Filmer, Sir Robert, 214, 221–24
Fiore, Robert L., 72
Fisher, Alan, 143, 218
Flecknoe, Richard: *Damoiselles a la Mode*, 115
Fletcher, John (and Francis Beaumont), 11, 42–43, 54, 62, 62n, 69, 71, 73, 86, 108n, 109n, 110, 166, 229, 263. Works: —*Bloody Brother, The*, 96; —*Chances, The*, 62n; —*Coxcomb, The*, 122, 125; —*Humorous Lieutenant, The*, 55–56, 60–61, 67, 73, 96; —*Island Princess, The*, 62n; —*King and No King, A*, 45, 45n, 243; —*Love's Pilgrimage*, 65n; —*Mad Lover, The*, 263; —*Maid in the Mill, The*, 56, 73, 263; —*Maid's Tragedy, The*, 46–47, 96; —*Monsieur

Thomas (*Father's Own Son*), 73, 166–67; —*Philaster (Love Lies a Bleeding)*, 61, 169, 194; —*Rule a Wife and Have a Wife*, 55, 60, 62n, 64, 91, 96, 125, 263; —*Scornful Lady, The*, 47–51, 55, 60, 64, 67, 73–74, 122; —*Sea Voyage, The*, 243; —*Spanish Curate, The*, 62n, 263; —*Tamer Tamed, The*, 60, 64, 73; —*Wild Goose Chase, The*, 66, 91; —*Wit Without Money*, 60, 72–73

Fletcherian mode, 42, 55–67, 69–73, 75–77, 82–83, 85–88, 92, 94, 97, 103, 105–9, 113–15, 117–27, 132–33, 136, 175–78, 182, 186, 198–200, 229; defined, 43–52

Ford, John, 108n

Foreign comedy, 108, 166, 183; defined, 109–10

Freehafer, John, 261n, 262–63, 262n, 263n, 266–67, 266n, 267n

Freud, Sigmund, 8

Fujimura, Thomas H., 28, 74

Furness, Horace, 85

Geertz, Clifford, 26n
Genest, John, 212
Gewirtz, Arthur, 98, 190
Gilder, Rosamund, 59
Gildon, Charles, 38
Girard, René, 27
Glanville, Joseph, 193
God's Revenge Against Punning, 1
Greg, W. W., 267n
Guardian's Instruction, The, 19
Gwyn, Nell, 19–20

Habington, William, 109n
Harris, Henry, 264, 264n
Harris, William, 220n
Hart, Charles: as actor, 143, 262; as manager, 264
Harth, Phillip, 20
Harwood, John T., 10
Hawkins, Harriet, 15n
Hazard, Paul, 11
Herbert, Sir Henry, 266n
Heroic drama/tragedy, 73, 83, 90, 166
Hill, Christopher, 13–14
Hobbes, Thomas (Hobbesian thought), 11–13, 22, 63, 183, 192
Holland, Norman, 81n, 82n, 197
Holland, Peter, 191–92, 199

Horkheimer, Max and Theodor Adorno, 14–15, 258
Hotson, Leslie, 262
Howard family, 115, 115n
Howard, Edward, 108. Works: —*Man of Newmarket*, 169, 173; —*Six Days' Adventure*, 109–10, 170; —*Women's Conquest, The*, 109–10
Howard, James: *All Mistaken*, 2, 74
Howard, Sir Robert: 69, 124; mocked in *The Sullen Lovers*, 115n. Works: —*Committee, The*, 56–68, 65n, 66n, 70, 75, 83, 118, 123, 126, 138, 167, 228–29, 241; —*Great Favourite, The*, 96; —*Indian-Queen, The*, 80, 96. See under Dryden, John; —*Surprisal, The*, 2, 56–61, 67–69, 73, 75
Hughes, Leo, 75–76
Hume, Robert D., 2, 15, 33, 122, 190, 210, 214, 231, 243, 261, 261n, 262n, 265, 266n
Hunt, Thomas [?], 19

Jauss, Hans Robert, 1–2
Jessey, Henry, 12
Jolly, George, 262
Jonson, Ben, 42, 108n, 232, 262. Works: —*Alchemist, The*, 52–55, 60, 77, 175; —*Bartholomew Fair*, 52, 61, 175; —*Eastward Ho*, 243; —*Epicoene*, 52–55, 60–61, 67, 79, 82, 175; —*Every Man in His Humour*, 175; —*Volpone*, 52–55, 77, 175
Jonsonian comedy, 42, 50–51, 56, 60–61, 67, 69, 71, 75–78, 82, 116, 123–25, 165, 175, 180; defined, 52–55

Killigrew, Charles, 264, 264n
Killigrew, Thomas: as manager, 20, 261–64, 261n, 262n, 264n; —*Thomaso*, 165, 242
King, Bruce, 214
King's Company, The, 52, 56, 70, 108n, 261–65, 263n, 264n, 266n
Kirsch, Arthur C., 43, 45–47, 83
Knepp, Mary, 24, 156n
Knight, David, 6
Kracauer, Siegfried, 31
Kunz, Don R., 179
Kynaston, Edward: as actor, 143, 262–63; as manager, 264

Lacan, Jacques, 21
Lacy, John: as actor, 59, 61, 113, 118, 262; as playwright, 75, 108. Works: —*Old*

Index

293

Troop, The, 74, 76; —Sauny the Scot, 30, 76; —Sir Hercules Buffoon, 243
Lancaster, Henry Carrington, 111
Lanson, Gustave, 133
La Rochefoucauld, François, duc de, 129–33, 130n, 136, 197
Laslett, Peter, 221–22
Leanerd, John: –Counterfeits, The, 168; —Rambling Justice, The, 172, 208, 220
Lee, Nathaniel, 18; —Princess of Cleve, The, 203–4, 229–30
Leigh, Anthony, 212, 220, 230, 234, 238, 247
Lewis, Philip E., 31
Lindenberger, Herbert, 34
Locke, John, 13, 221–22
Loftis, John, 62n, 65n, 71n, 72, 111, 126n
London comedy, 111, 126, 166
Long, Jane, 61, 105
Lovejoy, A. O., 46, 195

McCarthy, B. Eugene, 196
McKeon, Michael, 13, 15, 145n
Macpherson, C. B., 13
Maidwell, Lewis: Loving Enemies, The, 247
Mandel, Ernest, 257
Marriage, 9, 125–26, 134, 170–73
Marriage Promoted, 19
Marshall, Rebecca, 143, 156n
Marston, John: Dutch Courtesan, The, 242
Massinger, Philip, 166. Works: —Bondman, The, 263; —Guardian, The, 242
Maus, Katharine Eisaman, 29, 96
Medbourne, Matthew: Tartuffe, 111, 113, 115, 173
Méré, Antoine Gombaud, Chevalier de, 129, 133
Middleton, Thomas, 42, 166, 208; —Mad World, My Masters, A, 242; —No Wit, No Help Like a Womans, 208; —Widow, The, 74
Middleton, Thomas and William Rowley: Changeling, The, 263
Milhous, Judith, 41, 210, 214, 253, 261n, 264n, 266n
Milhous, Judith and Robert D. Hume, 24, 199
Millett, Kate, 92
Mistaken Husband, The, 167, 173
Mr. Turbulent, 172–73, 251–52
Mizener, Arthur, 43–44

Mohun, Michael: as actor, 143, 262, 262n; as manager, 264
Molière (Jean-Baptiste Poquelin): as actor, 114n, 119; as playwright, 16, 107–8, 111n, 114, 123n, 128, 229. Works: —L'Avare, 107, 114n; —Le Bourgeois gentilhomme, 107, 111, 114, 114n; —Don Juan, 114; —L'École des femmes, 107, 113, 115, 118–20, 119n, 124; —L'Étourdi, 111, 113–14, 116n, 120; compiled with Sir Martin Mar-all, 115–18; —Les Fâcheux, 111, 113–14; —Les Fourberies de Scapin, 114n, 168; —George Dandin, 11, 115, 120–22, 124, 134–35; —Le Malade imaginaire, 114n; —Le Médecin malgré lui, 114n; —Le Misanthrope, 113–15, 165, 193–94; —Les Précieuses ridicules, 114, 120; —Tartuffe, 107, 111, 113–14
Molière-based comedies, 109–29; defined, 110–15
Moore, W. G., 197
Moraliste wit, 31, 123–37, 154–55, 167–68, 174, 190–91, 198, 200–201, 229, 236, 244–45; defined, 123–31
Moreto y Cabaña, Augustìn: No puede ser, 71, 243
Morris, Herbert, 98
Moseley, Humphrey, 262n
Multi-plot comedy, 71, 73–75, 84, 88, 108, 166
Murray, John Tucker, 262
Musser, Joseph F., Jr., 182

Nagel, Thomas, 102
Newcastle, William Cavendish, Duke of: —Country Captain, The, 79, 122, 126; —Humorous Lovers, The, 76, 129; —Triumphant Widow, The, 168
Nicoll, Allardyce, 182, 263n
Nokes, James, 74, 79n, 113, 117–19, 212, 218, 238
Novak, Maximillian E., 19, 71, 90, 96–98, 207

Opera/Pastoral, 166
Ornstein, Robert, 53
Otway, Thomas, 36, 229, 242. Works: —Atheist, The, 230, 235, 238–41; —Cheats of Scapin, The, 111, 168; —Friendship in Fashion, 229, 235–38; —Orphan, The, 238 —Souldiers Fortune, The, 3, 205, 229, 235,

237–38, 240, 249–50; —*Venice Preserv'd*, 35, 239–40

Parody/Burlesque, 166
Pascal, Blaise, 129; —*Lettres provinciales*, 196
Payne, Nevil: *Morning Ramble, The*, 168–69, 171
Pechter, Edward, 2
Pepys, Samuel, 16, 42, 59, 101, 108, 115n, 265–67, 266n
Piaget, Jean, 31
Pope, Alexander, 128, 199
Pope, Walter, 19
Popish Plot, 228, 264, 266
"Popish Politics Unmasked," 251
Pordage, John, 14
Porter, Thomas: *French Conjurer, The*, 168, 173
Powell, Jocelyn, 81n, 105, 156n, 220n
Price, Joseph, 74
"Protean" characters, 45–47, 58, 124
Provincial comedy, 166

Racine, Jean: *Bérénice*, 139
Ranters, 13–14
Ravenscroft, Edward, 108, 203, 242. Works: —*Careless Lovers, The*, 168, 170; —*Citizen Turned Gentleman, The*, 115, 124; —*Dame Dobson*, 242–43, 249–50; —*English Lawyer, The*, 168; —*London Cuckolds, The*, 3, 16, 220, 242–43, 248–50
Rawlins, Thomas: —*Tom Essence*, 173, 220; —*Tunbridge Wells*, 172
Rawls, John: *A Theory of Justice*, 196
Rhodes, John, 262
Rochester, John Wilmot, Earl of, 18, 174, 196
Rodes, David, 150, 155
Rogers, Katharine M., 193
Rostand, Jean, 131
Ruggle, George: *Ignoramus*, 166, 168
Rundle, James Urvin, 126n
Rymer, Thomas, 96

Sablé, Mme. de, 129
Sablière, Mme. de la, 129
Sahlins, Marshall, 12
Sandford, Samuel, 74
Scarron, Paul: *Jodelet, ou le maître valet*, 71
Scenery/setting, 59–60, 63, 77–78, 123, 123n

Schneider, Ben Ross, 192
Scouten, Arthur H., 15n
Scouten, Arthur H. and Robert D. Hume, 15
Scudéry, Madame de, 110
Sedgwick, Eve, 36
Sedley, Sir Charles, 18; —*Mulberry Garden, The*, 74–5, 111n
Settle, Elkanah: *Empress of Morocco, The*, 220n
Shadwell, Thomas, 35, 108, 179n, 229. Works: —*Epsom Wells*, 125, 173; —*Humorists, The*, 173, 181; —*Hypocrite, The*, 113, 115; —*Lancashire Witches, The*, 220, 230, 233–36, 240, 246, 251; —*Libertine, The*, 20, 173, 204, 220, 232; —*Miser, The*, 113, 115; —*Sullen Lovers, The*, 79, 111, 114–15, 115n; —*Timon of Athens*, 232; —*True Widow, A*, 220, 229–33, 236–37; —*Virtuoso, The*, 4, 165, 173–82, 187, 189–91, 193, 201, 245–46; —*Woman-Captain, The*, 16, 37, 229, 232–34, 236, 238, 242
Shaftesbury, Anthony Ashley Cooper, Earl of, 222
Shakespeare, William, 39, 42, 69, 86, 128, 263, 263n; types of comic scenes in, 23–24. Works: —*Antony and Cleopatra*, 59–60; —*Cymbeline*, 51–52, 243; —*Measure for Measure*, 52n; —*Merry Wives of Windsor, The*, 52n; —*Midsummer Night's Dream, A*, 52n; —*Much Ado About Nothing*, 52, 52n; —*Othello*, 247; —*Pericles*, 51; —*Taming of the Shrew, The*, 30, 51; —*Tempest, The*, 51, 85–107; —*Troilus and Cressida*, 205; —*Twelfth Night*, 52n; —*Two Noble Kinsmen, The*, 52n, 86; —*Winter's Tale, The*, 51–52
Shakespeare, William and John Fletcher: —*Cardenio*, 86; —*Henry VIII*, 86
Shakespearean comedy, 47, 50–51, 55, 75; defined, 51–52
Shirley, James, 42, 108n
Simon, Herbert, 8
Smith, John Harrington, 64, 66n
Smith, John Harrington and Dougald MacMillan, 66n
Smith, William: as actor, 212, 220; as manager, 264
Sorelius, Gunnar, 262, 265
Southerne, Thomas: *Disappointment, The*, 242, 246–48

Index

Spanish plot/Spanish comedy, 56, 67, 70–73, 75, 108–10; defined, 62–63
Spencer, Hazelton, 85, 263n
Spufford, Margaret, 16
Staves, Susan, 11–13, 18, 67, 173
Steele, Sir Richard, 24, 249
Stone, George W., Jr., 41, 265, 266n
Stone, Lawrence, 11
"Strange's Case", 251
Summers, Montague, 212
Swift, Jonathan, 16; —*Tale of a Tub, A*, 223
Sydserf, Sir Thomas: *Tarugo's Wiles*, 71, 243
Symons, Donald, 29

Tate, Nahum, 242. Works: —*Cuckolds-Haven*, 243; —*Duke and No Duke, A*, 243
Tatham, John: *Rump, The*, 242
Teague, Frances, 53
Thomas, Keith, 11
Thompson, James, 8, 25–26
Tilley, Morris Palmer, 128, 198
Traugott, John, 23
Tuke, Sir Samuel, 65n, 71; —*Adventures of Five Hours, The*, 20, 36, 56–58, 62–64, 67–73, 75, 83, 109, 138, 183, 228–29, 241
Tupper, James W., 265

Underhill, Cave, 61, 74, 117–18
Underwood, Dale, 77

United Company, 20, 242, 264–65
Urfe, Honoré d': *L'Astrée*, 134

Vanbrugh, Sir John, 165
Vieth, David, 8
Visé, Donneau de and Thomas Corneille: *La Divineresse*, 242
Visser, Colin, 63

Wadsworth, Philip A., 114, 114n, 116n
Waith, Eugene M., 45, 45n, 47
Ward, Adolphus William, 216
Weber, Harold, 235
Webster, John, 263, 263n
Wilcox, John, 111–12
Wilde, Oscar: *Importance of Being Earnest, The*, 11
Wilson, John: *Cheats, The*, 228
Wilson, John Harold, 59, 169, 265
Woman Turn'd Bully, The, 168
Wood, Anthony à, 16
Wycherley, William, 3, 35, 108, 129. Works: —*Country-Wife, The*, 7, 13, 22, 27, 36–38, 67, 82, 115, 119n, 129, 135–36, 170, 181, 190, 206, 229, 244–45, 248; —*Gentleman Dancing-Master, The*, 30, 109; —*Love in a Wood*, 126–28; —*Plain-Dealer, The*, 4, 16, 27, 34–35, 37–38, 111, 115, 130, 165, 168, 174, 187, 190–201, 204–5

Zimbardo, Rose, 1, 89

Eric Rothstein, born in Brooklyn, New York, in 1936, attended public schools in New York City, Rockville (Indiana), Milwaukee, and Dayton (Ohio) before taking his A.B. at Harvard in 1957. He holds a Ph.D. from Princeton (1962). He became an instructor at the University of Wisconsin-Madison in 1961, an Assistant Professor (1963–66), Associate Professor (1966–70), Professor (1970–82), and Edgar W. Lacy Professor of English (1982–).

Professor Rothstein's first two books, in 1967, dealt with Restoration drama: *Restoration Tragedy: Form and the Process of Change* and *George Farquhar*. In *The Designs of Carolean Comedy*, he returns to and very much elaborates the relation between form and change with which he had dealt in both these earlier books. He is also the author of *Systems of Order and Inquiry in Later Eighteenth-Century Fiction* (1975) and *Restoration and Eighteenth-Century Poetry, 1660–1780* (1981). In addition, he has written articles on later seventeenth- and eighteenth-century aesthetics, fiction, poetry, and drama, and he served as editor of *Literary Monographs* (1967–79). Professor Rothstein's chief scholarly concerns are with the theory and practice of cultural history, especially the literary history of England, 1660–1800.

Frances M. Kavenik was born in Brownwood, Texas, in 1944, but stayed only a few weeks before leaving for the Midwest where she has spent most of her remaining years, with brief excursions eastward and westward. She received a B.A. from Lake Forest College (1966), an M.A. from Northwestern University (1968), and a Ph.D. from the University of Wisconsin-Madison (1977). She taught at Indiana University Northwest, Roosevelt University, and Northeastern Illinois University before settling in at the University of Wisconsin-Parkside in 1979, where she is currently an Assistant Professor of English and Humanities and Director of the ACCESS Program.

The Designs of Carolean Comedy, which grew out of work for her dissertation, is her first book; other works are "Aphra Behn: The Playwright as 'Breeches Part'" in *Curtain Calls: Women in the British and American Theatre, 1660–1800*, ed. Mary Anne Schofield and Cecilia Macheski (forthcoming) and *An Encyclopedic Handbook of U.S. Women's History*, ed. Angela Howard Zophy (forthcoming), for which she is associate editor. She has presented conference papers on Elizabeth Gaskell, Jane Austen, and film as well as on Jacobean and Carolean drama. Ms. Kavenik's chief scholarly interest is in the intersection of social and cultural history with various forms of popular culture, especially as directed to women.

She has been active in MMLA and in the Women's Caucus for the Modern Languages, for which she has recently become editor of *Concerns*, the Caucus newsletter.